Robert Jordan's
the WHEEL of TIME®
the EYE of the WORLD

The Wheel of Time®
Graphic Novels

Based on the Novels by Robert Jordan

**New Spring:
The Graphic Novel**
Robert Jordan, Chuck Dixon, Mike Miller, Harvey Tolibao

**The Eye of the World:
The Graphic Novel, Volume One**
Robert Jordan, Chuck Dixon, Chase Conley

**The Eye of the World:
The Graphic Novel, Volume Two**
Robert Jordan, Chuck Dixon, Andie Tong

**The Eye of the World:
The Graphic Novel, Volume Three**
Robert Jordan, Chuck Dixon, Marcio Fiorito, Francis Nuguit

**The Eye of the World:
The Graphic Novel, Volume Four**
Robert Jordan, Chuck Dixon, Andie Tong

**The Eye of the World:
The Graphic Novel, Volume Five**
Robert Jordan, Chuck Dixon, Andie Tong

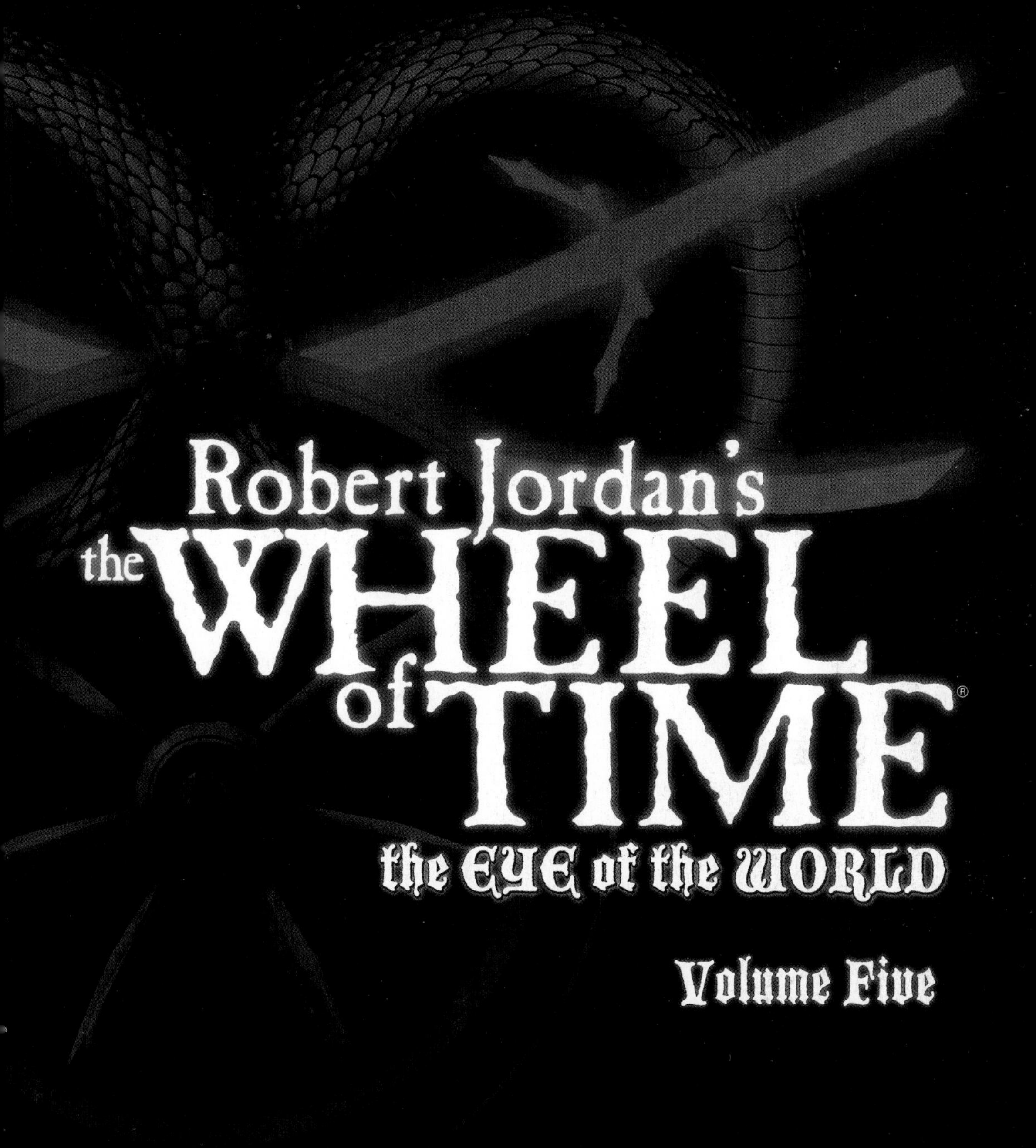

Robert Jordan's

the WHEEL of TIME®

the EYE of the WORLD

Volume Five

TOR®

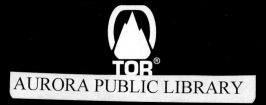

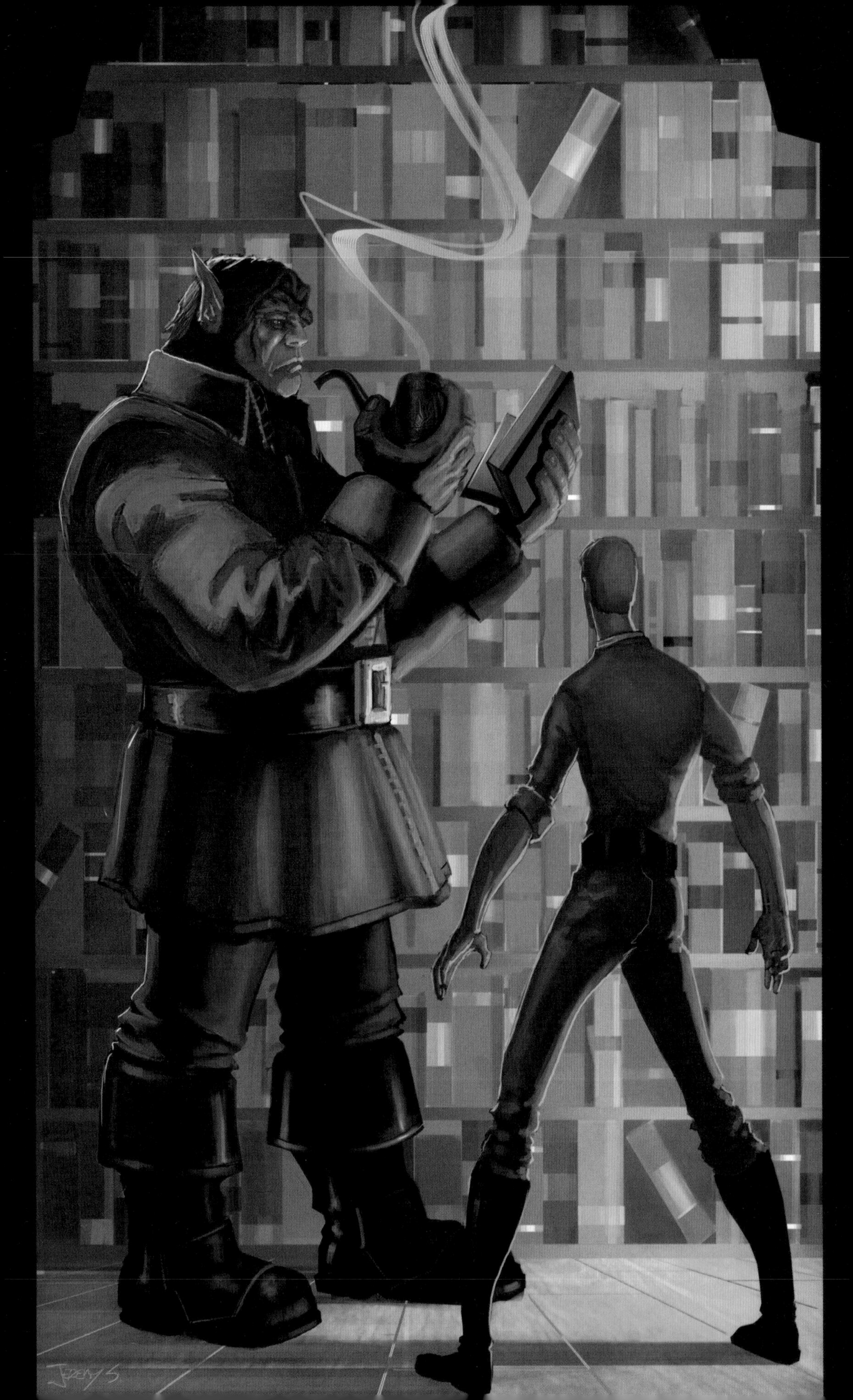

written by
ROBERT JORDAN

adapted by
CHUCK DIXON

artwork by
ANDIE TONG

colors by
NICOLAS CHAPUIS

lettered by
BILL TORTOLINI

original series edited by
ERNST DABEL
RICH YOUNG

consultation
ERNST DABEL
LES DABEL

thematic consultants
MARIA SIMONS
BOB KLUTTZ
ALAN ROMANCZUK

Covers by Andie Tong
Collection edits by Rich Young
Collection design by Bill Tortolini

DYNAMITE ENTERTAINMENT:

NICK BARRUCCI	• CEO / PUBLISHER	SARAH LITT	• DIGITAL EDITOR
JUAN COLLADO	• PRESIDENT / COO	JOSH GREEN	• TRAFFIC COORDINATOR
RICH YOUNG	• DIRECTOR BUSINESS DEVELOPMENT	JOSH JOHNSON	• ART DIRECTOR
KEITH DAVIDSEN	• MARKETING MANAGER	JASON ULLMEYER	• SENIOR GRAPHIC DESIGNER
JOSEPH RYBANDT	• SENIOR EDITOR	CHRIS CANIANO	• PRODUCTION ASSISTANT

WWW.DYNAMITE.COM
VISIT US ONLINE AT WWW.DYNAMITE.COM
FOLLOW US ON TWITTER @DYNAMITECOMICS
LIKE US ON FACEBOOK /DYNAMITECOMICS
WATCH US ON YOUTUBE /DYNAMITECOMICS

Published in comic book form by Dynamite Entertainment, 133 Gaither Dr, STE 205, Mt. Laurel, NJ 08054.
Dynamite, Dynamite Entertainment and the Dynamite Entertainment colophon are ® and © 2013 DFI. All rights reserved.

A Tor Book
Published by Tom Doherty Associates, LLC
175 Fifth Avenue
New York, NY 10010

www.tor-forge.com

Tor® is a registered trademark of Tom Doherty Associates, LLC.
ISBN 978-0-7653-7425-7
First Edition: July 2014
Printed in the United States of America

Table of
Contents

WHAT CAME BEFORE...

On the run from the forces of Ba'alzamon, Moiraine
leads the Emond's Fielders to the dead city of Aridhol,
a place of sleeping evil so great that even the Trollocs
fear to set foot inside its walls.

Believing themselves safe from danger, at least during
the day, Rand, Mat, and Perrin decide to strike out
from the group for a while to explore the city and
search for treasure.

What they find is someone named Mordeth, a man of
the shadows who does his best to trick the young men
into bringing some of the city's vast treasure out past
the city walls.

When temptation doesn't work, he reveals himself
as the cursed thing that he is, sending the boys
scrambling.

Against their will, the Trollocs have entered Aridhol –
also known as the cursed Shadar Logoth – to find their
prey. What they find instead is the mindless, seeping
evil of Mashadar, the foglike thing that devoured all
life in the city in the first place.

In their hurry to escape both the Trollocs and
Mashadar, the Emond's Fielders are separated. Perrin
and Egwene are washed across the river, where they
meet the enigmatic Elyas.

Thom Merrilin brings Rand and Mat to a river ship,
booking them all passage as gleemen.

Moiraine can sense that the others are heading in two
separate directions and must decide which one she, Lan,
and Nynaeve will follow...

chapter one

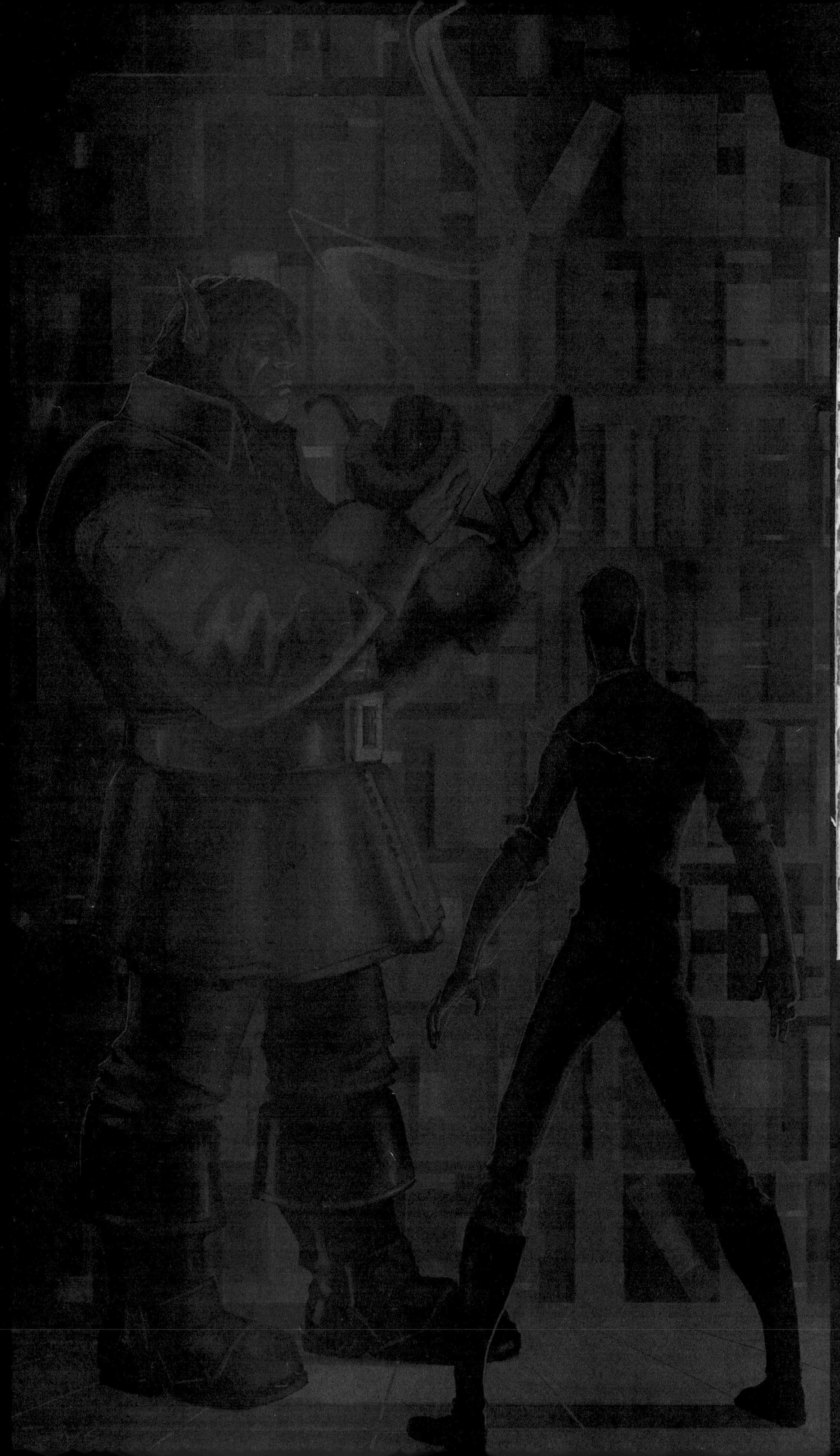

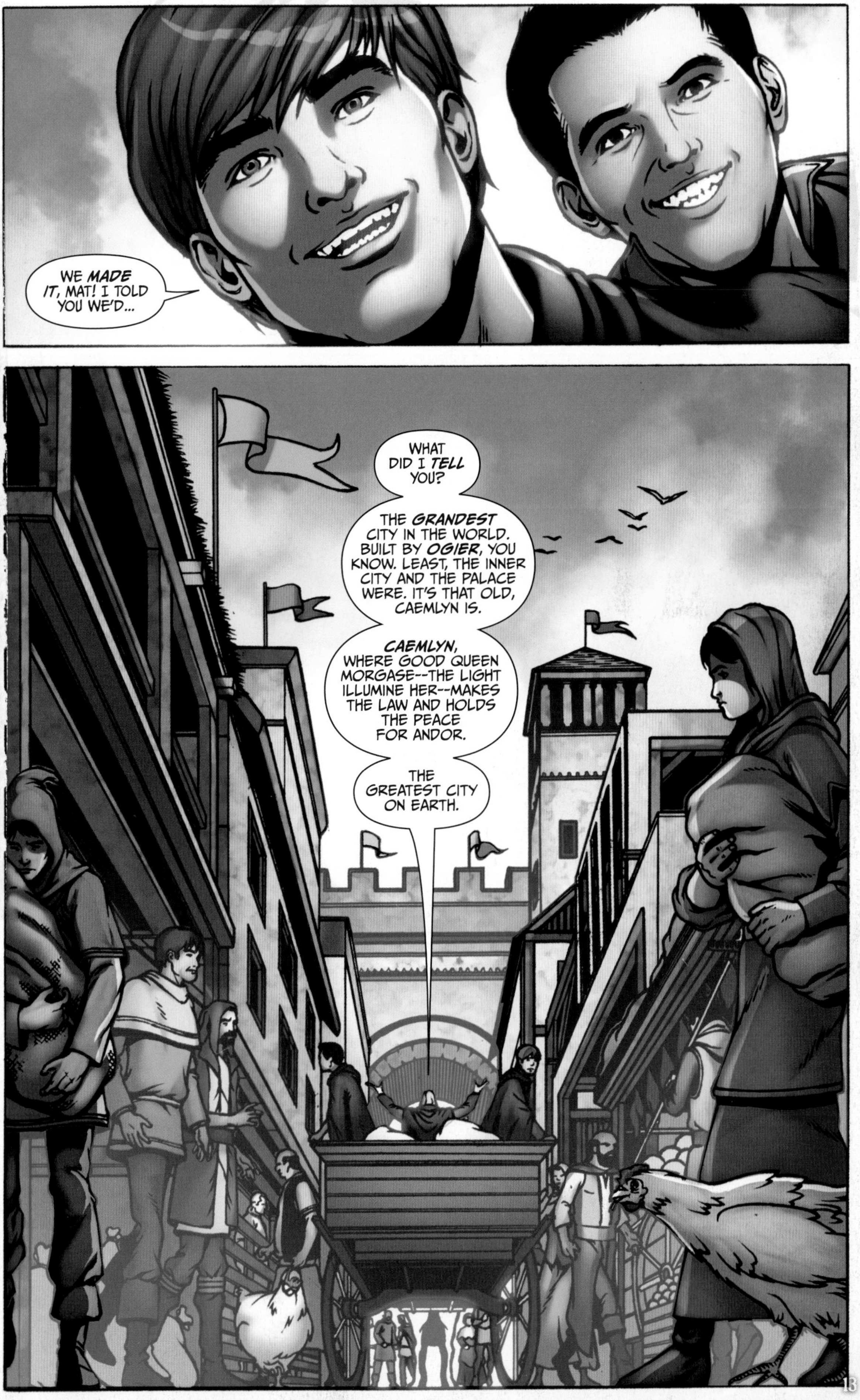
WE MADE IT, MAT! I TOLD YOU WE'D...
WHAT DID I TELL YOU?
THE GRANDEST CITY IN THE WORLD. BUILT BY OGIER, YOU KNOW. LEAST, THE INNER CITY AND THE PALACE WERE. IT'S THAT OLD, CAEMLYN IS.
CAEMLYN, WHERE GOOD QUEEN MORGASE--THE LIGHT ILLUMINE HER--MAKES THE LAW AND HOLDS THE PEACE FOR ANDOR.
THE GREATEST CITY ON EARTH.

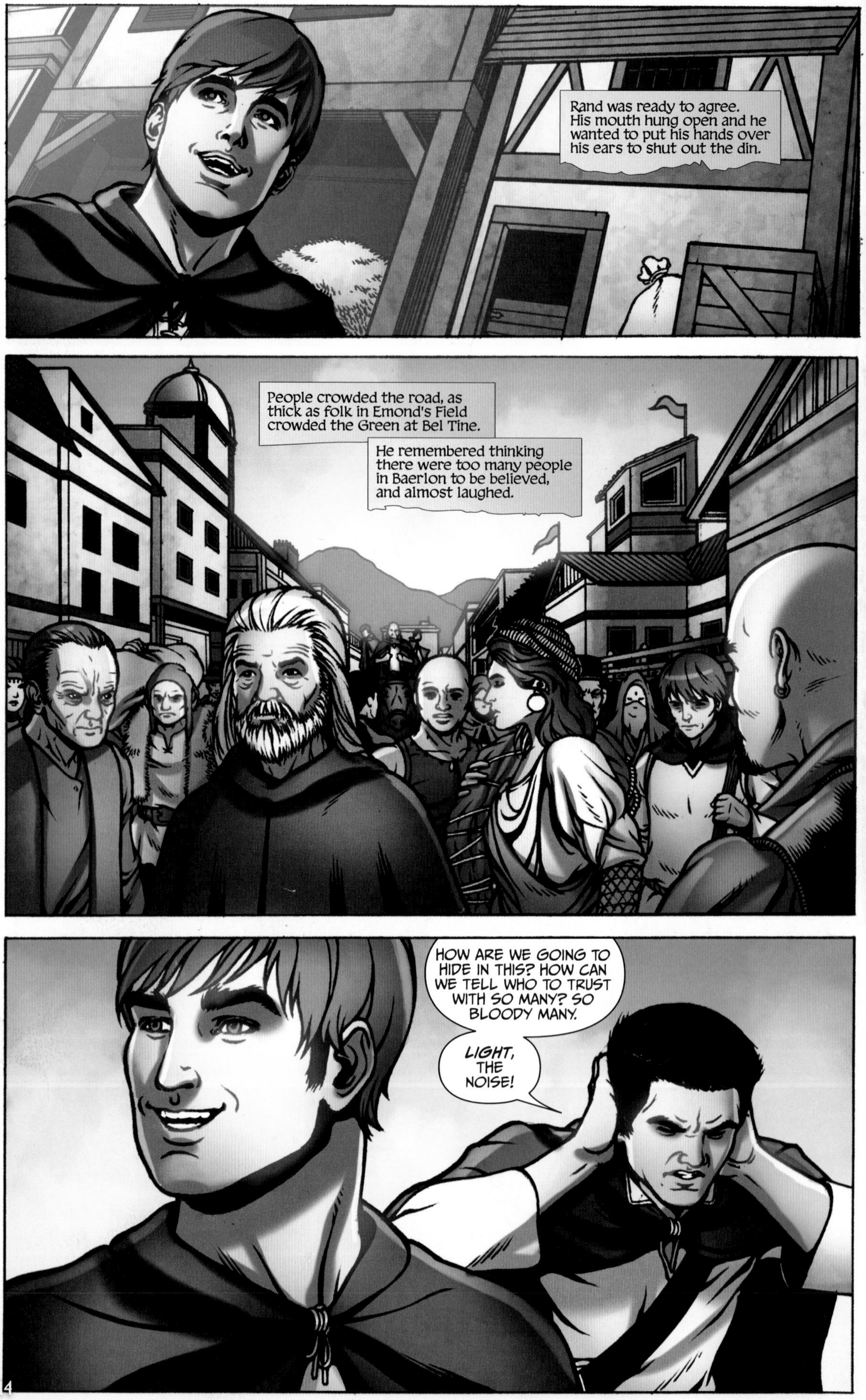
Rand was ready to agree. His mouth hung open and he wanted to put his hands over his ears to shut out the din.
People crowded the road, as thick as folk in Emond's Field crowded the Green at Bel Tine.
He remembered thinking there were too many people in Baerlon to be believed, and almost laughed.
HOW ARE WE GOING TO HIDE IN THIS? HOW CAN WE TELL WHO TO TRUST WITH SO MANY? SO BLOODY MANY.
LIGHT, THE NOISE!

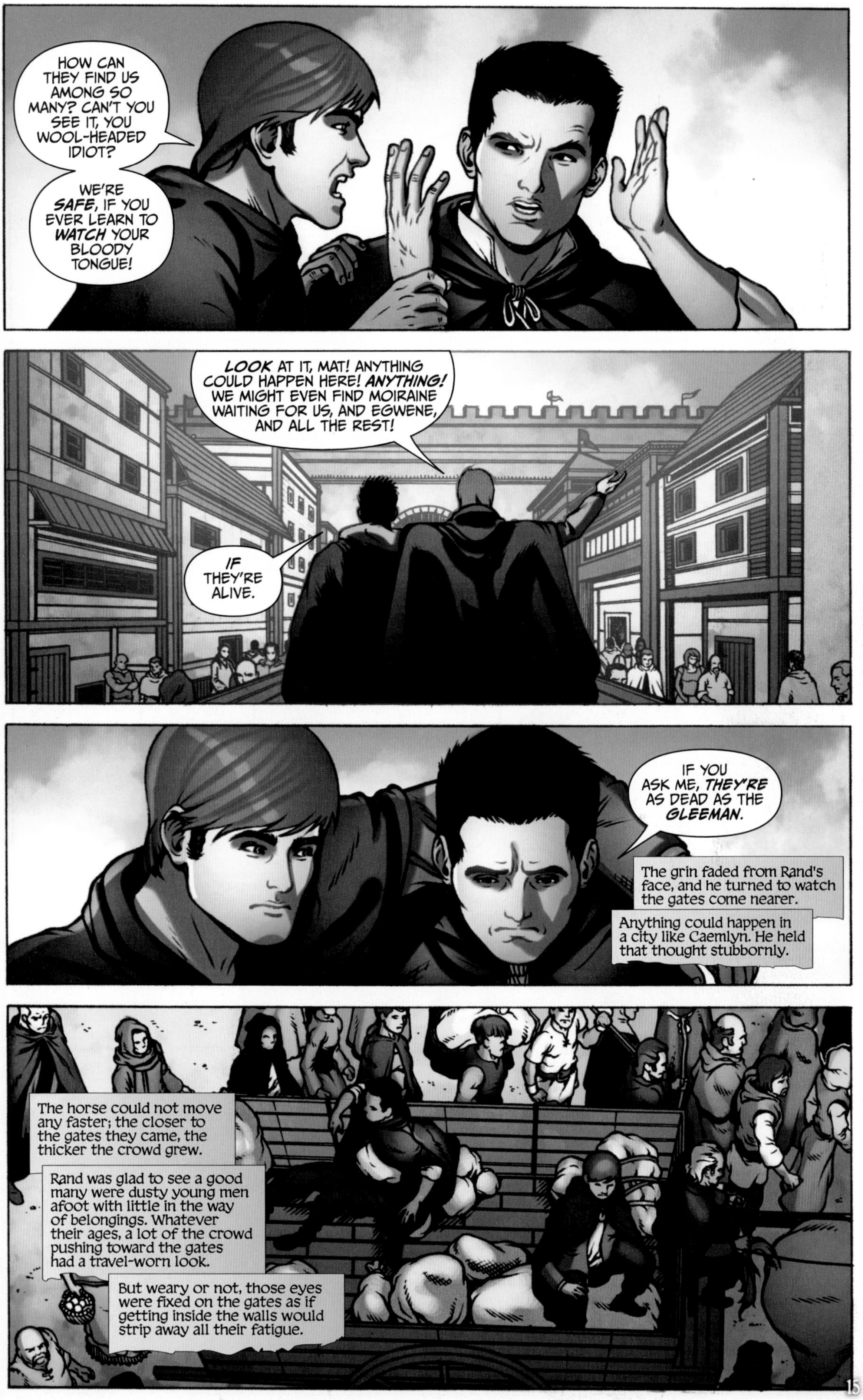
HOW CAN THEY FIND US AMONG SO MANY? CAN'T YOU SEE IT, YOU WOOL-HEADED IDIOT?
WE'RE SAFE, IF YOU EVER LEARN TO WATCH YOUR BLOODY TONGUE!
LOOK AT IT, MAT! ANYTHING COULD HAPPEN HERE! ANYTHING! WE MIGHT EVEN FIND MOIRAINE WAITING FOR US, AND EGWENE, AND ALL THE REST!
IF THEY'RE ALIVE.
IF YOU ASK ME, THEY'RE AS DEAD AS THE GLEEMAN.
The grin faded from Rand's face, and he turned to watch the gates come nearer.
Anything could happen in a city like Caemlyn. He held that thought stubbornly.
The horse could not move any faster; the closer to the gates they came, the thicker the crowd grew.
Rand was glad to see a good many were dusty young men afoot with little in the way of belongings. Whatever their ages, a lot of the crowd pushing toward the gates had a travel-worn look.
But weary or not, those eyes were fixed on the gates as if getting inside the walls would strip away all their fatigue.

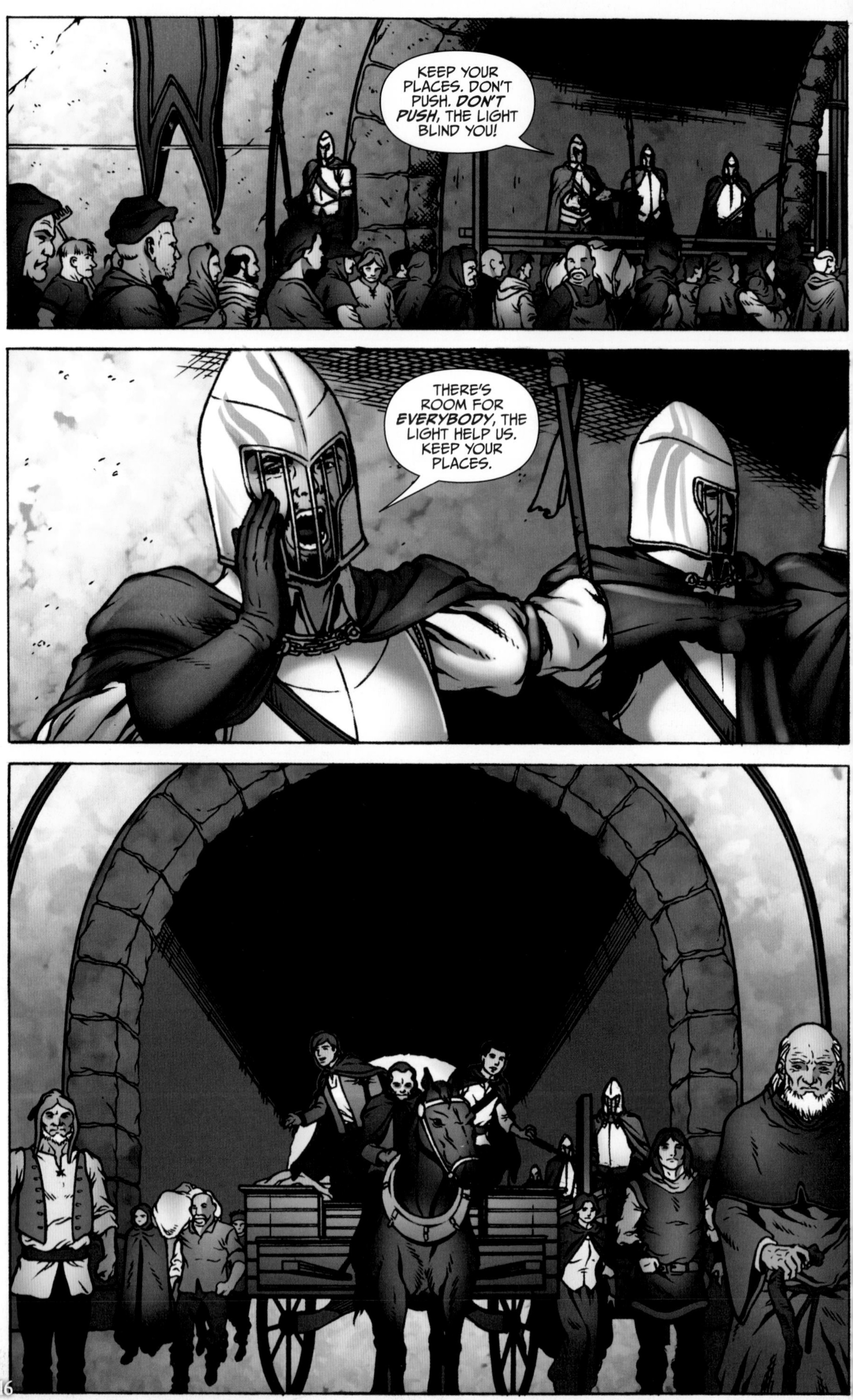
KEEP YOUR PLACES. DON'T PUSH. DON'T PUSH, THE LIGHT BLIND YOU!
THERE'S ROOM FOR EVERYBODY, THE LIGHT HELP US. KEEP YOUR PLACES.

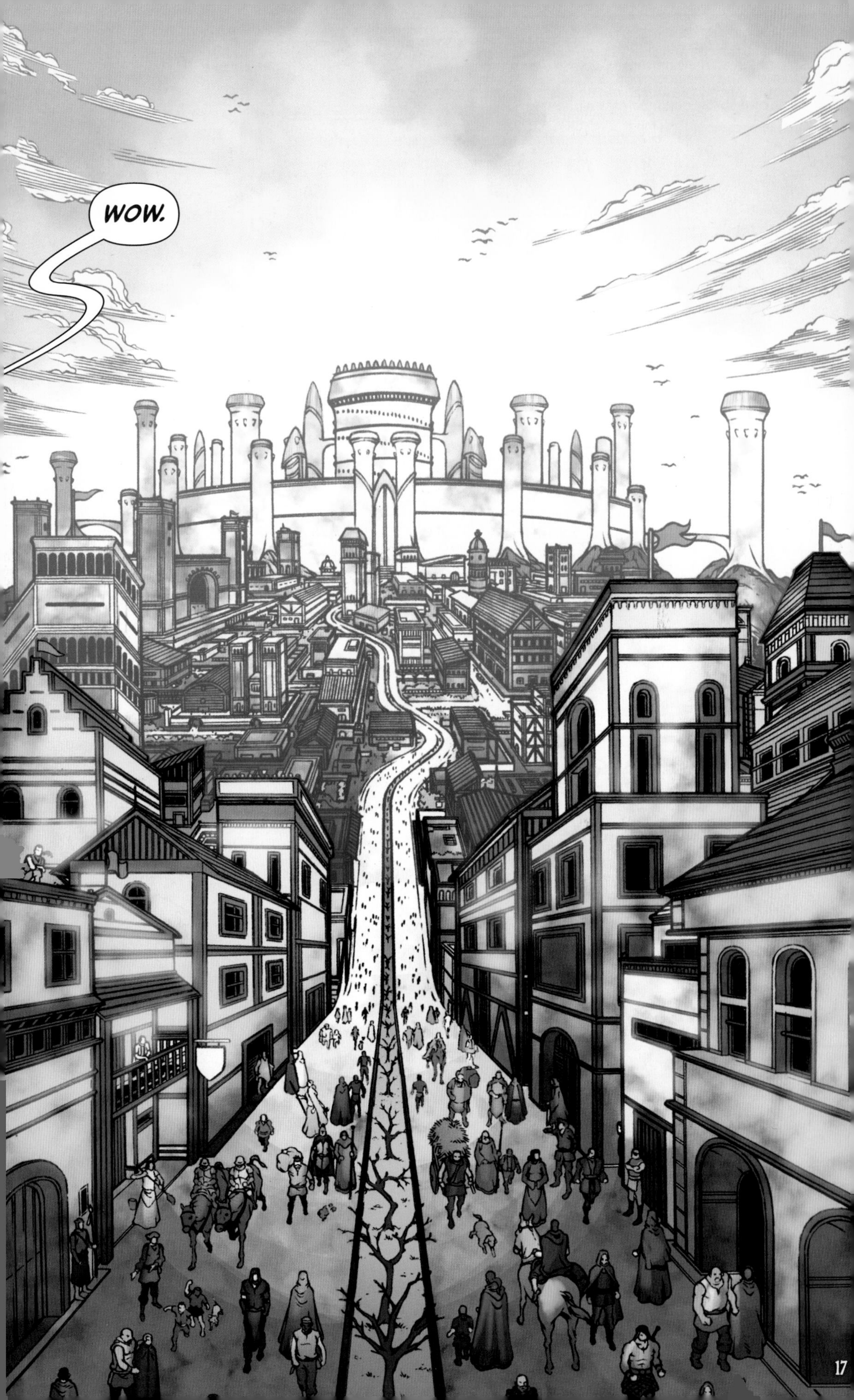
WOW.

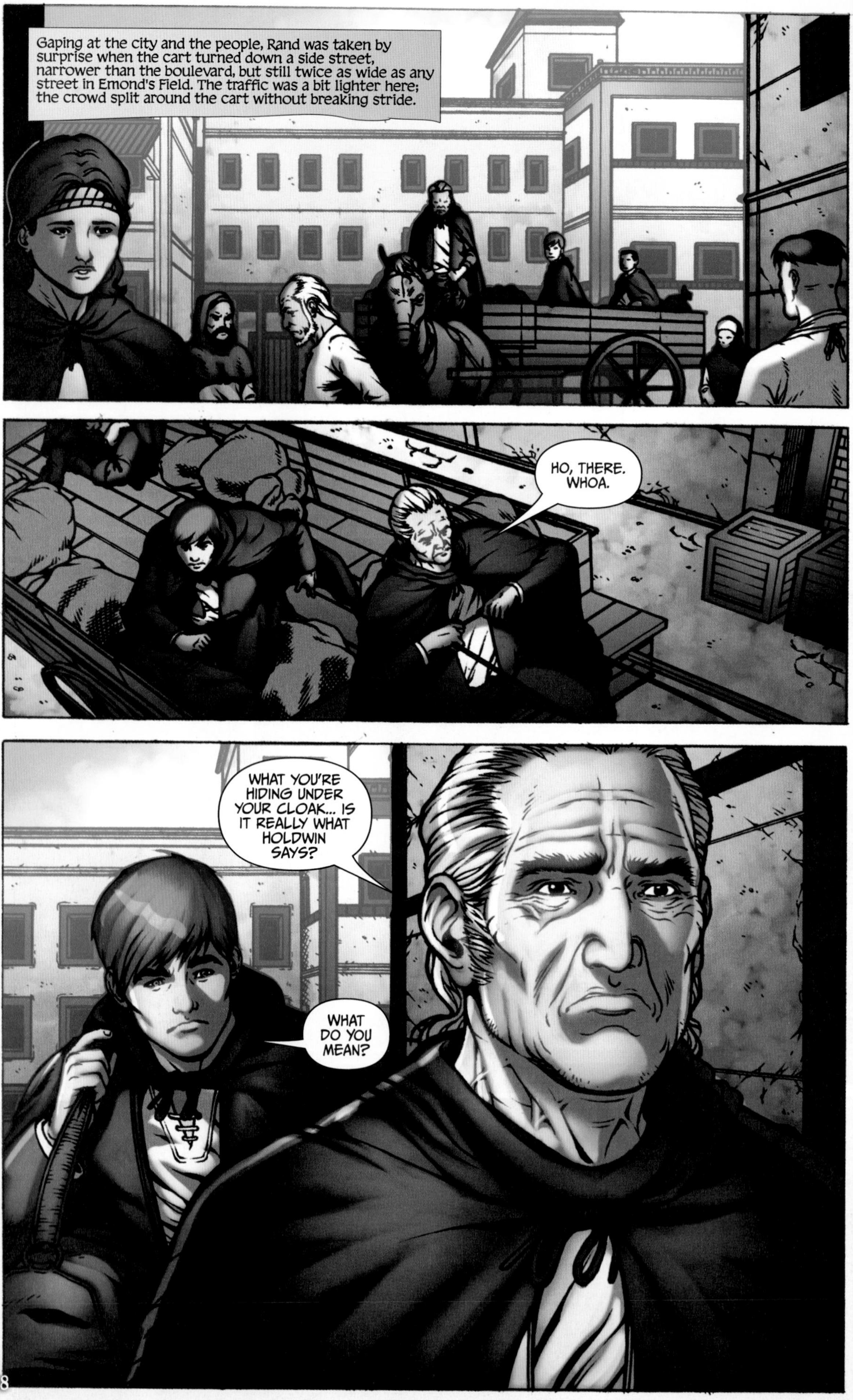
Gaping at the city and the people, Rand was taken by surprise when the cart turned down a side street, narrower than the boulevard, but still twice as wide as any street in Emond's Field. The traffic was a bit lighter here; the crowd split around the cart without breaking stride.
HO, THERE. WHOA.
WHAT YOU'RE HIDING UNDER YOUR CLOAK... IS IT REALLY WHAT HOLDWIN SAYS?
WHAT DO YOU MEAN?

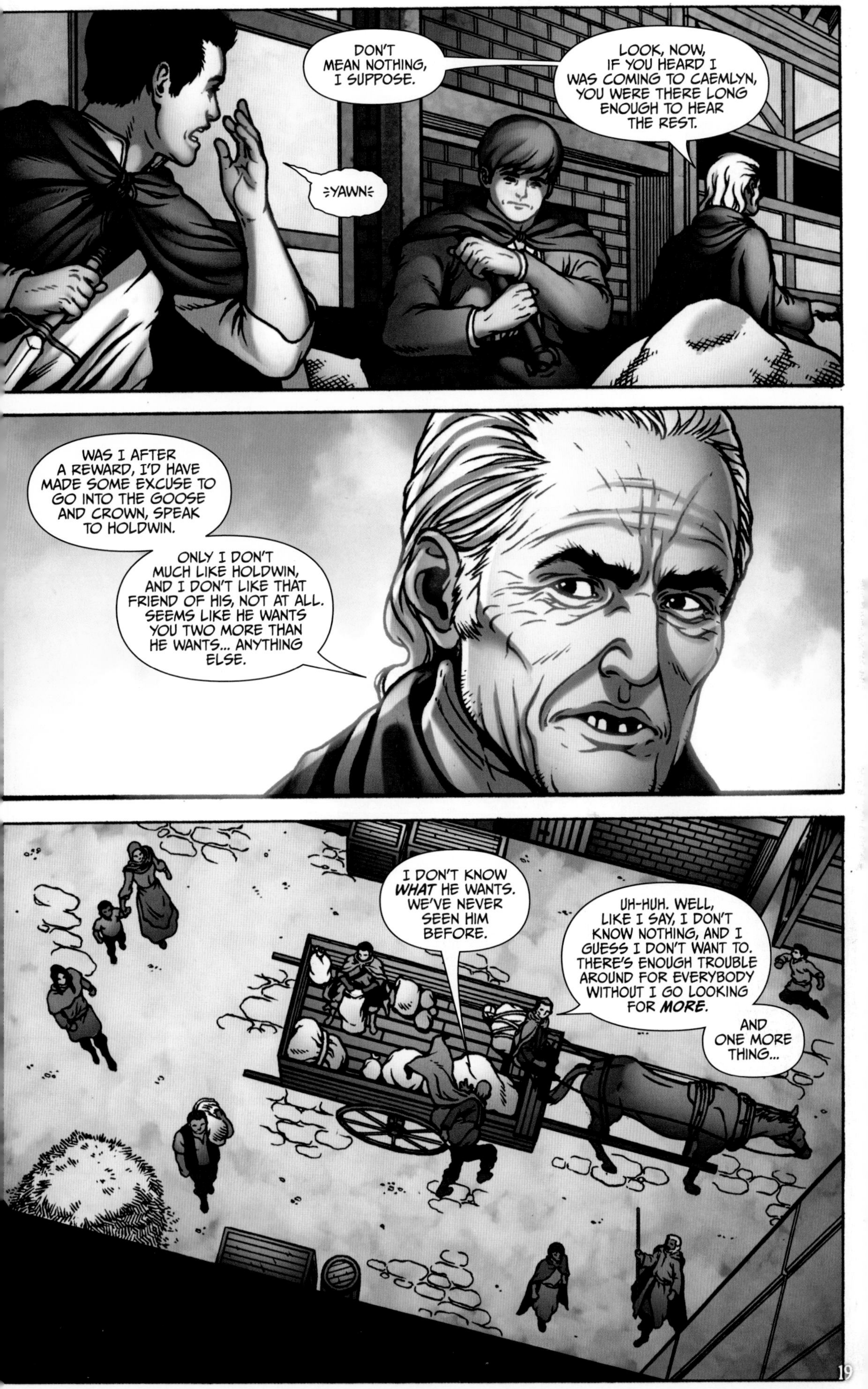
DON'T MEAN NOTHING, I SUPPOSE.
LOOK, NOW, IF YOU HEARD I WAS COMING TO CAEMLYN, YOU WERE THERE LONG ENOUGH TO HEAR THE REST.
YAWN
WAS I AFTER A REWARD, I'D HAVE MADE SOME EXCUSE TO GO INTO THE GOOSE AND CROWN, SPEAK TO HOLDWIN.
ONLY I DON'T MUCH LIKE HOLDWIN, AND I DON'T LIKE THAT FRIEND OF HIS, NOT AT ALL. SEEMS LIKE HE WANTS YOU TWO MORE THAN HE WANTS... ANYTHING ELSE.
I DON'T KNOW *WHAT* HE WANTS. WE'VE NEVER SEEN HIM BEFORE.
UH-HUH. WELL, LIKE I SAY, I DON'T KNOW NOTHING, AND I GUESS I DON'T WANT TO. THERE'S ENOUGH TROUBLE AROUND FOR EVERYBODY WITHOUT I GO LOOKING FOR *MORE*.
AND ONE MORE THING...

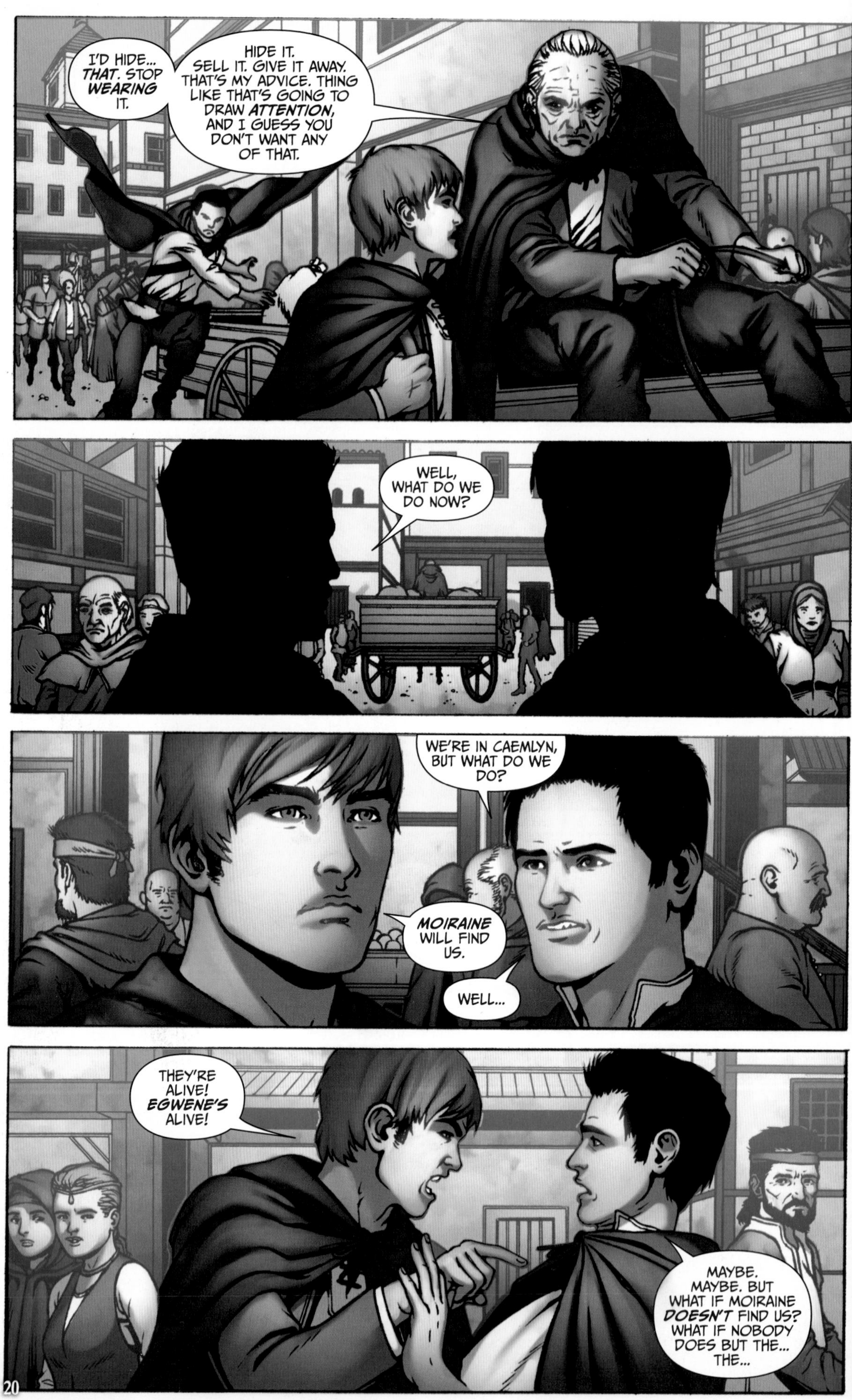
I'D HIDE... THAT. STOP WEARING IT.
HIDE IT. SELL IT. GIVE IT AWAY. THAT'S MY ADVICE. THING LIKE THAT'S GOING TO DRAW ATTENTION, AND I GUESS YOU DON'T WANT ANY OF THAT.
WELL, WHAT DO WE DO NOW?
WE'RE IN CAEMLYN, BUT WHAT DO WE DO?
MOIRAINE WILL FIND US.
WELL...
THEY'RE ALIVE! EGWENE'S ALIVE!
MAYBE. MAYBE. BUT WHAT IF MOIRAINE DOESN'T FIND US? WHAT IF NOBODY DOES BUT THE... THE...

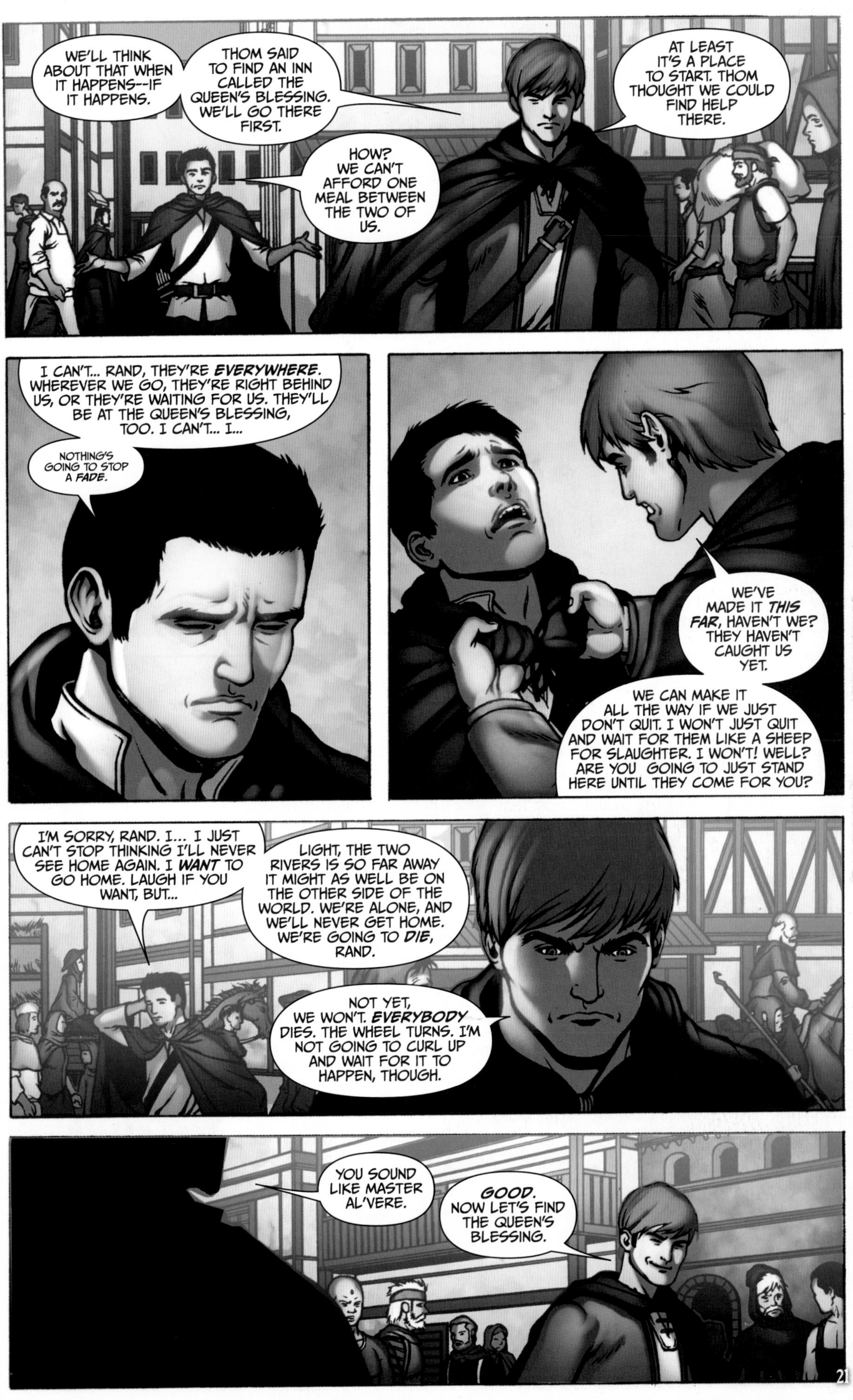

WE'LL THINK ABOUT THAT WHEN IT HAPPENS--IF IT HAPPENS.
THOM SAID TO FIND AN INN CALLED THE QUEEN'S BLESSING. WE'LL GO THERE FIRST.
HOW? WE CAN'T AFFORD ONE MEAL BETWEEN THE TWO OF US.
AT LEAST IT'S A PLACE TO START. THOM THOUGHT WE COULD FIND HELP THERE.
I CAN'T... RAND, THEY'RE *EVERYWHERE*. WHEREVER WE GO, THEY'RE RIGHT BEHIND US, OR THEY'RE WAITING FOR US. THEY'LL BE AT THE QUEEN'S BLESSING, TOO. I CAN'T... I...
NOTHING'S GOING TO STOP A *FADE*.
WE'VE MADE IT *THIS FAR*, HAVEN'T WE? THEY HAVEN'T CAUGHT US YET.
WE CAN MAKE IT ALL THE WAY IF WE JUST DON'T QUIT. I WON'T JUST QUIT AND WAIT FOR THEM LIKE A SHEEP FOR SLAUGHTER. I WON'T! WELL? ARE YOU GOING TO JUST STAND HERE UNTIL THEY COME FOR YOU?
I'M SORRY, RAND. I... I JUST CAN'T STOP THINKING I'LL NEVER SEE HOME AGAIN. I *WANT* TO GO HOME. LAUGH IF YOU WANT, BUT...
LIGHT, THE TWO RIVERS IS SO FAR AWAY IT MIGHT AS WELL BE ON THE OTHER SIDE OF THE WORLD. WE'RE ALONE, AND WE'LL NEVER GET HOME. WE'RE GOING TO *DIE*, RAND.
NOT YET, WE WON'T. *EVERYBODY* DIES. THE WHEEL TURNS. I'M NOT GOING TO CURL UP AND WAIT FOR IT TO HAPPEN, THOUGH.
YOU SOUND LIKE MASTER AL'VERE.
GOOD. NOW LET'S FIND THE QUEEN'S BLESSING.

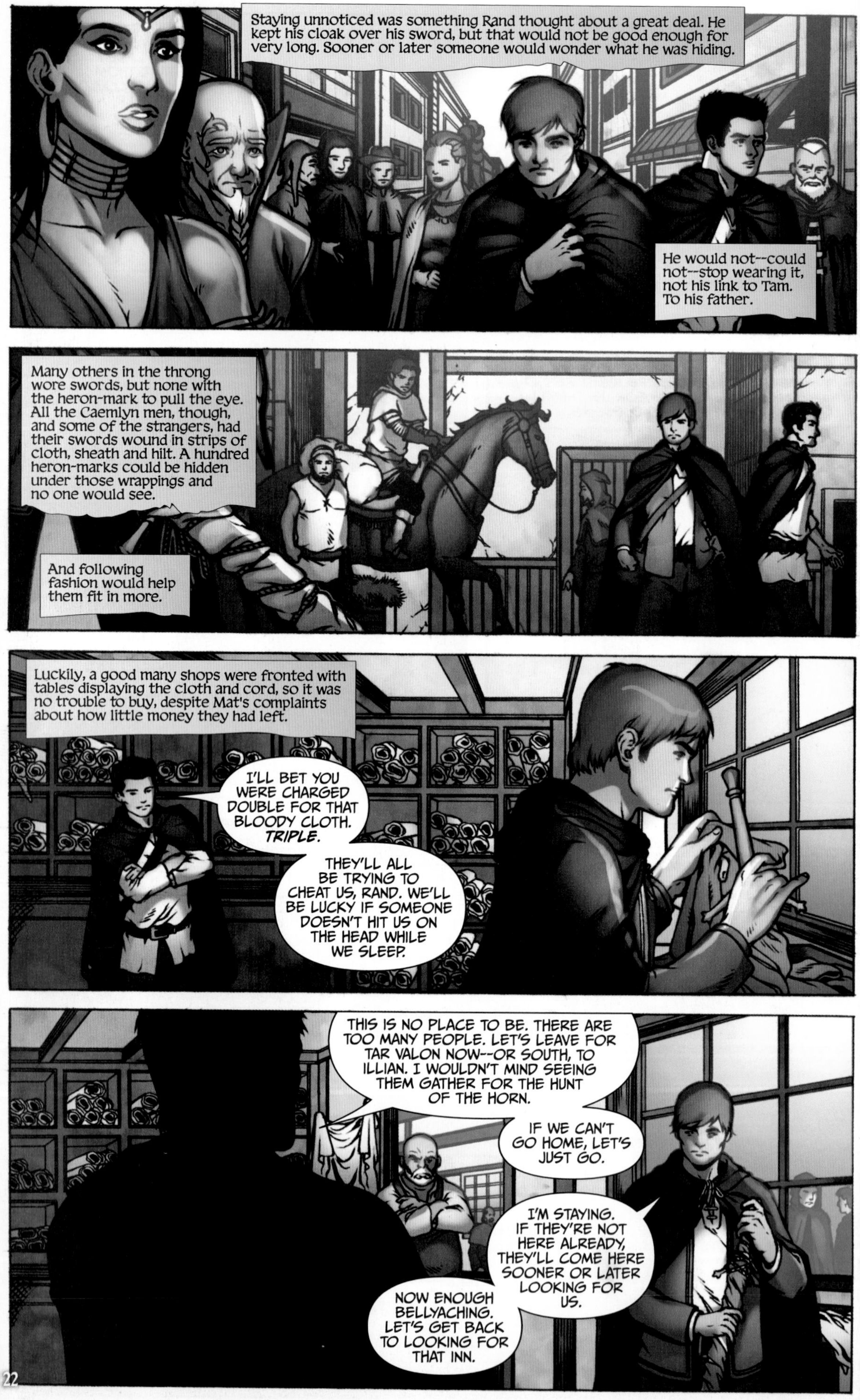

Staying unnoticed was something Rand thought about a great deal. He kept his cloak over his sword, but that would not be good enough for very long. Sooner or later someone would wonder what he was hiding.
He would not--could not--stop wearing it, not his link to Tam. To his father.
Many others in the throng wore swords, but none with the heron-mark to pull the eye. All the Caemlyn men, though, and some of the strangers, had their swords wound in strips of cloth, sheath and hilt. A hundred heron-marks could be hidden under those wrappings and no one would see.
And following fashion would help them fit in more.
Luckily, a good many shops were fronted with tables displaying the cloth and cord, so it was no trouble to buy, despite Mat's complaints about how little money they had left.
I'LL BET YOU WERE CHARGED DOUBLE FOR THAT BLOODY CLOTH. *TRIPLE*.
THEY'LL ALL BE TRYING TO CHEAT US, RAND. WE'LL BE LUCKY IF SOMEONE DOESN'T HIT US ON THE HEAD WHILE WE SLEEP.
THIS IS NO PLACE TO BE. THERE ARE TOO MANY PEOPLE. LET'S LEAVE FOR TAR VALON NOW--OR SOUTH, TO ILLIAN. I WOULDN'T MIND SEEING THEM GATHER FOR THE HUNT OF THE HORN.
IF WE CAN'T GO HOME, LET'S JUST GO.
I'M STAYING. IF THEY'RE NOT HERE ALREADY, THEY'LL COME HERE SOONER OR LATER LOOKING FOR US.
NOW ENOUGH BELLYACHING. LET'S GET BACK TO LOOKING FOR THAT INN.

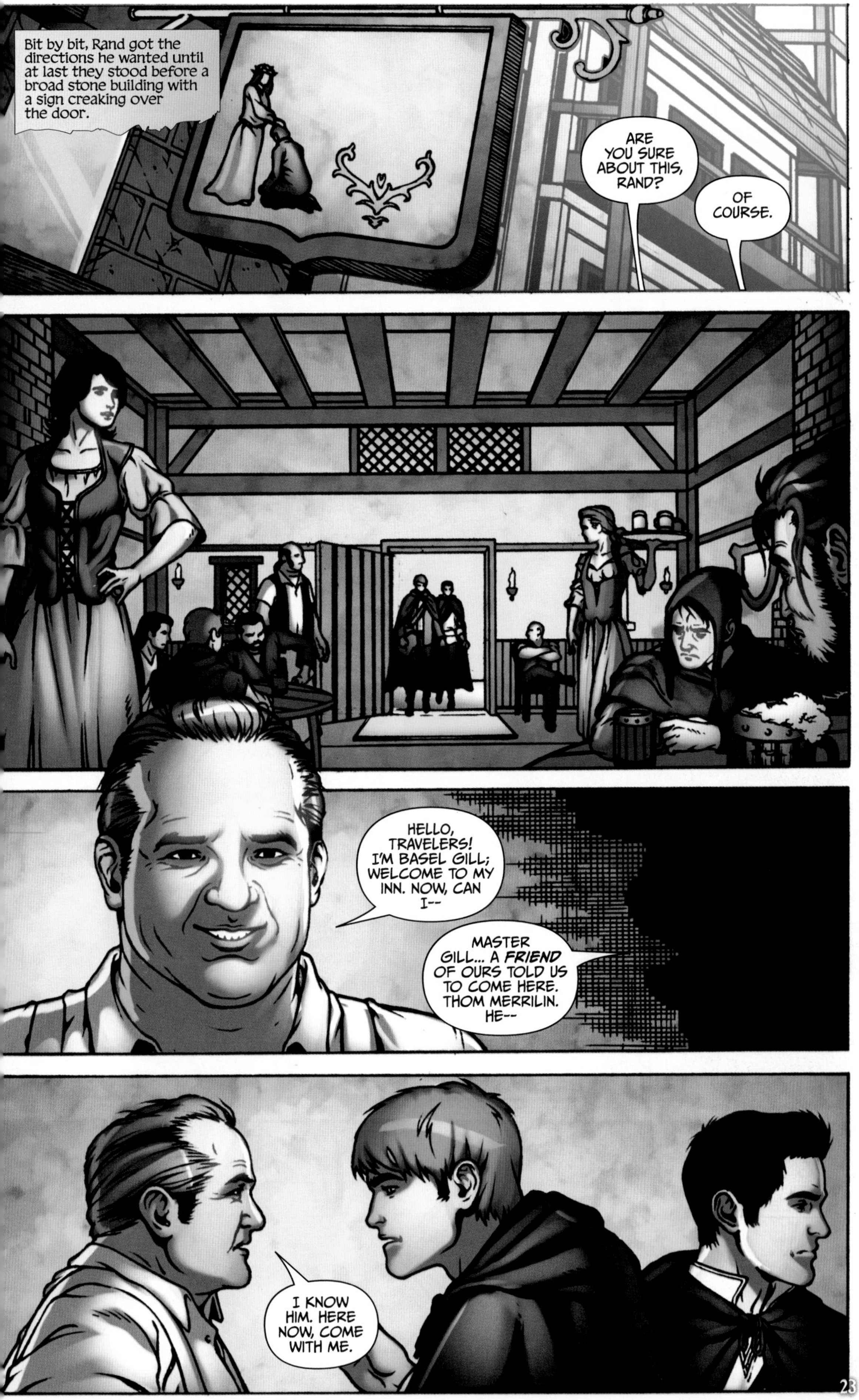
Bit by bit, Rand got the directions he wanted until at last they stood before a broad stone building with a sign creaking over the door.
ARE YOU SURE ABOUT THIS, RAND?
OF COURSE.
HELLO, TRAVELERS! I'M BASEL GILL; WELCOME TO MY INN. NOW, CAN I--
MASTER GILL... A *FRIEND* OF OURS TOLD US TO COME HERE. THOM MERRILIN. HE--
I KNOW HIM. HERE NOW, COME WITH ME.

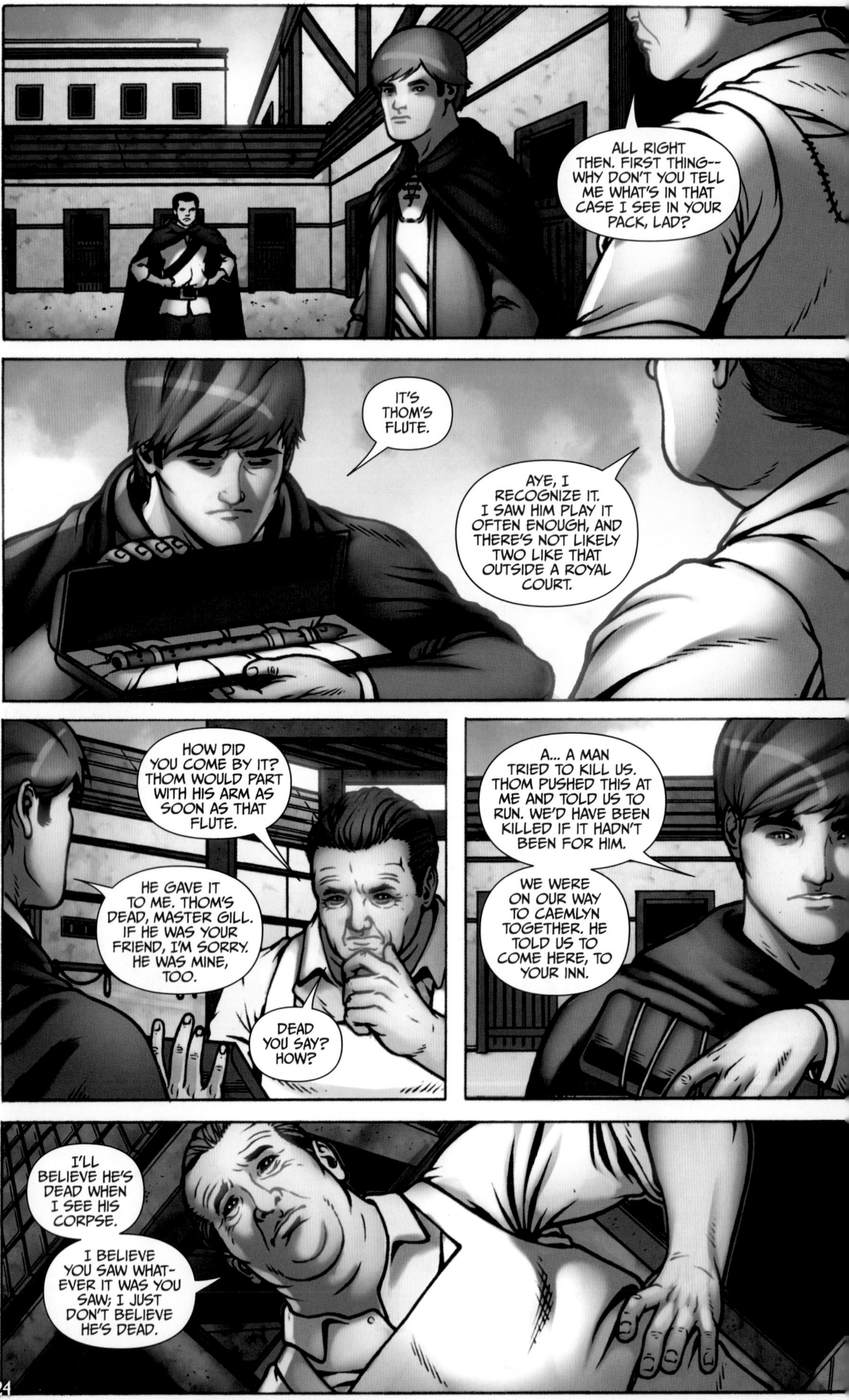
ALL RIGHT THEN. FIRST THING-- WHY DON'T YOU TELL ME WHAT'S IN THAT CASE I SEE IN YOUR PACK, LAD?
IT'S THOM'S FLUTE.
AYE, I RECOGNIZE IT. I SAW HIM PLAY IT OFTEN ENOUGH, AND THERE'S NOT LIKELY TWO LIKE THAT OUTSIDE A ROYAL COURT.
HOW DID YOU COME BY IT? THOM WOULD PART WITH HIS ARM AS SOON AS THAT FLUTE.
HE GAVE IT TO ME. THOM'S DEAD, MASTER GILL. IF HE WAS YOUR FRIEND, I'M SORRY. HE WAS MINE, TOO.
DEAD YOU SAY? HOW?
A... A MAN TRIED TO KILL US. THOM PUSHED THIS AT ME AND TOLD US TO RUN. WE'D HAVE BEEN KILLED IF IT HADN'T BEEN FOR HIM.
WE WERE ON OUR WAY TO CAEMLYN TOGETHER. HE TOLD US TO COME HERE, TO YOUR INN.
I'LL BELIEVE HE'S DEAD WHEN I SEE HIS CORPSE.
I BELIEVE YOU SAW WHAT-EVER IT WAS YOU SAW; I JUST DON'T BELIEVE HE'S DEAD.

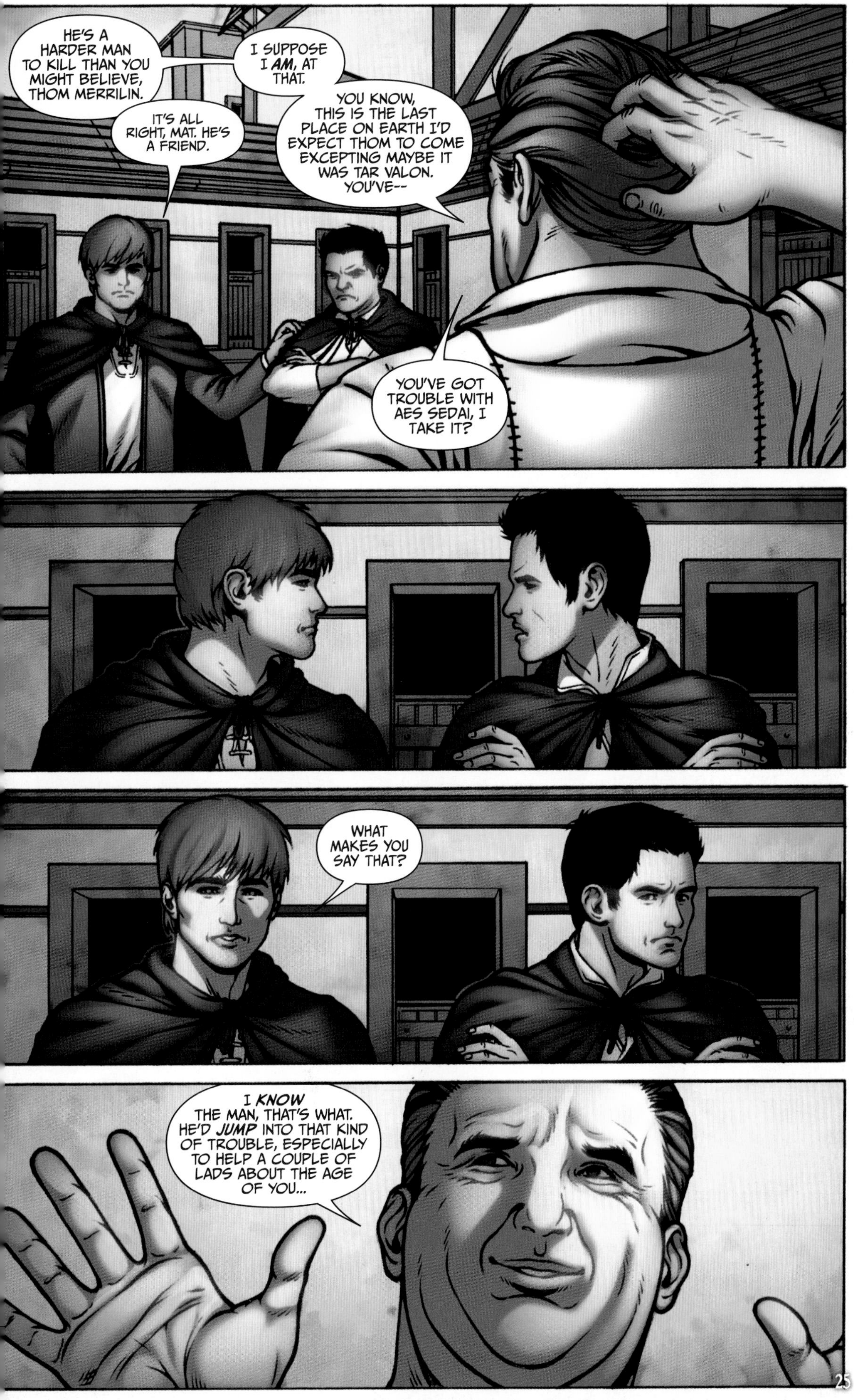
HE'S A HARDER MAN TO KILL THAN YOU MIGHT BELIEVE, THOM MERRILIN.
I SUPPOSE I *AM*, AT THAT.
IT'S ALL RIGHT, MAT. HE'S A FRIEND.
YOU KNOW, THIS IS THE LAST PLACE ON EARTH I'D EXPECT THOM TO COME EXCEPTING MAYBE IT WAS TAR VALON. YOU'VE--
YOU'VE GOT TROUBLE WITH AES SEDAI, I TAKE IT?
WHAT MAKES YOU SAY THAT?
I *KNOW* THE MAN, THAT'S WHAT. HE'D *JUMP* INTO THAT KIND OF TROUBLE, ESPECIALLY TO HELP A COUPLE OF LADS ABOUT THE AGE OF YOU...

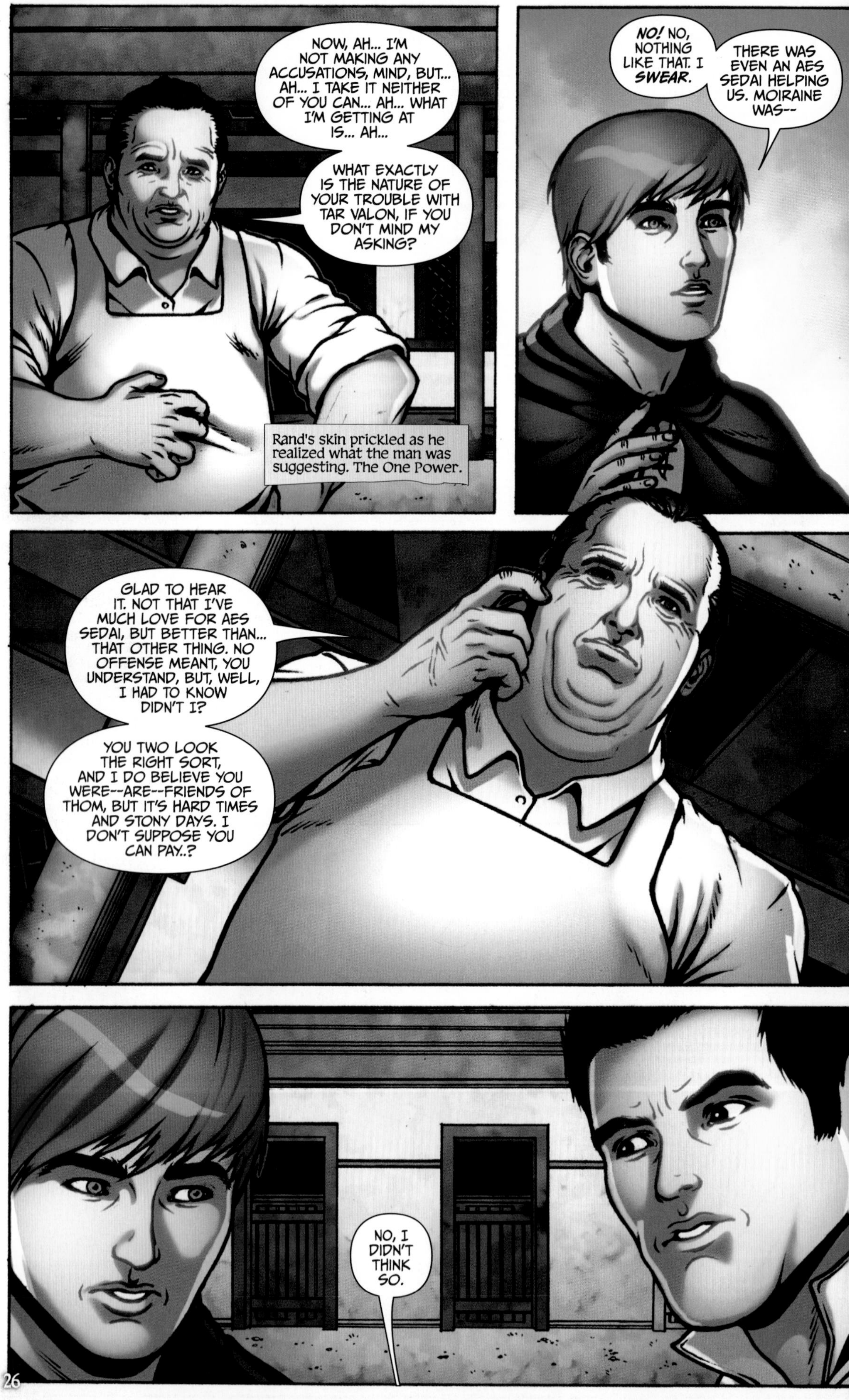
NOW, AH... I'M NOT MAKING ANY ACCUSATIONS, MIND, BUT... AH... I TAKE IT NEITHER OF YOU CAN... AH... WHAT I'M GETTING AT IS... AH...
WHAT EXACTLY IS THE NATURE OF YOUR TROUBLE WITH TAR VALON, IF YOU DON'T MIND MY ASKING?
Rand's skin prickled as he realized what the man was suggesting. The One Power.
NO! NO, NOTHING LIKE THAT. I SWEAR.
THERE WAS EVEN AN AES SEDAI HELPING US. MOIRAINE WAS--
GLAD TO HEAR IT. NOT THAT I'VE MUCH LOVE FOR AES SEDAI, BUT BETTER THAN... THAT OTHER THING. NO OFFENSE MEANT, YOU UNDERSTAND, BUT, WELL, I HAD TO KNOW DIDN'T I?
YOU TWO LOOK THE RIGHT SORT, AND I DO BELIEVE YOU WERE--ARE--FRIENDS OF THOM, BUT IT'S HARD TIMES AND STONY DAYS. I DON'T SUPPOSE YOU CAN PAY..?
NO, I DIDN'T THINK SO.

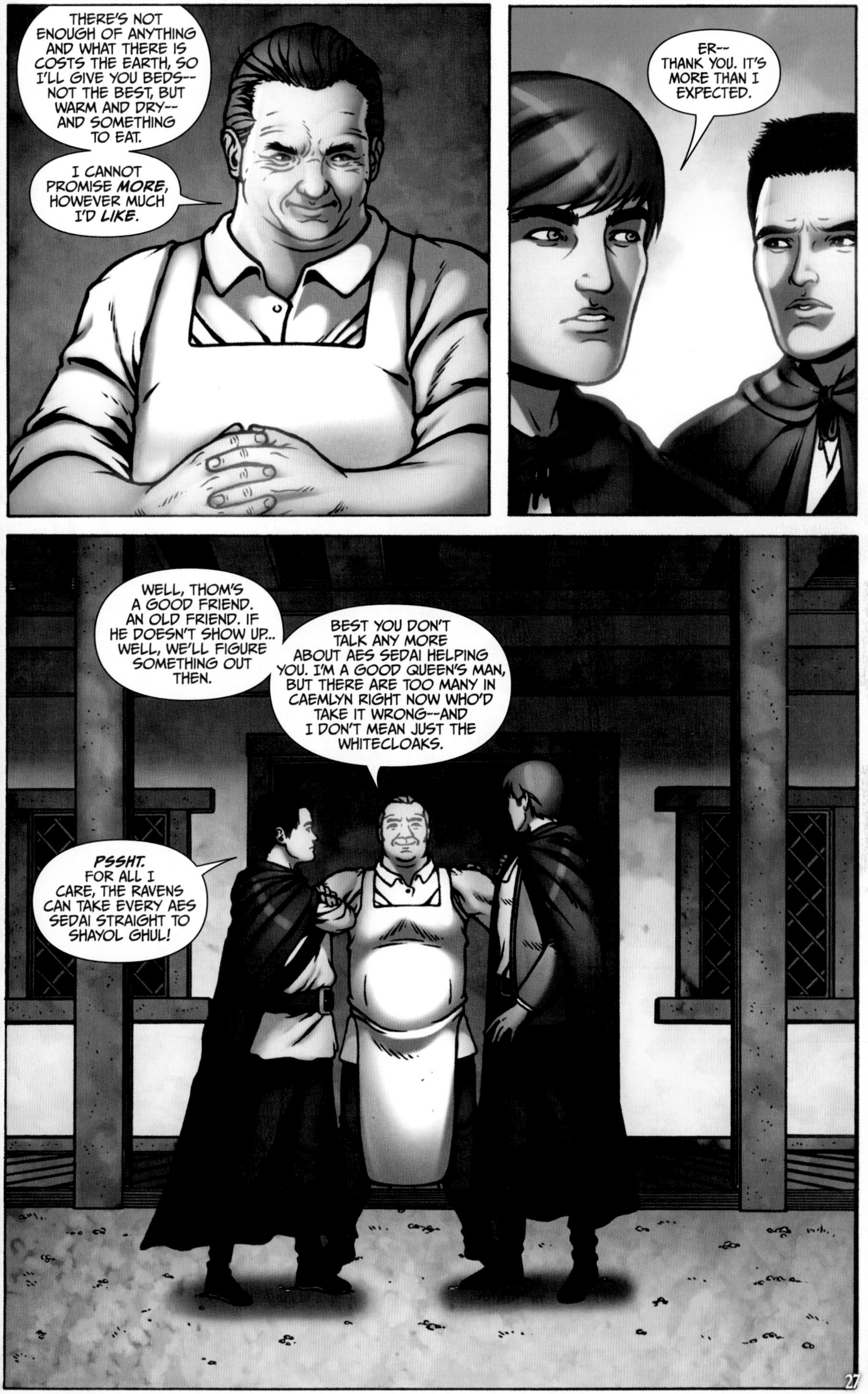
THERE'S NOT ENOUGH OF ANYTHING AND WHAT THERE IS COSTS THE EARTH, SO I'LL GIVE YOU BEDS-- NOT THE BEST, BUT WARM AND DRY-- AND SOMETHING TO EAT.
I CANNOT PROMISE MORE, HOWEVER MUCH I'D LIKE.
ER-- THANK YOU. IT'S MORE THAN I EXPECTED.
WELL, THOM'S A GOOD FRIEND. AN OLD FRIEND. IF HE DOESN'T SHOW UP... WELL, WE'LL FIGURE SOMETHING OUT THEN.
BEST YOU DON'T TALK ANY MORE ABOUT AES SEDAI HELPING YOU. I'M A GOOD QUEEN'S MAN, BUT THERE ARE TOO MANY IN CAEMLYN RIGHT NOW WHO'D TAKE IT WRONG--AND I DON'T MEAN JUST THE WHITECLOAKS.
PSSHT. FOR ALL I CARE, THE RAVENS CAN TAKE EVERY AES SEDAI STRAIGHT TO SHAYOL GHUL!

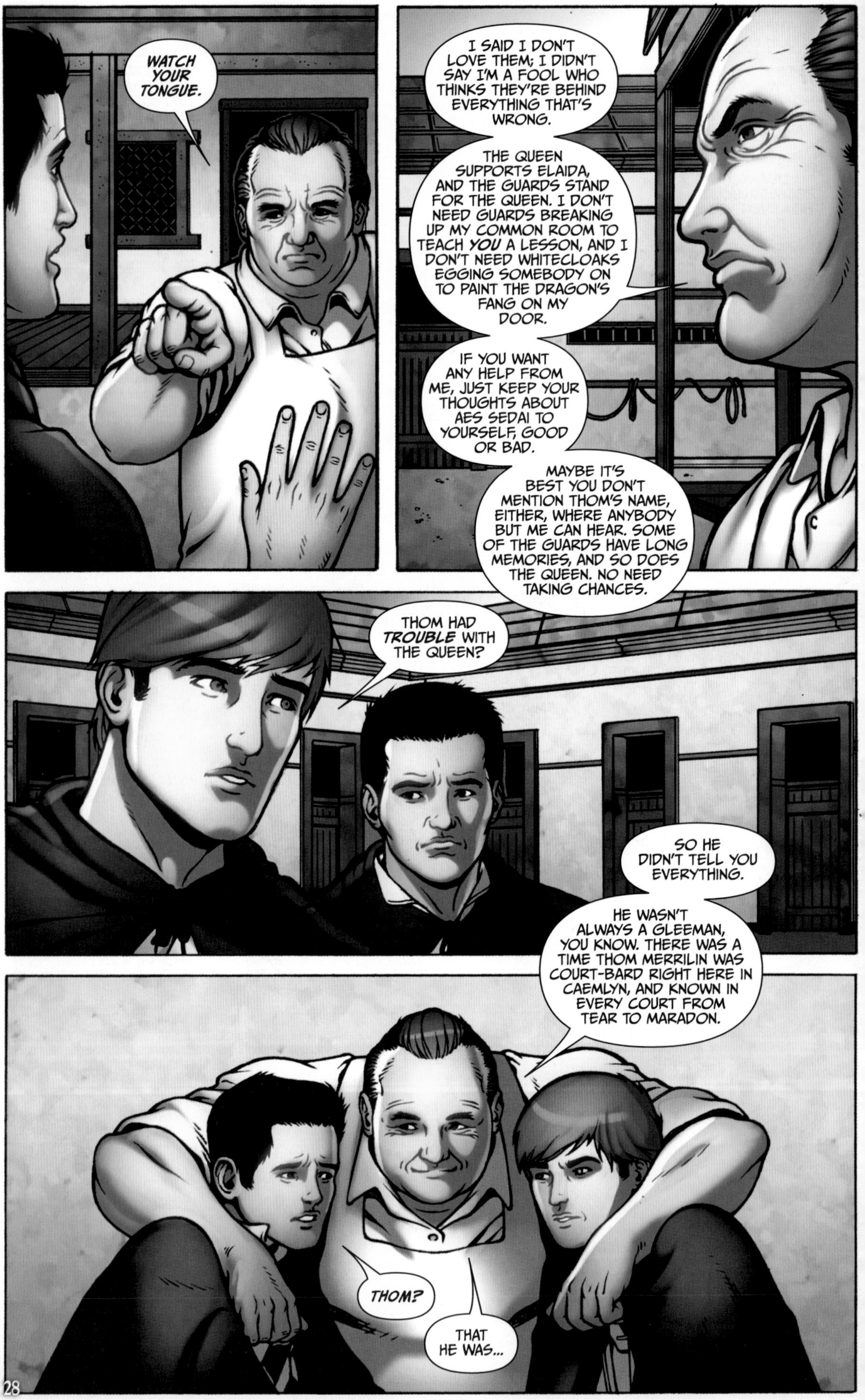
WATCH YOUR TONGUE.
I SAID I DON'T LOVE THEM; I DIDN'T SAY I'M A FOOL WHO THINKS THEY'RE BEHIND EVERYTHING THAT'S WRONG.
THE QUEEN SUPPORTS ELAIDA, AND THE GUARDS STAND FOR THE QUEEN. I DON'T NEED GUARDS BREAKING UP MY COMMON ROOM TO TEACH YOU A LESSON, AND I DON'T NEED WHITECLOAKS EGGING SOMEBODY ON TO PAINT THE DRAGON'S FANG ON MY DOOR.
IF YOU WANT ANY HELP FROM ME, JUST KEEP YOUR THOUGHTS ABOUT AES SEDAI TO YOURSELF, GOOD OR BAD.
MAYBE IT'S BEST YOU DON'T MENTION THOM'S NAME, EITHER, WHERE ANYBODY BUT ME CAN HEAR. SOME OF THE GUARDS HAVE LONG MEMORIES, AND SO DOES THE QUEEN. NO NEED TAKING CHANCES.
THOM HAD TROUBLE WITH THE QUEEN?
SO HE DIDN'T TELL YOU EVERYTHING.
HE WASN'T ALWAYS A GLEEMAN, YOU KNOW. THERE WAS A TIME THOM MERRILIN WAS COURT-BARD RIGHT HERE IN CAEMLYN, AND KNOWN IN EVERY COURT FROM TEAR TO MARADON.
THOM?
THAT HE WAS...

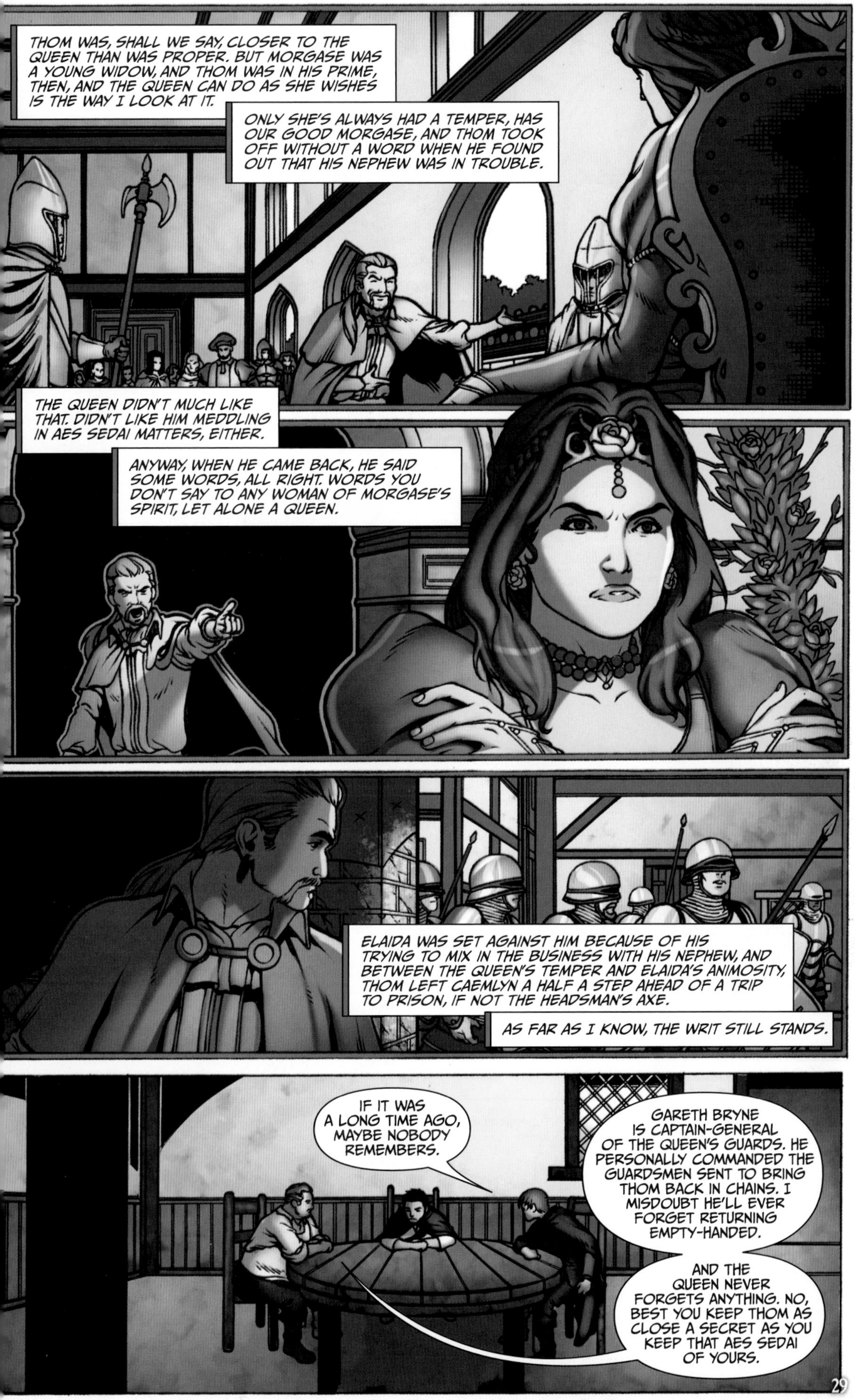
THOM WAS, SHALL WE SAY, CLOSER TO THE QUEEN THAN WAS PROPER. BUT MORGASE WAS A YOUNG WIDOW, AND THOM WAS IN HIS PRIME, THEN, AND THE QUEEN CAN DO AS SHE WISHES IS THE WAY I LOOK AT IT.
ONLY SHE'S ALWAYS HAD A TEMPER, HAS OUR GOOD MORGASE, AND THOM TOOK OFF WITHOUT A WORD WHEN HE FOUND OUT THAT HIS NEPHEW WAS IN TROUBLE.
THE QUEEN DIDN'T MUCH LIKE THAT. DIDN'T LIKE HIM MEDDLING IN AES SEDAI MATTERS, EITHER.
ANYWAY, WHEN HE CAME BACK, HE SAID SOME WORDS, ALL RIGHT. WORDS YOU DON'T SAY TO ANY WOMAN OF MORGASE'S SPIRIT, LET ALONE A QUEEN.
ELAIDA WAS SET AGAINST HIM BECAUSE OF HIS TRYING TO MIX IN THE BUSINESS WITH HIS NEPHEW, AND BETWEEN THE QUEEN'S TEMPER AND ELAIDA'S ANIMOSITY, THOM LEFT CAEMLYN A HALF A STEP AHEAD OF A TRIP TO PRISON, IF NOT THE HEADSMAN'S AXE.
AS FAR AS I KNOW, THE WRIT STILL STANDS.
IF IT WAS A LONG TIME AGO, MAYBE NOBODY REMEMBERS.
GARETH BRYNE IS CAPTAIN-GENERAL OF THE QUEEN'S GUARDS. HE PERSONALLY COMMANDED THE GUARDSMEN SENT TO BRING THOM BACK IN CHAINS. I MISDOUBT HE'LL EVER FORGET RETURNING EMPTY-HANDED.
AND THE QUEEN NEVER FORGETS ANYTHING. NO, BEST YOU KEEP THOM AS CLOSE A SECRET AS YOU KEEP THAT AES SEDAI OF YOURS.

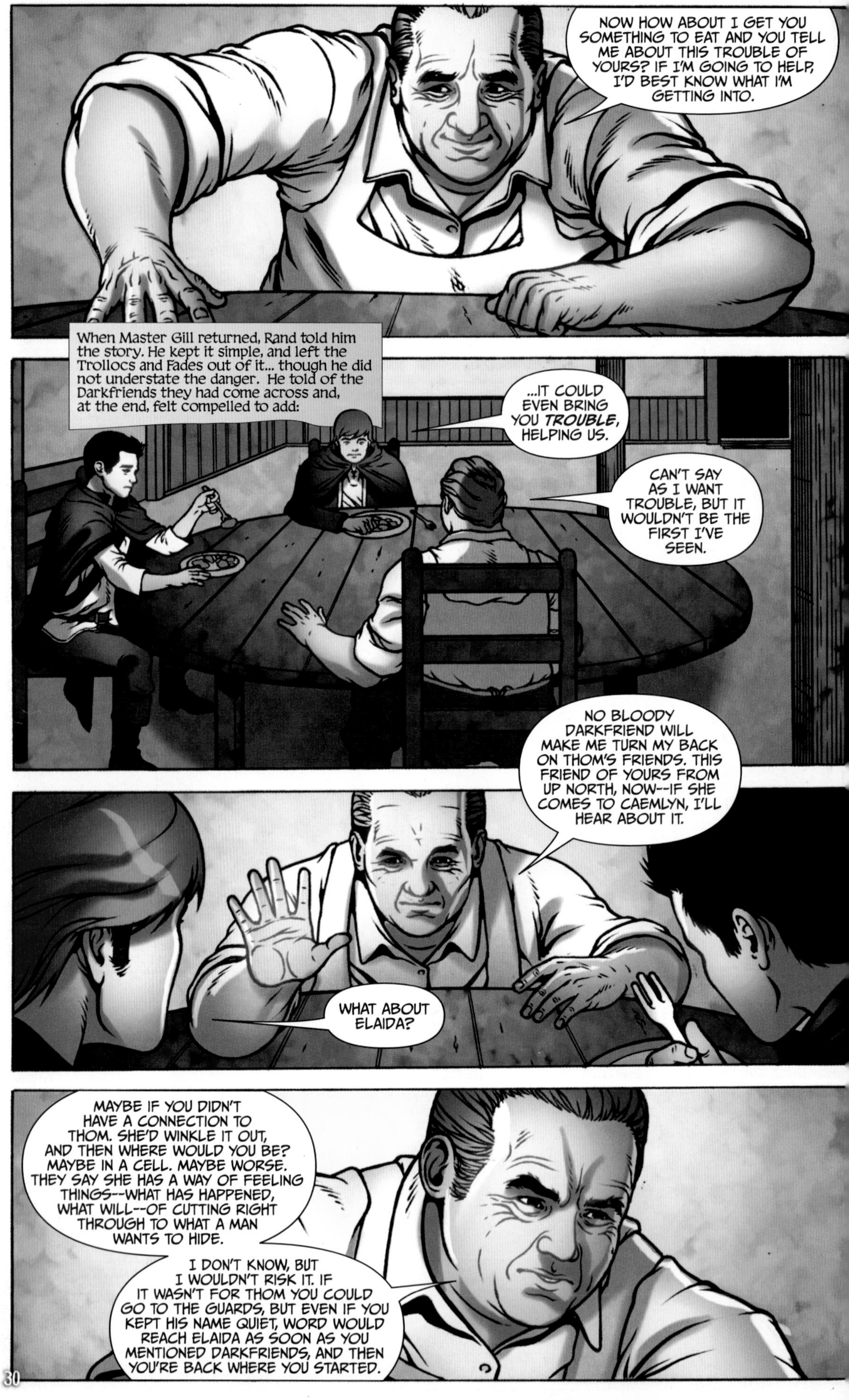
NOW HOW ABOUT I GET YOU SOMETHING TO EAT AND YOU TELL ME ABOUT THIS TROUBLE OF YOURS? IF I'M GOING TO HELP, I'D BEST KNOW WHAT I'M GETTING INTO.
When Master Gill returned, Rand told him the story. He kept it simple, and left the Trollocs and Fades out of it... though he did not understate the danger. He told of the Darkfriends they had come across and, at the end, felt compelled to add:
...IT COULD EVEN BRING YOU TROUBLE, HELPING US.
CAN'T SAY AS I WANT TROUBLE, BUT IT WOULDN'T BE THE FIRST I'VE SEEN.
NO BLOODY DARKFRIEND WILL MAKE ME TURN MY BACK ON THOM'S FRIENDS. THIS FRIEND OF YOURS FROM UP NORTH, NOW--IF SHE COMES TO CAEMLYN, I'LL HEAR ABOUT IT.
WHAT ABOUT ELAIDA?
MAYBE IF YOU DIDN'T HAVE A CONNECTION TO THOM. SHE'D WINKLE IT OUT, AND THEN WHERE WOULD YOU BE? MAYBE IN A CELL. MAYBE WORSE. THEY SAY SHE HAS A WAY OF FEELING THINGS--WHAT HAS HAPPENED, WHAT WILL--OF CUTTING RIGHT THROUGH TO WHAT A MAN WANTS TO HIDE.
I DON'T KNOW, BUT I WOULDN'T RISK IT. IF IT WASN'T FOR THOM YOU COULD GO TO THE GUARDS, BUT EVEN IF YOU KEPT HIS NAME QUIET, WORD WOULD REACH ELAIDA AS SOON AS YOU MENTIONED DARKFRIENDS, AND THEN YOU'RE BACK WHERE YOU STARTED.

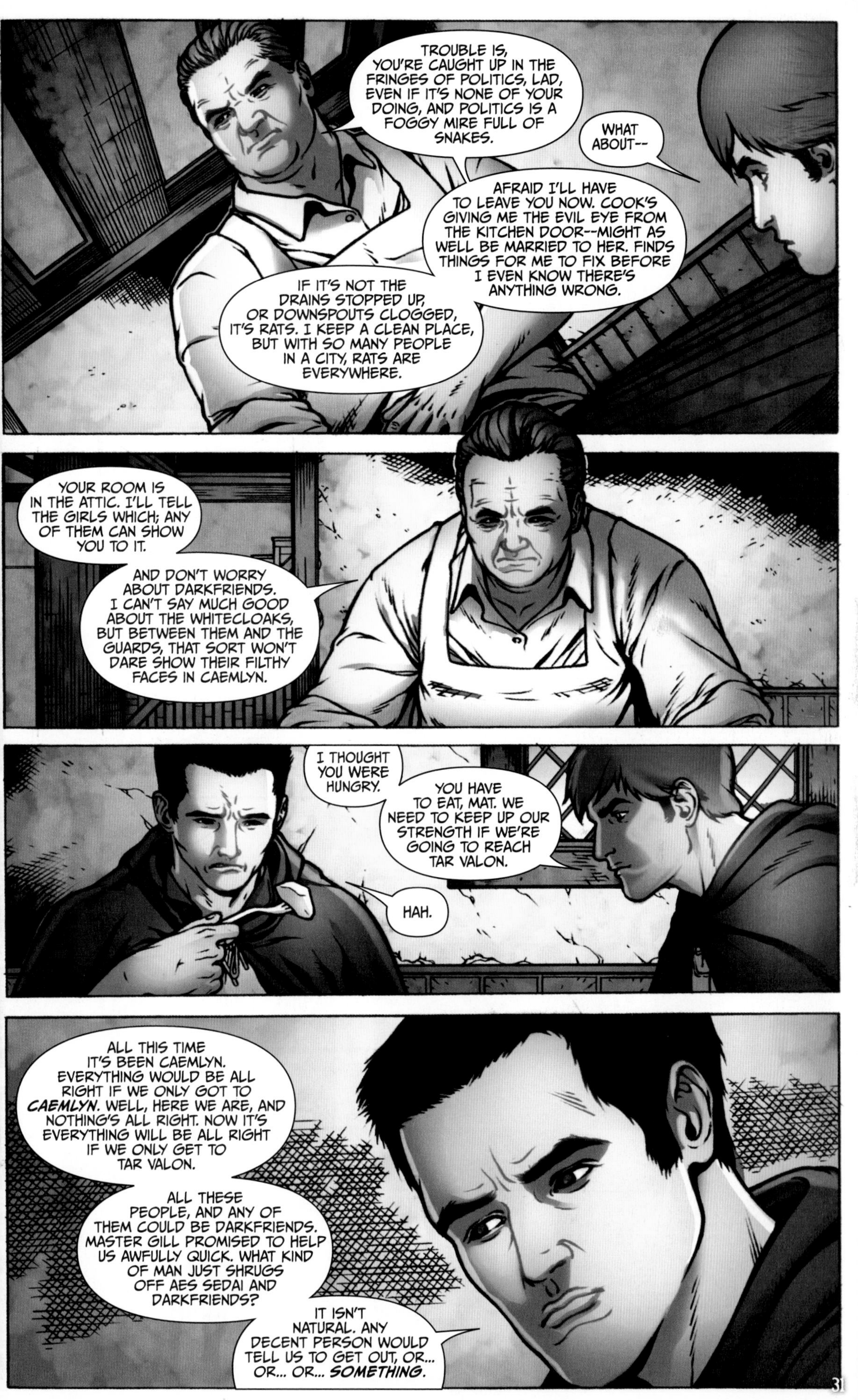
TROUBLE IS, YOU'RE CAUGHT UP IN THE FRINGES OF POLITICS, LAD, EVEN IF IT'S NONE OF YOUR DOING, AND POLITICS IS A FOGGY MIRE FULL OF SNAKES.
WHAT ABOUT--
AFRAID I'LL HAVE TO LEAVE YOU NOW. COOK'S GIVING ME THE EVIL EYE FROM THE KITCHEN DOOR--MIGHT AS WELL BE MARRIED TO HER. FINDS THINGS FOR ME TO FIX BEFORE I EVEN KNOW THERE'S ANYTHING WRONG.
IF IT'S NOT THE DRAINS STOPPED UP, OR DOWNSPOUTS CLOGGED, IT'S RATS. I KEEP A CLEAN PLACE, BUT WITH SO MANY PEOPLE IN A CITY, RATS ARE EVERYWHERE.
YOUR ROOM IS IN THE ATTIC. I'LL TELL THE GIRLS WHICH; ANY OF THEM CAN SHOW YOU TO IT.
AND DON'T WORRY ABOUT DARKFRIENDS. I CAN'T SAY MUCH GOOD ABOUT THE WHITECLOAKS, BUT BETWEEN THEM AND THE GUARDS, THAT SORT WON'T DARE SHOW THEIR FILTHY FACES IN CAEMLYN.
I THOUGHT YOU WERE HUNGRY.
YOU HAVE TO EAT, MAT. WE NEED TO KEEP UP OUR STRENGTH IF WE'RE GOING TO REACH TAR VALON.
HAH.
ALL THIS TIME IT'S BEEN CAEMLYN. EVERYTHING WOULD BE ALL RIGHT IF WE ONLY GOT TO ***CAEMLYN***. WELL, HERE WE ARE, AND NOTHING'S ALL RIGHT. NOW IT'S EVERYTHING WILL BE ALL RIGHT IF WE ONLY GET TO TAR VALON.
ALL THESE PEOPLE, AND ANY OF THEM COULD BE DARKFRIENDS. MASTER GILL PROMISED TO HELP US AWFULLY QUICK. WHAT KIND OF MAN JUST SHRUGS OFF AES SEDAI AND DARKFRIENDS?
IT ISN'T NATURAL. ANY DECENT PERSON WOULD TELL US TO GET OUT, OR... OR... OR... ***SOMETHING***.

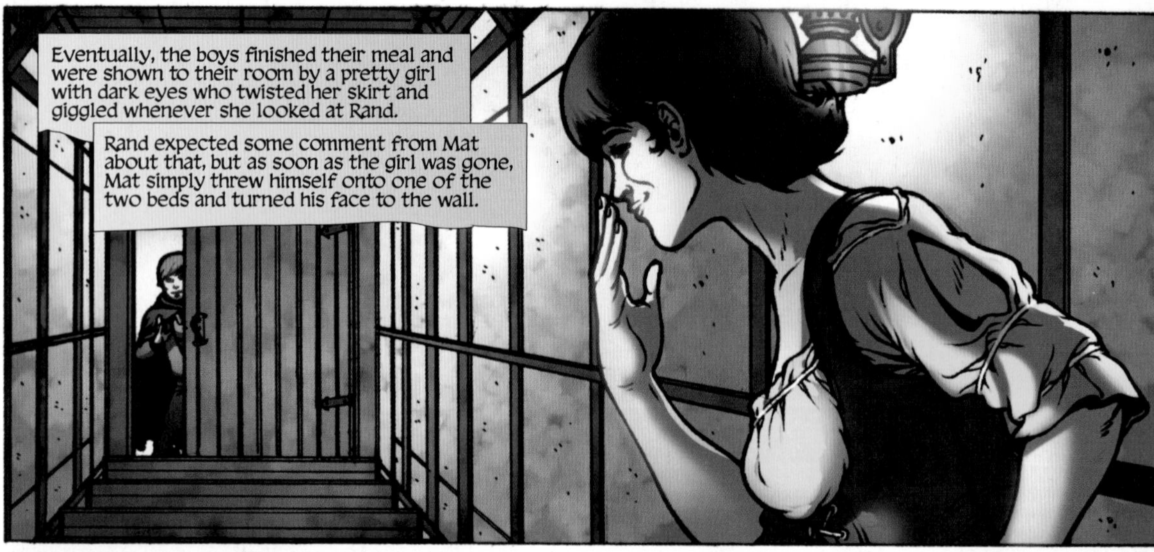
Eventually, the boys finished their meal and were shown to their room by a pretty girl with dark eyes who twisted her skirt and giggled whenever she looked at Rand.
Rand expected some comment from Mat about that, but as soon as the girl was gone, Mat simply threw himself onto one of the two beds and turned his face to the wall.

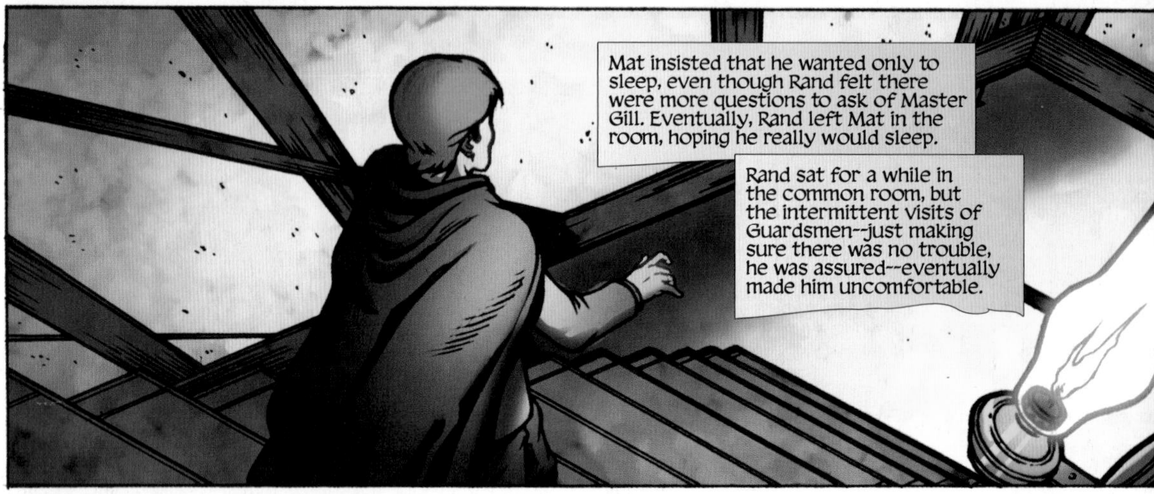
Mat insisted that he wanted only to sleep, even though Rand felt there were more questions to ask of Master Gill. Eventually, Rand left Mat in the room, hoping he really would sleep.
Rand sat for a while in the common room, but the intermittent visits of Guardsmen--just making sure there was no trouble, he was assured--eventually made him uncomfortable.

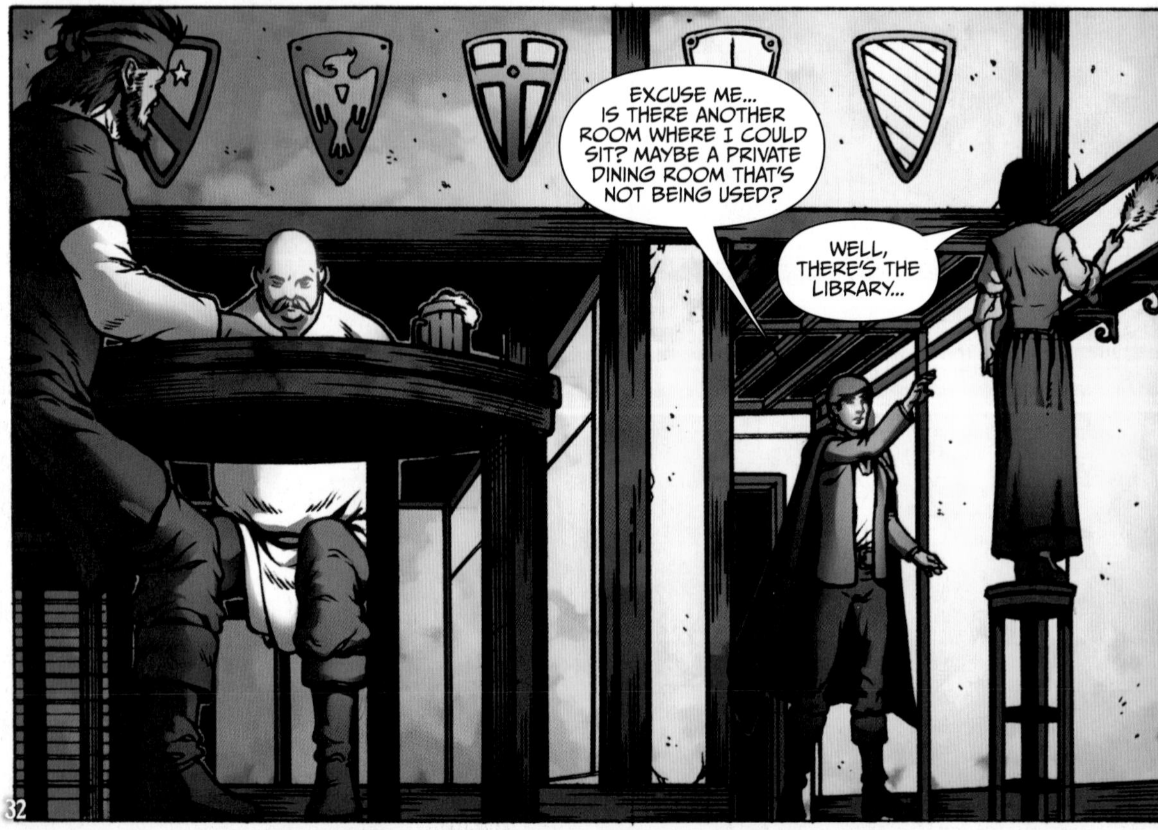
EXCUSE ME... IS THERE ANOTHER ROOM WHERE I COULD SIT? MAYBE A PRIVATE DINING ROOM THAT'S NOT BEING USED?
WELL, THERE'S THE LIBRARY...

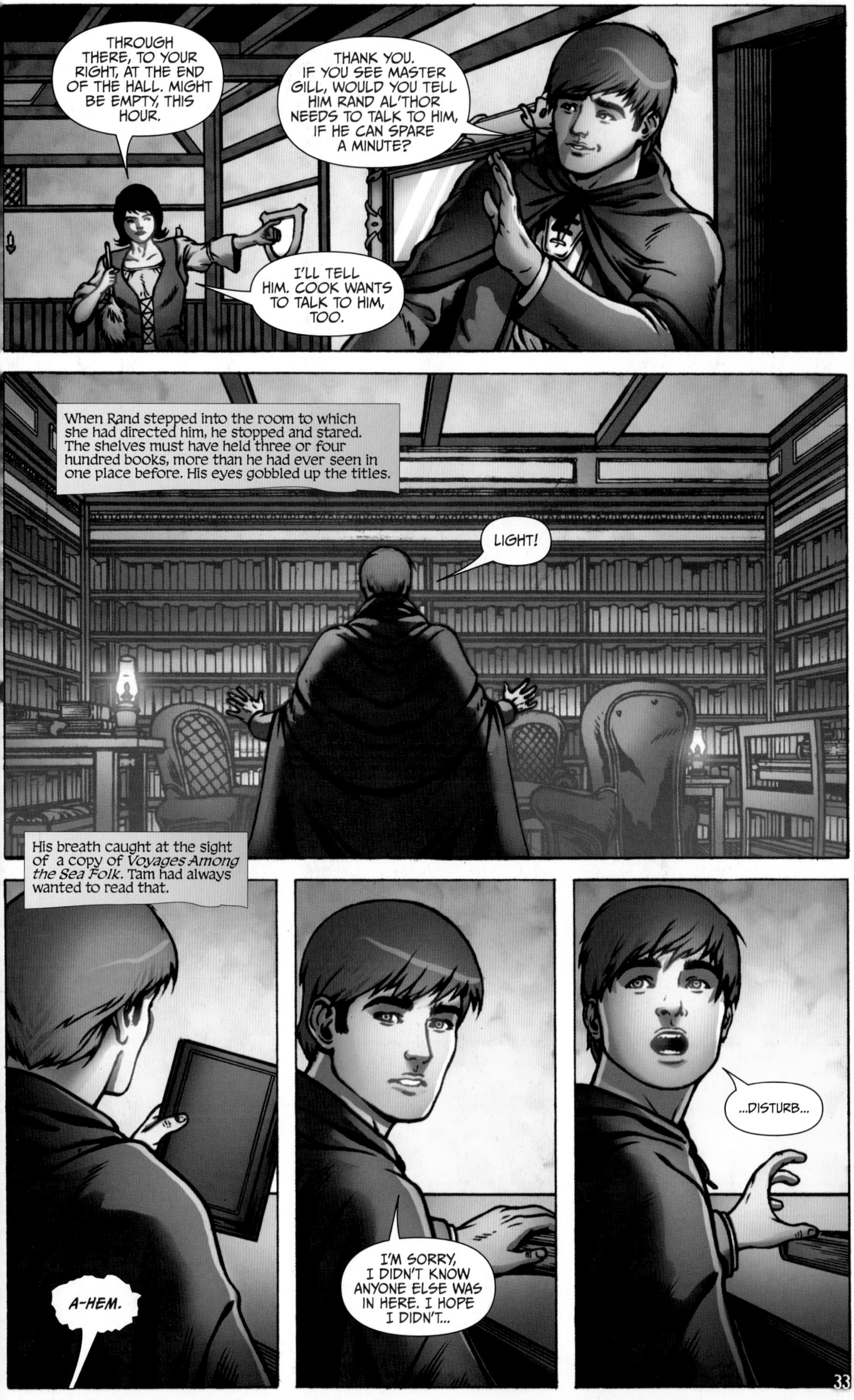
THROUGH THERE, TO YOUR RIGHT, AT THE END OF THE HALL. MIGHT BE EMPTY, THIS HOUR.
THANK YOU. IF YOU SEE MASTER GILL, WOULD YOU TELL HIM RAND AL'THOR NEEDS TO TALK TO HIM, IF HE CAN SPARE A MINUTE?
I'LL TELL HIM. COOK WANTS TO TALK TO HIM, TOO.
When Rand stepped into the room to which she had directed him, he stopped and stared. The shelves must have held three or four hundred books, more than he had ever seen in one place before. His eyes gobbled up the titles.
LIGHT!
His breath caught at the sight of a copy of *Voyages Among the Sea Folk*. Tam had always wanted to read that.
A-HEM.
I'M SORRY, I DIDN'T KNOW ANYONE ELSE WAS IN HERE. I HOPE I DIDN'T...
...DISTURB...

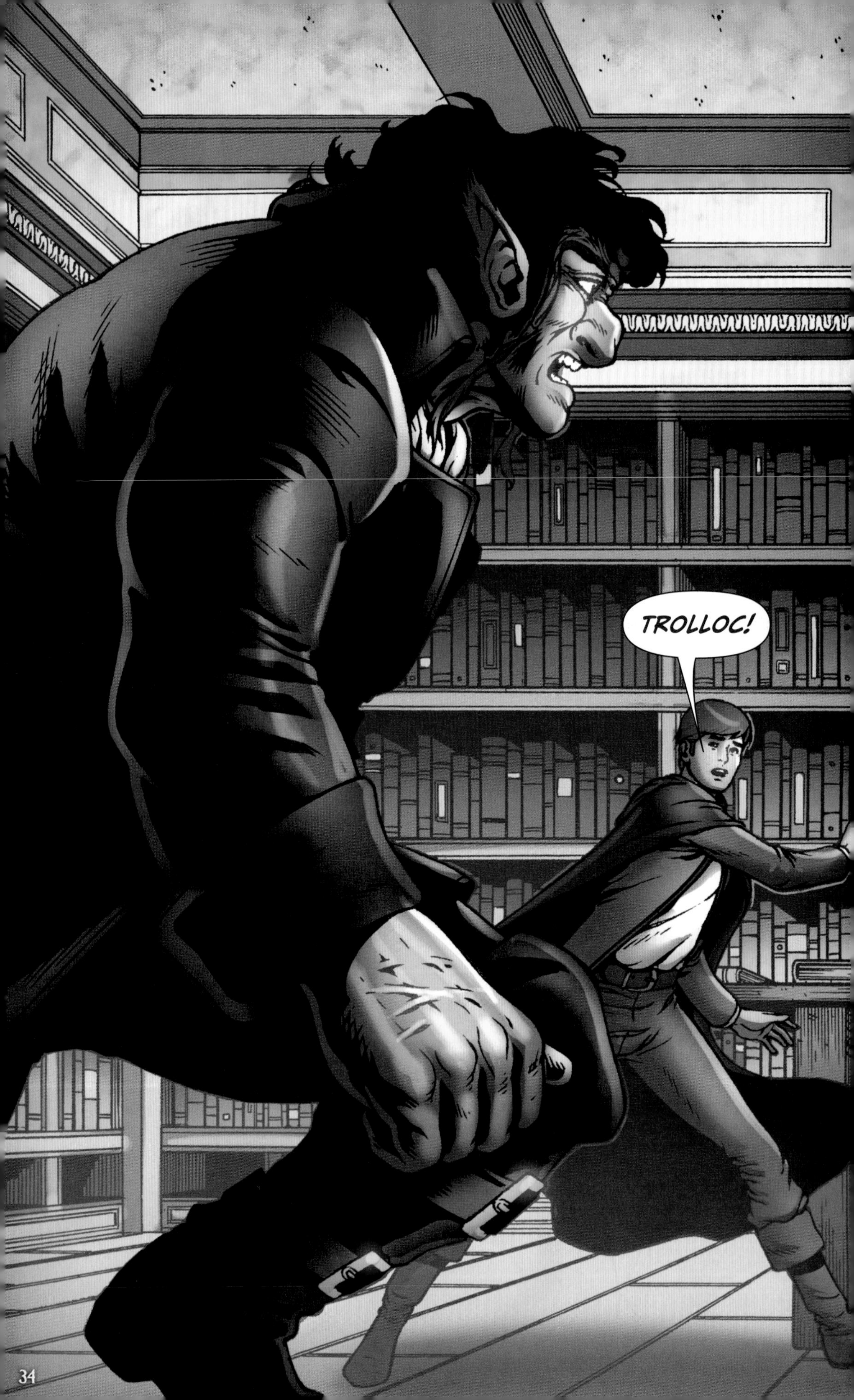
TROLLOC!

chapter two

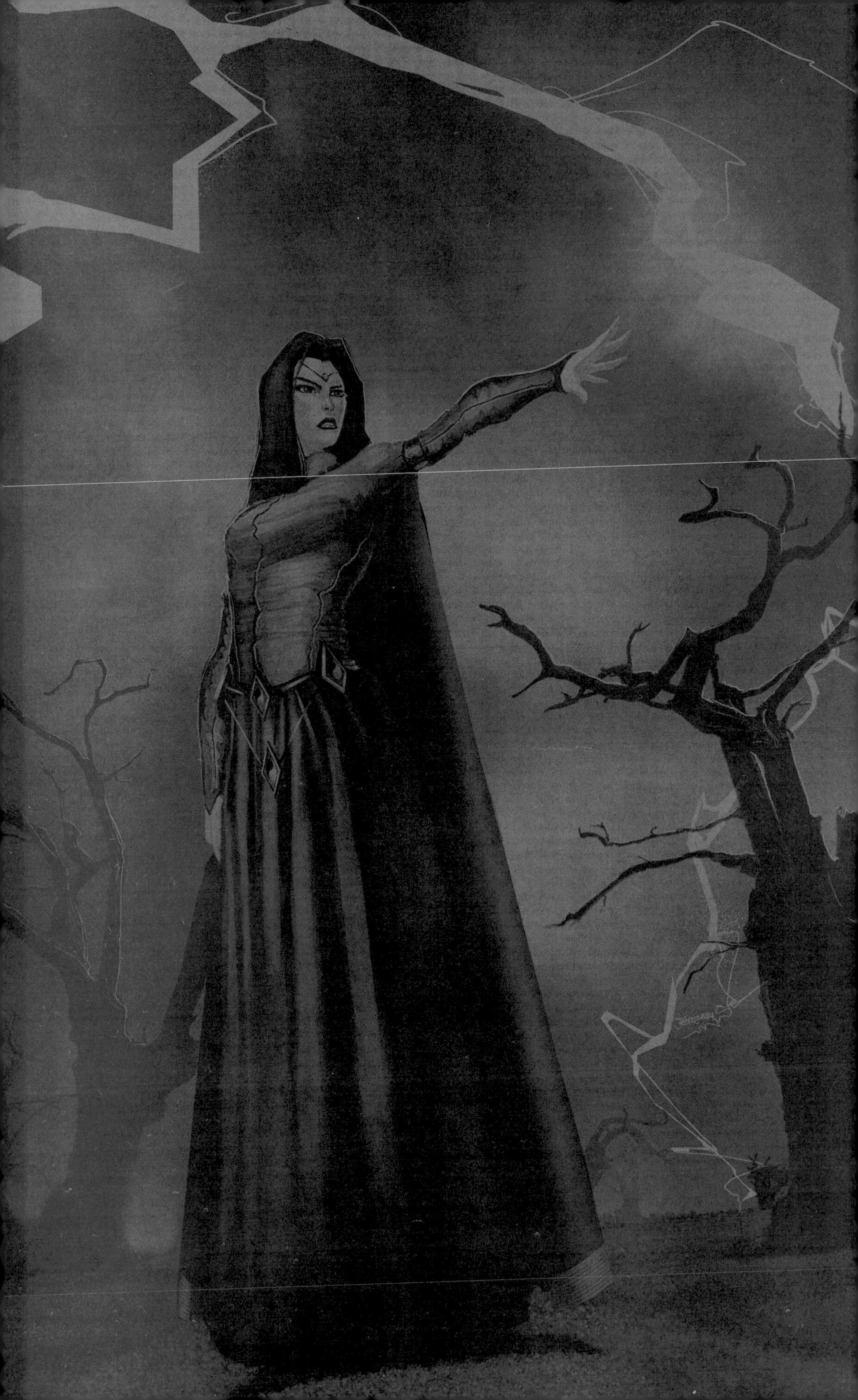

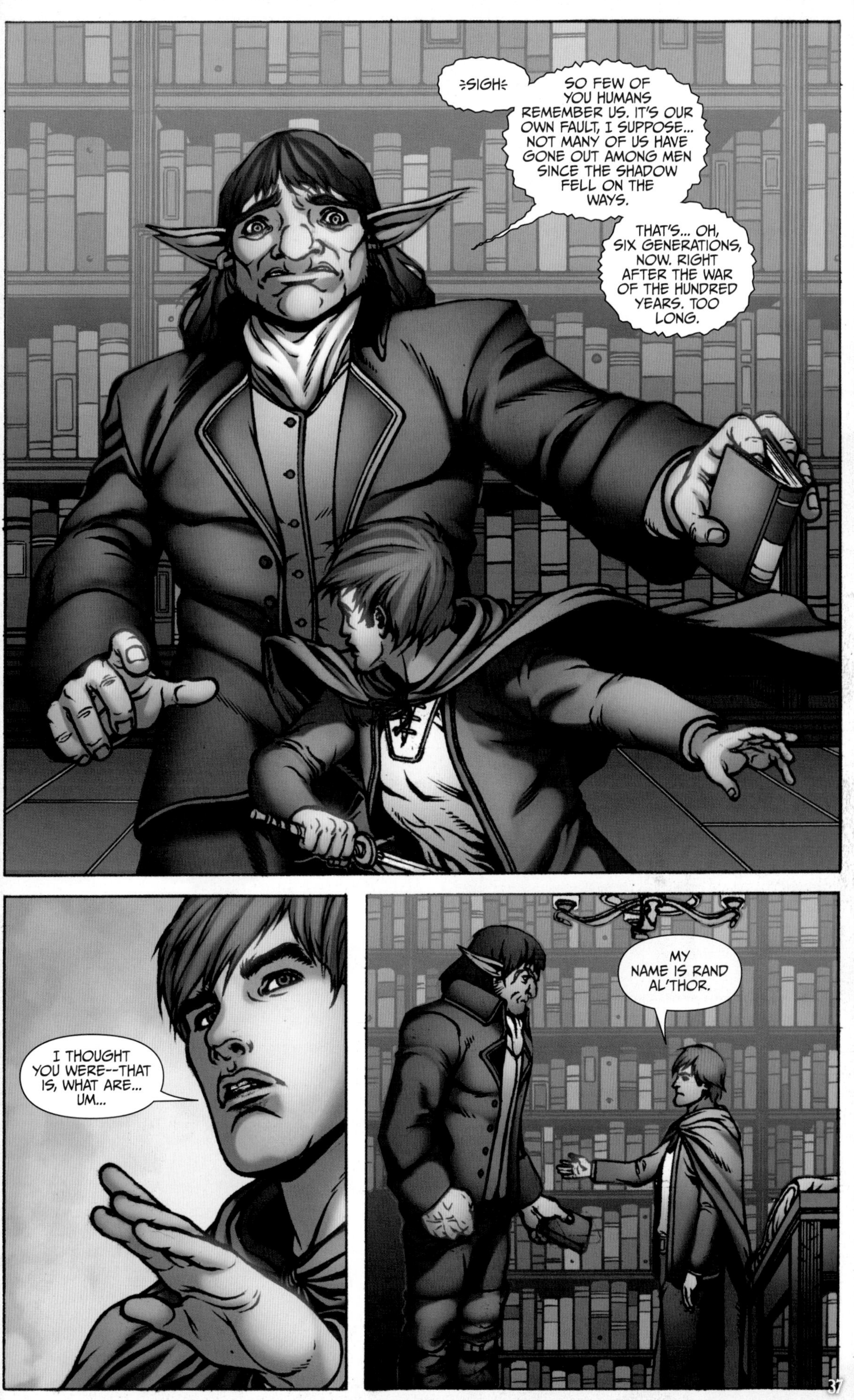

≡SIGH≡
SO FEW OF YOU HUMANS REMEMBER US. IT'S OUR OWN FAULT, I SUPPOSE... NOT MANY OF US HAVE GONE OUT AMONG MEN SINCE THE SHADOW FELL ON THE WAYS.
THAT'S... OH, SIX GENERATIONS, NOW. RIGHT AFTER THE WAR OF THE HUNDRED YEARS. TOO LONG.
I THOUGHT YOU WERE--THAT IS, WHAT ARE... UM...
MY NAME IS RAND AL'THOR.

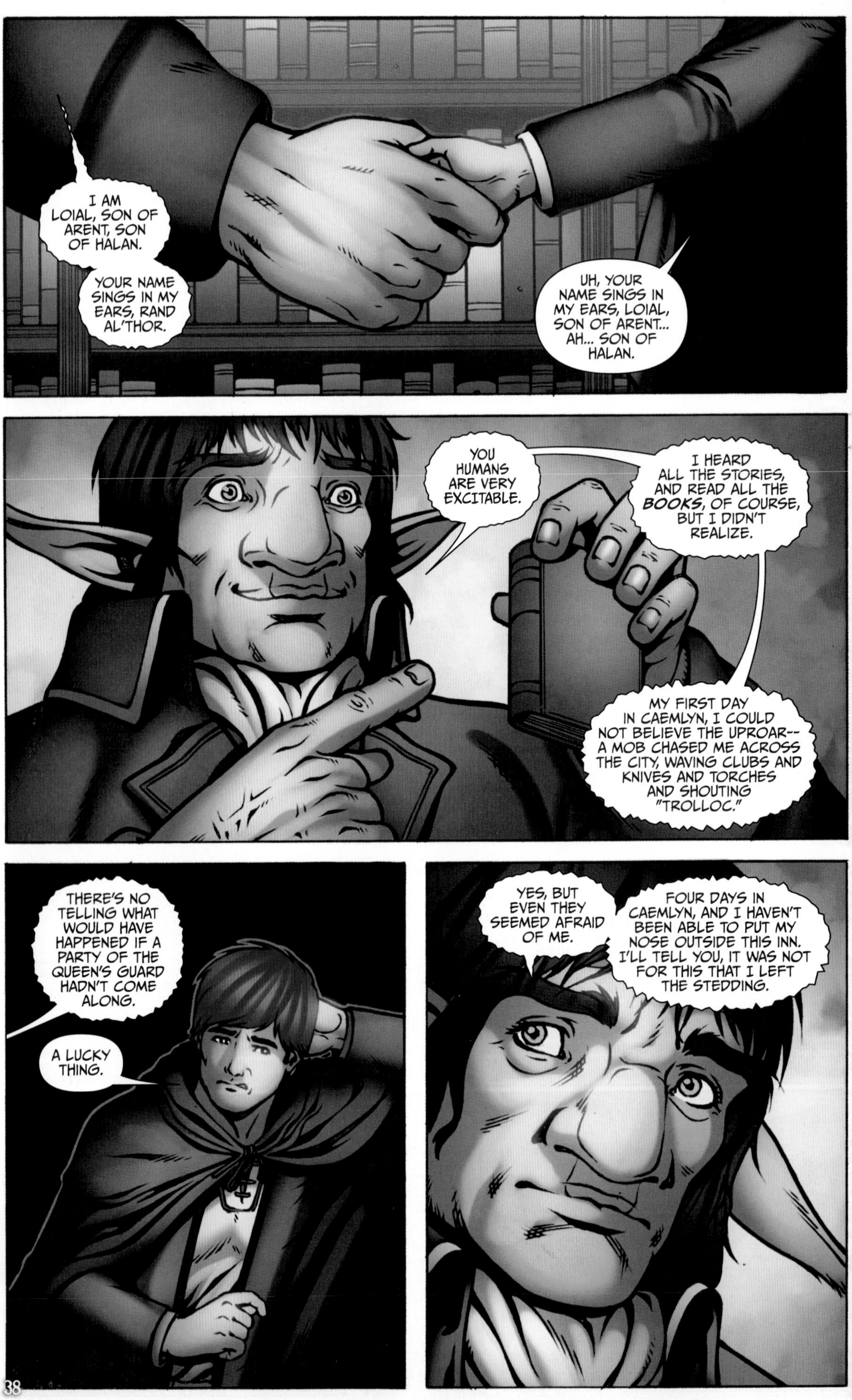
I AM LOIAL, SON OF ARENT, SON OF HALAN.
YOUR NAME SINGS IN MY EARS, RAND AL'THOR.
UH, YOUR NAME SINGS IN MY EARS, LOIAL, SON OF ARENT... AH... SON OF HALAN.
YOU HUMANS ARE VERY EXCITABLE.
I HEARD ALL THE STORIES, AND READ ALL THE *BOOKS*, OF COURSE, BUT I DIDN'T REALIZE.
MY FIRST DAY IN CAEMLYN, I COULD NOT BELIEVE THE UPROAR-- A MOB CHASED ME ACROSS THE CITY, WAVING CLUBS AND KNIVES AND TORCHES AND SHOUTING "TROLLOC."
THERE'S NO TELLING WHAT WOULD HAVE HAPPENED IF A PARTY OF THE QUEEN'S GUARD HADN'T COME ALONG.
A LUCKY THING.
YES, BUT EVEN THEY SEEMED AFRAID OF ME.
FOUR DAYS IN CAEMLYN, AND I HAVEN'T BEEN ABLE TO PUT MY NOSE OUTSIDE THIS INN. I'LL TELL YOU, IT WAS NOT FOR THIS THAT I LEFT THE STEDDING.

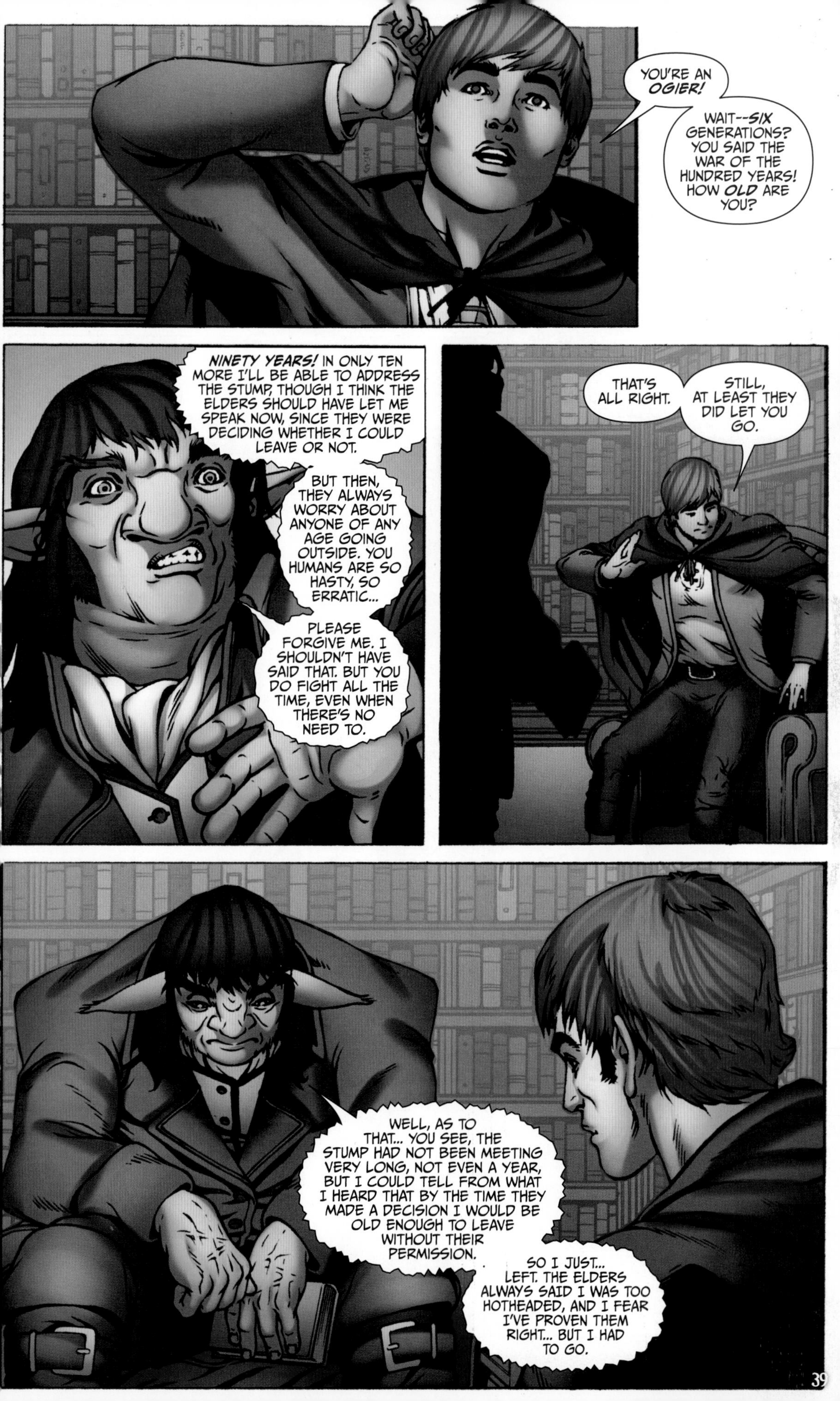
YOU'RE AN *OGIER!*
WAIT--*SIX* GENERATIONS? YOU SAID THE WAR OF THE HUNDRED YEARS! HOW *OLD* ARE YOU?
NINETY YEARS! IN ONLY TEN MORE I'LL BE ABLE TO ADDRESS THE STUMP, THOUGH I THINK THE ELDERS SHOULD HAVE LET ME SPEAK NOW, SINCE THEY WERE DECIDING WHETHER I COULD LEAVE OR NOT.
BUT THEN, THEY ALWAYS WORRY ABOUT ANYONE OF ANY AGE GOING OUTSIDE. YOU HUMANS ARE SO HASTY, SO ERRATIC...
PLEASE FORGIVE ME. I SHOULDN'T HAVE SAID THAT. BUT YOU DO FIGHT ALL THE TIME, EVEN WHEN THERE'S NO NEED TO.
THAT'S ALL RIGHT.
STILL, AT LEAST THEY DID LET YOU GO.
WELL, AS TO THAT... YOU SEE, THE STUMP HAD NOT BEEN MEETING VERY LONG, NOT EVEN A YEAR, BUT I COULD TELL FROM WHAT I HEARD THAT BY THE TIME THEY MADE A DECISION I WOULD BE OLD ENOUGH TO LEAVE WITHOUT THEIR PERMISSION.
SO I JUST... LEFT. THE ELDERS ALWAYS SAID I WAS TOO HOTHEADED, AND I FEAR I'VE PROVEN THEM RIGHT... BUT I HAD TO GO.

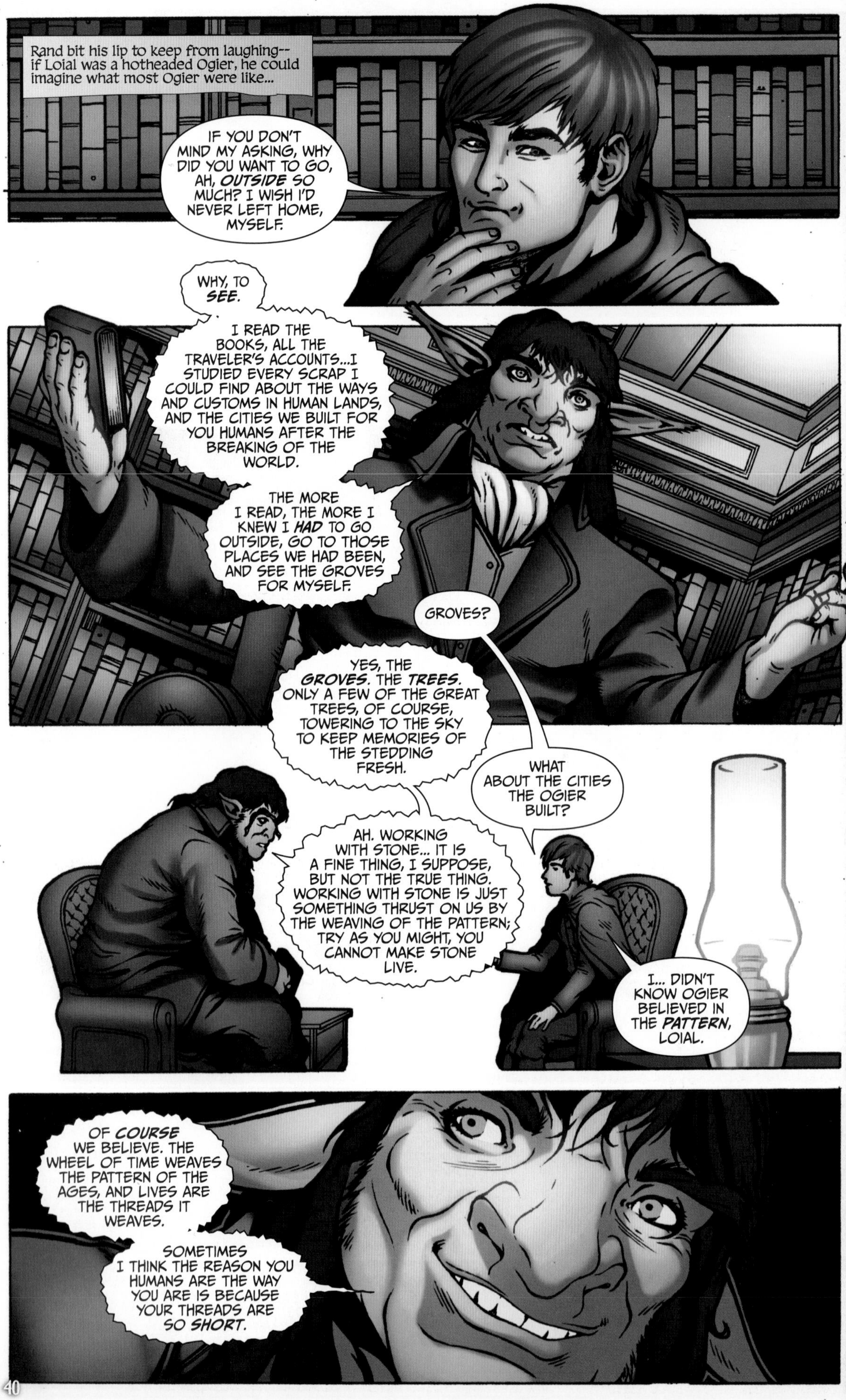

Rand bit his lip to keep from laughing--if Loial was a hotheaded Ogier, he could imagine what most Ogier were like...
IF YOU DON'T MIND MY ASKING, WHY DID YOU WANT TO GO, AH, *OUTSIDE* SO MUCH? I WISH I'D NEVER LEFT HOME, MYSELF.
WHY, TO *SEE*.
I READ THE BOOKS, ALL THE TRAVELER'S ACCOUNTS...I STUDIED EVERY SCRAP I COULD FIND ABOUT THE WAYS AND CUSTOMS IN HUMAN LANDS, AND THE CITIES WE BUILT FOR YOU HUMANS AFTER THE BREAKING OF THE WORLD.
THE MORE I READ, THE MORE I KNEW I *HAD* TO GO OUTSIDE, GO TO THOSE PLACES WE HAD BEEN, AND SEE THE GROVES FOR MYSELF.
GROVES?
YES, THE *GROVES*. THE *TREES*. ONLY A FEW OF THE GREAT TREES, OF COURSE, TOWERING TO THE SKY TO KEEP MEMORIES OF THE STEDDING FRESH.
WHAT ABOUT THE CITIES THE OGIER BUILT?
AH. WORKING WITH STONE... IT IS A FINE THING, I SUPPOSE, BUT NOT THE TRUE THING. WORKING WITH STONE IS JUST SOMETHING THRUST ON US BY THE WEAVING OF THE PATTERN; TRY AS YOU MIGHT, YOU CANNOT MAKE STONE LIVE.
I... DIDN'T KNOW OGIER BELIEVED IN THE *PATTERN*, LOIAL.
OF *COURSE* WE BELIEVE. THE WHEEL OF TIME WEAVES THE PATTERN OF THE AGES, AND LIVES ARE THE THREADS IT WEAVES.
SOMETIMES I THINK THE REASON YOU HUMANS ARE THE WAY YOU ARE IS BECAUSE YOUR THREADS ARE SO *SHORT*.

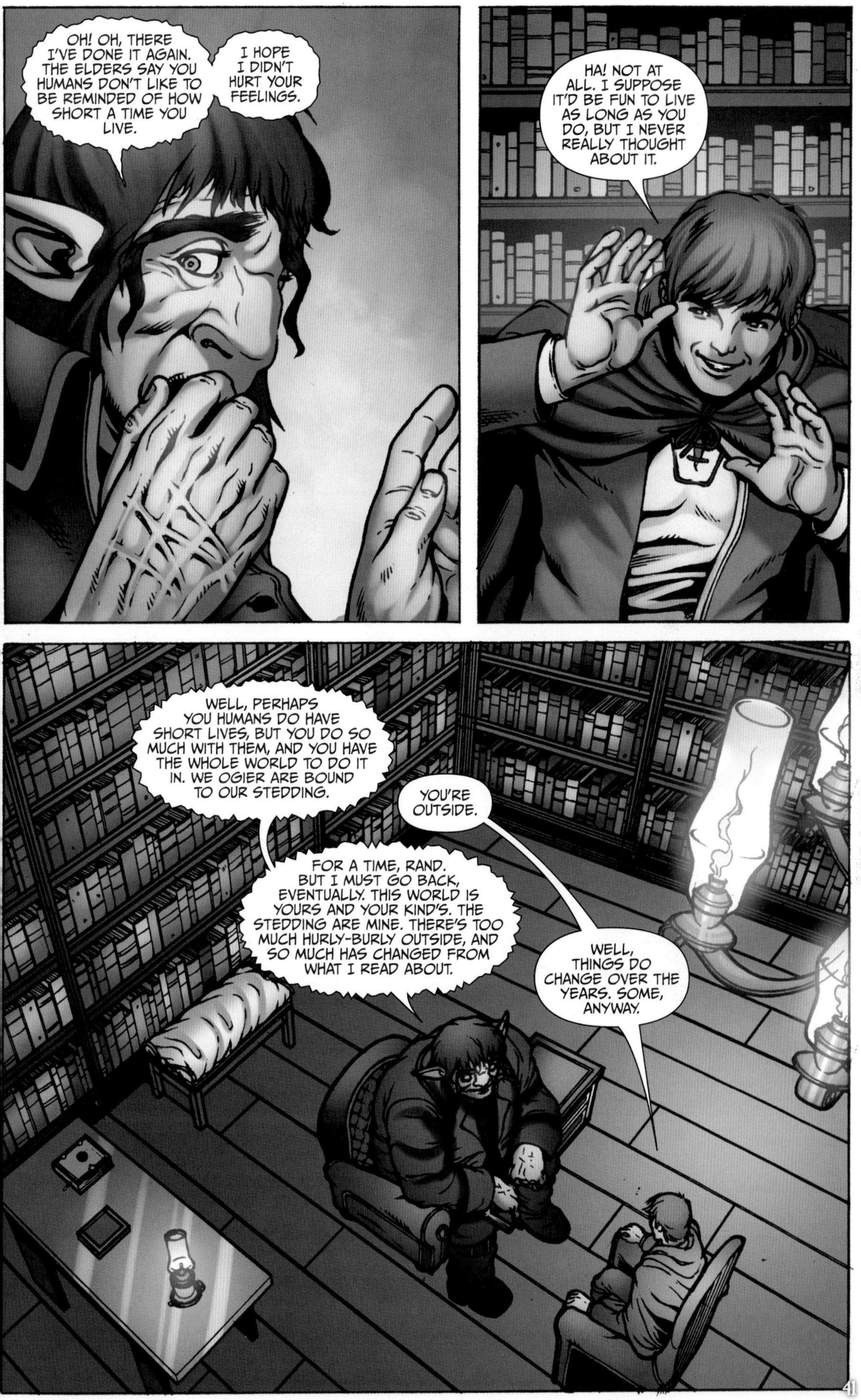
OH! OH, THERE I'VE DONE IT AGAIN. THE ELDERS SAY YOU HUMANS DON'T LIKE TO BE REMINDED OF HOW SHORT A TIME YOU LIVE.
I HOPE I DIDN'T HURT YOUR FEELINGS.
HA! NOT AT ALL. I SUPPOSE IT'D BE FUN TO LIVE AS LONG AS YOU DO, BUT I NEVER REALLY THOUGHT ABOUT IT.
WELL, PERHAPS YOU HUMANS DO HAVE SHORT LIVES, BUT YOU DO SO MUCH WITH THEM, AND YOU HAVE THE WHOLE WORLD TO DO IT IN. WE OGIER ARE BOUND TO OUR STEDDING.
YOU'RE OUTSIDE.
FOR A TIME, RAND. BUT I MUST GO BACK, EVENTUALLY. THIS WORLD IS YOURS AND YOUR KIND'S. THE STEDDING ARE MINE. THERE'S TOO MUCH HURLY-BURLY OUTSIDE, AND SO MUCH HAS CHANGED FROM WHAT I READ ABOUT.
WELL, THINGS DO CHANGE OVER THE YEARS. SOME, ANYWAY.

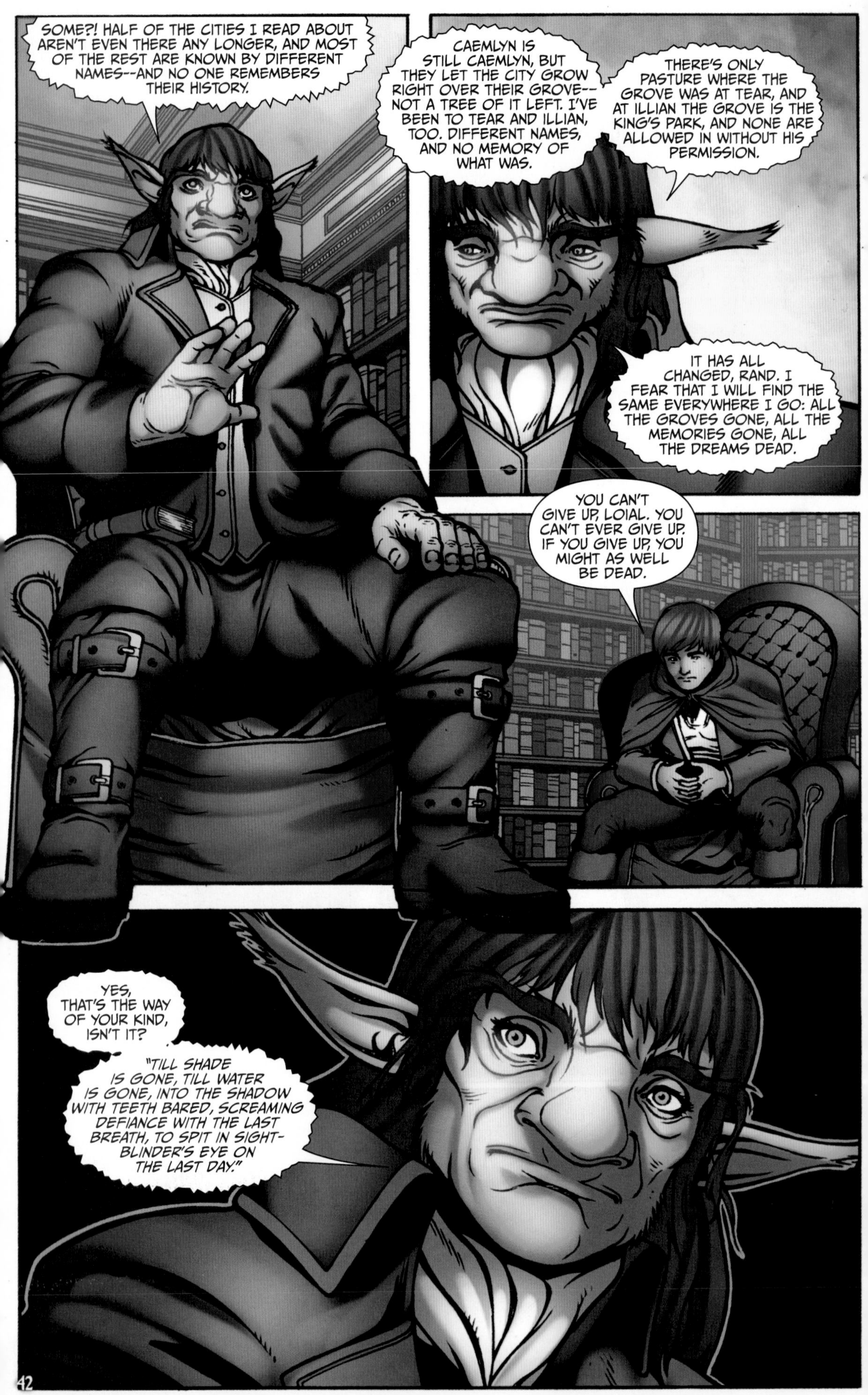
SOME?! HALF OF THE CITIES I READ ABOUT AREN'T EVEN THERE ANY LONGER, AND MOST OF THE REST ARE KNOWN BY DIFFERENT NAMES--AND NO ONE REMEMBERS THEIR HISTORY.
CAEMLYN IS STILL CAEMLYN, BUT THEY LET THE CITY GROW RIGHT OVER THEIR GROVE--NOT A TREE OF IT LEFT. I'VE BEEN TO TEAR AND ILLIAN, TOO. DIFFERENT NAMES, AND NO MEMORY OF WHAT WAS.
THERE'S ONLY PASTURE WHERE THE GROVE WAS AT TEAR, AND AT ILLIAN THE GROVE IS THE KING'S PARK, AND NONE ARE ALLOWED IN WITHOUT HIS PERMISSION.
IT HAS ALL CHANGED, RAND. I FEAR THAT I WILL FIND THE SAME EVERYWHERE I GO: ALL THE GROVES GONE, ALL THE MEMORIES GONE, ALL THE DREAMS DEAD.
YOU CAN'T GIVE UP, LOIAL. YOU CAN'T EVER GIVE UP. IF YOU GIVE UP, YOU MIGHT AS WELL BE DEAD.
YES, THAT'S THE WAY OF YOUR KIND, ISN'T IT?
"TILL SHADE IS GONE, TILL WATER IS GONE, INTO THE SHADOW WITH TEETH BARED, SCREAMING DEFIANCE WITH THE LAST BREATH, TO SPIT IN SIGHT-BLINDER'S EYE ON THE LAST DAY."

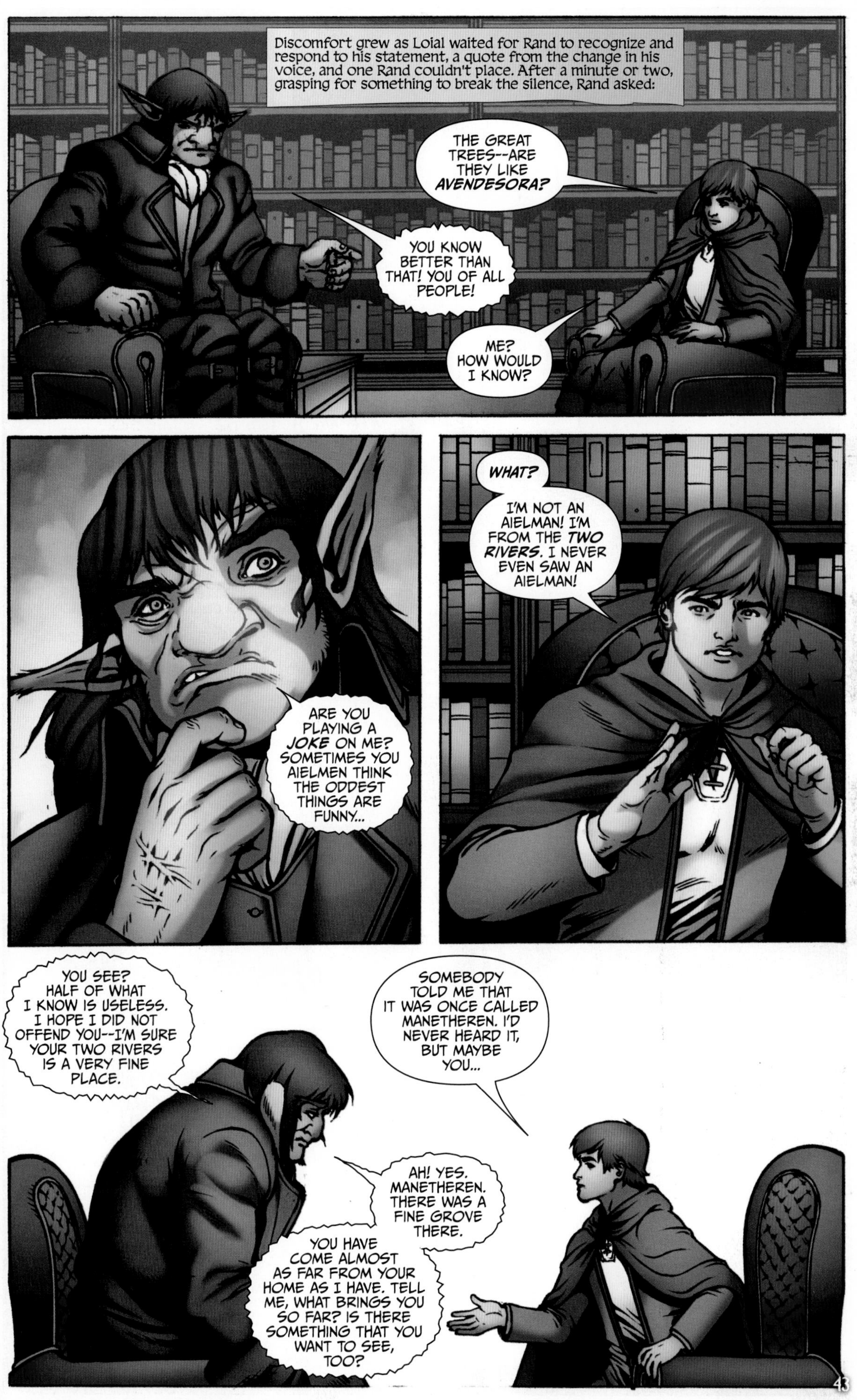

Discomfort grew as Loial waited for Rand to recognize and respond to his statement, a quote from the change in his voice, and one Rand couldn't place. After a minute or two, grasping for something to break the silence, Rand asked:
THE GREAT TREES--ARE THEY LIKE *AVENDESORA?*
YOU KNOW BETTER THAN THAT! YOU OF ALL PEOPLE!
ME? HOW WOULD I KNOW?
ARE YOU PLAYING A *JOKE* ON ME? SOMETIMES YOU AIELMEN THINK THE ODDEST THINGS ARE FUNNY...
WHAT?
I'M NOT AN AIELMAN! I'M FROM THE *TWO RIVERS*. I NEVER EVEN SAW AN AIELMAN!
YOU SEE? HALF OF WHAT I KNOW IS USELESS. I HOPE I DID NOT OFFEND YOU--I'M SURE YOUR TWO RIVERS IS A VERY FINE PLACE.
SOMEBODY TOLD ME THAT IT WAS ONCE CALLED MANETHEREN. I'D NEVER HEARD IT, BUT MAYBE YOU...
AH! YES. MANETHEREN. THERE WAS A FINE GROVE THERE.
YOU HAVE COME ALMOST AS FAR FROM YOUR HOME AS I HAVE. TELL ME, WHAT BRINGS YOU SO FAR? IS THERE SOMETHING THAT YOU WANT TO SEE, TOO?

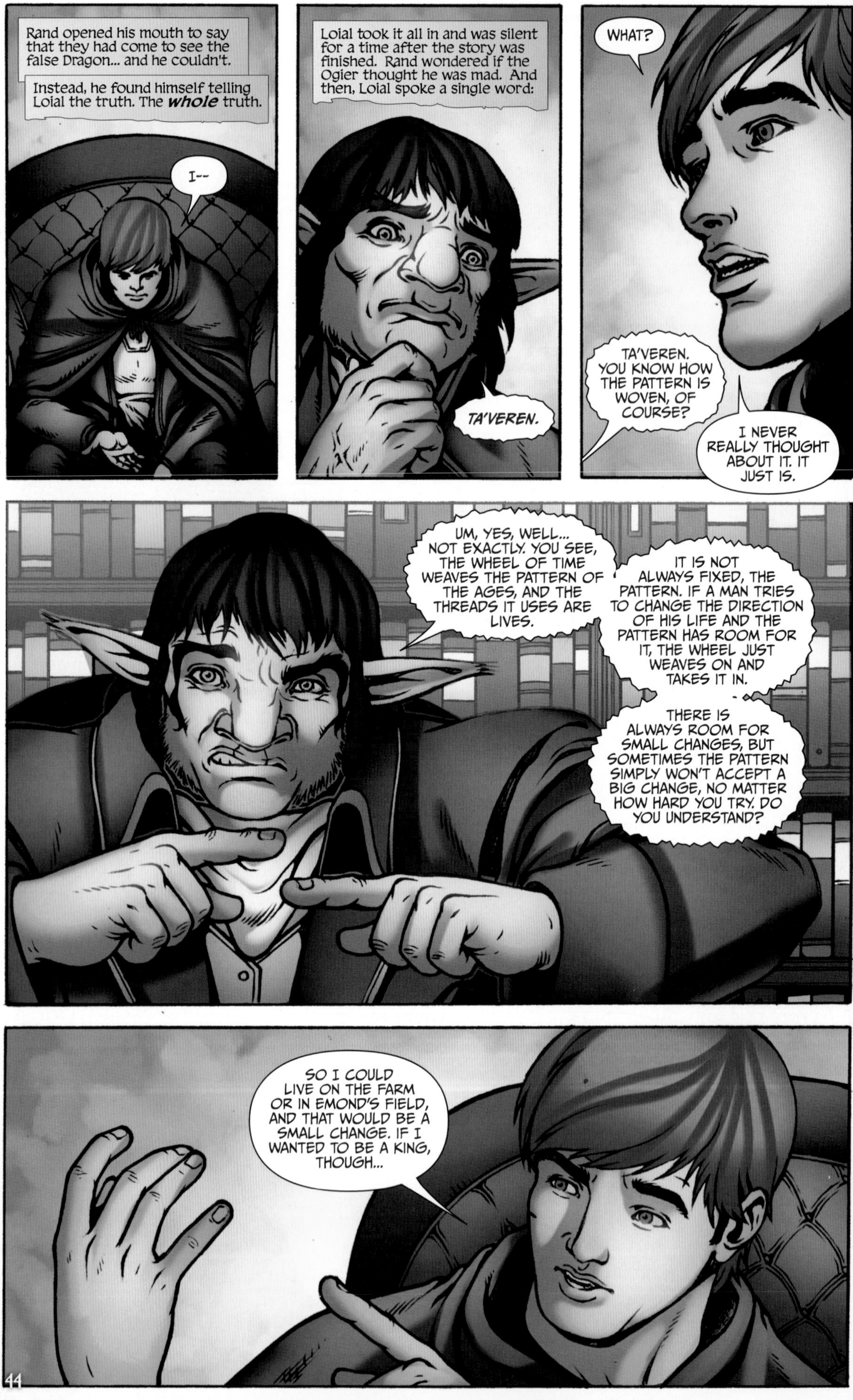

Rand opened his mouth to say that they had come to see the false Dragon... and he couldn't.
Instead, he found himself telling Loial the truth. The *whole* truth.
I--
Loial took it all in and was silent for a time after the story was finished. Rand wondered if the Ogier thought he was mad. And then, Loial spoke a single word:
TA'VEREN.
WHAT?
TA'VEREN. YOU KNOW HOW THE PATTERN IS WOVEN, OF COURSE?
I NEVER REALLY THOUGHT ABOUT IT. IT JUST IS.
UM, YES, WELL... NOT EXACTLY. YOU SEE, THE WHEEL OF TIME WEAVES THE PATTERN OF THE AGES, AND THE THREADS IT USES ARE LIVES.
IT IS NOT ALWAYS FIXED, THE PATTERN. IF A MAN TRIES TO CHANGE THE DIRECTION OF HIS LIFE AND THE PATTERN HAS ROOM FOR IT, THE WHEEL JUST WEAVES ON AND TAKES IT IN.
THERE IS ALWAYS ROOM FOR SMALL CHANGES, BUT SOMETIMES THE PATTERN SIMPLY WON'T ACCEPT A BIG CHANGE, NO MATTER HOW HARD YOU TRY. DO YOU UNDERSTAND?
SO I COULD LIVE ON THE FARM OR IN EMOND'S FIELD, AND THAT WOULD BE A SMALL CHANGE. IF I WANTED TO BE A KING, THOUGH...

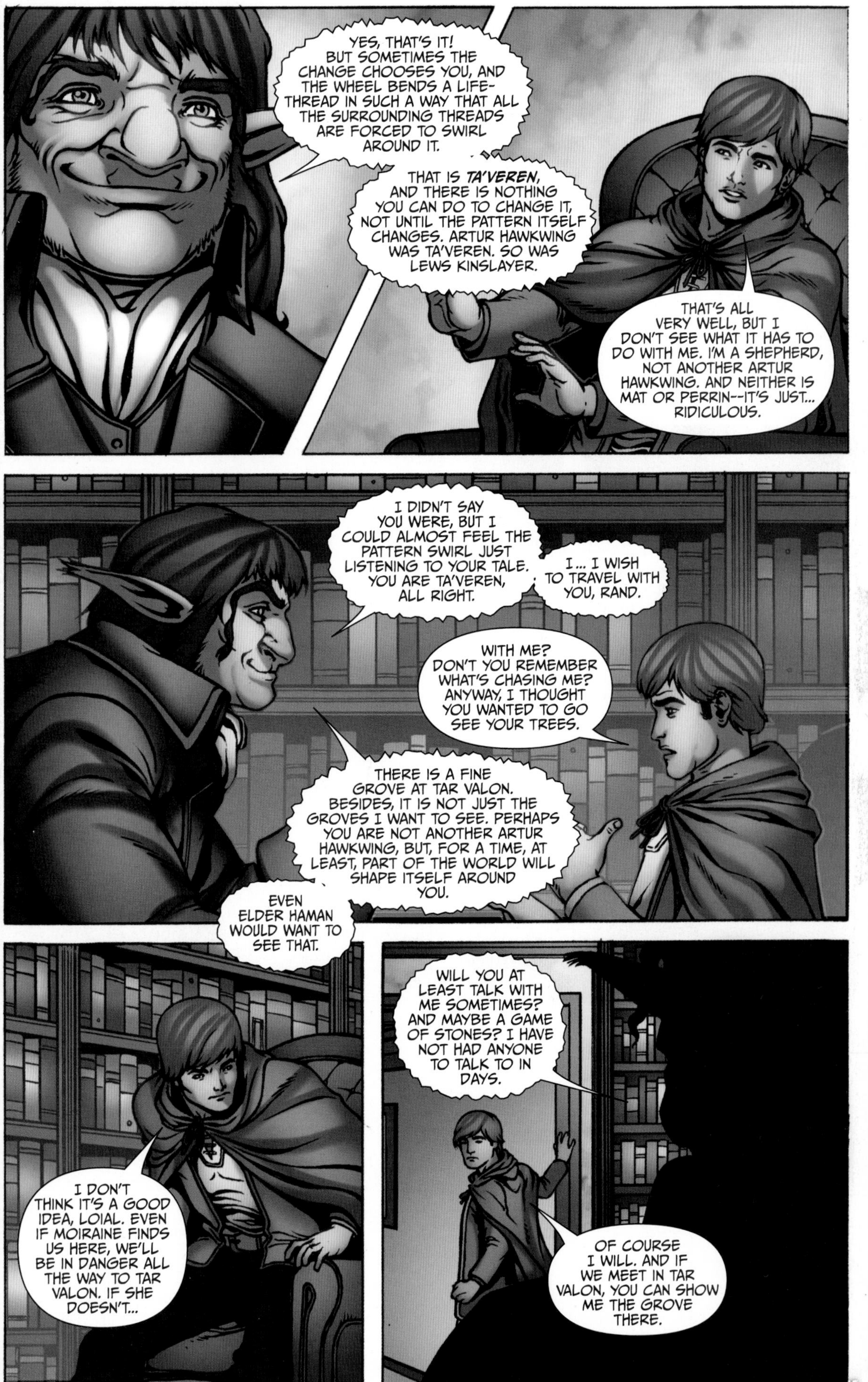
YES, THAT'S IT! BUT SOMETIMES THE CHANGE CHOOSES YOU, AND THE WHEEL BENDS A LIFE-THREAD IN SUCH A WAY THAT ALL THE SURROUNDING THREADS ARE FORCED TO SWIRL AROUND IT.
THAT IS *TA'VEREN*, AND THERE IS NOTHING YOU CAN DO TO CHANGE IT, NOT UNTIL THE PATTERN ITSELF CHANGES. ARTUR HAWKWING WAS TA'VEREN. SO WAS LEWS KINSLAYER.
THAT'S ALL VERY WELL, BUT I DON'T SEE WHAT IT HAS TO DO WITH ME. I'M A SHEPHERD, NOT ANOTHER ARTUR HAWKWING. AND NEITHER IS MAT OR PERRIN--IT'S JUST... RIDICULOUS.
I DIDN'T SAY YOU WERE, BUT I COULD ALMOST FEEL THE PATTERN SWIRL JUST LISTENING TO YOUR TALE. YOU ARE TA'VEREN, ALL RIGHT.
I... I WISH TO TRAVEL WITH YOU, RAND.
WITH ME? DON'T YOU REMEMBER WHAT'S CHASING ME? ANYWAY, I THOUGHT YOU WANTED TO GO SEE YOUR TREES.
THERE IS A FINE GROVE AT TAR VALON. BESIDES, IT IS NOT JUST THE GROVES I WANT TO SEE. PERHAPS YOU ARE NOT ANOTHER ARTUR HAWKWING, BUT, FOR A TIME, AT LEAST, PART OF THE WORLD WILL SHAPE ITSELF AROUND YOU.
EVEN ELDER HAMAN WOULD WANT TO SEE THAT.
I DON'T THINK IT'S A GOOD IDEA, LOIAL. EVEN IF MOIRAINE FINDS US HERE, WE'LL BE IN DANGER ALL THE WAY TO TAR VALON. IF SHE DOESN'T...
WILL YOU AT LEAST TALK WITH ME SOMETIMES? AND MAYBE A GAME OF STONES? I HAVE NOT HAD ANYONE TO TALK TO IN DAYS.
OF COURSE I WILL. AND IF WE MEET IN TAR VALON, YOU CAN SHOW ME THE GROVE THERE.

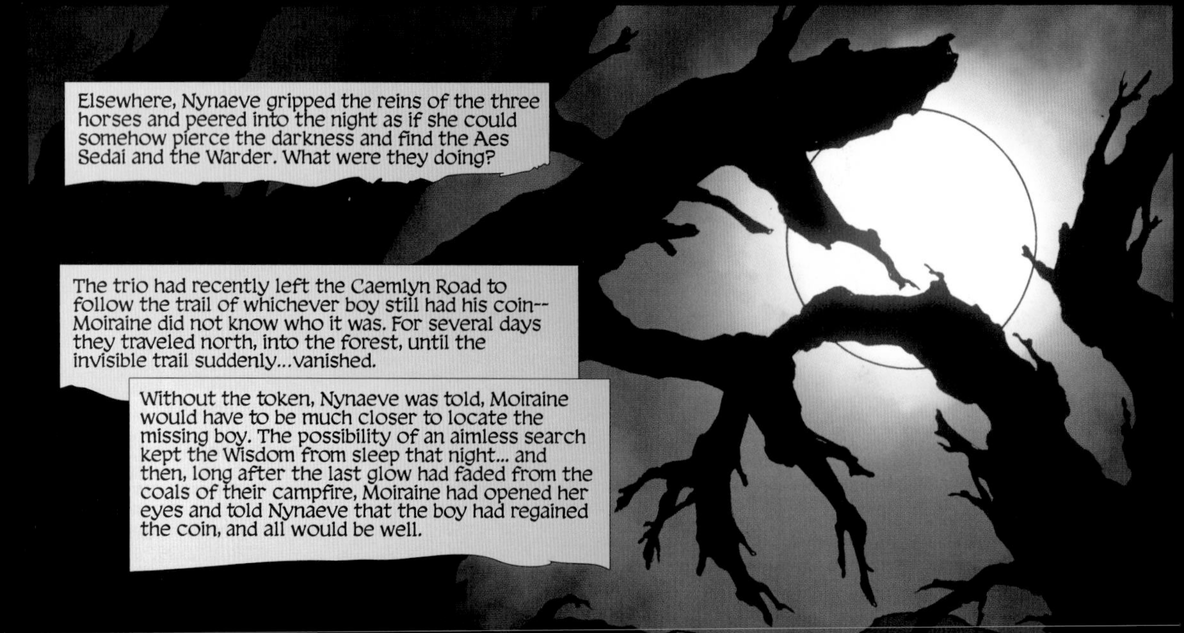
Elsewhere, Nynaeve gripped the reins of the three horses and peered into the night as if she could somehow pierce the darkness and find the Aes Sedai and the Warder. What were they doing?
The trio had recently left the Caemlyn Road to follow the trail of whichever boy still had his coin--Moiraine did not know who it was. For several days they traveled north, into the forest, until the invisible trail suddenly...vanished.
Without the token, Nynaeve was told, Moiraine would have to be much closer to locate the missing boy. The possibility of an aimless search kept the Wisdom from sleep that night... and then, long after the last glow had faded from the coals of their campfire, Moiraine had opened her eyes and told Nynaeve that the boy had regained the coin, and all would be well.

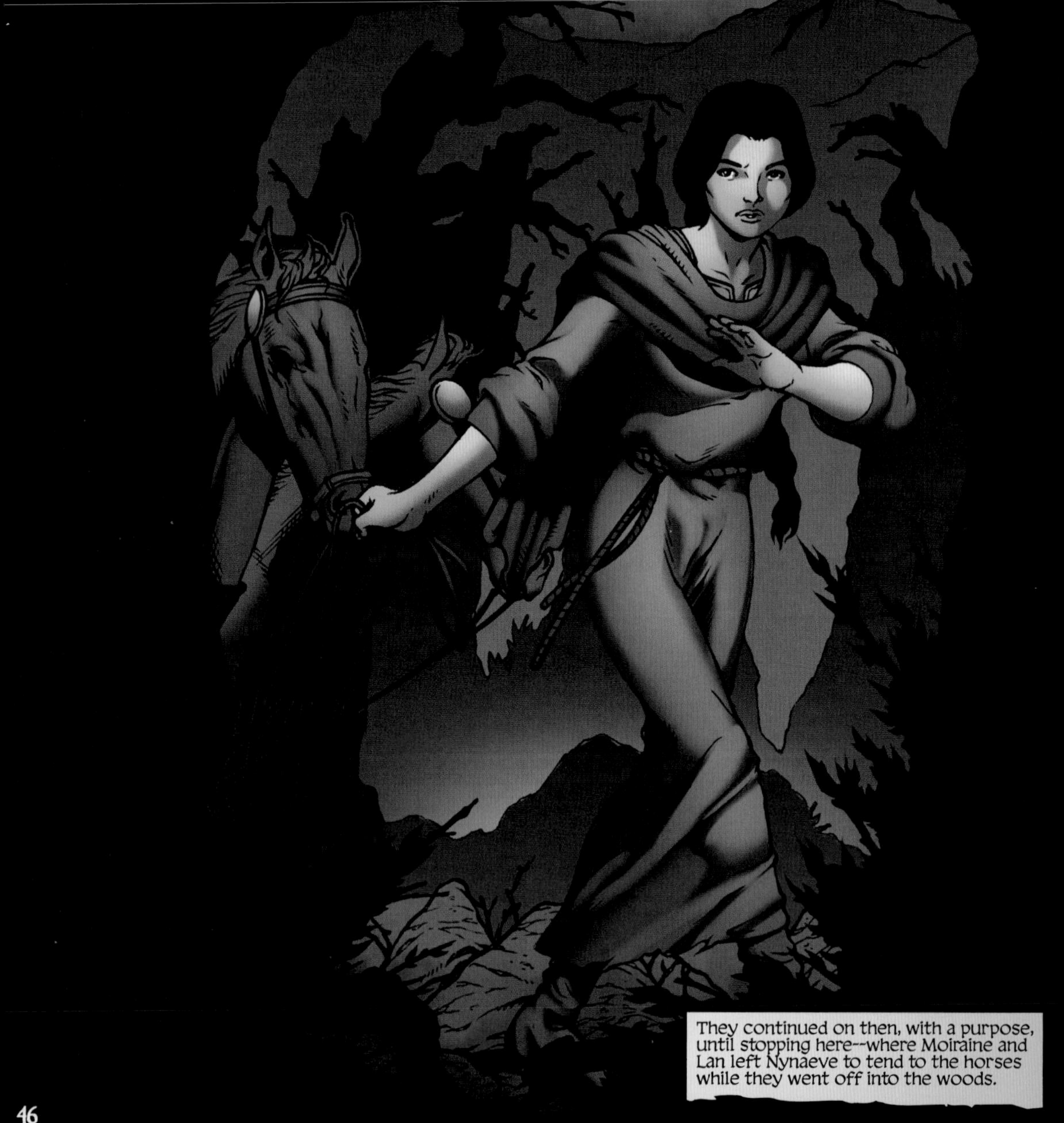
They continued on then, with a purpose, until stopping here--where Moiraine and Lan left Nynaeve to tend to the horses while they went off into the woods.

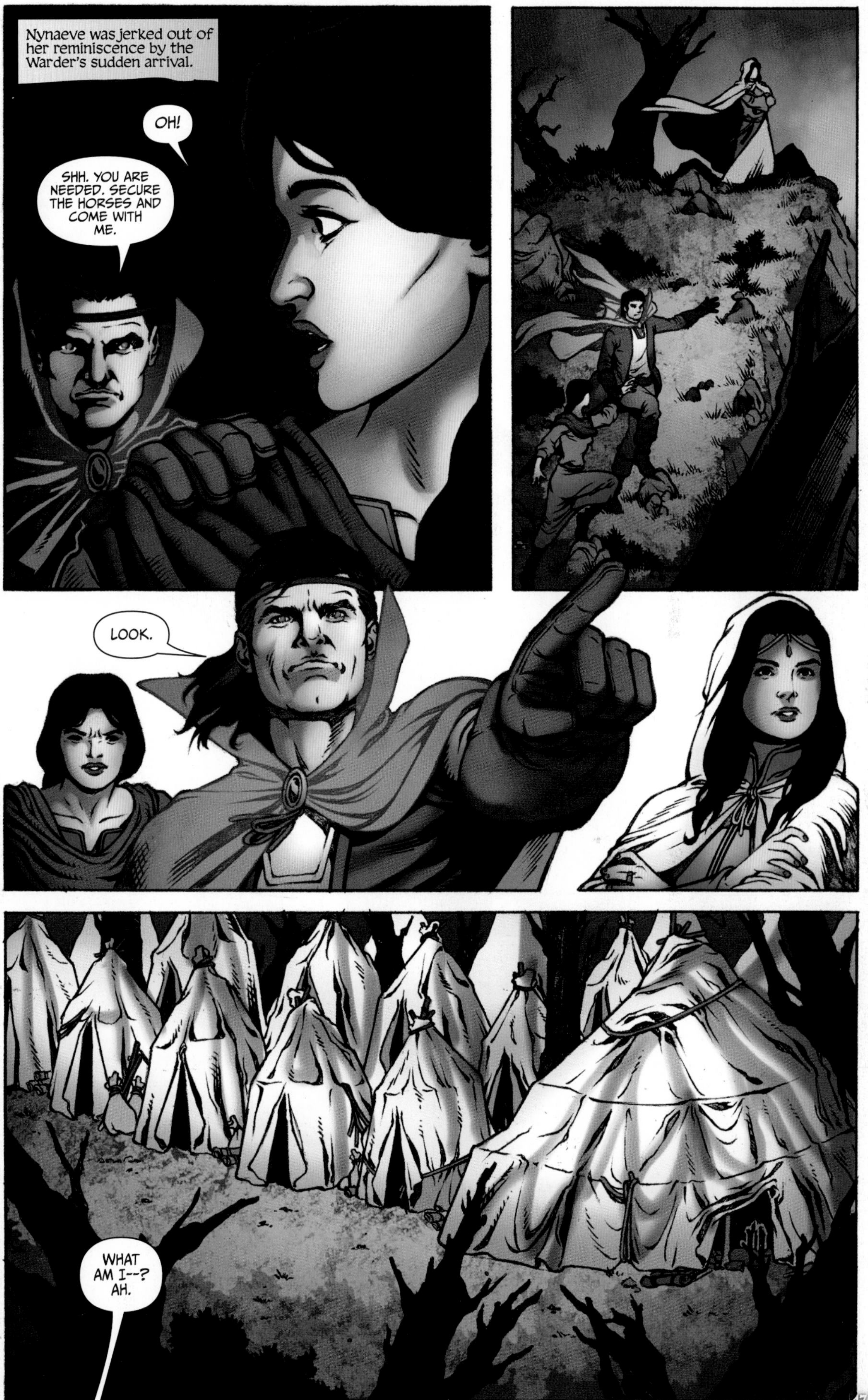
Nynaeve was jerked out of her reminiscence by the Warder's sudden arrival.
OH!
SHH. YOU ARE NEEDED. SECURE THE HORSES AND COME WITH ME.
LOOK.
WHAT AM I--? AH.

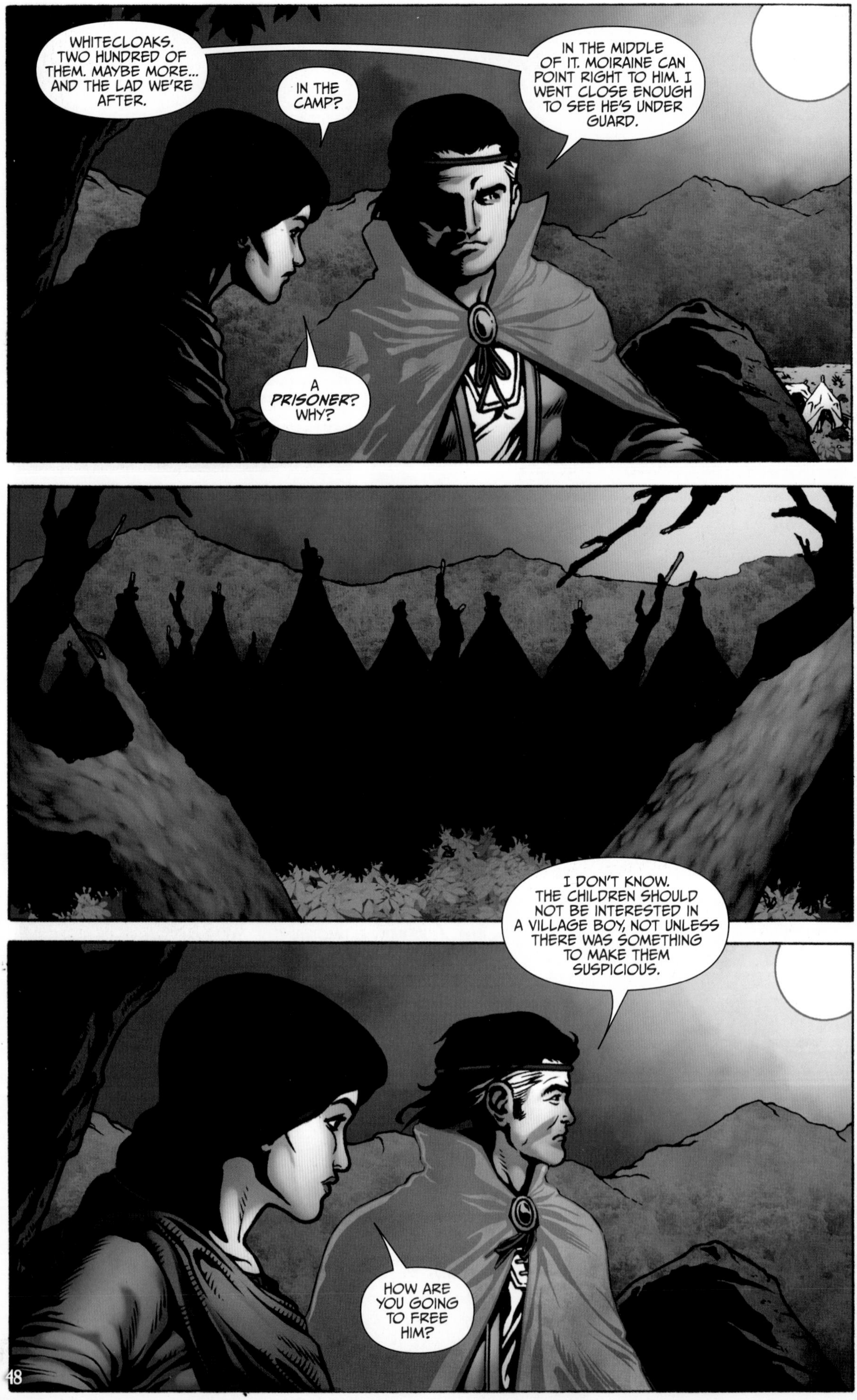
WHITECLOAKS. TWO HUNDRED OF THEM. MAYBE MORE... AND THE LAD WE'RE AFTER.
IN THE CAMP?
IN THE MIDDLE OF IT. MOIRAINE CAN POINT RIGHT TO HIM. I WENT CLOSE ENOUGH TO SEE HE'S UNDER GUARD.
A *PRISONER?* WHY?
I DON'T KNOW. THE CHILDREN SHOULD NOT BE INTERESTED IN A VILLAGE BOY, NOT UNLESS THERE WAS SOMETHING TO MAKE THEM SUSPICIOUS.
HOW ARE YOU GOING TO FREE HIM?

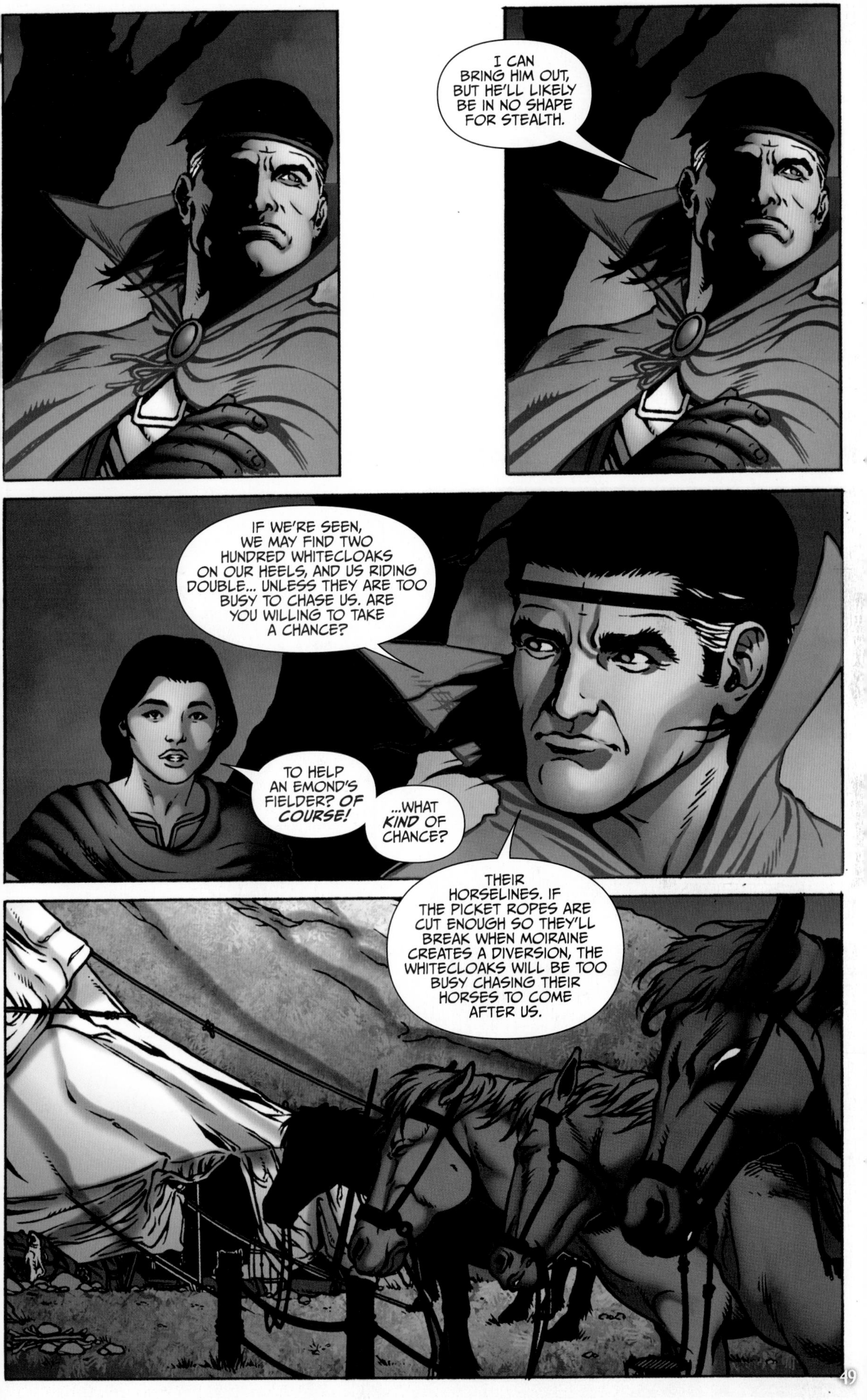
I CAN BRING HIM OUT, BUT HE'LL LIKELY BE IN NO SHAPE FOR STEALTH.
IF WE'RE SEEN, WE MAY FIND TWO HUNDRED WHITECLOAKS ON OUR HEELS, AND US RIDING DOUBLE... UNLESS THEY ARE TOO BUSY TO CHASE US. ARE YOU WILLING TO TAKE A CHANCE?
TO HELP AN EMOND'S FIELDER? *OF COURSE!*
...WHAT *KIND* OF CHANCE?
THEIR HORSELINES. IF THE PICKET ROPES ARE CUT ENOUGH SO THEY'LL BREAK WHEN MOIRAINE CREATES A DIVERSION, THE WHITECLOAKS WILL BE TOO BUSY CHASING THEIR HORSES TO COME AFTER US.

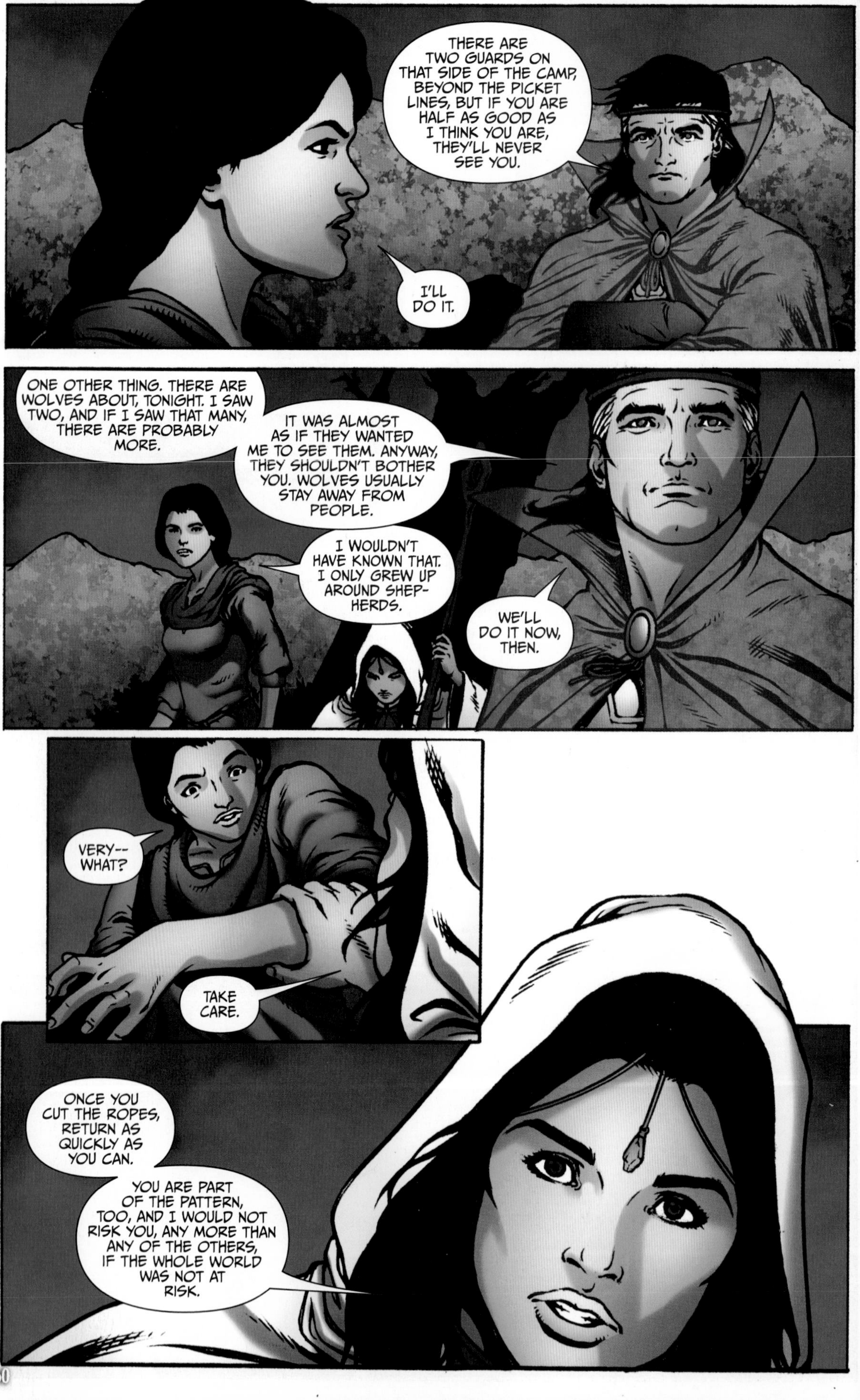
THERE ARE TWO GUARDS ON THAT SIDE OF THE CAMP, BEYOND THE PICKET LINES, BUT IF YOU ARE HALF AS GOOD AS I THINK YOU ARE, THEY'LL NEVER SEE YOU.
I'LL DO IT.
ONE OTHER THING. THERE ARE WOLVES ABOUT, TONIGHT. I SAW TWO, AND IF I SAW THAT MANY, THERE ARE PROBABLY MORE.
IT WAS ALMOST AS IF THEY WANTED ME TO SEE THEM. ANYWAY, THEY SHOULDN'T BOTHER YOU. WOLVES USUALLY STAY AWAY FROM PEOPLE.
I WOULDN'T HAVE KNOWN THAT. I ONLY GREW UP AROUND SHEP-HERDS.
WE'LL DO IT NOW, THEN.
VERY-- WHAT?
TAKE CARE.
ONCE YOU CUT THE ROPES, RETURN AS QUICKLY AS YOU CAN.
YOU ARE PART OF THE PATTERN, TOO, AND I WOULD NOT RISK YOU, ANY MORE THAN ANY OF THE OTHERS, IF THE WHOLE WORLD WAS NOT AT RISK.

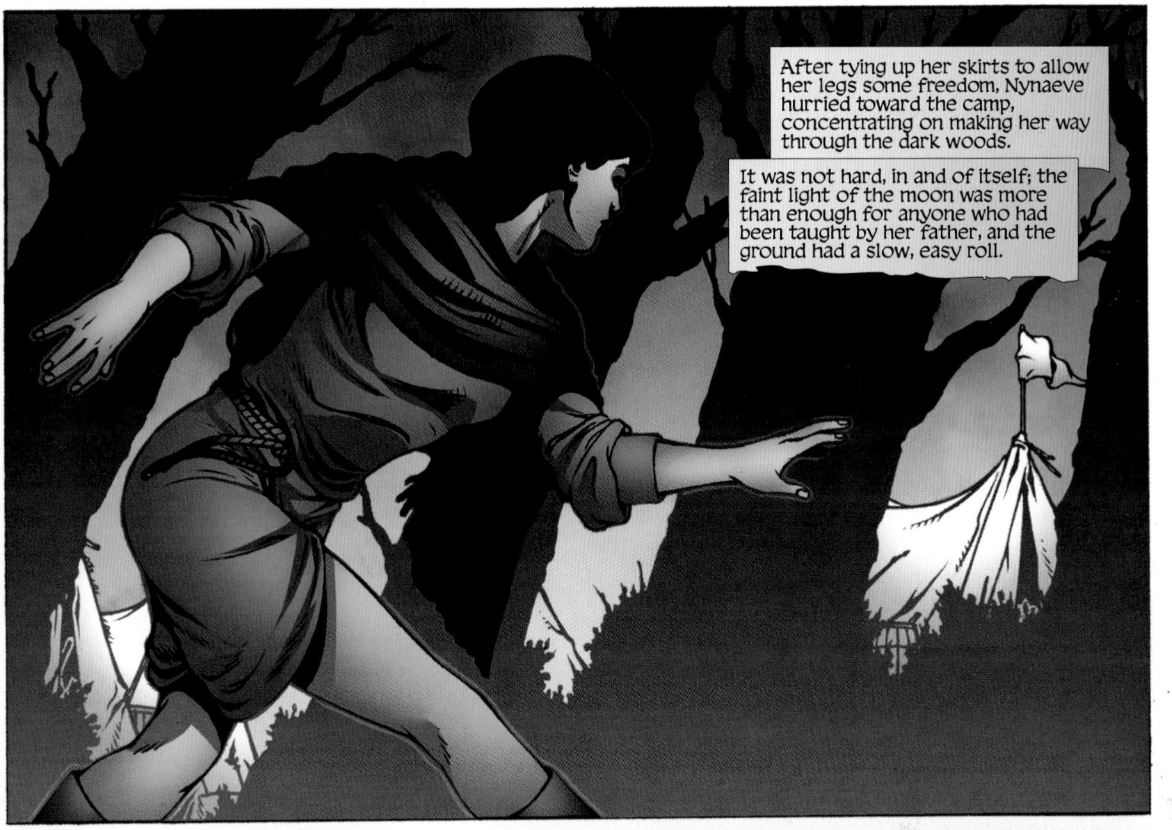
After tying up her skirts to allow her legs some freedom, Nynaeve hurried toward the camp, concentrating on making her way through the dark woods.
It was not hard, in and of itself; the faint light of the moon was more than enough for anyone who had been taught by her father, and the ground had a slow, easy roll.

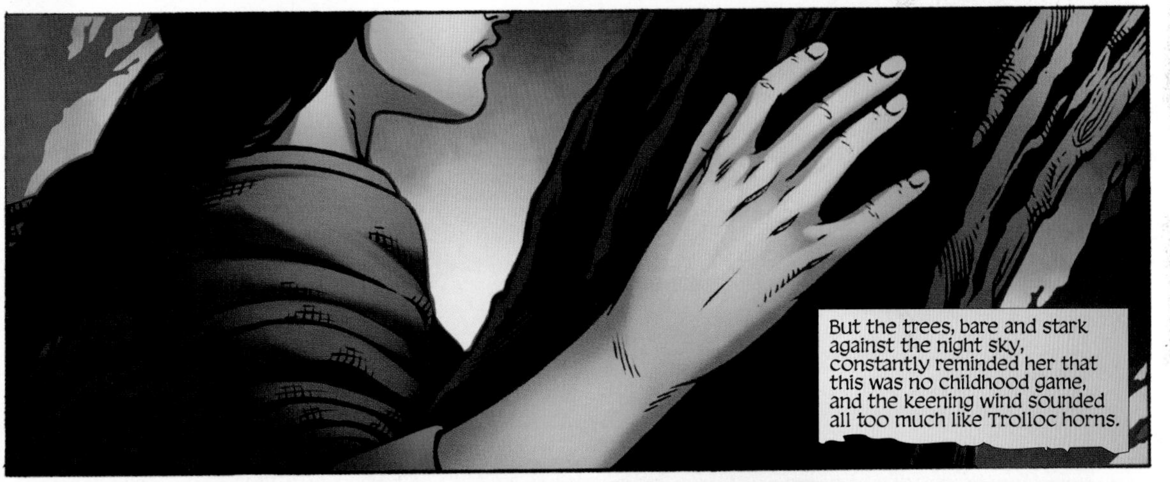
But the trees, bare and stark against the night sky, constantly reminded her that this was no childhood game, and the keening wind sounded all too much like Trolloc horns.

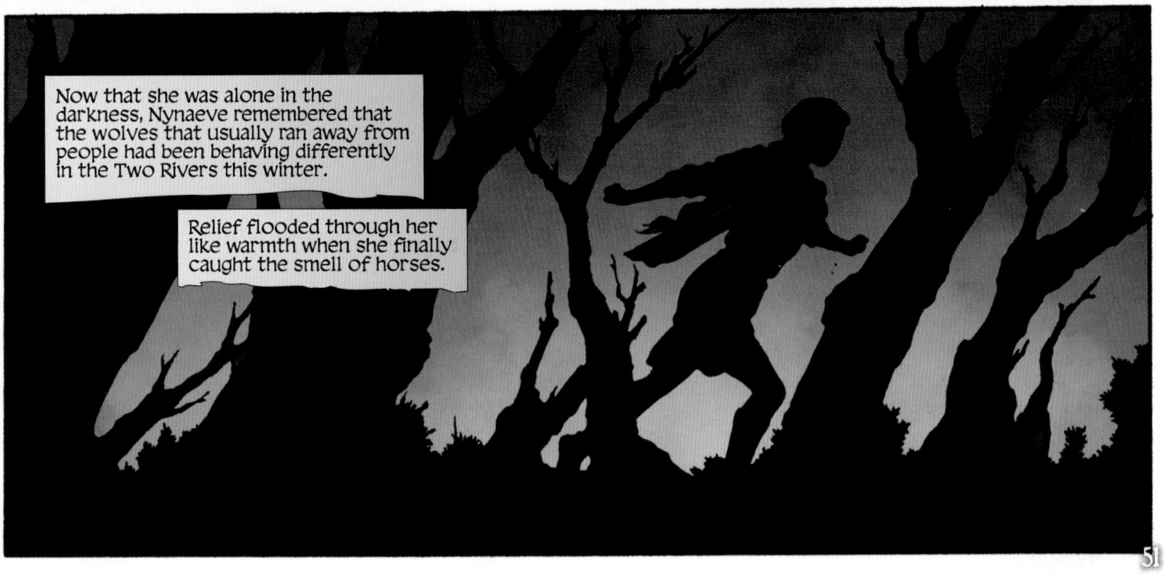
Now that she was alone in the darkness, Nynaeve remembered that the wolves that usually ran away from people had been behaving differently in the Two Rivers this winter.
Relief flooded through her like warmth when she finally caught the smell of horses.

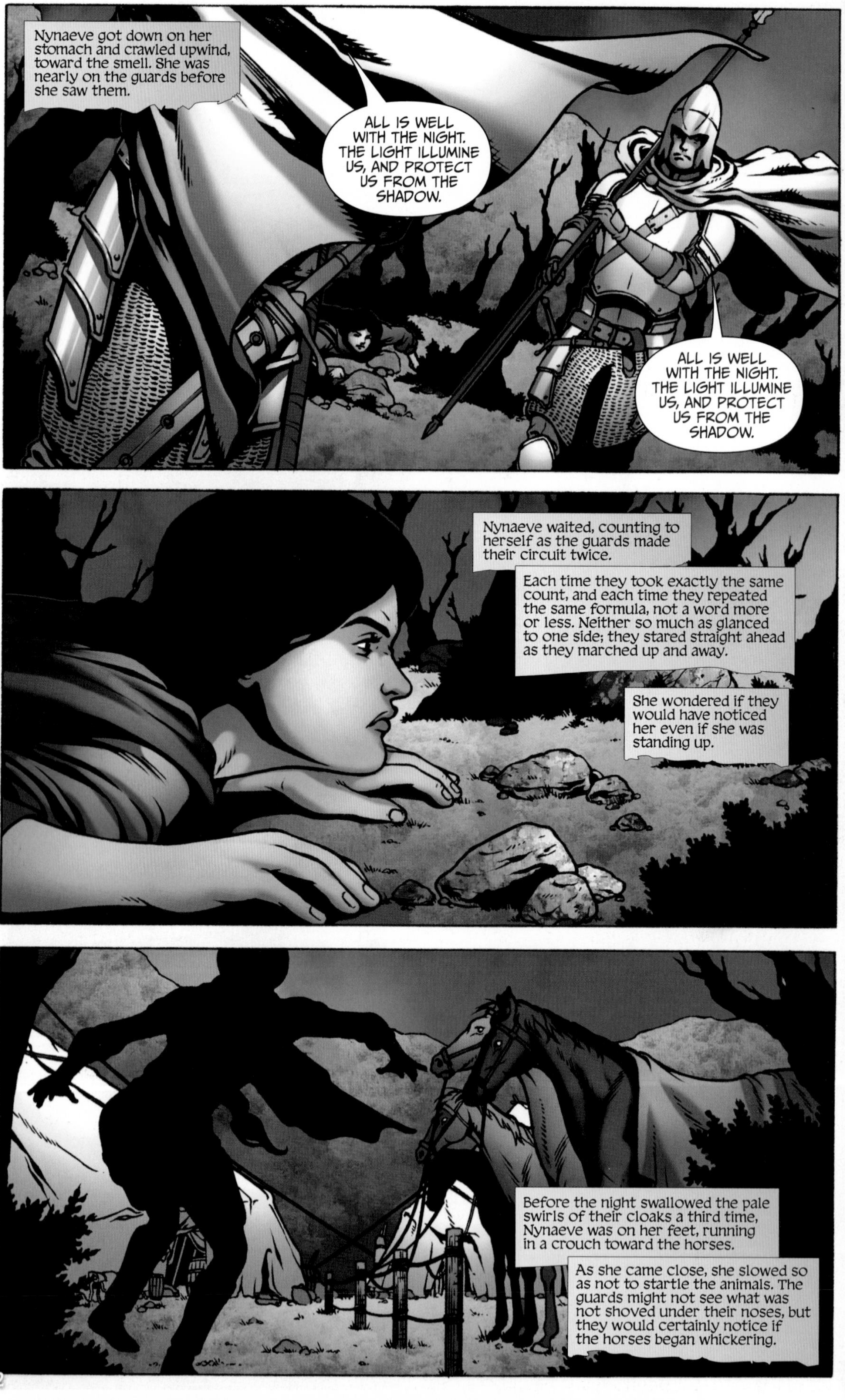
Nynaeve got down on her stomach and crawled upwind, toward the smell. She was nearly on the guards before she saw them.
ALL IS WELL WITH THE NIGHT. THE LIGHT ILLUMINE US, AND PROTECT US FROM THE SHADOW.
ALL IS WELL WITH THE NIGHT. THE LIGHT ILLUMINE US, AND PROTECT US FROM THE SHADOW.
Nynaeve waited, counting to herself as the guards made their circuit twice.
Each time they took exactly the same count, and each time they repeated the same formula, not a word more or less. Neither so much as glanced to one side; they stared straight ahead as they marched up and away.
She wondered if they would have noticed her even if she was standing up.
Before the night swallowed the pale swirls of their cloaks a third time, Nynaeve was on her feet, running in a crouch toward the horses.
As she came close, she slowed so as not to startle the animals. The guards might not see what was not shoved under their noses, but they would certainly notice if the horses began whickering.

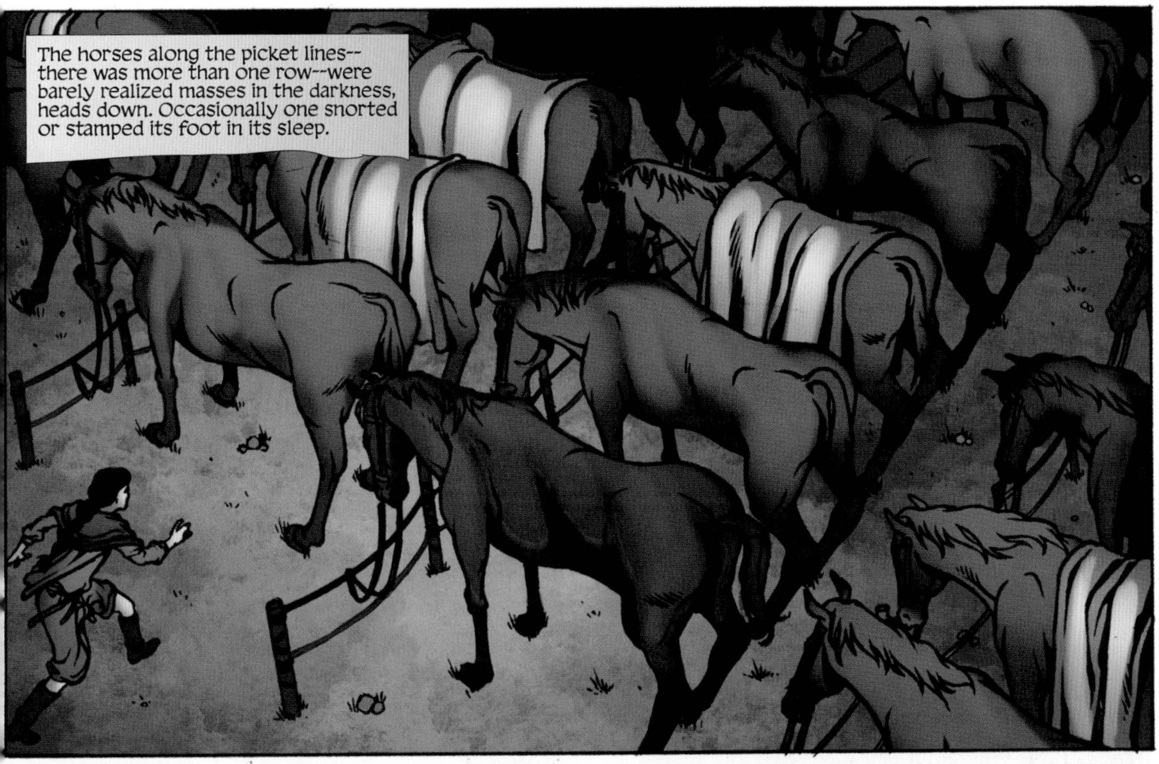
The horses along the picket lines--there was more than one row--were barely realized masses in the darkness, heads down. Occasionally one snorted or stamped its foot in its sleep.

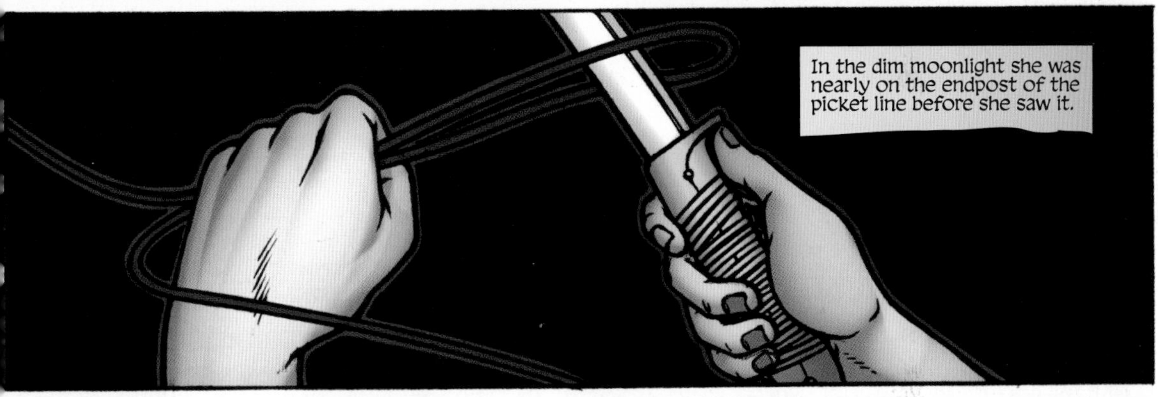
In the dim moonlight she was nearly on the endpost of the picket line before she saw it.

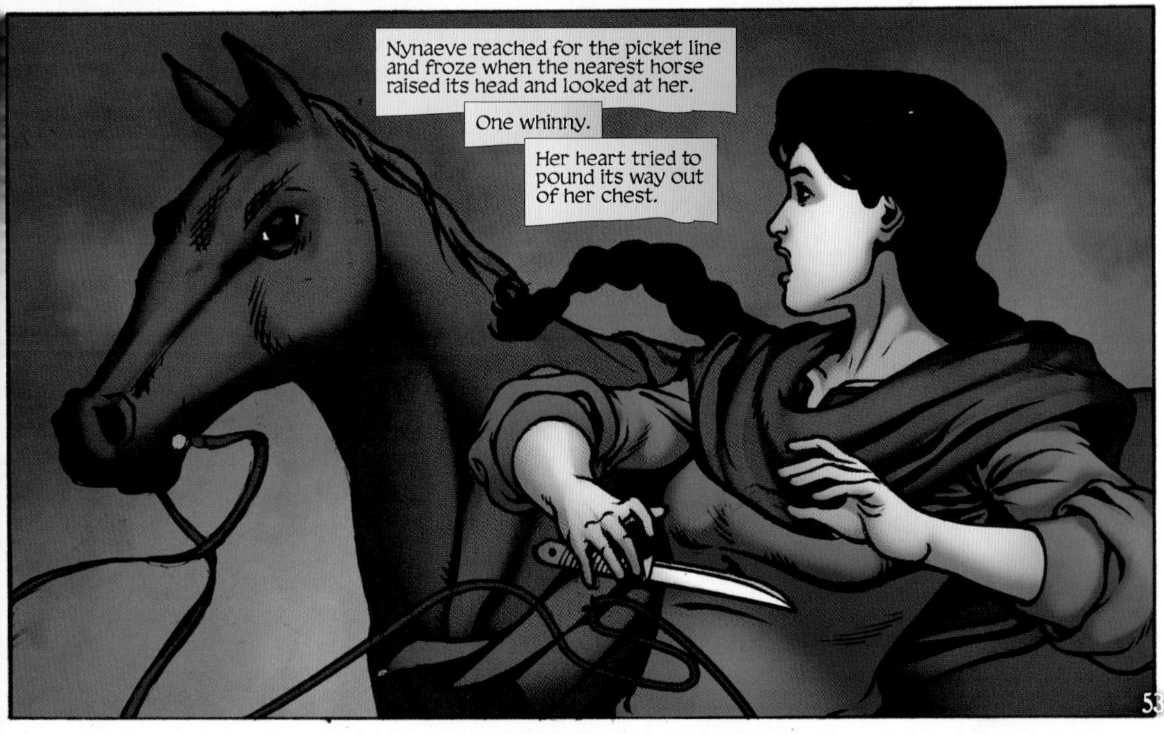
Nynaeve reached for the picket line and froze when the nearest horse raised its head and looked at her.
One whinny.
Her heart tried to pound its way out of her chest.

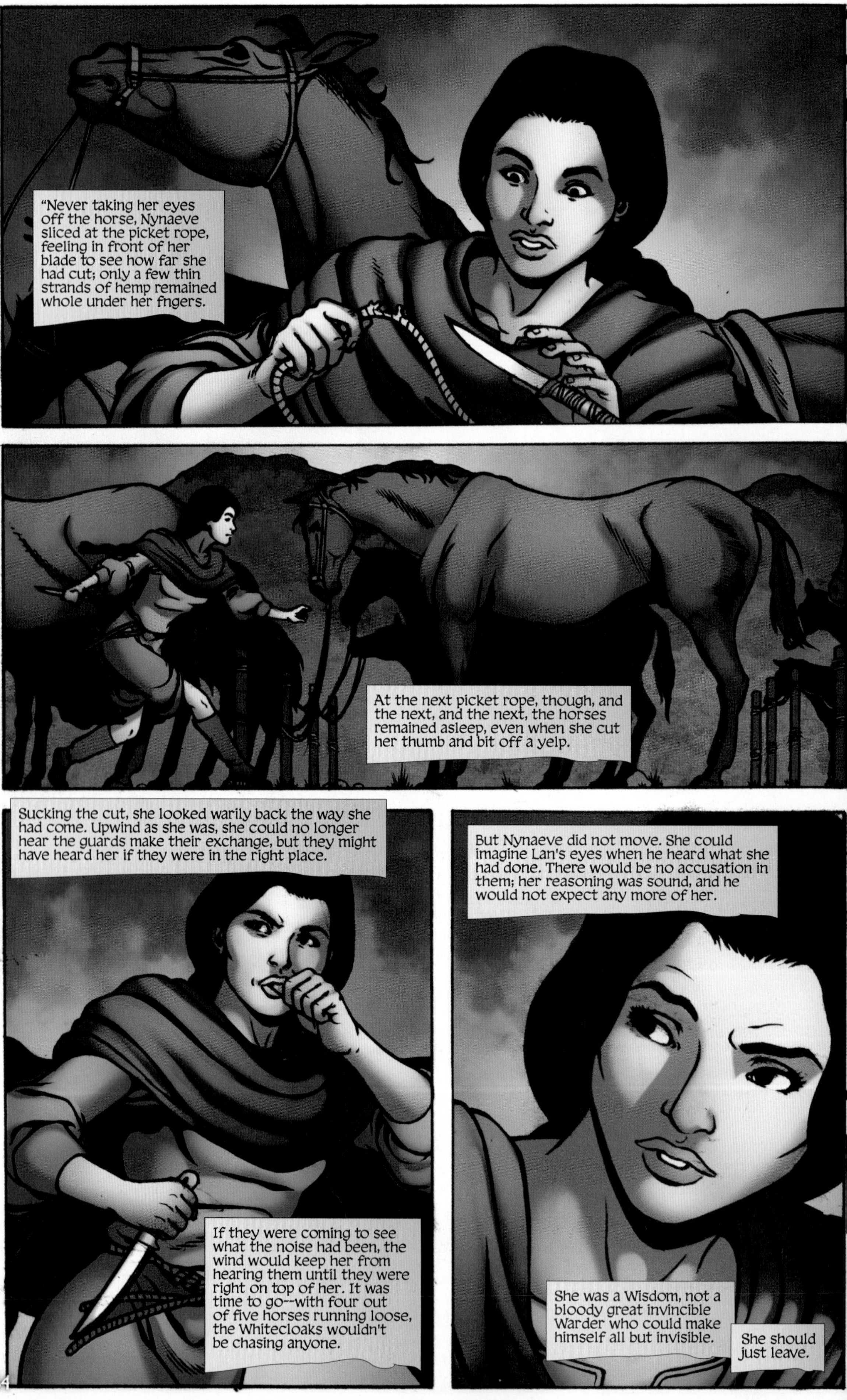
"Never taking her eyes off the horse, Nynaeve sliced at the picket rope, feeling in front of her blade to see how far she had cut; only a few thin strands of hemp remained whole under her fngers.
At the next picket rope, though, and the next, and the next, the horses remained asleep, even when she cut her thumb and bit off a yelp.
Sucking the cut, she looked warily back the way she had come. Upwind as she was, she could no longer hear the guards make their exchange, but they might have heard her if they were in the right place.
If they were coming to see what the noise had been, the wind would keep her from hearing them until they were right on top of her. It was time to go--with four out of five horses running loose, the Whitecloaks wouldn't be chasing anyone.
But Nynaeve did not move. She could imagine Lan's eyes when he heard what she had done. There would be no accusation in them; her reasoning was sound, and he would not expect any more of her.
She was a Wisdom, not a bloody great invincible Warder who could make himself all but invisible.
She should just leave.

Jaw set, Nynaeve moved on to the last picket line...

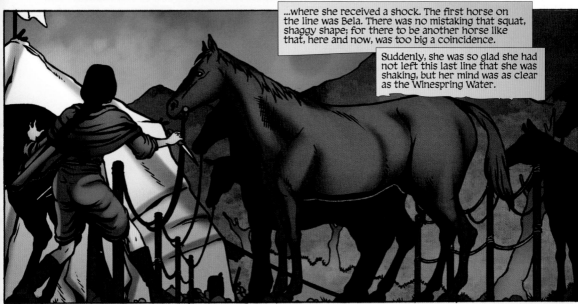

...where she received a shock. The first horse on the line was Bela. There was no mistaking that squat, shaggy shape; for there to be another horse like that, here and now, was too big a coincidence.

Suddenly, she was so glad she had not left this last line that she was shaking, but her mind was as clear as the Winespring Water.

Whichever of the boys was in this camp, Egwene was there, too. And if they left riding double, some of the Children would catch them no matter how well the horses were scattered, and some of them would die.

She was as certain as if she were listening to the wind, and it terrified her.

Strangely, the fear stilled her trembling. After cutting the rope, she resheathed her dagger and grabbed Bela's lead rein. The shaggy mare woke with a start, but Nynaeve stroked her nose and spoke comforting words... Bela gave a low snort and seemed content.

The next horse in the line was awake, too, and gave no objection to a strange hand grabbing its lead. Indeed, it seemed to want some of the muzzle-stroking that Bela had received.

Nynaeve gripped the leads tightly, all the while watching the camp nervously. The tents were only thirty yards off, and she could see men moving among them. Whatever the Aes Sedai was going to do, let her do it now.

Light, make her do it now, before...

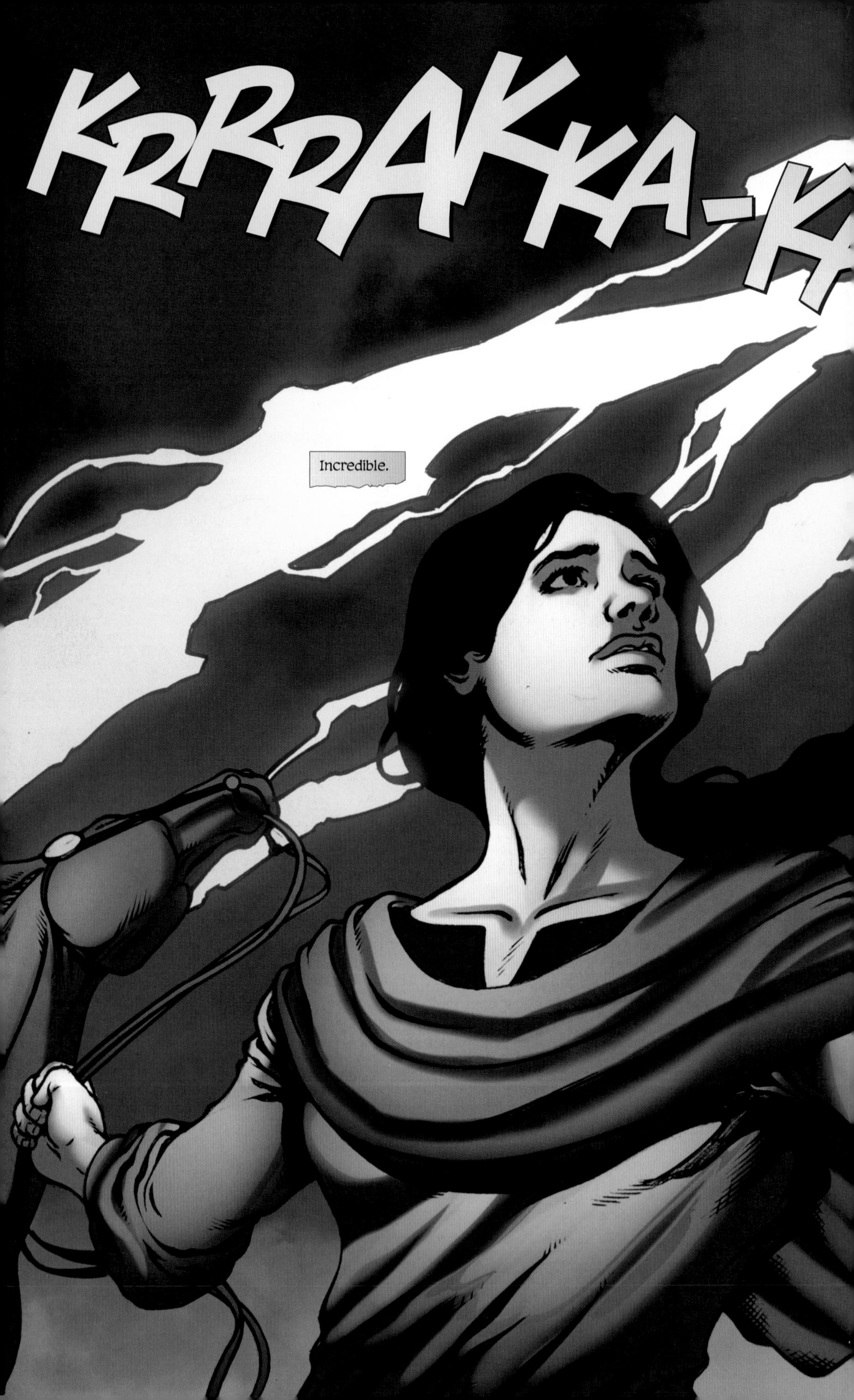
KRRRAKKA-KA
Incredible.

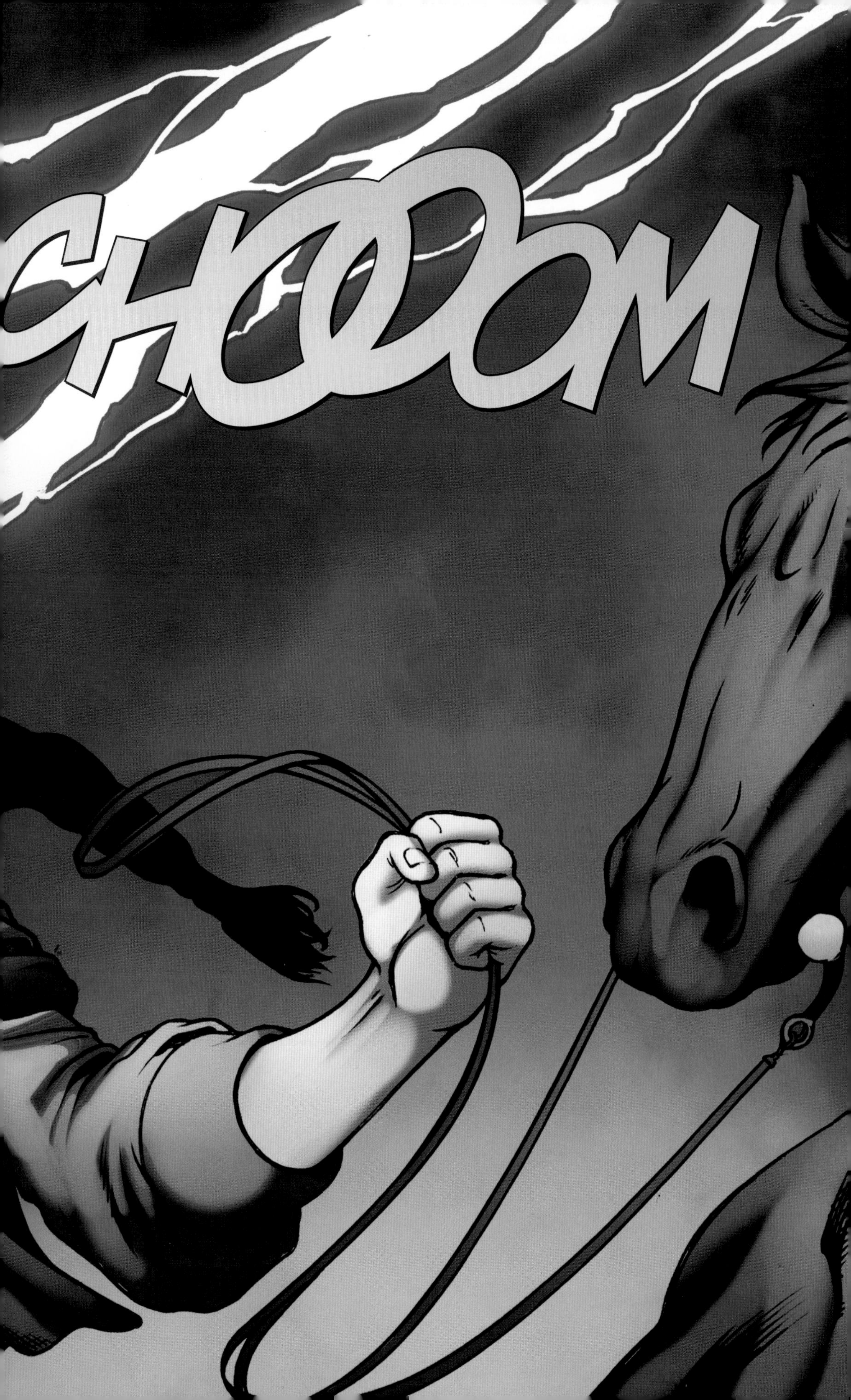
CHOOM

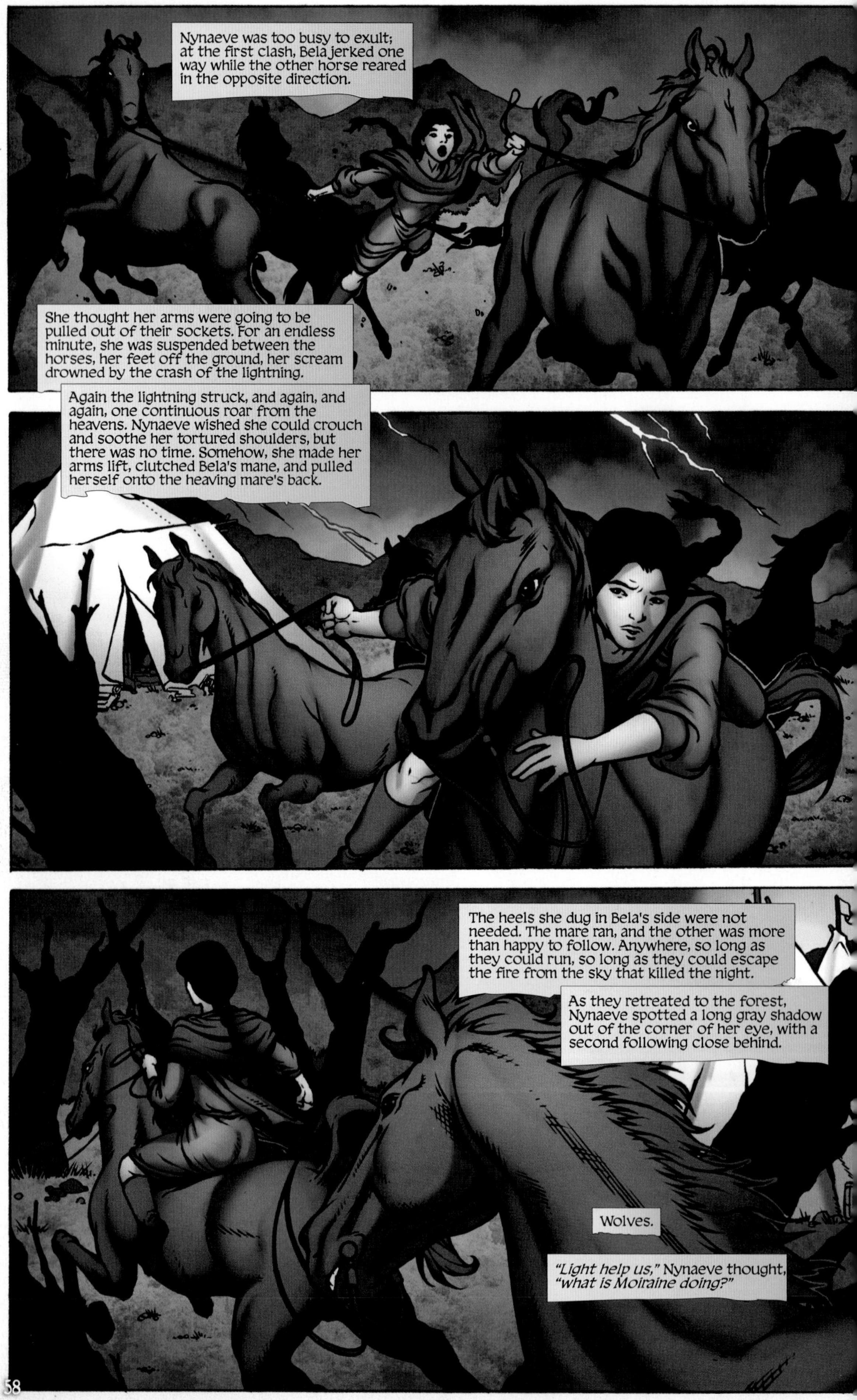

Nynaeve was too busy to exult; at the first clash, Bela jerked one way while the other horse reared in the opposite direction.
She thought her arms were going to be pulled out of their sockets. For an endless minute, she was suspended between the horses, her feet off the ground, her scream drowned by the crash of the lightning.
Again the lightning struck, and again, and again, one continuous roar from the heavens. Nynaeve wished she could crouch and soothe her tortured shoulders, but there was no time. Somehow, she made her arms lift, clutched Bela's mane, and pulled herself onto the heaving mare's back.
The heels she dug in Bela's side were not needed. The mare ran, and the other was more than happy to follow. Anywhere, so long as they could run, so long as they could escape the fire from the sky that killed the night.
As they retreated to the forest, Nynaeve spotted a long gray shadow out of the corner of her eye, with a second following close behind.
Wolves.
"Light help us," Nynaeve thought, *"what is Moiraine doing?"*

chapter three

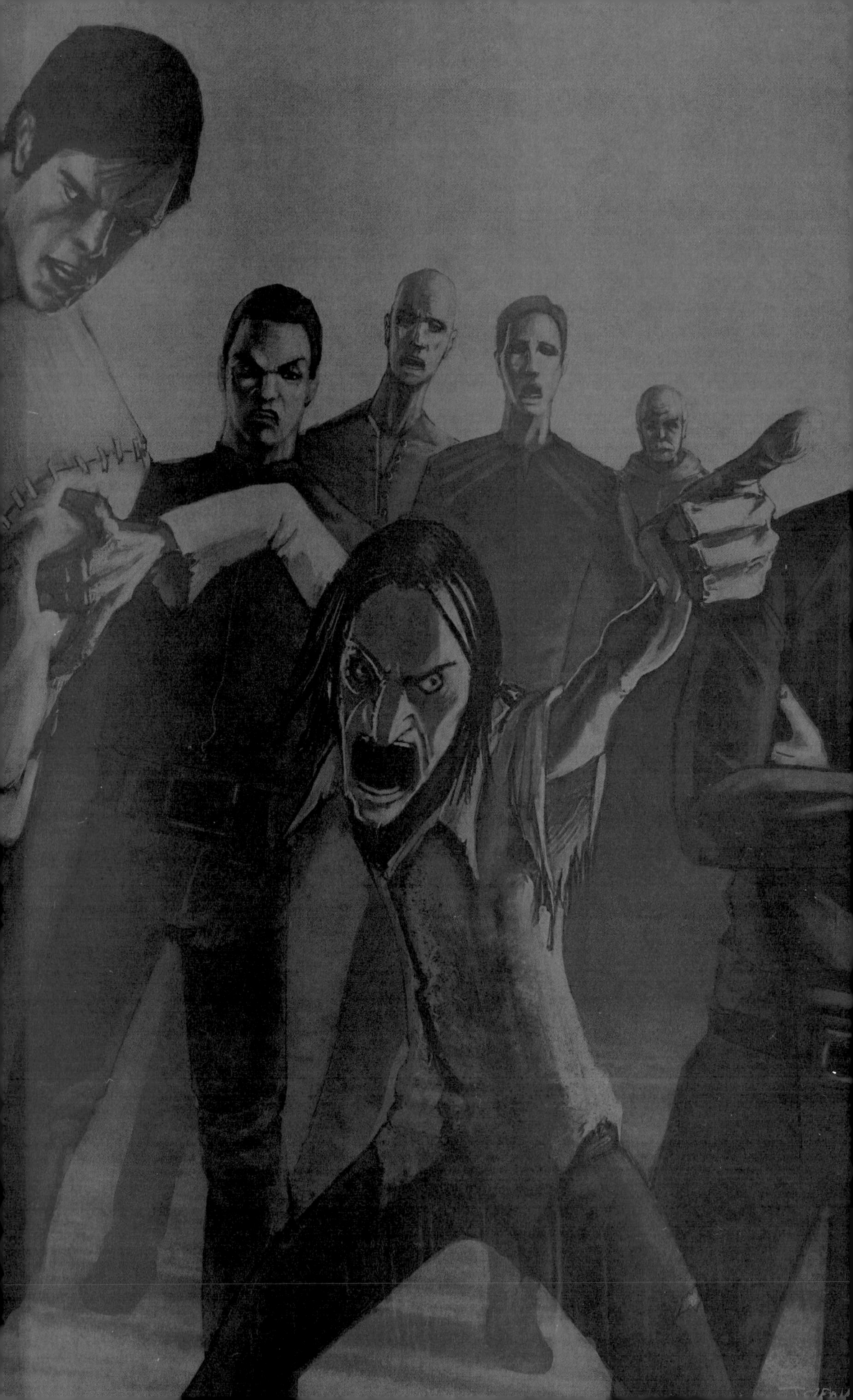

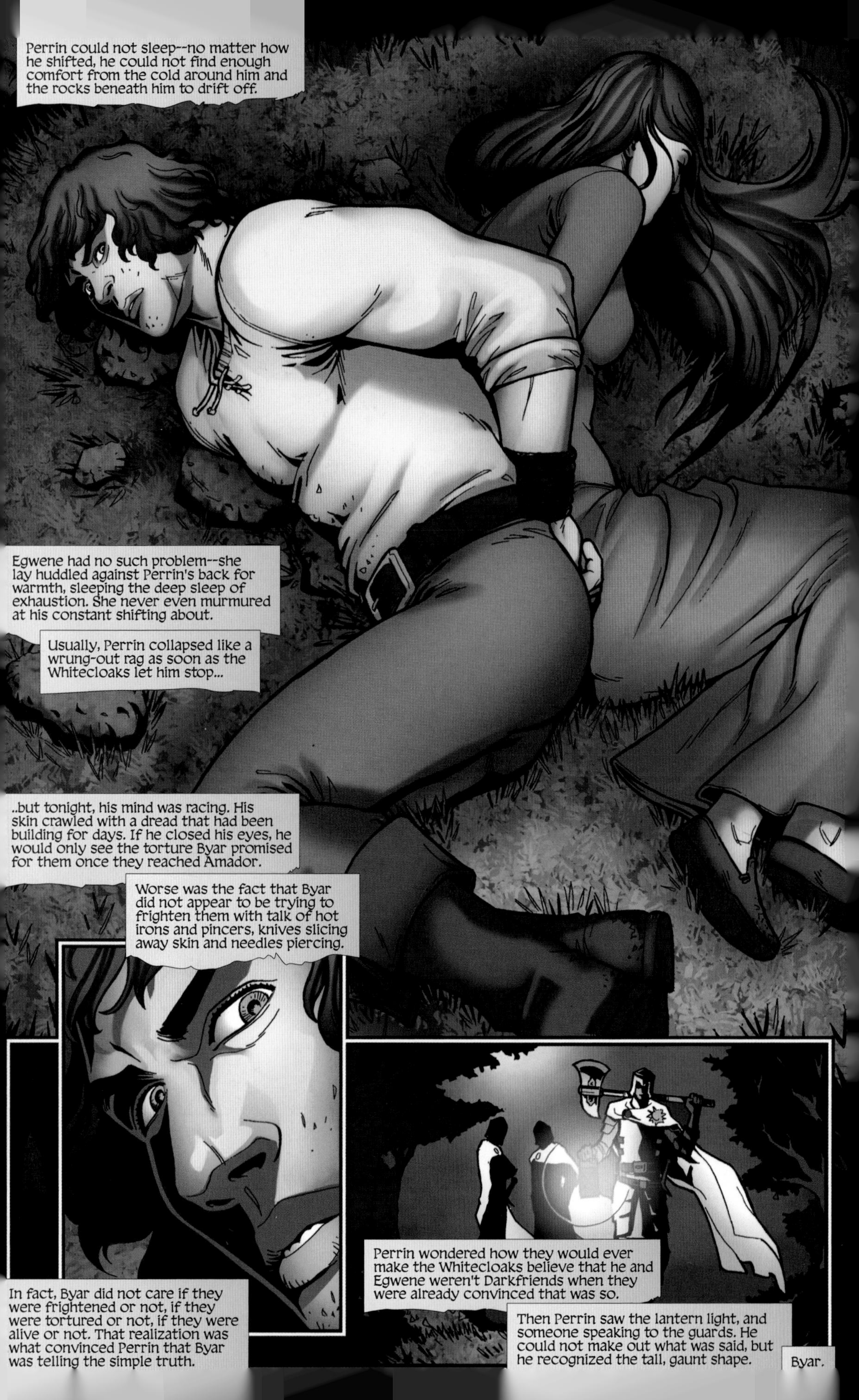
Perrin could not sleep--no matter how he shifted, he could not find enough comfort from the cold around him and the rocks beneath him to drift off.
Egwene had no such problem--she lay huddled against Perrin's back for warmth, sleeping the deep sleep of exhaustion. She never even murmured at his constant shifting about.
Usually, Perrin collapsed like a wrung-out rag as soon as the Whitecloaks let him stop...
..but tonight, his mind was racing. His skin crawled with a dread that had been building for days. If he closed his eyes, he would only see the torture Byar promised for them once they reached Amador.
Worse was the fact that Byar did not appear to be trying to frighten them with talk of hot irons and pincers, knives slicing away skin and needles piercing.
In fact, Byar did not care if they were frightened or not, if they were tortured or not, if they were alive or not. That realization was what convinced Perrin that Byar was telling the simple truth.
Perrin wondered how they would ever make the Whitecloaks believe that he and Egwene weren't Darkfriends when they were already convinced that was so.
Then Perrin saw the lantern light, and someone speaking to the guards. He could not make out what was said, but he recognized the tall, gaunt shape.
Byar.

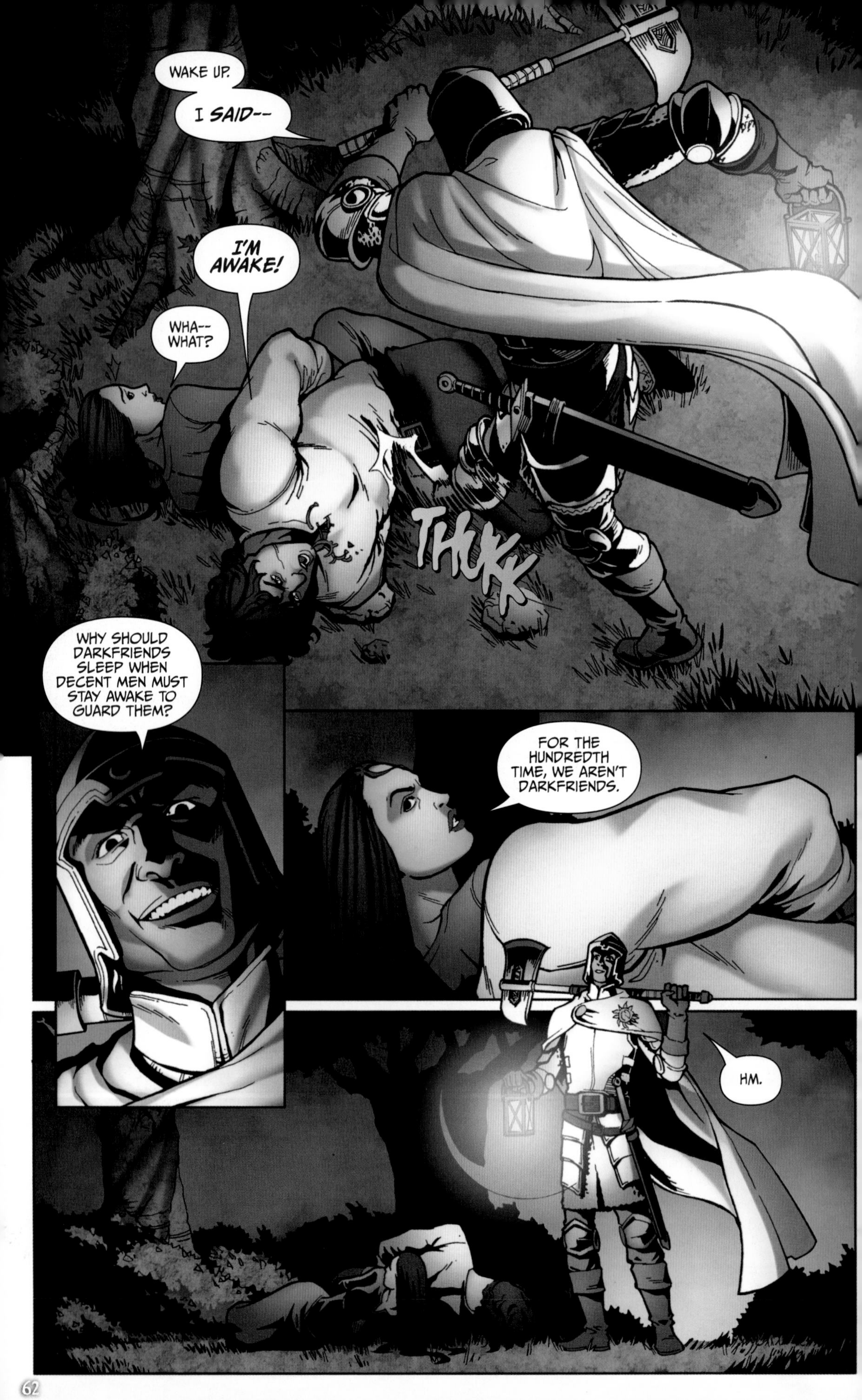
WAKE UP.
I SAID--
I'M AWAKE!
WHA-- WHAT?
THUKK
WHY SHOULD DARKFRIENDS SLEEP WHEN DECENT MEN MUST STAY AWAKE TO GUARD THEM?
FOR THE HUNDREDTH TIME, WE AREN'T DARKFRIENDS.
HM.

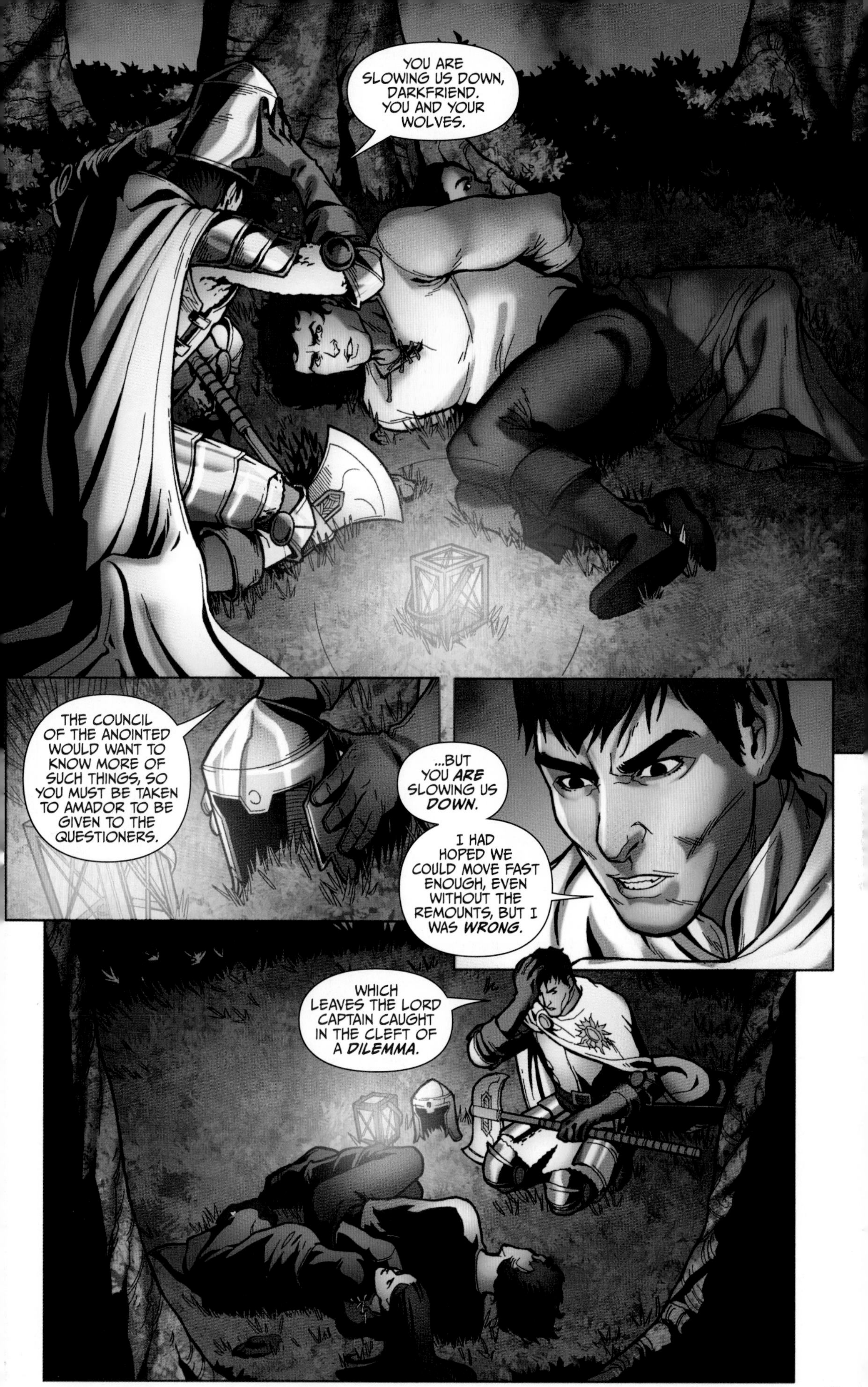
YOU ARE SLOWING US DOWN, DARKFRIEND. YOU AND YOUR WOLVES.
THE COUNCIL OF THE ANOINTED WOULD WANT TO KNOW MORE OF SUCH THINGS, SO YOU MUST BE TAKEN TO AMADOR TO BE GIVEN TO THE QUESTIONERS.
...BUT YOU *ARE* SLOWING US *DOWN*.
I HAD HOPED WE COULD MOVE FAST ENOUGH, EVEN WITHOUT THE REMOUNTS, BUT I WAS *WRONG*.
WHICH LEAVES THE LORD CAPTAIN CAUGHT IN THE CLEFT OF A *DILEMMA*.

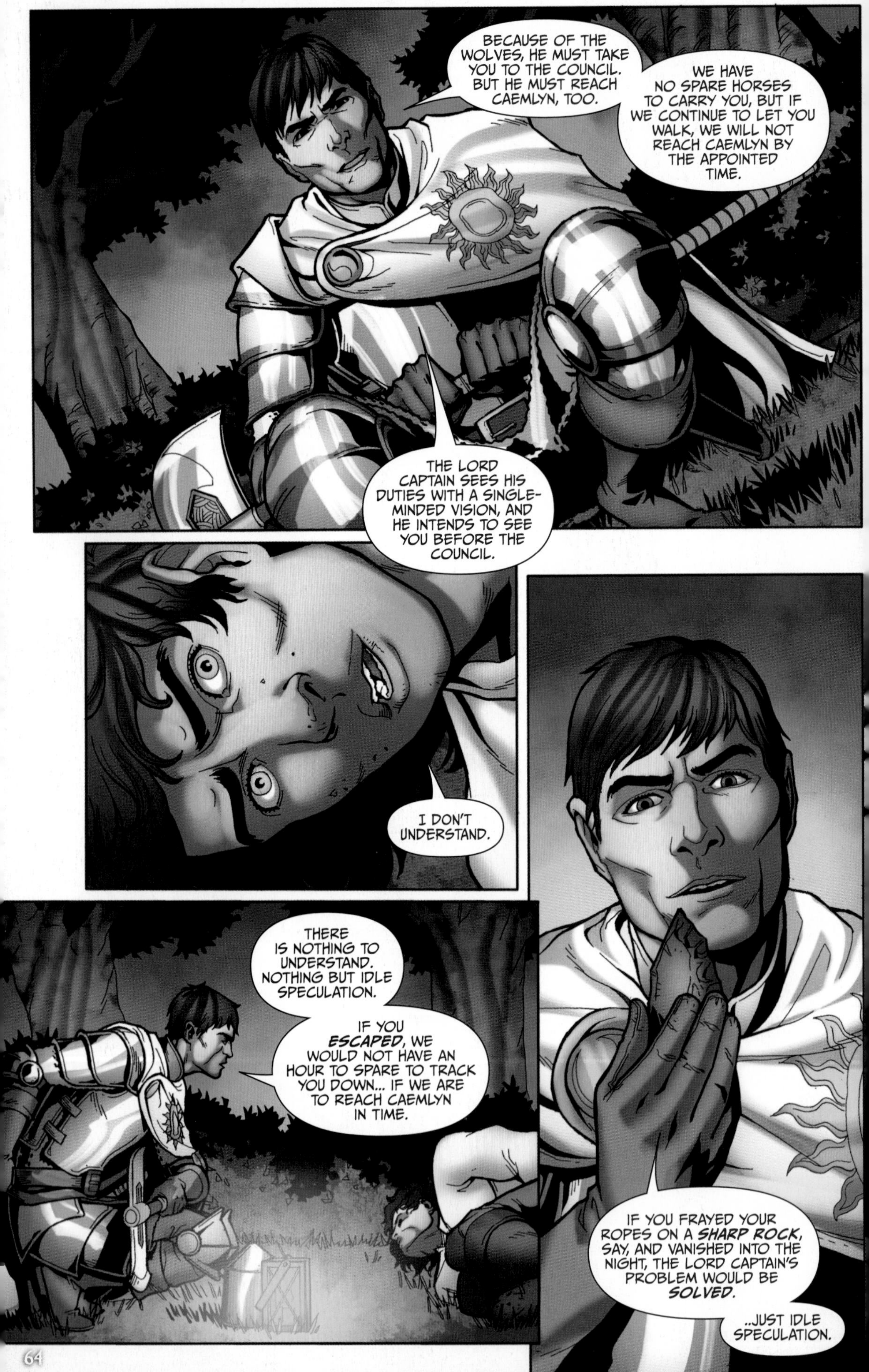
BECAUSE OF THE WOLVES, HE MUST TAKE YOU TO THE COUNCIL. BUT HE MUST REACH CAEMLYN, TOO.
WE HAVE NO SPARE HORSES TO CARRY YOU, BUT IF WE CONTINUE TO LET YOU WALK, WE WILL NOT REACH CAEMLYN BY THE APPOINTED TIME.
THE LORD CAPTAIN SEES HIS DUTIES WITH A SINGLE-MINDED VISION, AND HE INTENDS TO SEE YOU BEFORE THE COUNCIL.
I DON'T UNDERSTAND.
THERE IS NOTHING TO UNDERSTAND. NOTHING BUT IDLE SPECULATION.
IF YOU *ESCAPED*, WE WOULD NOT HAVE AN HOUR TO SPARE TO TRACK YOU DOWN... IF WE ARE TO REACH CAEMLYN IN TIME.
IF YOU FRAYED YOUR ROPES ON A *SHARP ROCK*, SAY, AND VANISHED INTO THE NIGHT, THE LORD CAPTAIN'S PROBLEM WOULD BE *SOLVED*.
..JUST IDLE SPECULATION.

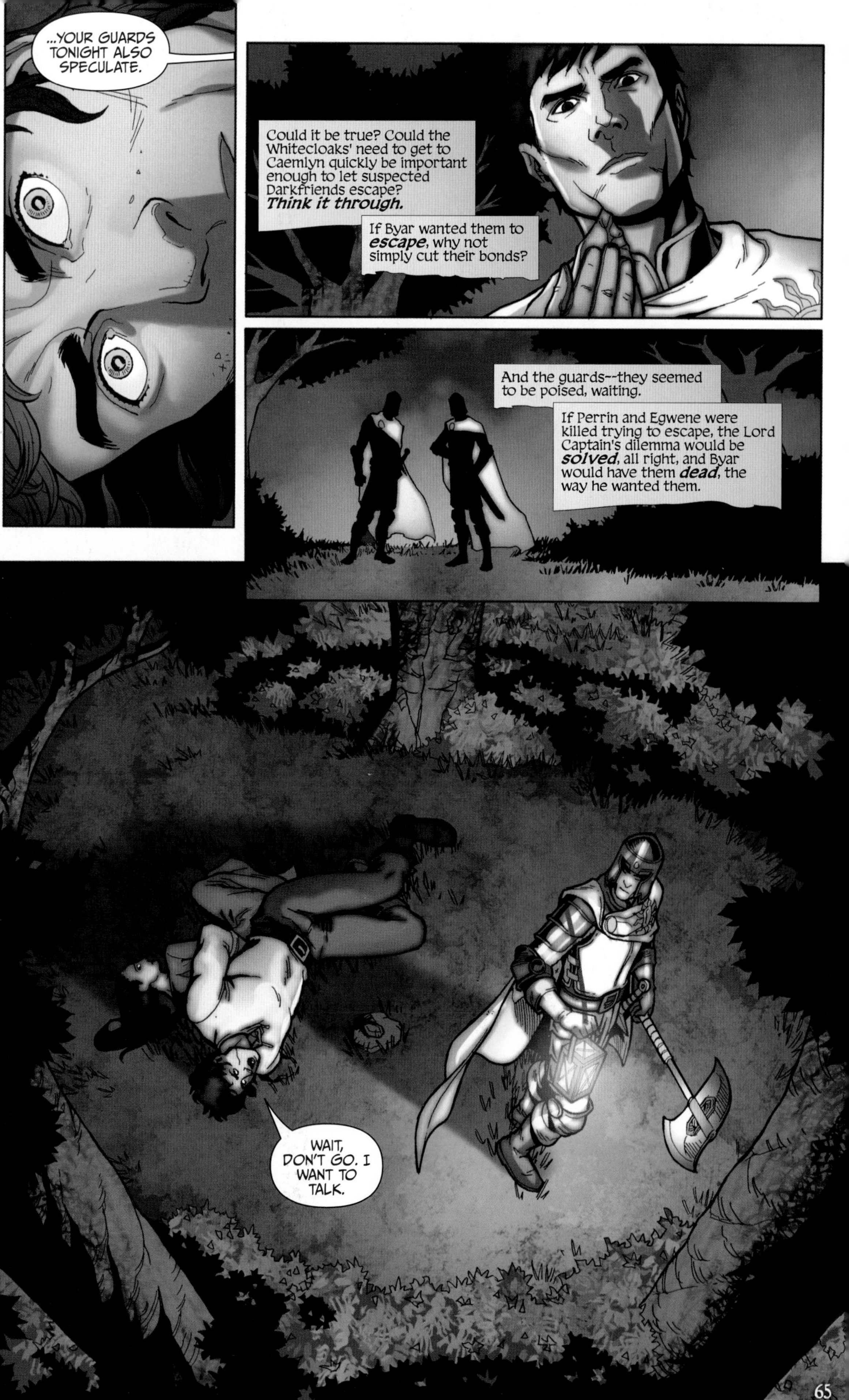
...YOUR GUARDS TONIGHT ALSO SPECULATE.
Could it be true? Could the Whitecloaks' need to get to Caemlyn quickly be important enough to let suspected Darkfriends escape? ***Think it through.***
If Byar wanted them to ***escape***, why not simply cut their bonds?
And the guards--they seemed to be poised, waiting.
If Perrin and Egwene were killed trying to escape, the Lord Captain's dilemma would be ***solved***, all right, and Byar would have them ***dead***, the way he wanted them.
WAIT, DON'T GO. I WANT TO TALK.

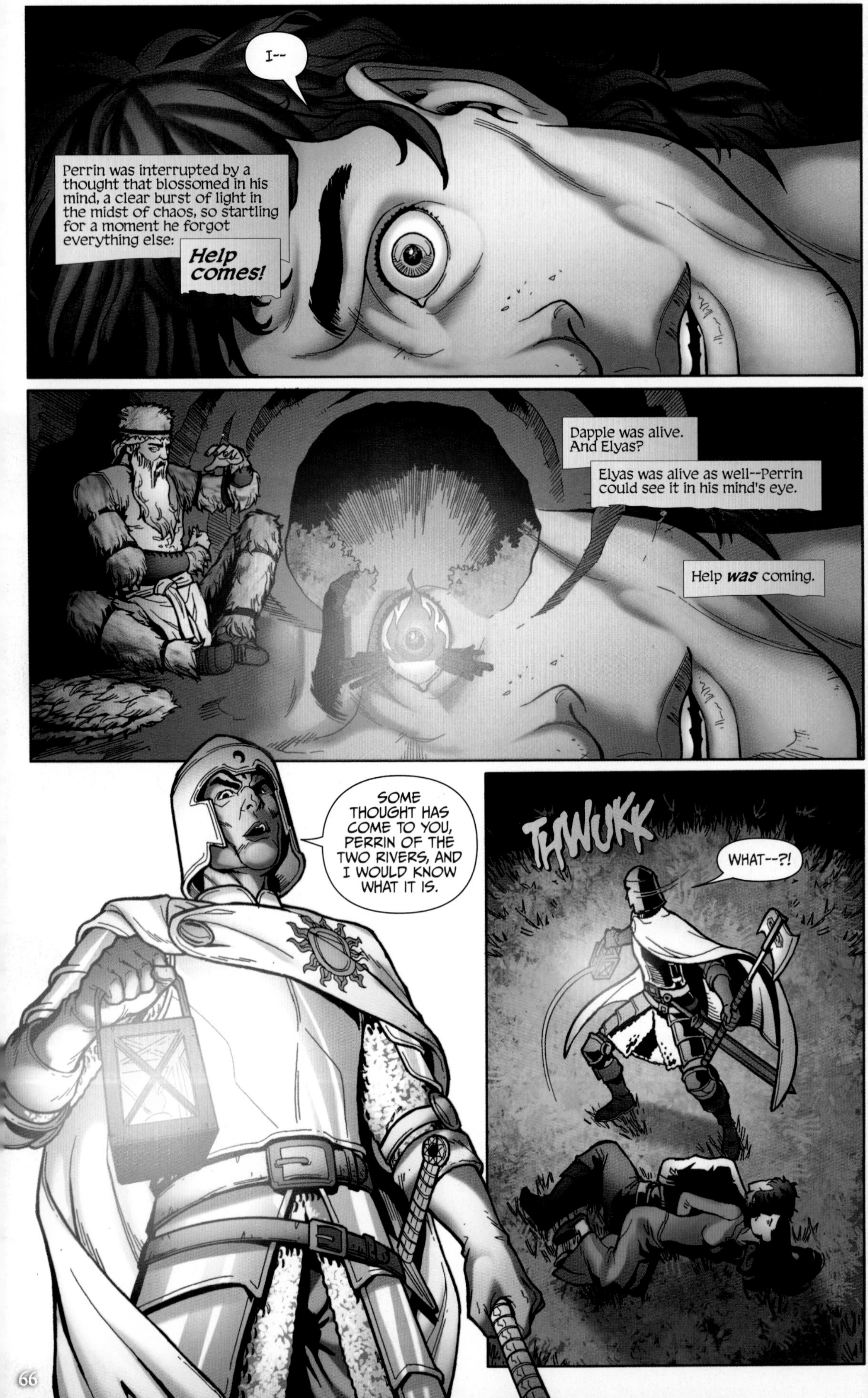

I--
Perrin was interrupted by a thought that blossomed in his mind, a clear burst of light in the midst of chaos, so startling for a moment he forgot everything else:
Help comes!
Dapple was alive. And Elyas?
Elyas was alive as well--Perrin could see it in his mind's eye.
Help was coming.
SOME THOUGHT HAS COME TO YOU, PERRIN OF THE TWO RIVERS, AND I WOULD KNOW WHAT IT IS.
THWUKK
WHAT--?!

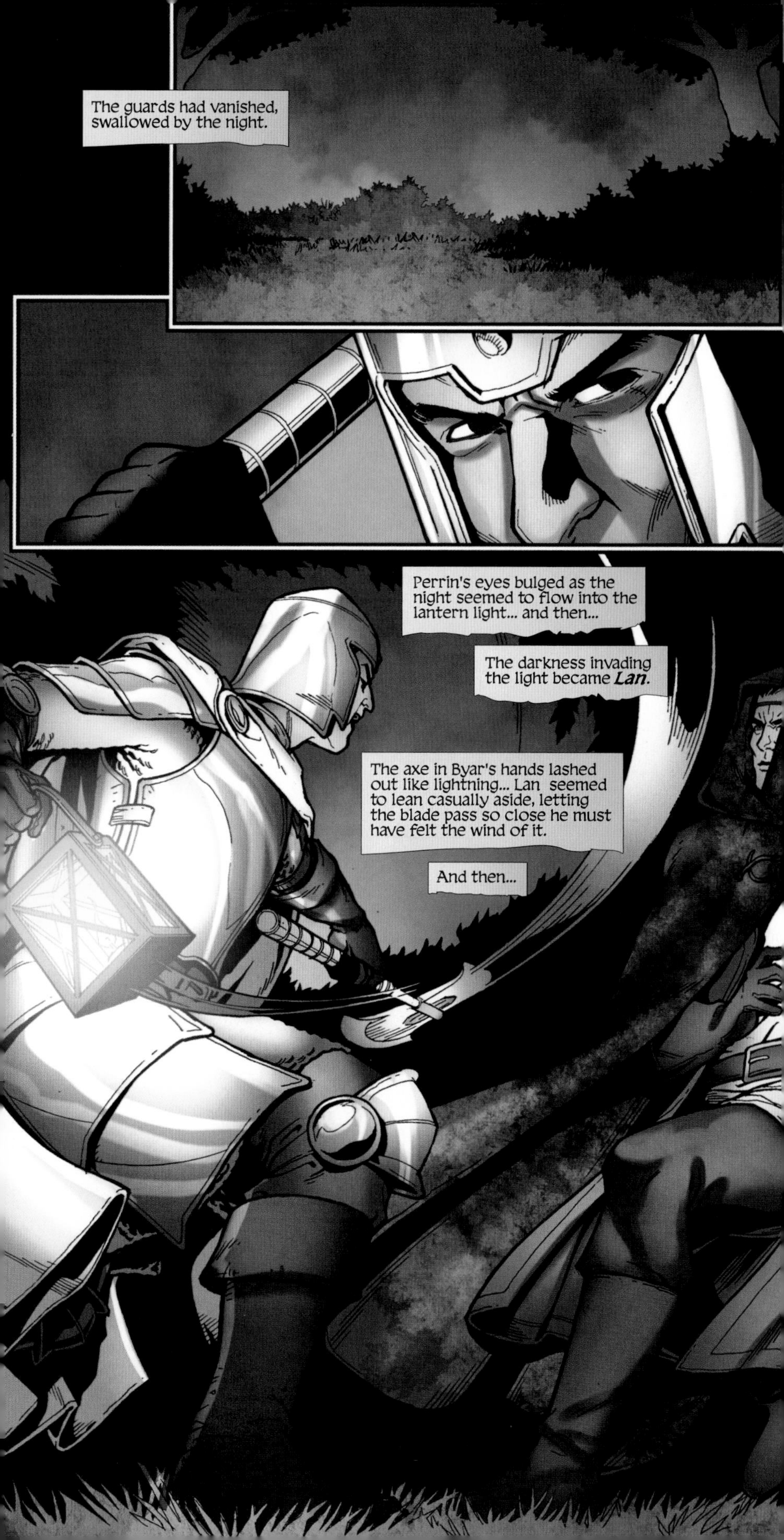
The guards had vanished, swallowed by the night.
Perrin's eyes bulged as the night seemed to flow into the lantern light... and then...
The darkness invading the light became *Lan*.
The axe in Byar's hands lashed out like lightning... Lan seemed to lean casually aside, letting the blade pass so close he must have felt the wind of it.
And then...

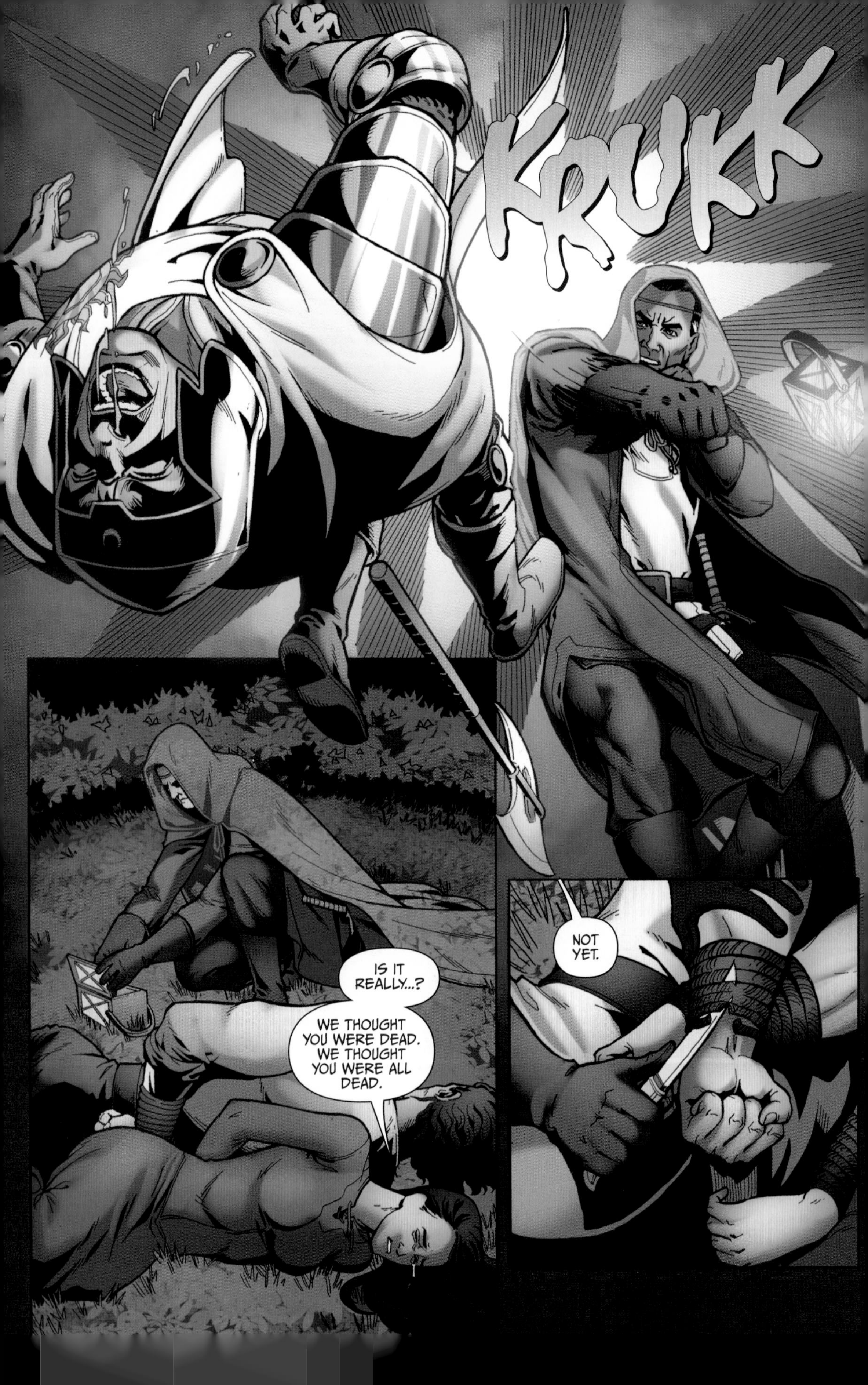
KRUKK
IS IT REALLY...?
WE THOUGHT YOU WERE DEAD. WE THOUGHT YOU WERE ALL DEAD.
NOT YET.

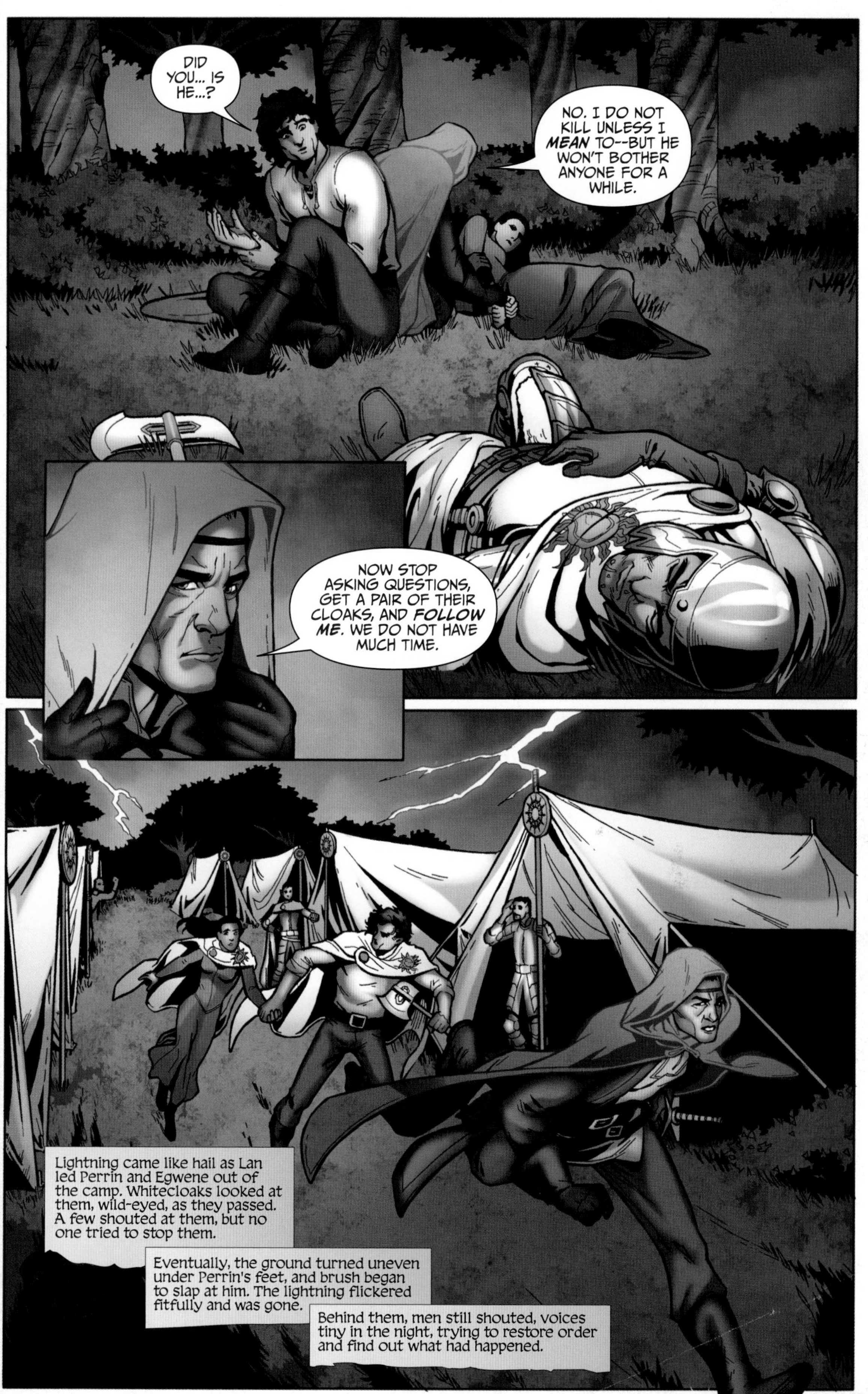
DID YOU... IS HE...?
NO. I DO NOT KILL UNLESS I MEAN TO--BUT HE WON'T BOTHER ANYONE FOR A WHILE.
NOW STOP ASKING QUESTIONS, GET A PAIR OF THEIR CLOAKS, AND FOLLOW ME. WE DO NOT HAVE MUCH TIME.
Lightning came like hail as Lan led Perrin and Egwene out of the camp. Whitecloaks looked at them, wild-eyed, as they passed. A few shouted at them, but no one tried to stop them.
Eventually, the ground turned uneven under Perrin's feet, and brush began to slap at him. The lightning flickered fitfully and was gone.
Behind them, men still shouted, voices tiny in the night, trying to restore order and find out what had happened.

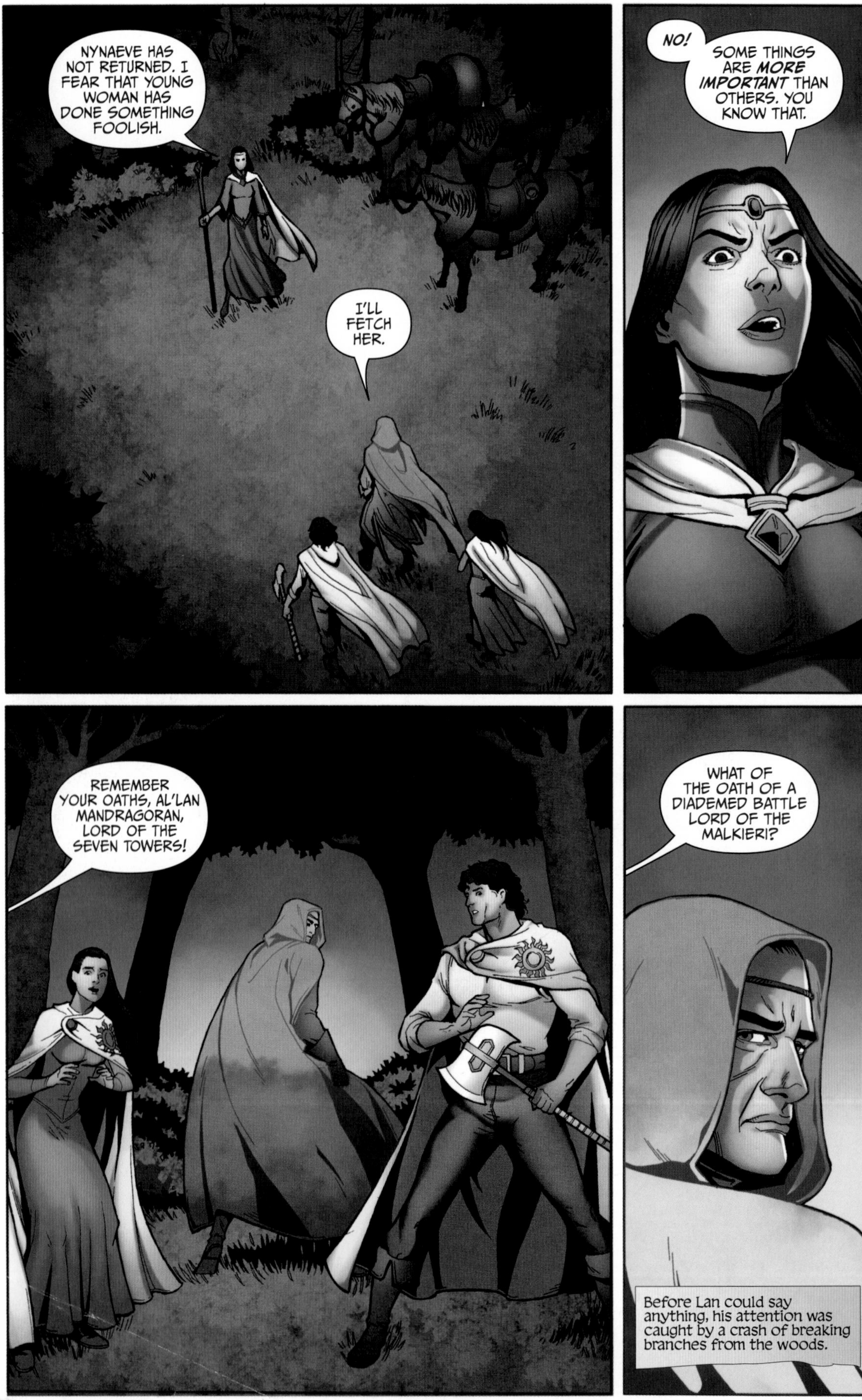
NYNAEVE HAS NOT RETURNED. I FEAR THAT YOUNG WOMAN HAS DONE SOMETHING FOOLISH.
I'LL FETCH HER.
NO!
SOME THINGS ARE *MORE IMPORTANT* THAN OTHERS. YOU KNOW THAT.
REMEMBER YOUR OATHS, AL'LAN MANDRAGORAN, LORD OF THE SEVEN TOWERS!
WHAT OF THE OATH OF A DIADEMED BATTLE LORD OF THE MALKIERI?
Before Lan could say anything, his attention was caught by a crash of breaking branches from the woods.

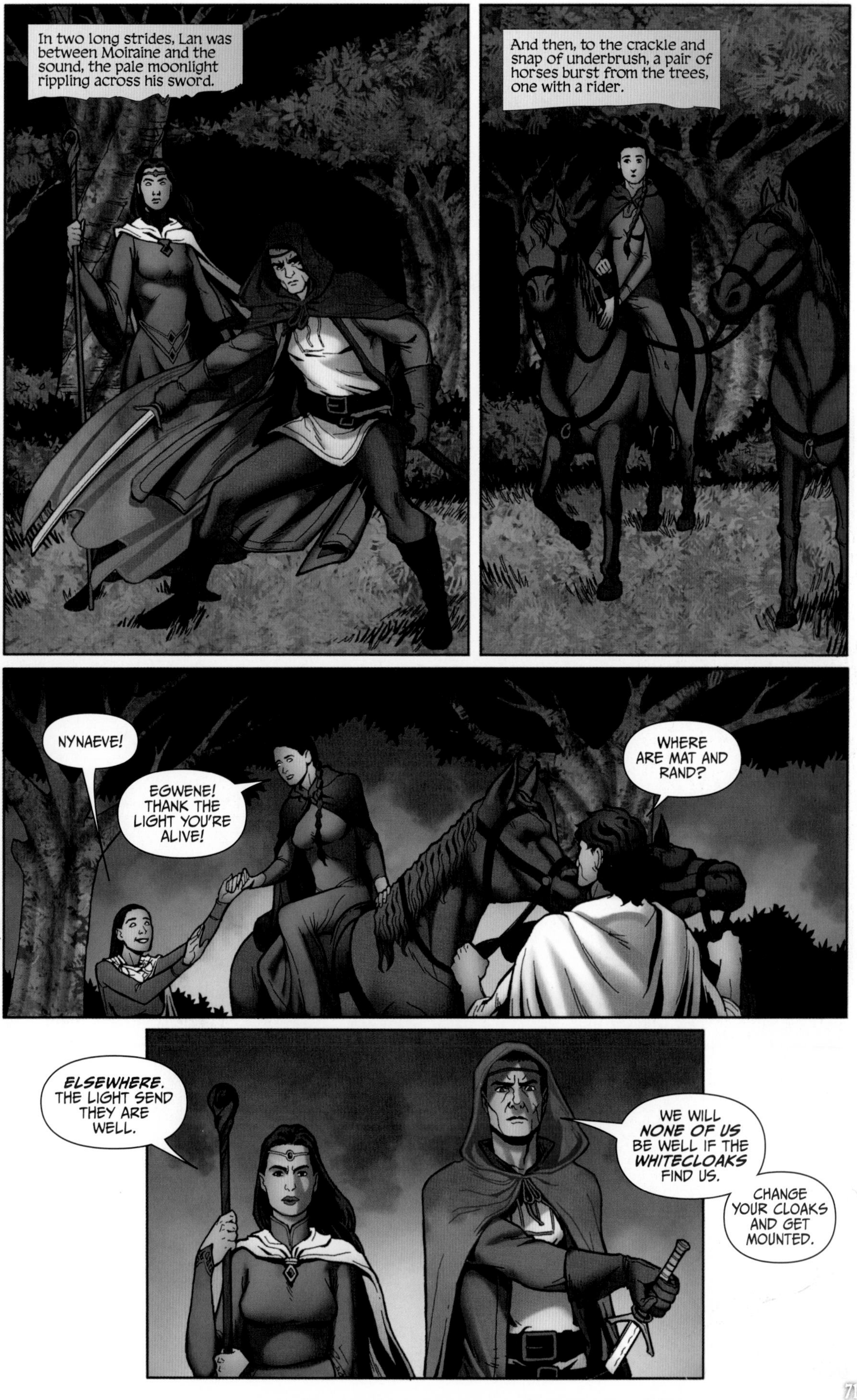
In two long strides, Lan was between Moiraine and the sound, the pale moonlight rippling across his sword.
And then, to the crackle and snap of underbrush, a pair of horses burst from the trees, one with a rider.
NYNAEVE!
EGWENE! THANK THE LIGHT YOU'RE ALIVE!
WHERE ARE MAT AND RAND?
ELSEWHERE. THE LIGHT SEND THEY ARE WELL.
WE WILL NONE OF US BE WELL IF THE WHITECLOAKS FIND US.
CHANGE YOUR CLOAKS AND GET MOUNTED.

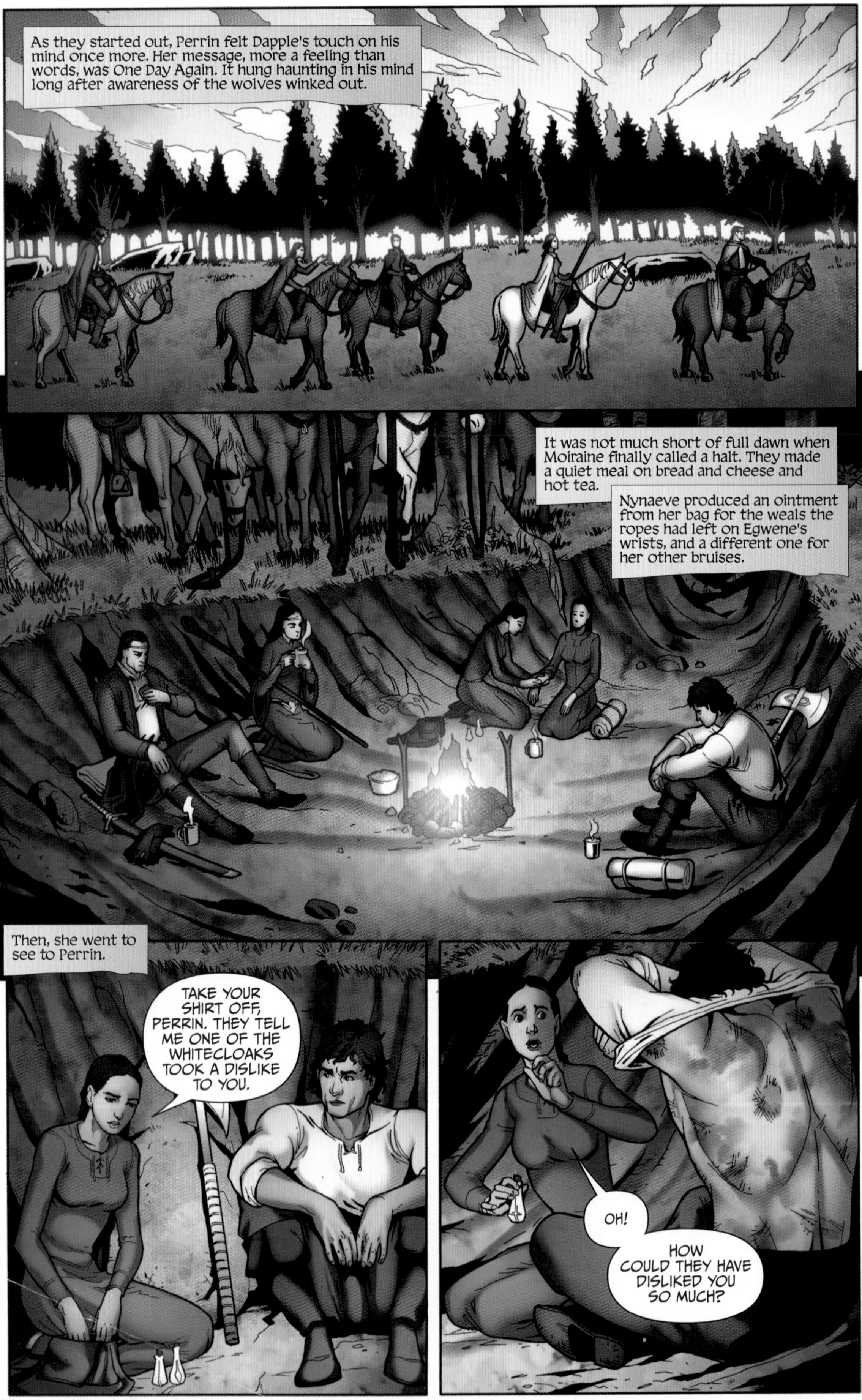
As they started out, Perrin felt Dapple's touch on his mind once more. Her message, more a feeling than words, was One Day Again. It hung haunting in his mind long after awareness of the wolves winked out.
It was not much short of full dawn when Moiraine finally called a halt. They made a quiet meal on bread and cheese and hot tea.
Nynaeve produced an ointment from her bag for the weals the ropes had left on Egwene's wrists, and a different one for her other bruises.
Then, she went to see to Perrin.
TAKE YOUR SHIRT OFF, PERRIN. THEY TELL ME ONE OF THE WHITECLOAKS TOOK A DISLIKE TO YOU.
OH!
HOW COULD THEY HAVE DISLIKED YOU SO MUCH?

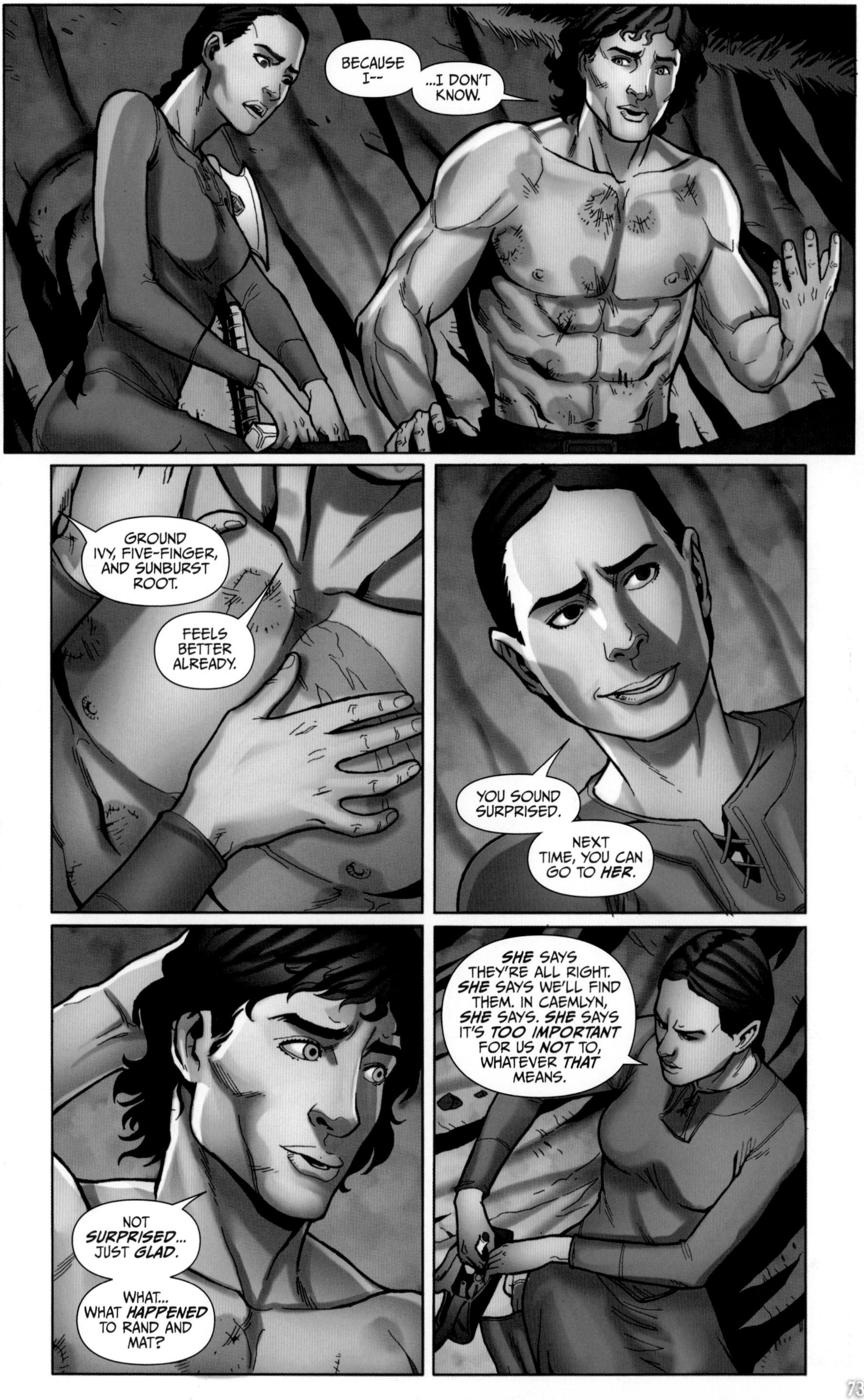
BECAUSE I--
...I DON'T KNOW.
GROUND IVY, FIVE-FINGER, AND SUNBURST ROOT.
FEELS BETTER ALREADY.
YOU SOUND SURPRISED.
NEXT TIME, YOU CAN GO TO HER.
NOT SURPRISED... JUST GLAD.
WHAT... WHAT HAPPENED TO RAND AND MAT?
SHE SAYS THEY'RE ALL RIGHT. SHE SAYS WE'LL FIND THEM. IN CAEMLYN, SHE SAYS. SHE SAYS IT'S TOO IMPORTANT FOR US NOT TO, WHATEVER THAT MEANS.

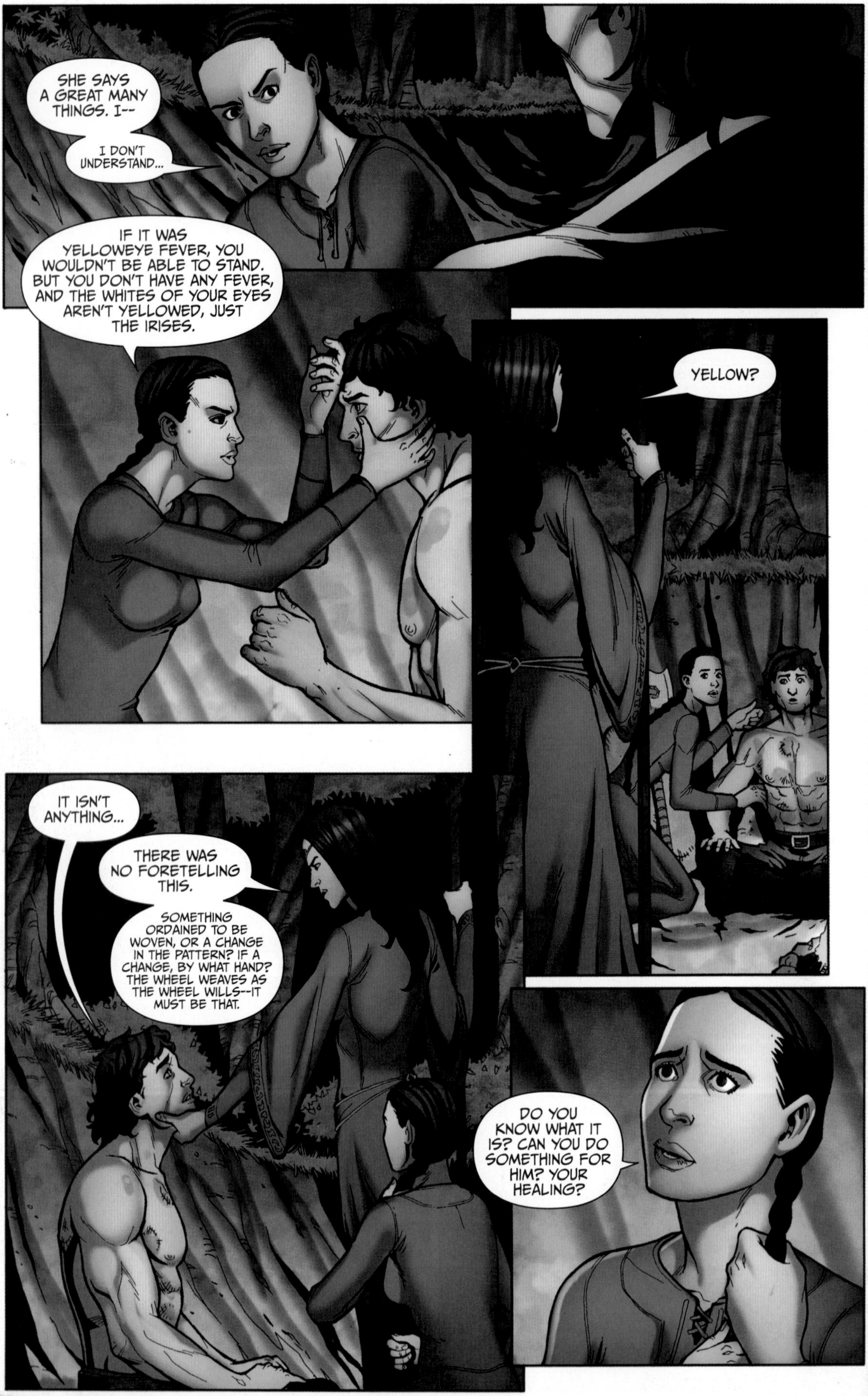
SHE SAYS A GREAT MANY THINGS. I--
I DON'T UNDERSTAND...
IF IT WAS YELLOWEYE FEVER, YOU WOULDN'T BE ABLE TO STAND. BUT YOU DON'T HAVE ANY FEVER, AND THE WHITES OF YOUR EYES AREN'T YELLOWED, JUST THE IRISES.
YELLOW?
IT ISN'T ANYTHING...
THERE WAS NO FORETELLING THIS.
SOMETHING ORDAINED TO BE WOVEN, OR A CHANGE IN THE PATTERN? IF A CHANGE, BY WHAT HAND? THE WHEEL WEAVES AS THE WHEEL WILLS--IT MUST BE THAT.
DO YOU KNOW WHAT IT IS? CAN YOU DO SOMETHING FOR HIM? YOUR HEALING?

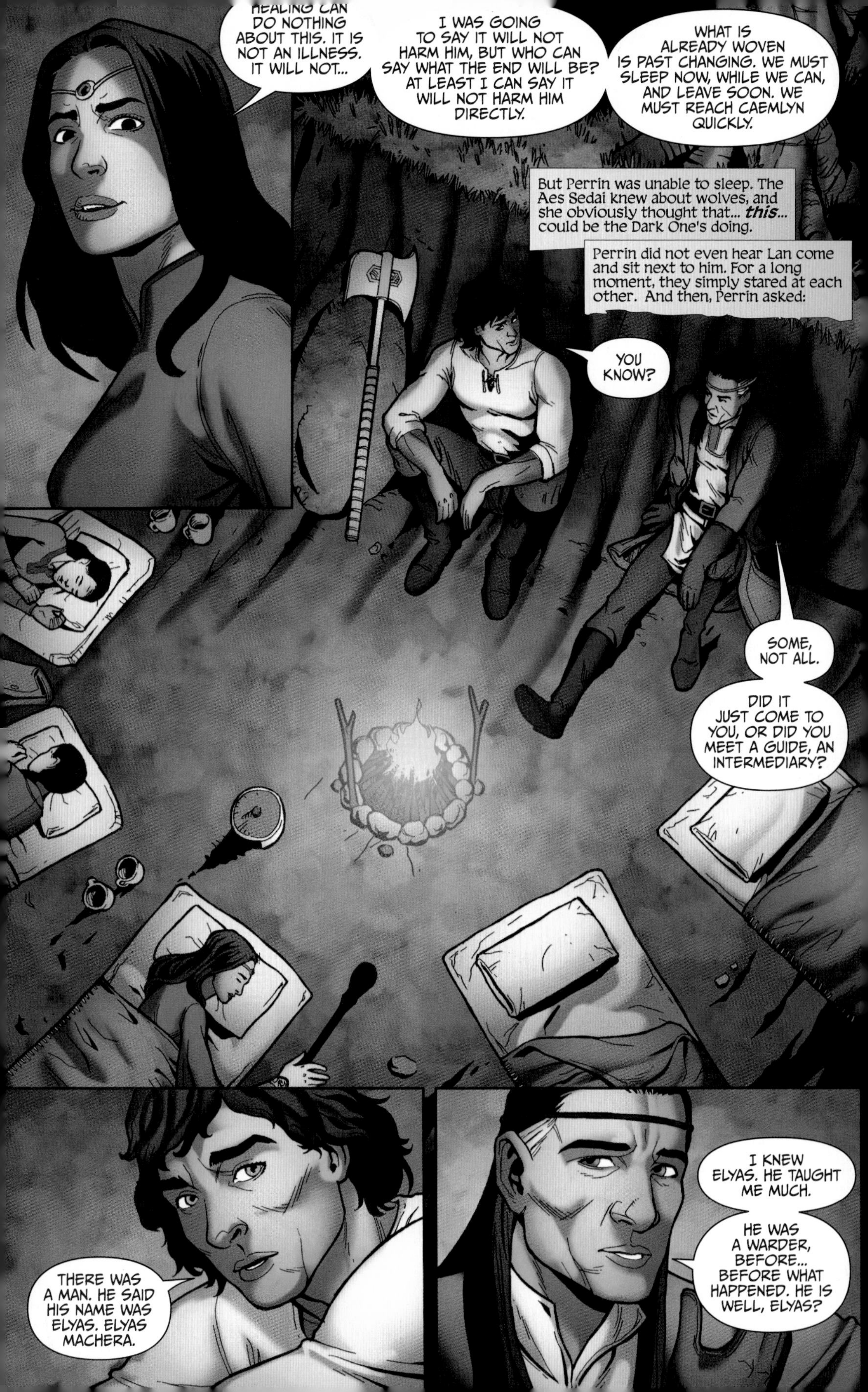
HEALING CAN DO NOTHING ABOUT THIS. IT IS NOT AN ILLNESS. IT WILL NOT...
I WAS GOING TO SAY IT WILL NOT HARM HIM, BUT WHO CAN SAY WHAT THE END WILL BE? AT LEAST I CAN SAY IT WILL NOT HARM HIM DIRECTLY.
WHAT IS ALREADY WOVEN IS PAST CHANGING. WE MUST SLEEP NOW, WHILE WE CAN, AND LEAVE SOON. WE MUST REACH CAEMLYN QUICKLY.
But Perrin was unable to sleep. The Aes Sedai knew about wolves, and she obviously thought that... *this*... could be the Dark One's doing.
Perrin did not even hear Lan come and sit next to him. For a long moment, they simply stared at each other. And then, Perrin asked:
YOU KNOW?
SOME, NOT ALL.
DID IT JUST COME TO YOU, OR DID YOU MEET A GUIDE, AN INTERMEDIARY?
THERE WAS A MAN. HE SAID HIS NAME WAS ELYAS. ELYAS MACHERA.
I KNEW ELYAS. HE TAUGHT ME MUCH.
HE WAS A WARDER, BEFORE... BEFORE WHAT HAPPENED. HE IS WELL, ELYAS?

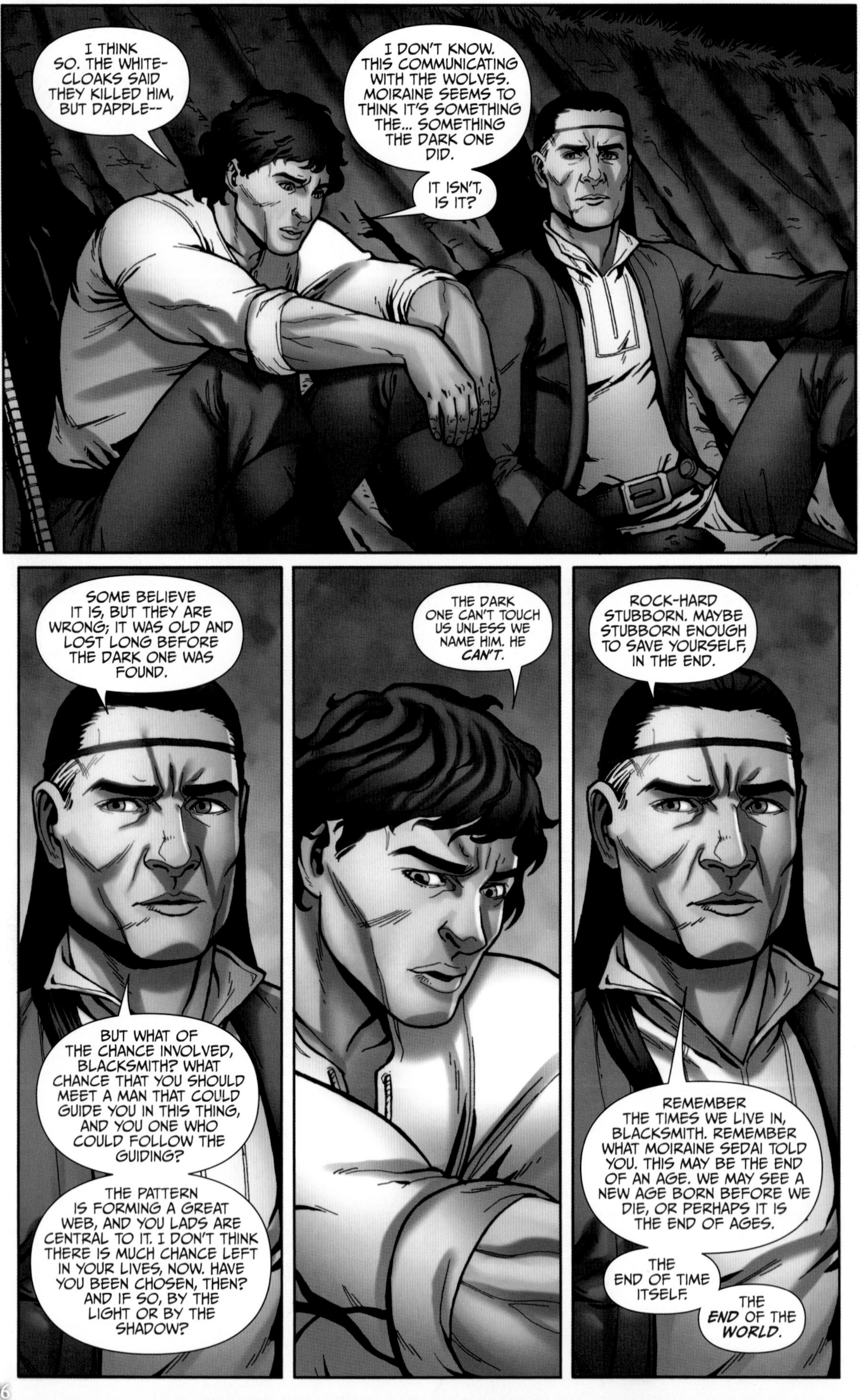
I THINK SO. THE WHITE-CLOAKS SAID THEY KILLED HIM, BUT DAPPLE--
I DON'T KNOW. THIS COMMUNICATING WITH THE WOLVES. MOIRAINE SEEMS TO THINK IT'S SOMETHING THE... SOMETHING THE DARK ONE DID.
IT ISN'T, IS IT?
SOME BELIEVE IT IS, BUT THEY ARE WRONG; IT WAS OLD AND LOST LONG BEFORE THE DARK ONE WAS FOUND.
BUT WHAT OF THE CHANCE INVOLVED, BLACKSMITH? WHAT CHANCE THAT YOU SHOULD MEET A MAN THAT COULD GUIDE YOU IN THIS THING, AND YOU ONE WHO COULD FOLLOW THE GUIDING?
THE PATTERN IS FORMING A GREAT WEB, AND YOU LADS ARE CENTRAL TO IT. I DON'T THINK THERE IS MUCH CHANCE LEFT IN YOUR LIVES, NOW. HAVE YOU BEEN CHOSEN, THEN? AND IF SO, BY THE LIGHT OR BY THE SHADOW?
THE DARK ONE CAN'T TOUCH US UNLESS WE NAME HIM. HE *CAN'T*.
ROCK-HARD STUBBORN. MAYBE STUBBORN ENOUGH TO SAVE YOURSELF, IN THE END.
REMEMBER THE TIMES WE LIVE IN, BLACKSMITH. REMEMBER WHAT MOIRAINE SEDAI TOLD YOU. THIS MAY BE THE END OF AN AGE. WE MAY SEE A NEW AGE BORN BEFORE WE DIE, OR PERHAPS IT IS THE END OF AGES.
THE END OF TIME ITSELF.
THE *END* OF THE *WORLD*.

BUT THAT'S NOT FOR US TO WORRY ABOUT, EH, BLACKSMITH? WE'LL FIGHT THE SHADOW AS LONG AS WE HAVE BREATH, AND IF IT OVERRUNS US, WE'LL GO UNDER BITING AND CLAWING.

YOU TWO RIVERS FOLK ARE TOO STUBBORN TO SURRENDER.

DON'T YOU WORRY WHETHER THE DARK ONE HAS STIRRED IN YOUR LIFE. YOU ARE AMONG FRIENDS, NOW.

REMEMBER, THE WHEEL WEAVES AS THE WHEEL WILLS, AND EVEN THE DARK ONE CANNOT CHANGE THAT, NOT WITH *MOIRAINE* TO WATCH OVER YOU. BUT WE HAD BETTER FIND YOUR FRIENDS SOON.

WHAT DO YOU MEAN?

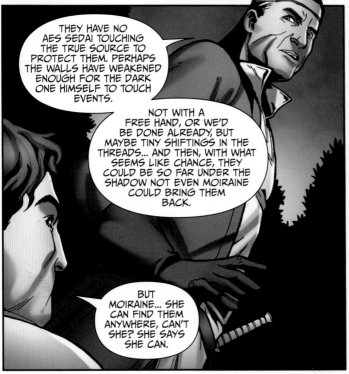

THEY HAVE NO AES SEDAI TOUCHING THE TRUE SOURCE TO PROTECT THEM. PERHAPS THE WALLS HAVE WEAKENED ENOUGH FOR THE DARK ONE HIMSELF TO TOUCH EVENTS.

NOT WITH A FREE HAND, OR WE'D BE DONE ALREADY, BUT MAYBE TINY SHIFTINGS IN THE THREADS... AND THEN, WITH WHAT SEEMS LIKE CHANCE, THEY COULD BE SO FAR UNDER THE SHADOW NOT EVEN MOIRAINE COULD BRING THEM BACK.

BUT MOIRAINE... SHE CAN FIND THEM ANYWHERE, CAN'T SHE? SHE SAYS SHE CAN.

BUT CAN SHE FIND THEM IN TIME? IF THE DARK ONE IS STRONG ENOUGH TO TAKE A HAND HIMSELF, TIME IS RUNNING OUT.

YOU PRAY WE FIND THEM IN CAEMLYN, BLACK-SMITH, OR WE MAY ALL BE LOST.

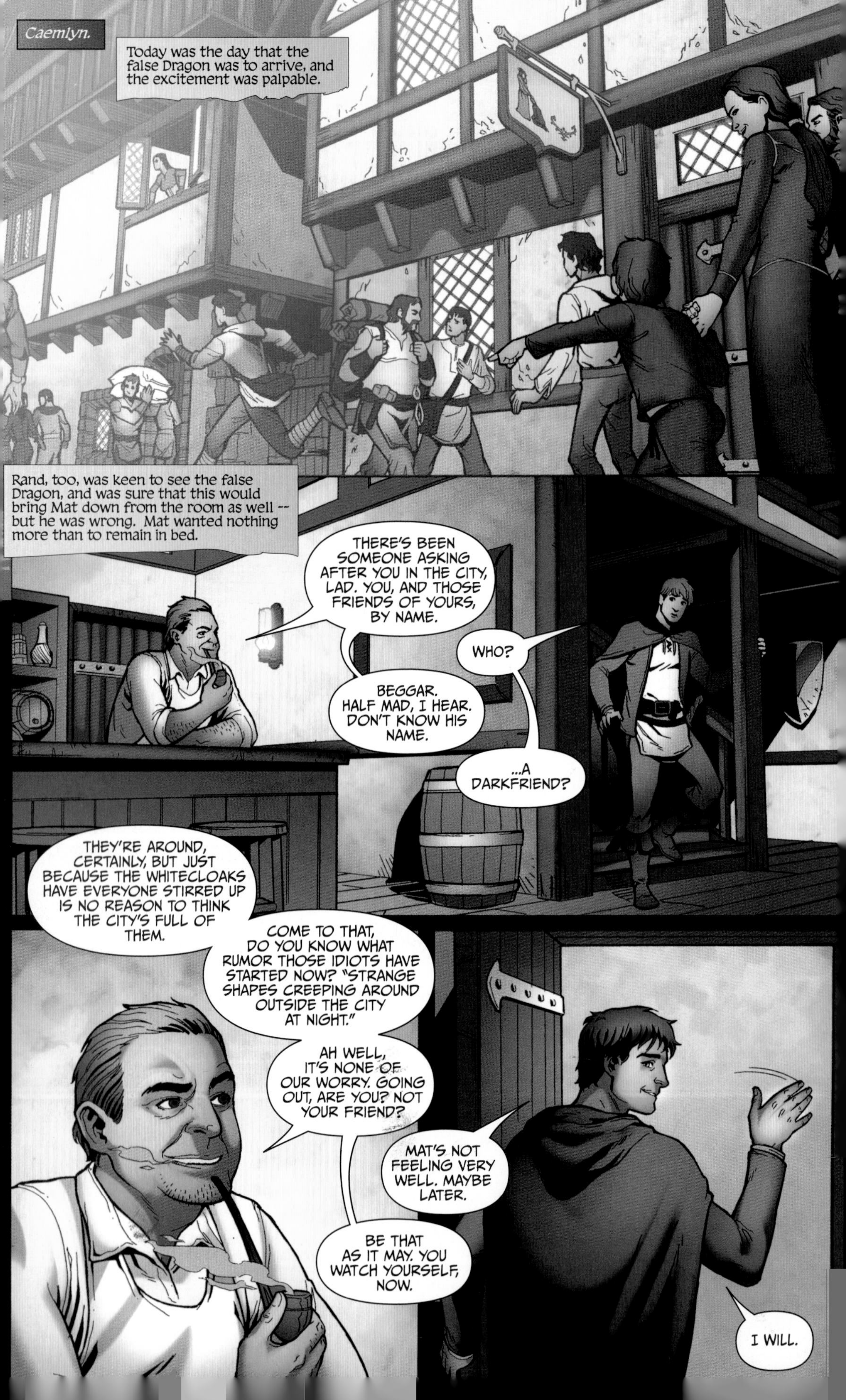
Caemlyn.
Today was the day that the false Dragon was to arrive, and the excitement was palpable.
Rand, too, was keen to see the false Dragon, and was sure that this would bring Mat down from the room as well -- but he was wrong. Mat wanted nothing more than to remain in bed.
THERE'S BEEN SOMEONE ASKING AFTER YOU IN THE CITY, LAD. YOU, AND THOSE FRIENDS OF YOURS, BY NAME.
WHO?
BEGGAR. HALF MAD, I HEAR. DON'T KNOW HIS NAME.
...A DARKFRIEND?
THEY'RE AROUND, CERTAINLY, BUT JUST BECAUSE THE WHITECLOAKS HAVE EVERYONE STIRRED UP IS NO REASON TO THINK THE CITY'S FULL OF THEM.
COME TO THAT, DO YOU KNOW WHAT RUMOR THOSE IDIOTS HAVE STARTED NOW? "STRANGE SHAPES CREEPING AROUND OUTSIDE THE CITY AT NIGHT."
AH WELL, IT'S NONE OF OUR WORRY. GOING OUT, ARE YOU? NOT YOUR FRIEND?
MAT'S NOT FEELING VERY WELL. MAYBE LATER.
BE THAT AS IT MAY. YOU WATCH YOURSELF, NOW.
I WILL.

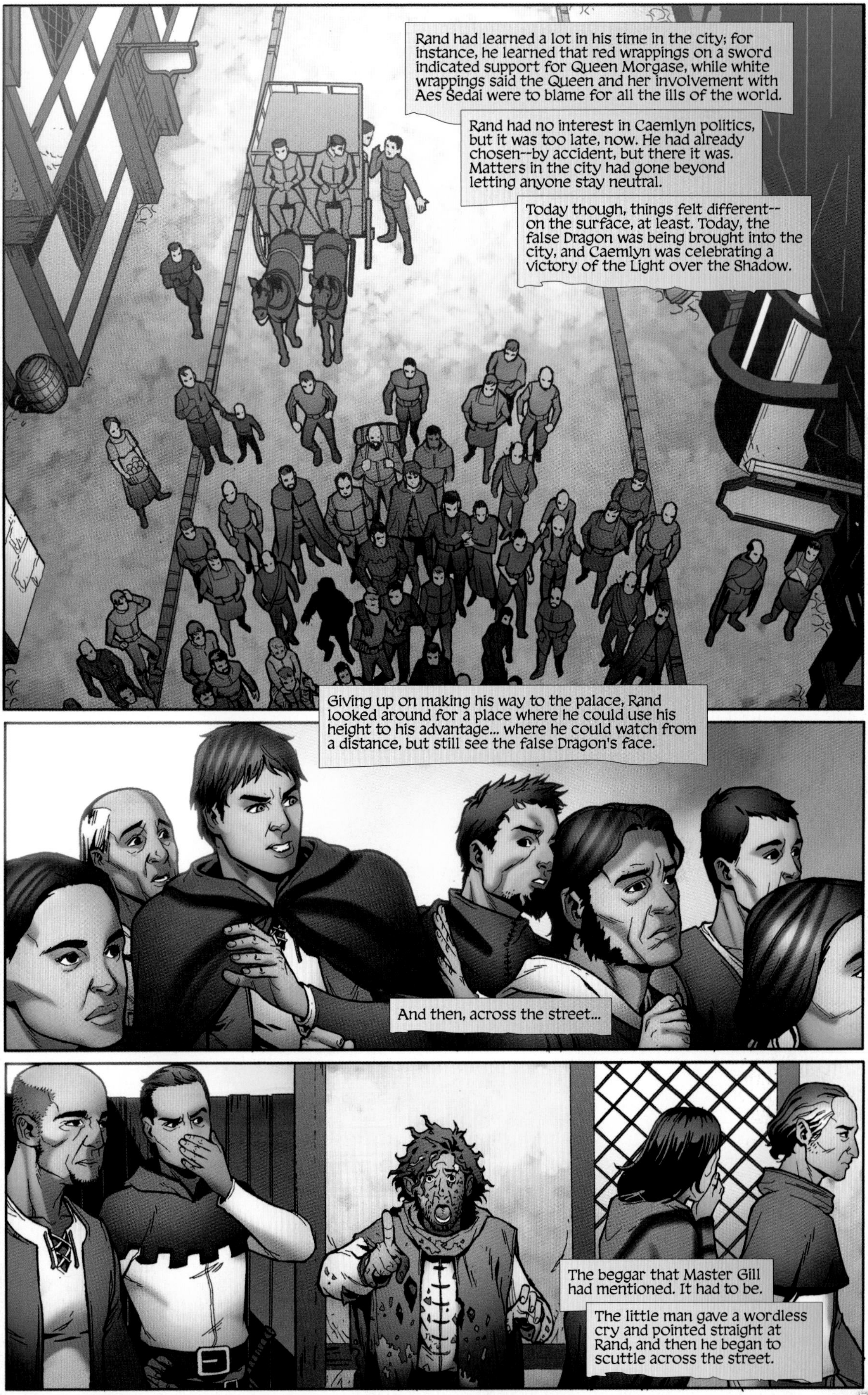
Rand had learned a lot in his time in the city; for instance, he learned that red wrappings on a sword indicated support for Queen Morgase, while white wrappings said the Queen and her involvement with Aes Sedai were to blame for all the ills of the world.
Rand had no interest in Caemlyn politics, but it was too late, now. He had already chosen--by accident, but there it was. Matters in the city had gone beyond letting anyone stay neutral.
Today though, things felt different--on the surface, at least. Today, the false Dragon was being brought into the city, and Caemlyn was celebrating a victory of the Light over the Shadow.
Giving up on making his way to the palace, Rand looked around for a place where he could use his height to his advantage... where he could watch from a distance, but still see the false Dragon's face.
And then, across the street...
The beggar that Master Gill had mentioned. It had to be.
The little man gave a wordless cry and pointed straight at Rand, and then he began to scuttle across the street.

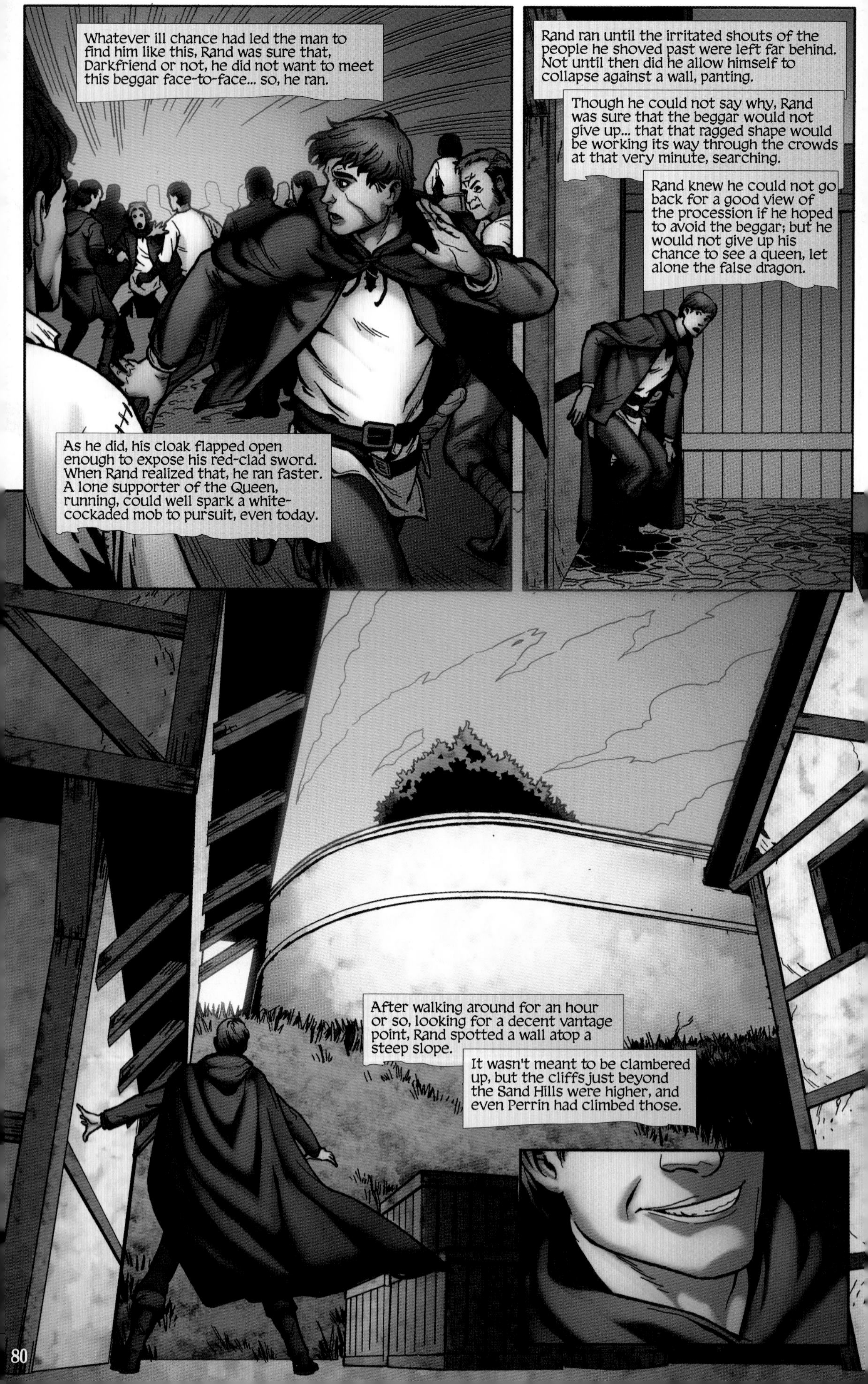

Whatever ill chance had led the man to find him like this, Rand was sure that, Darkfriend or not, he did not want to meet this beggar face-to-face... so, he ran.
As he did, his cloak flapped open enough to expose his red-clad sword. When Rand realized that, he ran faster. A lone supporter of the Queen, running, could well spark a white-cockaded mob to pursuit, even today.
Rand ran until the irritated shouts of the people he shoved past were left far behind. Not until then did he allow himself to collapse against a wall, panting.
Though he could not say why, Rand was sure that the beggar would not give up... that that ragged shape would be working its way through the crowds at that very minute, searching.
Rand knew he could not go back for a good view of the procession if he hoped to avoid the beggar; but he would not give up his chance to see a queen, let alone the false dragon.
After walking around for an hour or so, looking for a decent vantage point, Rand spotted a wall atop a steep slope.
It wasn't meant to be clambered up, but the cliffs just beyond the Sand Hills were higher, and even Perrin had climbed those.

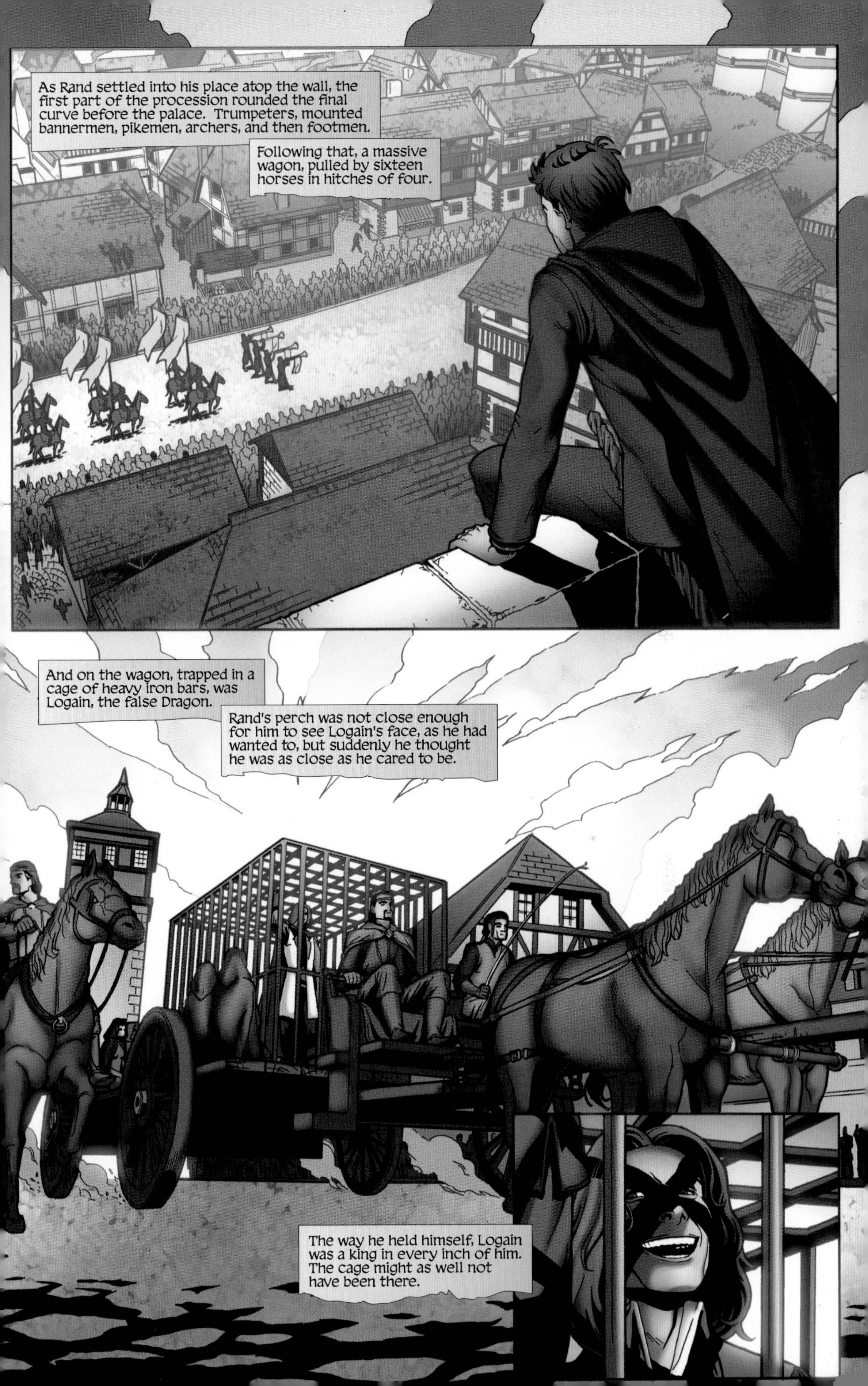
As Rand settled into his place atop the wall, the first part of the procession rounded the final curve before the palace. Trumpeters, mounted bannermen, pikemen, archers, and then footmen.
Following that, a massive wagon, pulled by sixteen horses in hitches of four.
And on the wagon, trapped in a cage of heavy iron bars, was Logain, the false Dragon.
Rand's perch was not close enough for him to see Logain's face, as he had wanted to, but suddenly he thought he was as close as he cared to be.
The way he held himself, Logain was a king in every inch of him. The cage might as well not have been there.

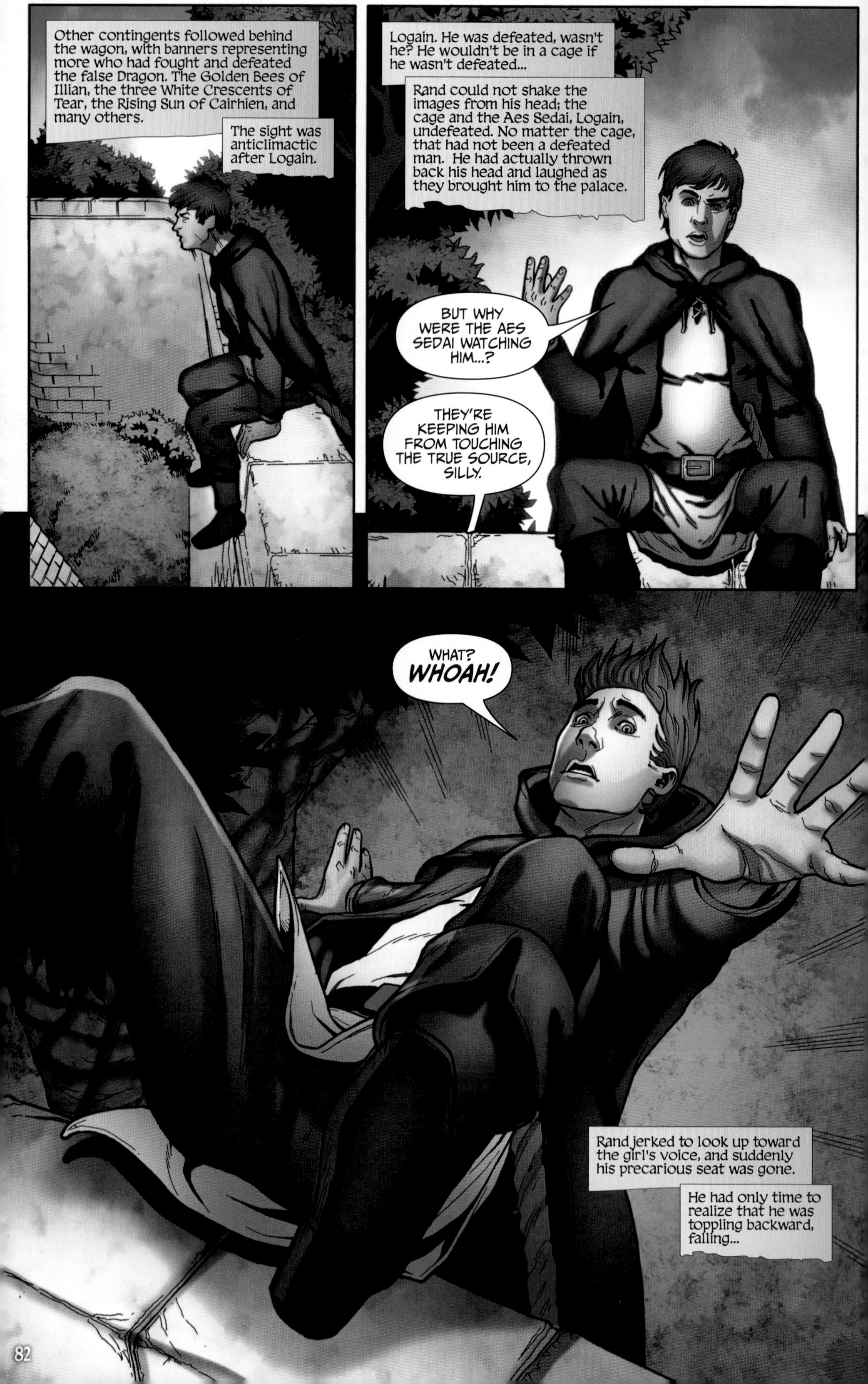
Other contingents followed behind the wagon, with banners representing more who had fought and defeated the false Dragon. The Golden Bees of Illian, the three White Crescents of Tear, the Rising Sun of Cairhien, and many others.
The sight was anticlimactic after Logain.
Logain. He was defeated, wasn't he? He wouldn't be in a cage if he wasn't defeated...
Rand could not shake the images from his head; the cage and the Aes Sedai, Logain, undefeated. No matter the cage, that had not been a defeated man. He had actually thrown back his head and laughed as they brought him to the palace.
BUT WHY WERE THE AES SEDAI WATCHING HIM...?
THEY'RE KEEPING HIM FROM TOUCHING THE TRUE SOURCE, SILLY.
WHAT? WHOAH!
Rand jerked to look up toward the girl's voice, and suddenly his precarious seat was gone.
He had only time to realize that he was toppling backward, falling...

chapter four

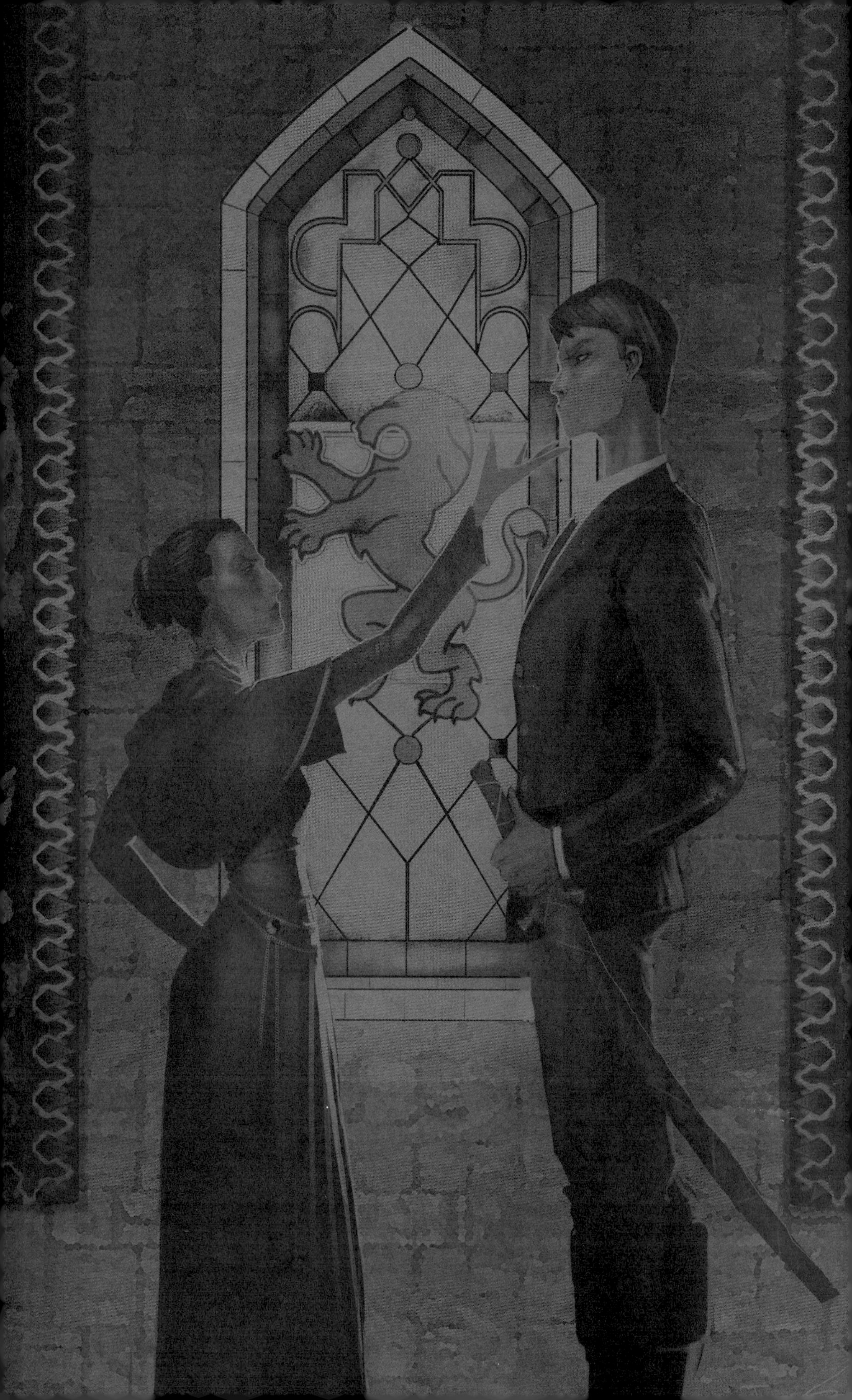

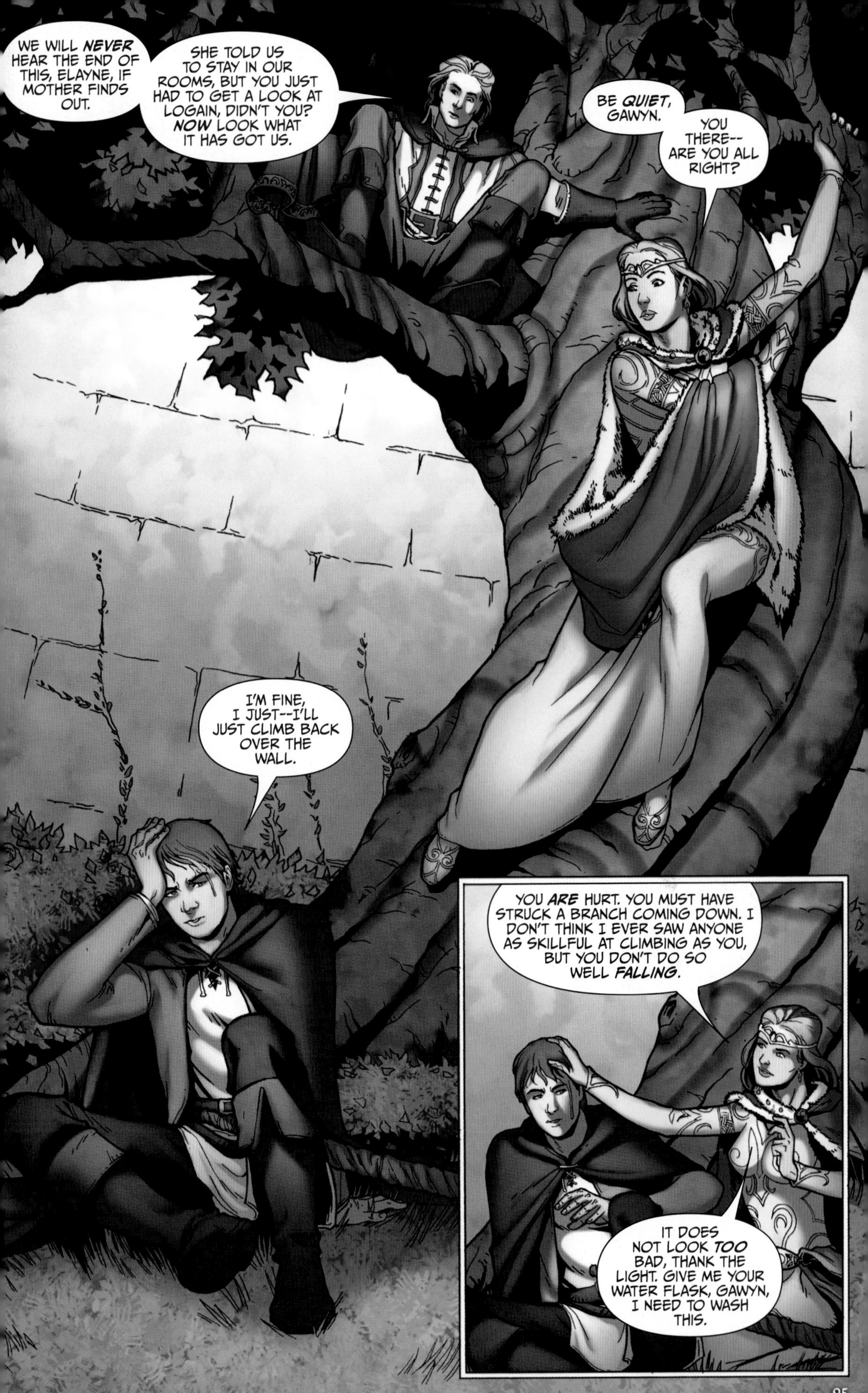

WE WILL NEVER HEAR THE END OF THIS, ELAYNE, IF MOTHER FINDS OUT.
SHE TOLD US TO STAY IN OUR ROOMS, BUT YOU JUST HAD TO GET A LOOK AT LOGAIN, DIDN'T YOU? NOW LOOK WHAT IT HAS GOT US.
BE QUIET, GAWYN.
YOU THERE-- ARE YOU ALL RIGHT?
I'M FINE, I JUST--I'LL JUST CLIMB BACK OVER THE WALL.
YOU ARE HURT. YOU MUST HAVE STRUCK A BRANCH COMING DOWN. I DON'T THINK I EVER SAW ANYONE AS SKILLFUL AT CLIMBING AS YOU, BUT YOU DON'T DO SO WELL FALLING.
IT DOES NOT LOOK TOO BAD, THANK THE LIGHT. GIVE ME YOUR WATER FLASK, GAWYN, I NEED TO WASH THIS.

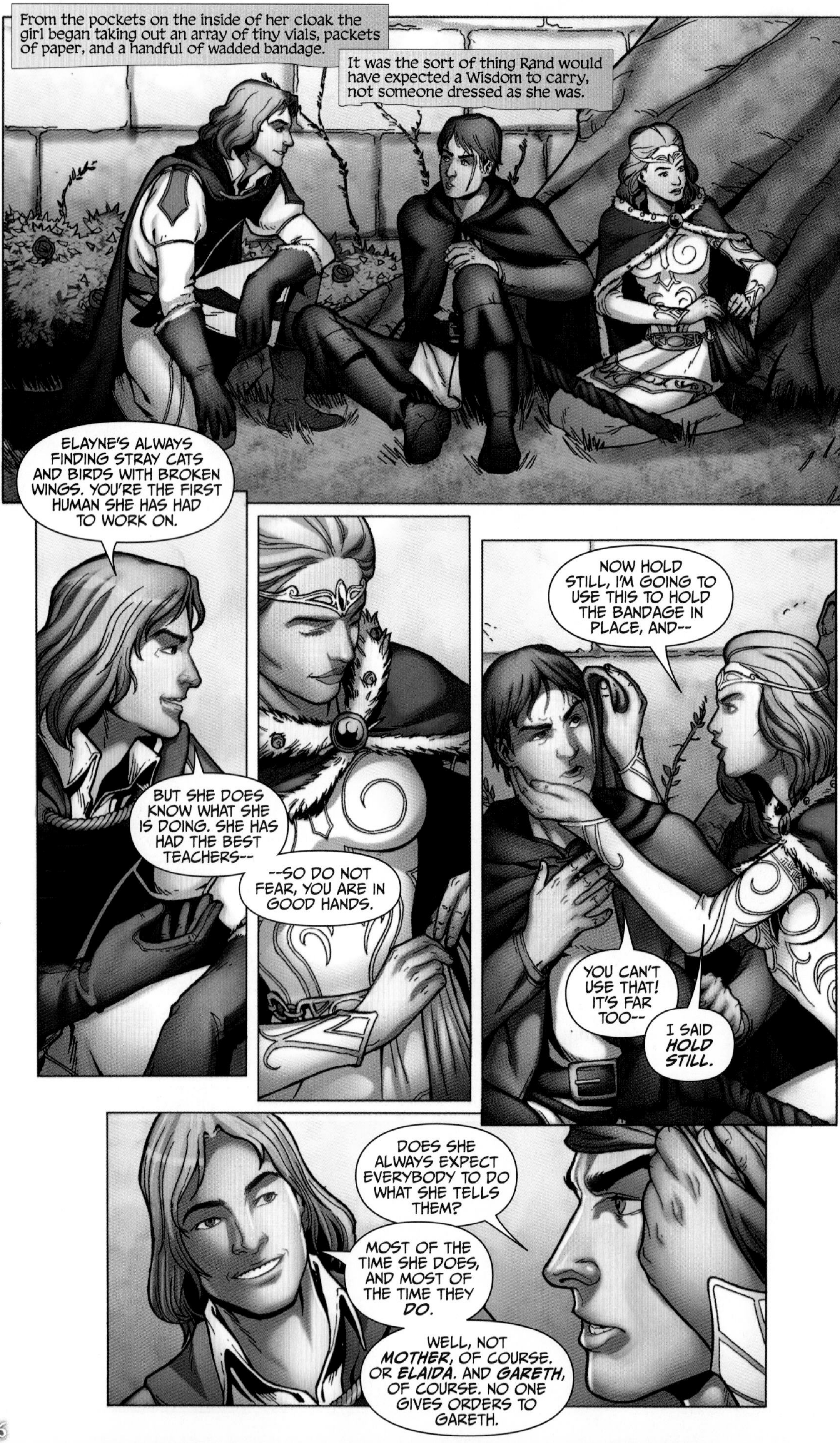
From the pockets on the inside of her cloak the girl began taking out an array of tiny vials, packets of paper, and a handful of wadded bandage.
It was the sort of thing Rand would have expected a Wisdom to carry, not someone dressed as she was.
ELAYNE'S ALWAYS FINDING STRAY CATS AND BIRDS WITH BROKEN WINGS. YOU'RE THE FIRST HUMAN SHE HAS HAD TO WORK ON.
BUT SHE DOES KNOW WHAT SHE IS DOING. SHE HAS HAD THE BEST TEACHERS--
--SO DO NOT FEAR, YOU ARE IN GOOD HANDS.
NOW HOLD STILL, I'M GOING TO USE THIS TO HOLD THE BANDAGE IN PLACE, AND--
YOU CAN'T USE THAT! IT'S FAR TOO--
I SAID *HOLD STILL.*
DOES SHE ALWAYS EXPECT EVERYBODY TO DO WHAT SHE TELLS THEM?
MOST OF THE TIME SHE DOES, AND MOST OF THE TIME THEY *DO.*
WELL, NOT *MOTHER,* OF COURSE. OR *ELAIDA.* AND *GARETH,* OF COURSE. NO ONE GIVES ORDERS TO GARETH.

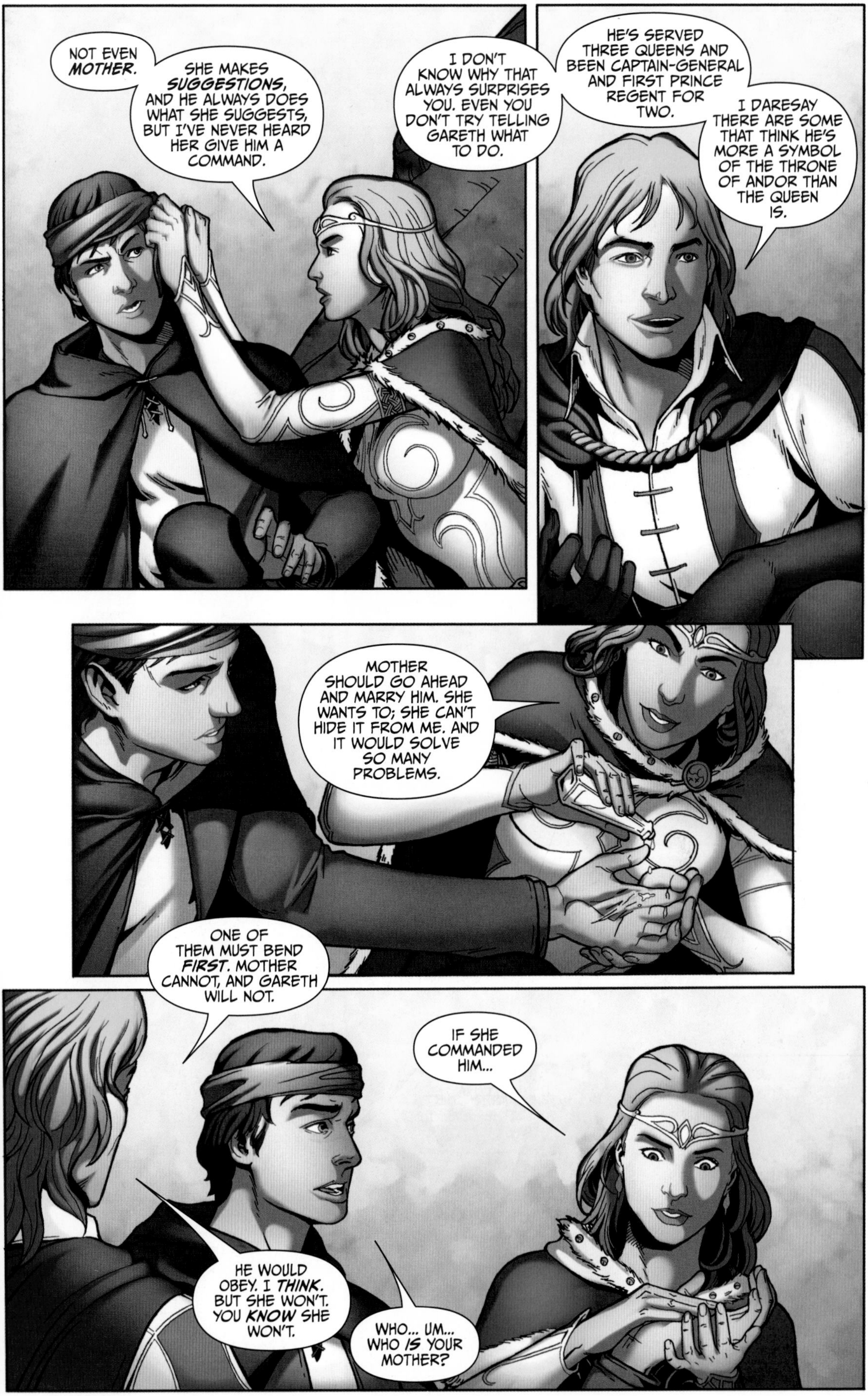
NOT EVEN *MOTHER.*
SHE MAKES *SUGGESTIONS,* AND HE ALWAYS DOES WHAT SHE SUGGESTS, BUT I'VE NEVER HEARD HER GIVE HIM A COMMAND.
I DON'T KNOW WHY THAT ALWAYS SURPRISES YOU. EVEN YOU DON'T TRY TELLING GARETH WHAT TO DO.
HE'S SERVED THREE QUEENS AND BEEN CAPTAIN-GENERAL AND FIRST PRINCE REGENT FOR TWO.
I DARESAY THERE ARE SOME THAT THINK HE'S MORE A SYMBOL OF THE THRONE OF ANDOR THAN THE QUEEN IS.
MOTHER SHOULD GO AHEAD AND MARRY HIM. SHE WANTS TO; SHE CAN'T HIDE IT FROM ME. AND IT WOULD SOLVE SO MANY PROBLEMS.
ONE OF THEM MUST BEND *FIRST.* MOTHER CANNOT, AND GARETH WILL NOT.
IF SHE COMMANDED HIM...
HE WOULD OBEY. I *THINK.* BUT SHE WON'T. YOU *KNOW* SHE WON'T.
WHO... UM... WHO *IS* YOUR MOTHER?

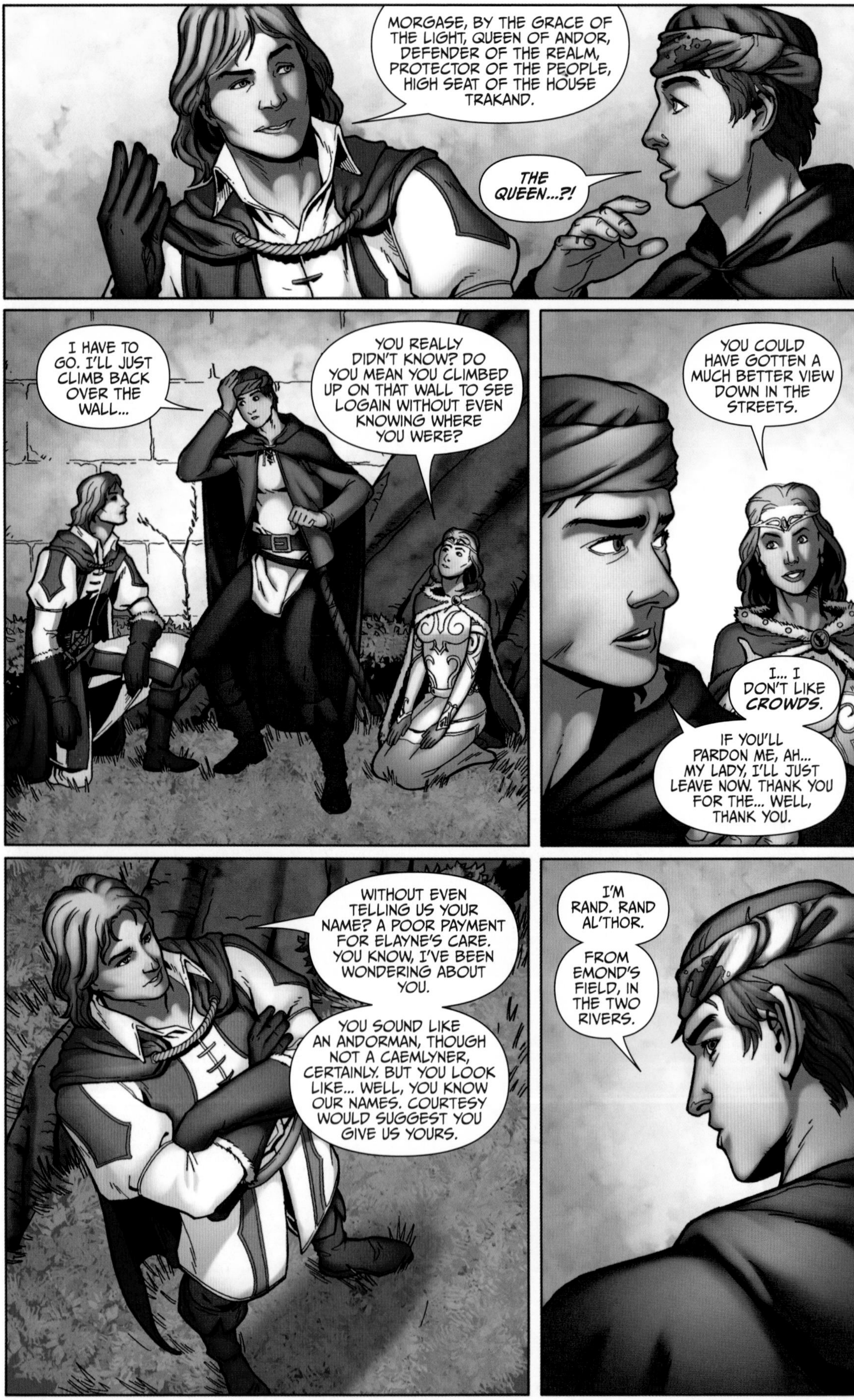
MORGASE, BY THE GRACE OF THE LIGHT, QUEEN OF ANDOR, DEFENDER OF THE REALM, PROTECTOR OF THE PEOPLE, HIGH SEAT OF THE HOUSE TRAKAND.
THE QUEEN...?!
I HAVE TO GO. I'LL JUST CLIMB BACK OVER THE WALL...
YOU REALLY DIDN'T KNOW? DO YOU MEAN YOU CLIMBED UP ON THAT WALL TO SEE LOGAIN WITHOUT EVEN KNOWING WHERE YOU WERE?
YOU COULD HAVE GOTTEN A MUCH BETTER VIEW DOWN IN THE STREETS.
I... I DON'T LIKE ***CROWDS***.
IF YOU'LL PARDON ME, AH... MY LADY, I'LL JUST LEAVE NOW. THANK YOU FOR THE... WELL, THANK YOU.
WITHOUT EVEN TELLING US YOUR NAME? A POOR PAYMENT FOR ELAYNE'S CARE. YOU KNOW, I'VE BEEN WONDERING ABOUT YOU.
YOU SOUND LIKE AN ANDORMAN, THOUGH NOT A CAEMLYNER, CERTAINLY. BUT YOU LOOK LIKE... WELL, YOU KNOW OUR NAMES. COURTESY WOULD SUGGEST YOU GIVE US YOURS.
I'M RAND. RAND AL'THOR.
FROM EMOND'S FIELD, IN THE TWO RIVERS.

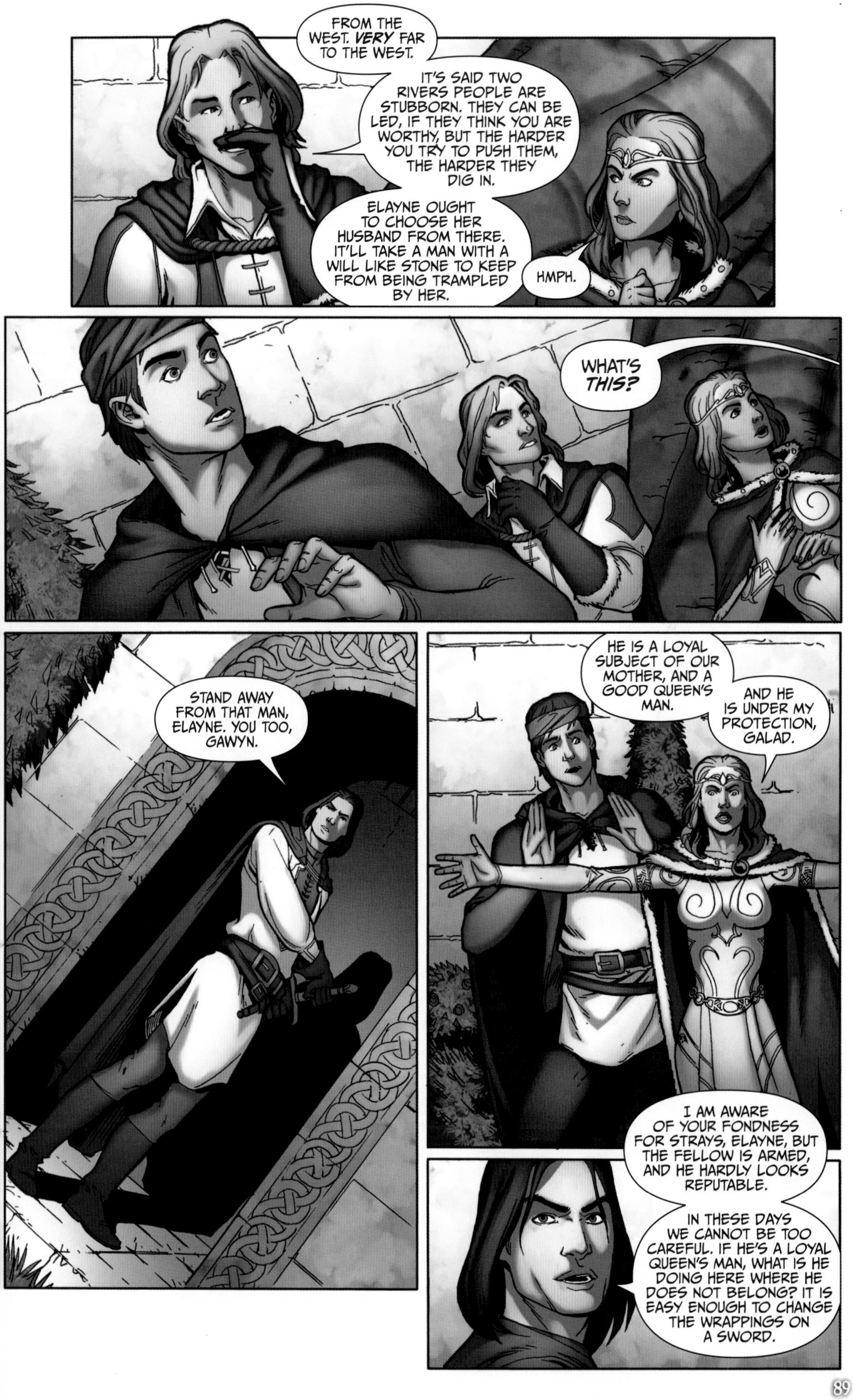
FROM THE WEST. *VERY* FAR TO THE WEST.
IT'S SAID TWO RIVERS PEOPLE ARE STUBBORN. THEY CAN BE LED, IF THEY THINK YOU ARE WORTHY, BUT THE HARDER YOU TRY TO PUSH THEM, THE HARDER THEY DIG IN.
ELAYNE OUGHT TO CHOOSE HER HUSBAND FROM THERE. IT'LL TAKE A MAN WITH A WILL LIKE STONE TO KEEP FROM BEING TRAMPLED BY HER.
HMPH.
WHAT'S *THIS?*
STAND AWAY FROM THAT MAN, ELAYNE. YOU TOO, GAWYN.
HE IS A LOYAL SUBJECT OF OUR MOTHER, AND A GOOD QUEEN'S MAN.
AND HE IS UNDER MY PROTECTION, GALAD.
I AM AWARE OF YOUR FONDNESS FOR STRAYS, ELAYNE, BUT THE FELLOW IS ARMED, AND HE HARDLY LOOKS REPUTABLE.
IN THESE DAYS WE CANNOT BE TOO CAREFUL. IF HE'S A LOYAL QUEEN'S MAN, WHAT IS HE DOING HERE WHERE HE DOES NOT BELONG? IT IS EASY ENOUGH TO CHANGE THE WRAPPINGS ON A SWORD.

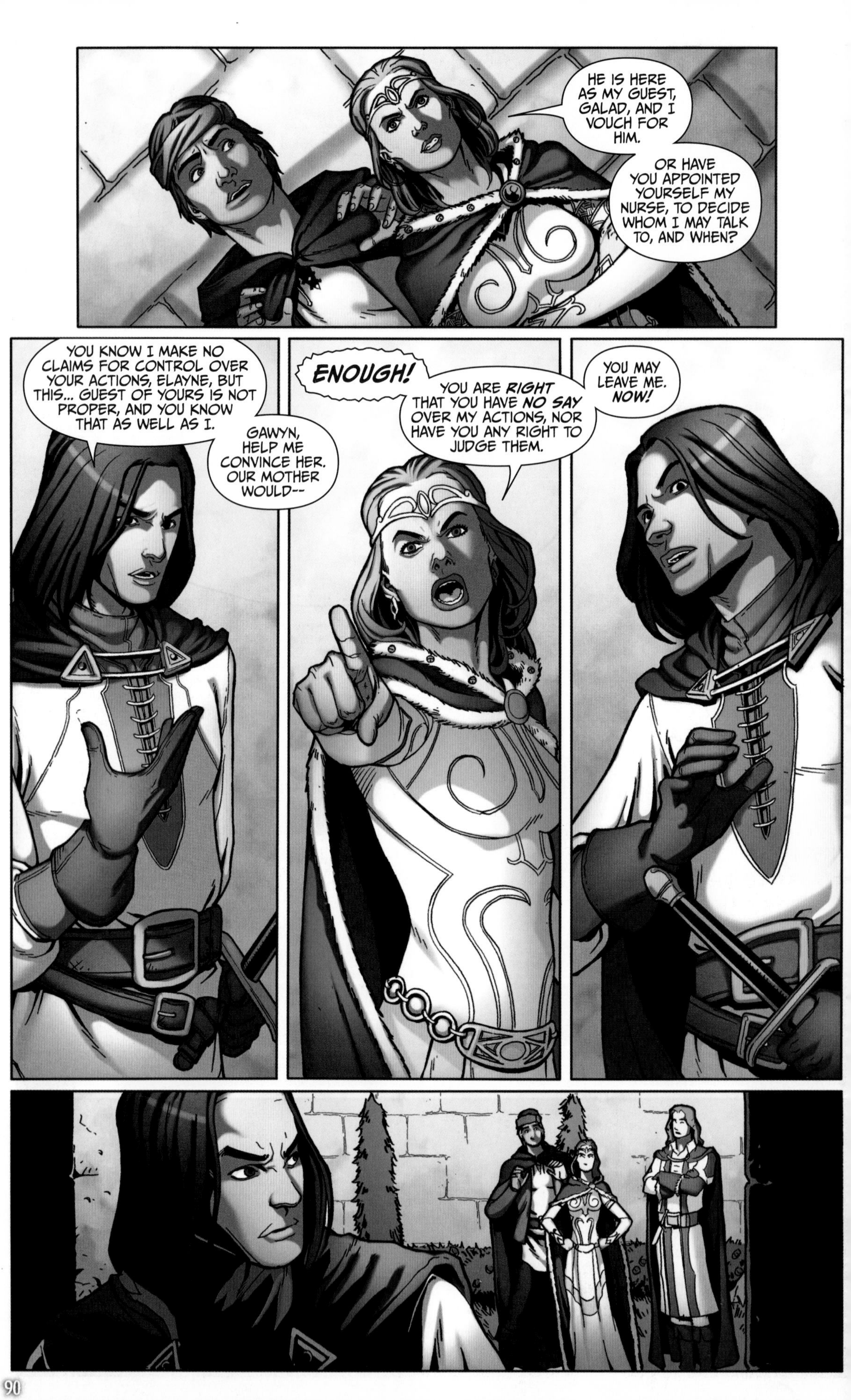
HE IS HERE AS MY GUEST, GALAD, AND I VOUCH FOR HIM.
OR HAVE YOU APPOINTED YOURSELF MY NURSE, TO DECIDE WHOM I MAY TALK TO, AND WHEN?
YOU KNOW I MAKE NO CLAIMS FOR CONTROL OVER YOUR ACTIONS, ELAYNE, BUT THIS... GUEST OF YOURS IS NOT PROPER, AND YOU KNOW THAT AS WELL AS I.
GAWYN, HELP ME CONVINCE HER. OUR MOTHER WOULD--
ENOUGH!
YOU ARE RIGHT THAT YOU HAVE NO SAY OVER MY ACTIONS, NOR HAVE YOU ANY RIGHT TO JUDGE THEM.
YOU MAY LEAVE ME. NOW!

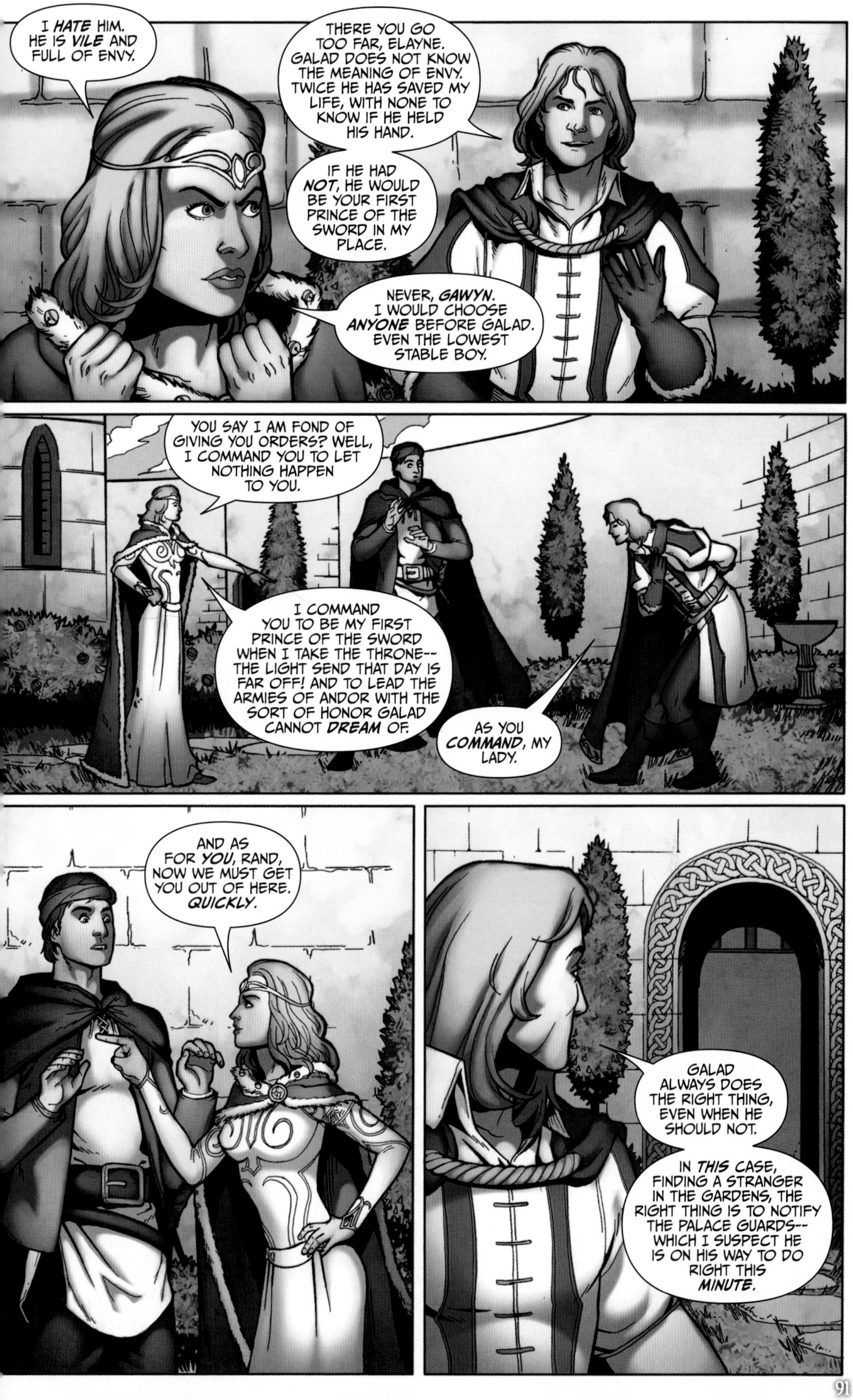
I HATE HIM. HE IS VILE AND FULL OF ENVY.
THERE YOU GO TOO FAR, ELAYNE. GALAD DOES NOT KNOW THE MEANING OF ENVY. TWICE HE HAS SAVED MY LIFE, WITH NONE TO KNOW IF HE HELD HIS HAND.
IF HE HAD NOT, HE WOULD BE YOUR FIRST PRINCE OF THE SWORD IN MY PLACE.
NEVER, GAWYN. I WOULD CHOOSE ANYONE BEFORE GALAD. EVEN THE LOWEST STABLE BOY.
YOU SAY I AM FOND OF GIVING YOU ORDERS? WELL, I COMMAND YOU TO LET NOTHING HAPPEN TO YOU.
I COMMAND YOU TO BE MY FIRST PRINCE OF THE SWORD WHEN I TAKE THE THRONE-- THE LIGHT SEND THAT DAY IS FAR OFF! AND TO LEAD THE ARMIES OF ANDOR WITH THE SORT OF HONOR GALAD CANNOT DREAM OF.
AS YOU COMMAND, MY LADY.
AND AS FOR YOU, RAND, NOW WE MUST GET YOU OUT OF HERE. QUICKLY.
GALAD ALWAYS DOES THE RIGHT THING, EVEN WHEN HE SHOULD NOT.
IN THIS CASE, FINDING A STRANGER IN THE GARDENS, THE RIGHT THING IS TO NOTIFY THE PALACE GUARDS-- WHICH I SUSPECT HE IS ON HIS WAY TO DO RIGHT THIS MINUTE.

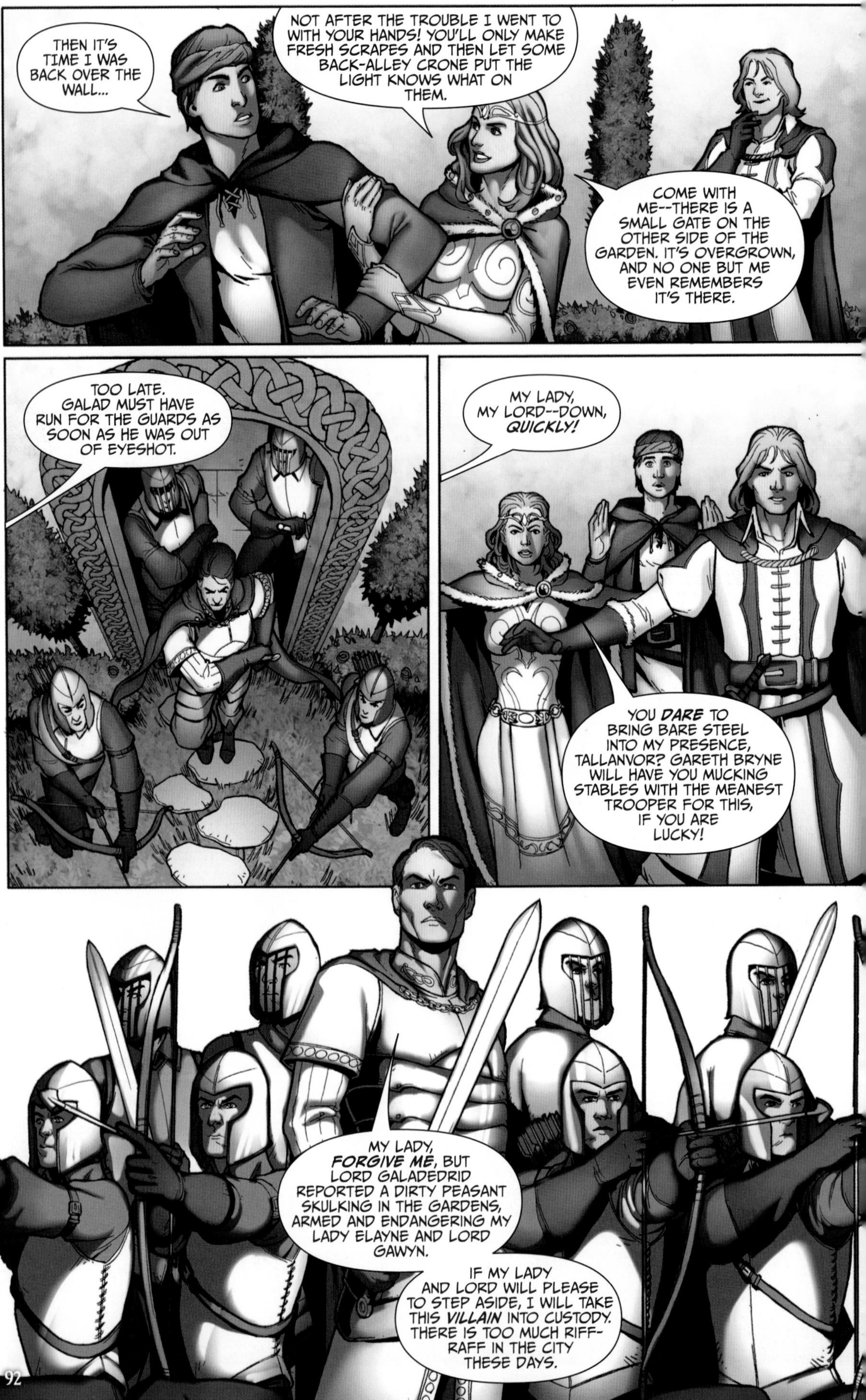
THEN IT'S TIME I WAS BACK OVER THE WALL...
NOT AFTER THE TROUBLE I WENT TO WITH YOUR HANDS! YOU'LL ONLY MAKE FRESH SCRAPES AND THEN LET SOME BACK-ALLEY CRONE PUT THE LIGHT KNOWS WHAT ON THEM.
COME WITH ME--THERE IS A SMALL GATE ON THE OTHER SIDE OF THE GARDEN. IT'S OVERGROWN, AND NO ONE BUT ME EVEN REMEMBERS IT'S THERE.
TOO LATE. GALAD MUST HAVE RUN FOR THE GUARDS AS SOON AS HE WAS OUT OF EYESHOT.
MY LADY, MY LORD--DOWN, *QUICKLY!*
YOU ***DARE*** TO BRING BARE STEEL INTO MY PRESENCE, TALLANVOR? GARETH BRYNE WILL HAVE YOU MUCKING STABLES WITH THE MEANEST TROOPER FOR THIS, IF YOU ARE LUCKY!
MY LADY, ***FORGIVE ME***, BUT LORD GALADEDRID REPORTED A DIRTY PEASANT SKULKING IN THE GARDENS, ARMED AND ENDANGERING MY LADY ELAYNE AND LORD GAWYN.
IF MY LADY AND LORD WILL PLEASE TO STEP ASIDE, I WILL TAKE THIS ***VILLAIN*** INTO CUSTODY. THERE IS TOO MUCH RIFF-RAFF IN THE CITY THESE DAYS.

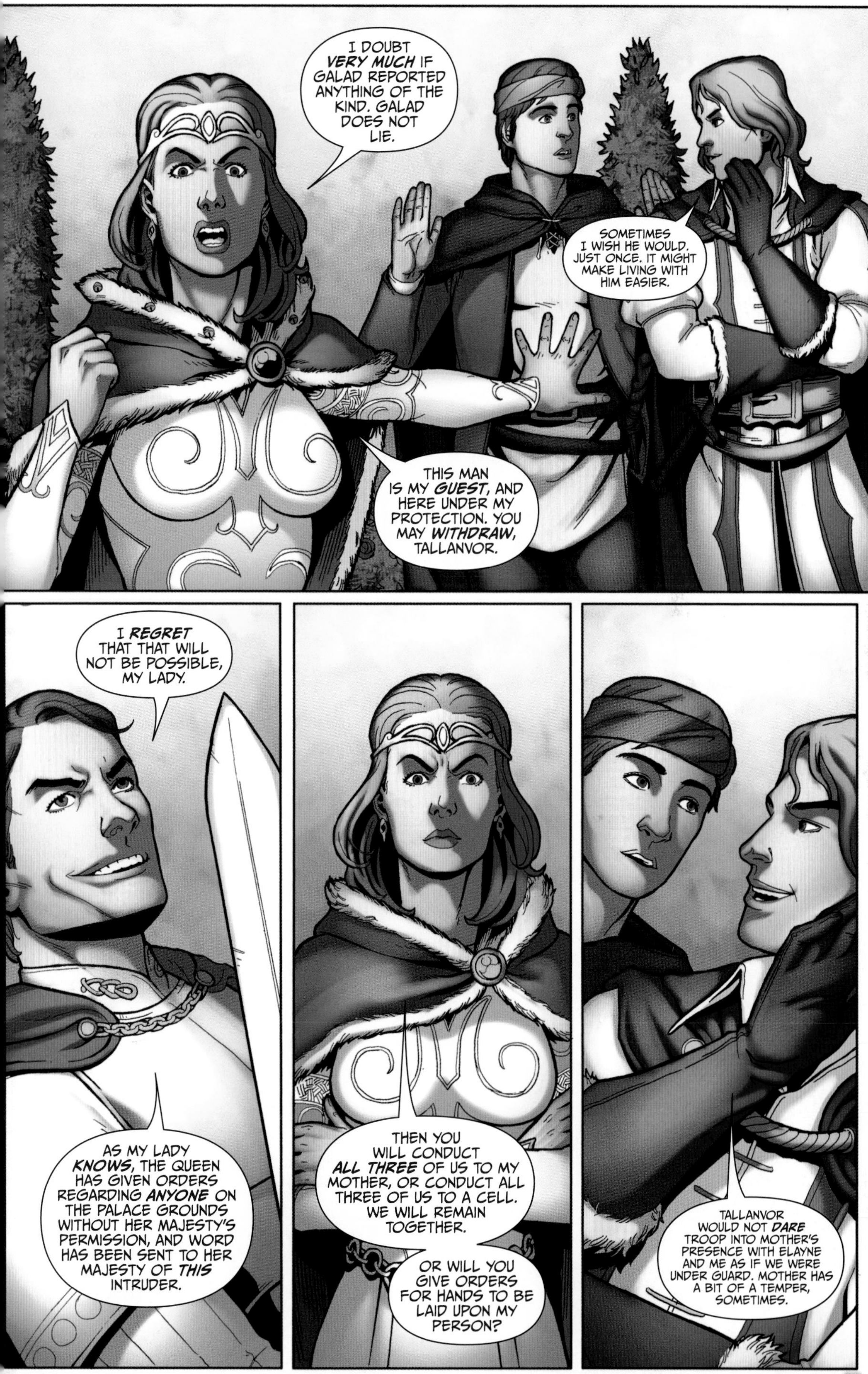
I DOUBT VERY MUCH IF GALAD REPORTED ANYTHING OF THE KIND. GALAD DOES NOT LIE.
SOMETIMES I WISH HE WOULD. JUST ONCE. IT MIGHT MAKE LIVING WITH HIM EASIER.
THIS MAN IS MY GUEST, AND HERE UNDER MY PROTECTION. YOU MAY WITHDRAW, TALLANVOR.
I REGRET THAT THAT WILL NOT BE POSSIBLE, MY LADY.
AS MY LADY KNOWS, THE QUEEN HAS GIVEN ORDERS REGARDING ANYONE ON THE PALACE GROUNDS WITHOUT HER MAJESTY'S PERMISSION, AND WORD HAS BEEN SENT TO HER MAJESTY OF THIS INTRUDER.
THEN YOU WILL CONDUCT ALL THREE OF US TO MY MOTHER, OR CONDUCT ALL THREE OF US TO A CELL. WE WILL REMAIN TOGETHER.
OR WILL YOU GIVE ORDERS FOR HANDS TO BE LAID UPON MY PERSON?
TALLANVOR WOULD NOT DARE TROOP INTO MOTHER'S PRESENCE WITH ELAYNE AND ME AS IF WE WERE UNDER GUARD. MOTHER HAS A BIT OF A TEMPER, SOMETIMES.

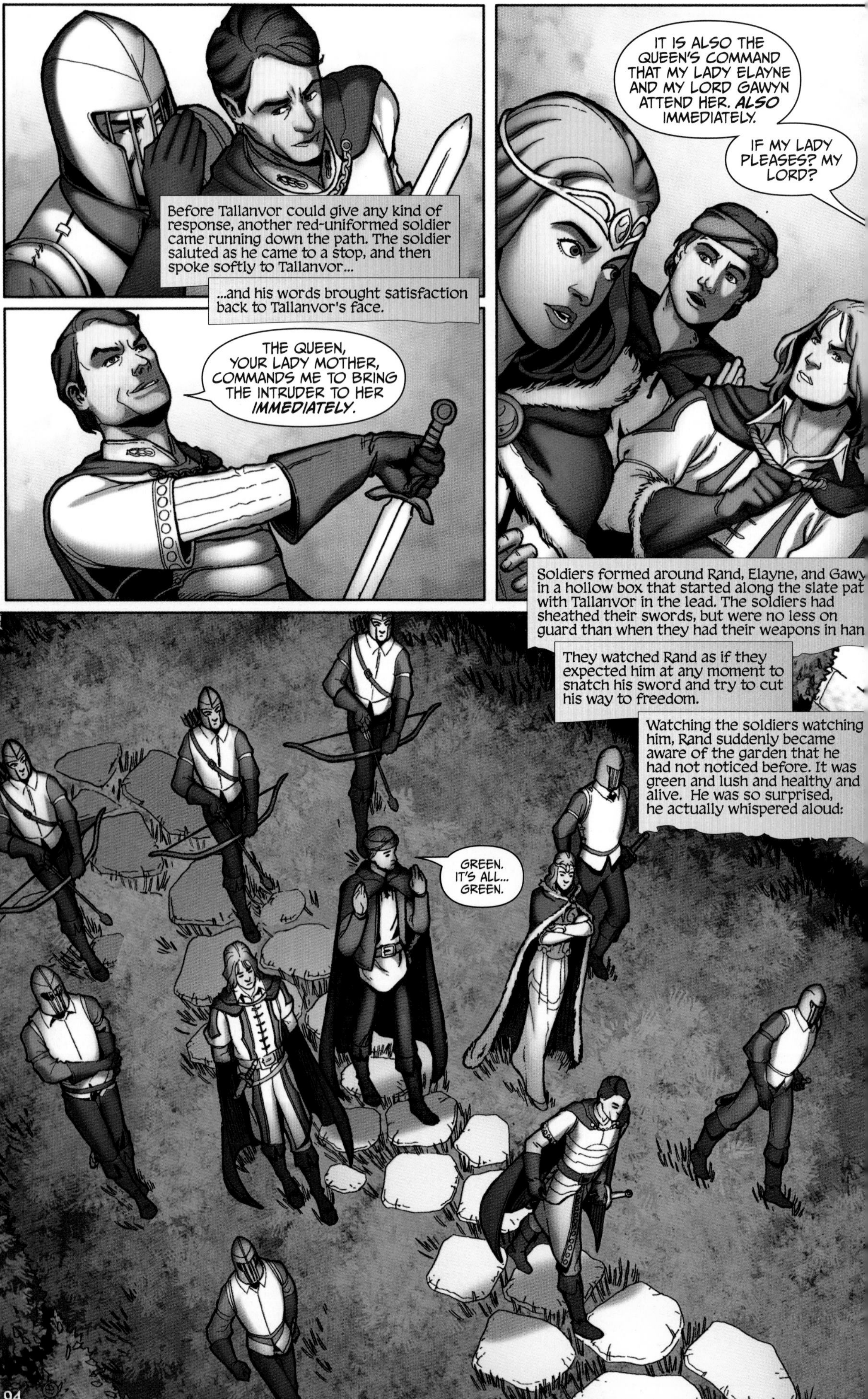
Before Tallanvor could give any kind of response, another red-uniformed soldier came running down the path. The soldier saluted as he came to a stop, and then spoke softly to Tallanvor...
...and his words brought satisfaction back to Tallanvor's face.
THE QUEEN, YOUR LADY MOTHER, COMMANDS ME TO BRING THE INTRUDER TO HER *IMMEDIATELY*.
IT IS ALSO THE QUEEN'S COMMAND THAT MY LADY ELAYNE AND MY LORD GAWYN ATTEND HER. *ALSO* IMMEDIATELY.
IF MY LADY PLEASES? MY LORD?
Soldiers formed around Rand, Elayne, and Gawy in a hollow box that started along the slate pat with Tallanvor in the lead. The soldiers had sheathed their swords, but were no less on guard than when they had their weapons in han
They watched Rand as if they expected him at any moment to snatch his sword and try to cut his way to freedom.
Watching the soldiers watching him, Rand suddenly became aware of the garden that he had not noticed before. It was green and lush and healthy and alive. He was so surprised, he actually whispered aloud:
GREEN. IT'S ALL... GREEN.

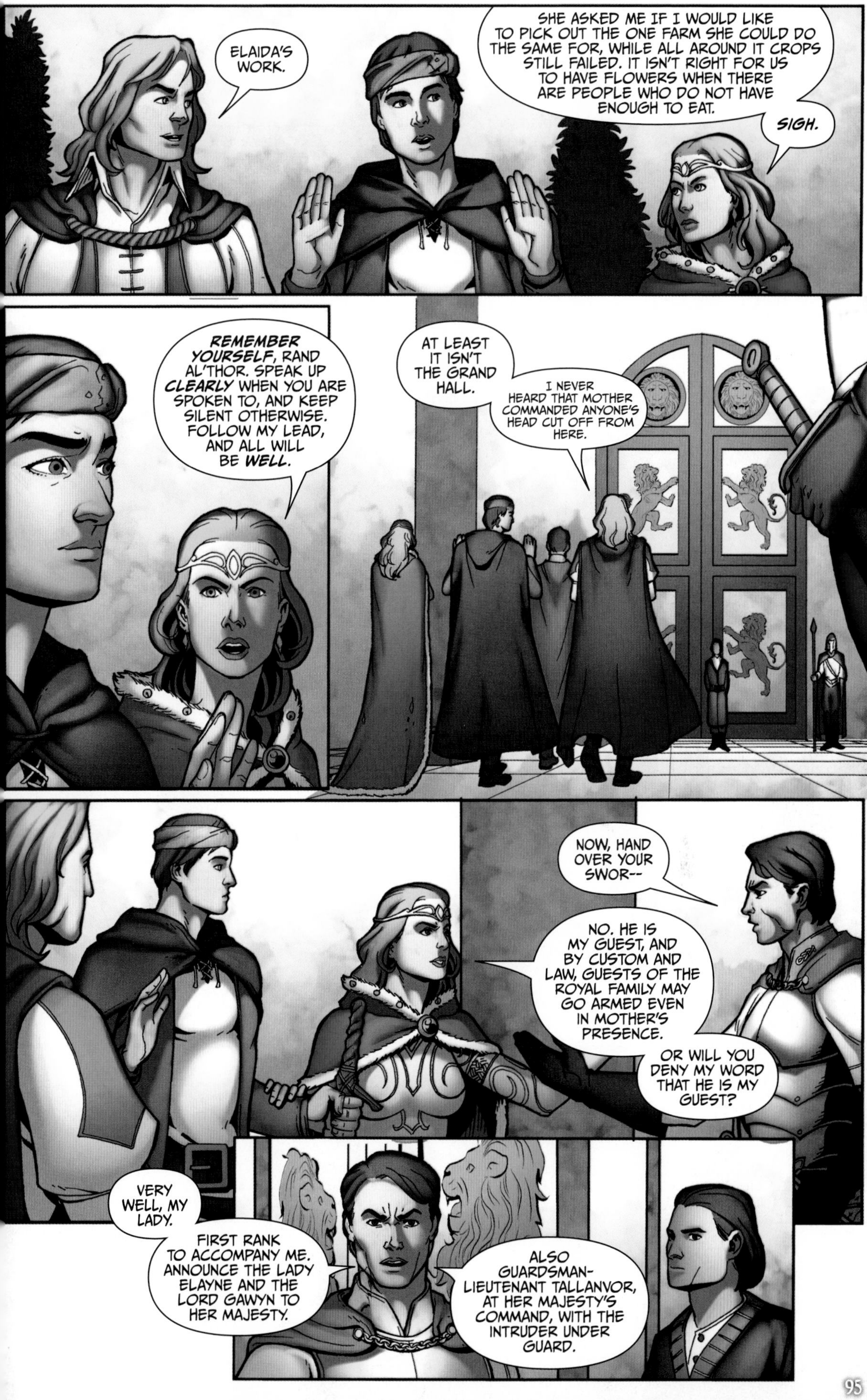

ELAIDA'S WORK.
SHE ASKED ME IF I WOULD LIKE TO PICK OUT THE ONE FARM SHE COULD DO THE SAME FOR, WHILE ALL AROUND IT CROPS STILL FAILED. IT ISN'T RIGHT FOR US TO HAVE FLOWERS WHEN THERE ARE PEOPLE WHO DO NOT HAVE ENOUGH TO EAT.
SIGH.
REMEMBER YOURSELF, RAND AL'THOR. SPEAK UP CLEARLY WHEN YOU ARE SPOKEN TO, AND KEEP SILENT OTHERWISE. FOLLOW MY LEAD, AND ALL WILL BE WELL.
AT LEAST IT ISN'T THE GRAND HALL.
I NEVER HEARD THAT MOTHER COMMANDED ANYONE'S HEAD CUT OFF FROM HERE.
NOW, HAND OVER YOUR SWOR--
NO. HE IS MY GUEST, AND BY CUSTOM AND LAW, GUESTS OF THE ROYAL FAMILY MAY GO ARMED EVEN IN MOTHER'S PRESENCE.
OR WILL YOU DENY MY WORD THAT HE IS MY GUEST?
VERY WELL, MY LADY.
FIRST RANK TO ACCOMPANY ME. ANNOUNCE THE LADY ELAYNE AND THE LORD GAWYN TO HER MAJESTY.
ALSO GUARDSMAN-LIEUTENANT TALLANVOR, AT HER MAJESTY'S COMMAND, WITH THE INTRUDER UNDER GUARD.

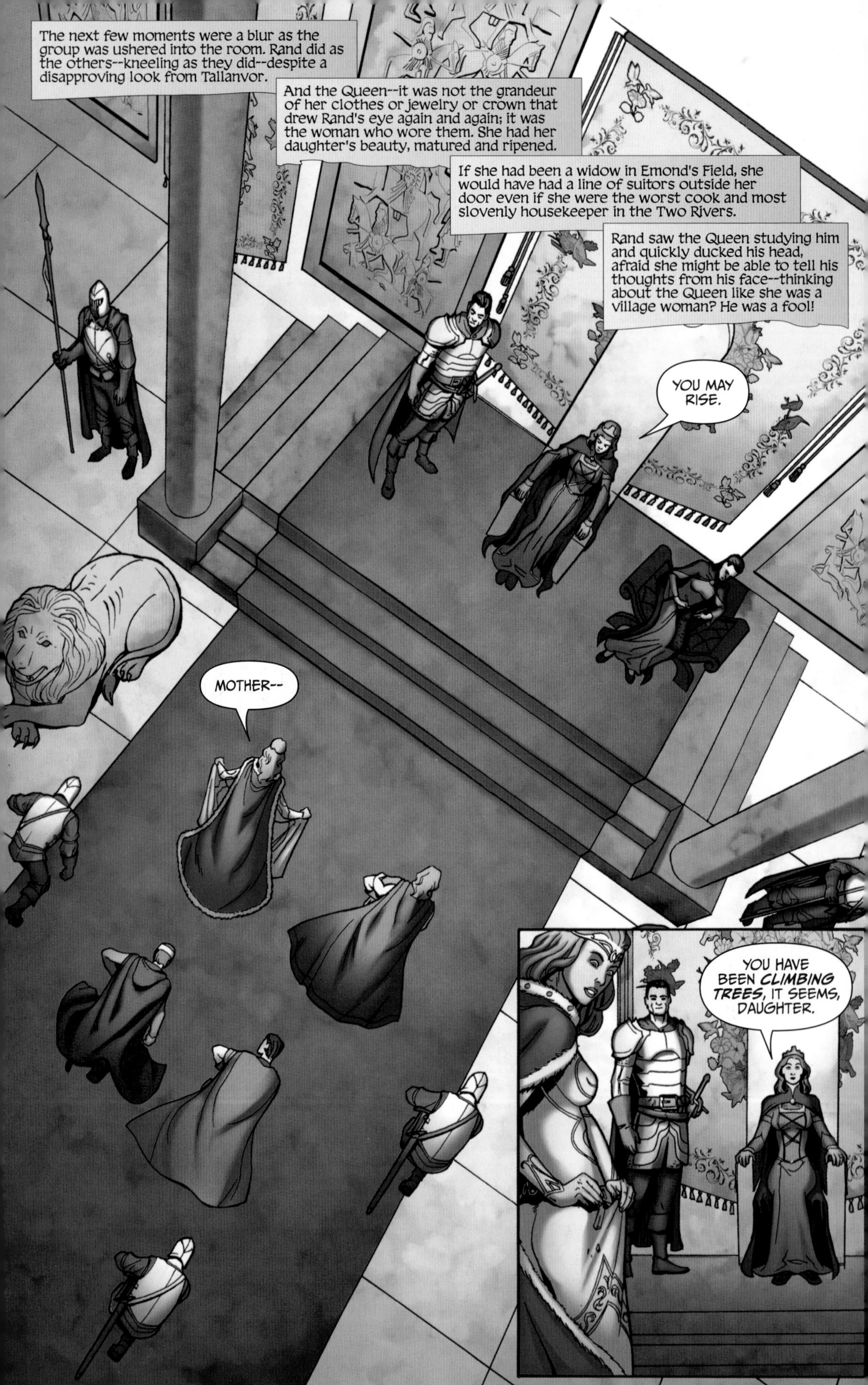
The next few moments were a blur as the group was ushered into the room. Rand did as the others--kneeling as they did--despite a disapproving look from Tallanvor.
And the Queen--it was not the grandeur of her clothes or jewelry or crown that drew Rand's eye again and again; it was the woman who wore them. She had her daughter's beauty, matured and ripened.
If she had been a widow in Emond's Field, she would have had a line of suitors outside her door even if she were the worst cook and most slovenly housekeeper in the Two Rivers.
Rand saw the Queen studying him and quickly ducked his head, afraid she might be able to tell his thoughts from his face--thinking about the Queen like she was a village woman? He was a fool!
YOU MAY RISE.
MOTHER--
YOU HAVE BEEN *CLIMBING TREES*, IT SEEMS, DAUGHTER.

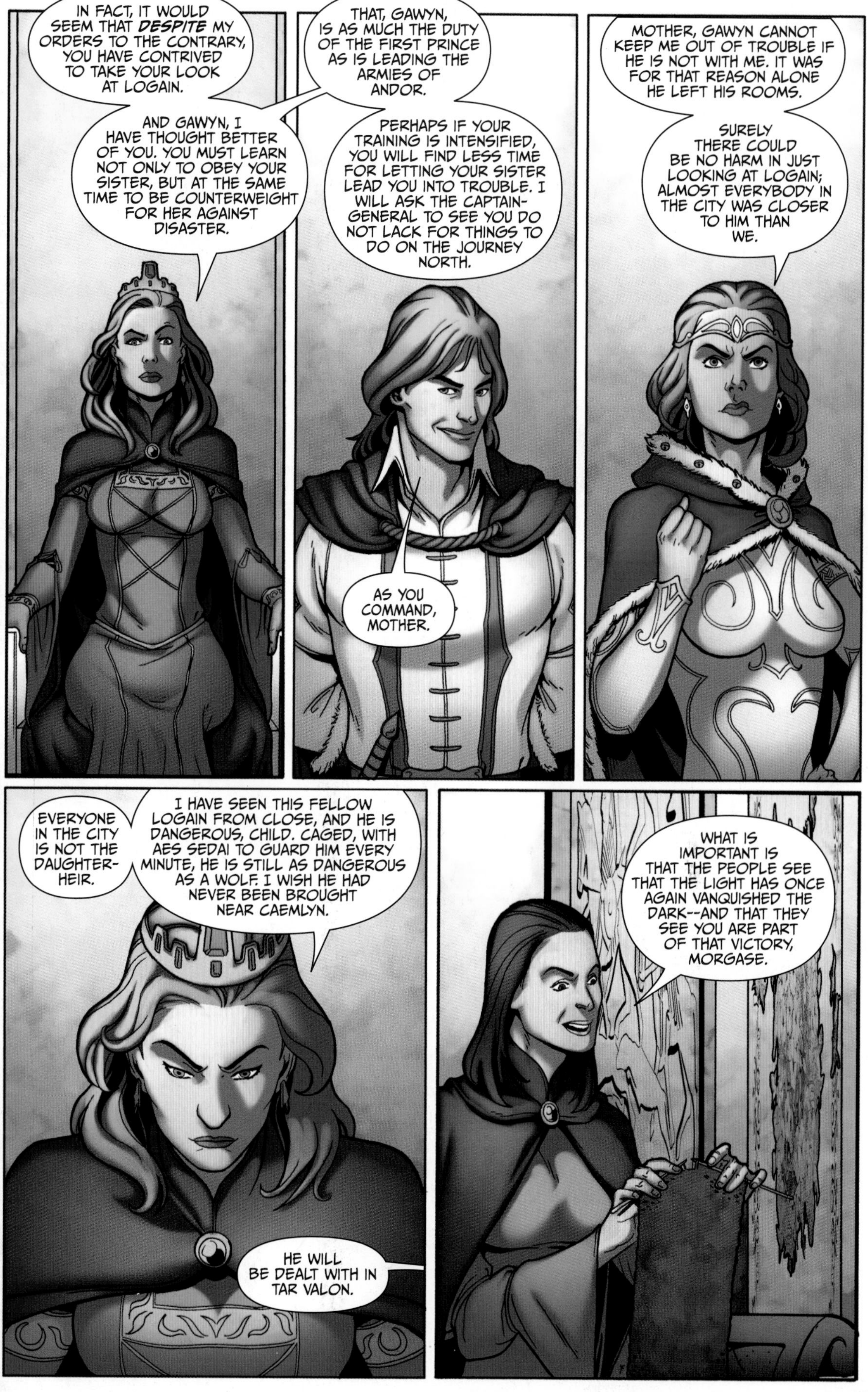
IN FACT, IT WOULD SEEM THAT DESPITE MY ORDERS TO THE CONTRARY, YOU HAVE CONTRIVED TO TAKE YOUR LOOK AT LOGAIN.
AND GAWYN, I HAVE THOUGHT BETTER OF YOU. YOU MUST LEARN NOT ONLY TO OBEY YOUR SISTER, BUT AT THE SAME TIME TO BE COUNTERWEIGHT FOR HER AGAINST DISASTER.
THAT, GAWYN, IS AS MUCH THE DUTY OF THE FIRST PRINCE AS IS LEADING THE ARMIES OF ANDOR.
PERHAPS IF YOUR TRAINING IS INTENSIFIED, YOU WILL FIND LESS TIME FOR LETTING YOUR SISTER LEAD YOU INTO TROUBLE. I WILL ASK THE CAPTAIN-GENERAL TO SEE YOU DO NOT LACK FOR THINGS TO DO ON THE JOURNEY NORTH.
AS YOU COMMAND, MOTHER.
MOTHER, GAWYN CANNOT KEEP ME OUT OF TROUBLE IF HE IS NOT WITH ME. IT WAS FOR THAT REASON ALONE HE LEFT HIS ROOMS.
SURELY THERE COULD BE NO HARM IN JUST LOOKING AT LOGAIN; ALMOST EVERYBODY IN THE CITY WAS CLOSER TO HIM THAN WE.
EVERYONE IN THE CITY IS NOT THE DAUGHTER-HEIR.
I HAVE SEEN THIS FELLOW LOGAIN FROM CLOSE, AND HE IS DANGEROUS, CHILD. CAGED, WITH AES SEDAI TO GUARD HIM EVERY MINUTE, HE IS STILL AS DANGEROUS AS A WOLF. I WISH HE HAD NEVER BEEN BROUGHT NEAR CAEMLYN.
HE WILL BE DEALT WITH IN TAR VALON.
WHAT IS IMPORTANT IS THAT THE PEOPLE SEE THAT THE LIGHT HAS ONCE AGAIN VANQUISHED THE DARK--AND THAT THEY SEE YOU ARE PART OF THAT VICTORY, MORGASE.

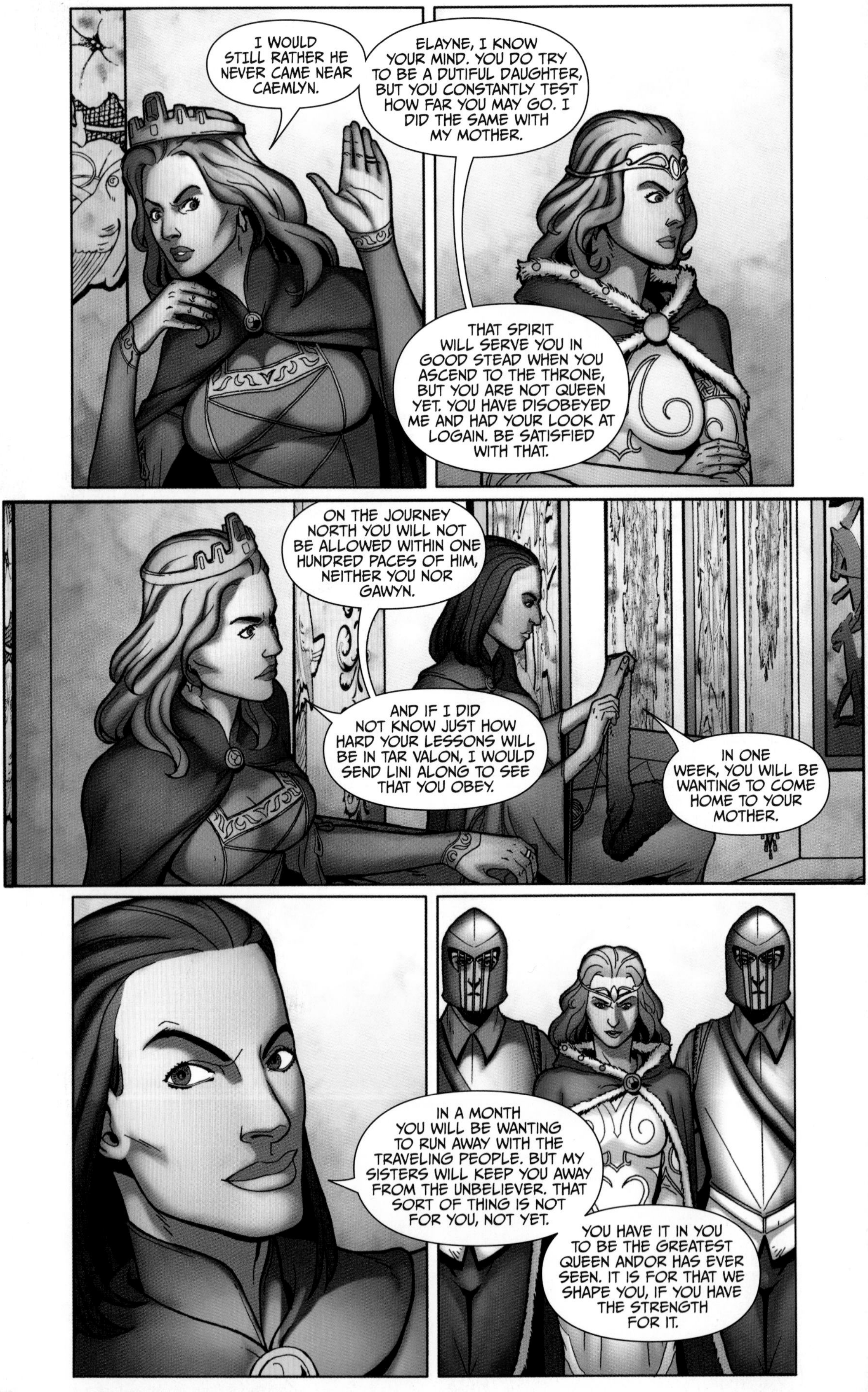
I WOULD STILL RATHER HE NEVER CAME NEAR CAEMLYN.
ELAYNE, I KNOW YOUR MIND. YOU DO TRY TO BE A DUTIFUL DAUGHTER, BUT YOU CONSTANTLY TEST HOW FAR YOU MAY GO. I DID THE SAME WITH MY MOTHER.
THAT SPIRIT WILL SERVE YOU IN GOOD STEAD WHEN YOU ASCEND TO THE THRONE, BUT YOU ARE NOT QUEEN YET. YOU HAVE DISOBEYED ME AND HAD YOUR LOOK AT LOGAIN. BE SATISFIED WITH THAT.
ON THE JOURNEY NORTH YOU WILL NOT BE ALLOWED WITHIN ONE HUNDRED PACES OF HIM, NEITHER YOU NOR GAWYN.
AND IF I DID NOT KNOW JUST HOW HARD YOUR LESSONS WILL BE IN TAR VALON, I WOULD SEND LINI ALONG TO SEE THAT YOU OBEY.
IN ONE WEEK, YOU WILL BE WANTING TO COME HOME TO YOUR MOTHER.
IN A MONTH YOU WILL BE WANTING TO RUN AWAY WITH THE TRAVELING PEOPLE. BUT MY SISTERS WILL KEEP YOU AWAY FROM THE UNBELIEVER. THAT SORT OF THING IS NOT FOR YOU, NOT YET.
YOU HAVE IT IN YOU TO BE THE GREATEST QUEEN ANDOR HAS EVER SEEN. IT IS FOR THAT WE SHAPE YOU, IF YOU HAVE THE STRENGTH FOR IT.

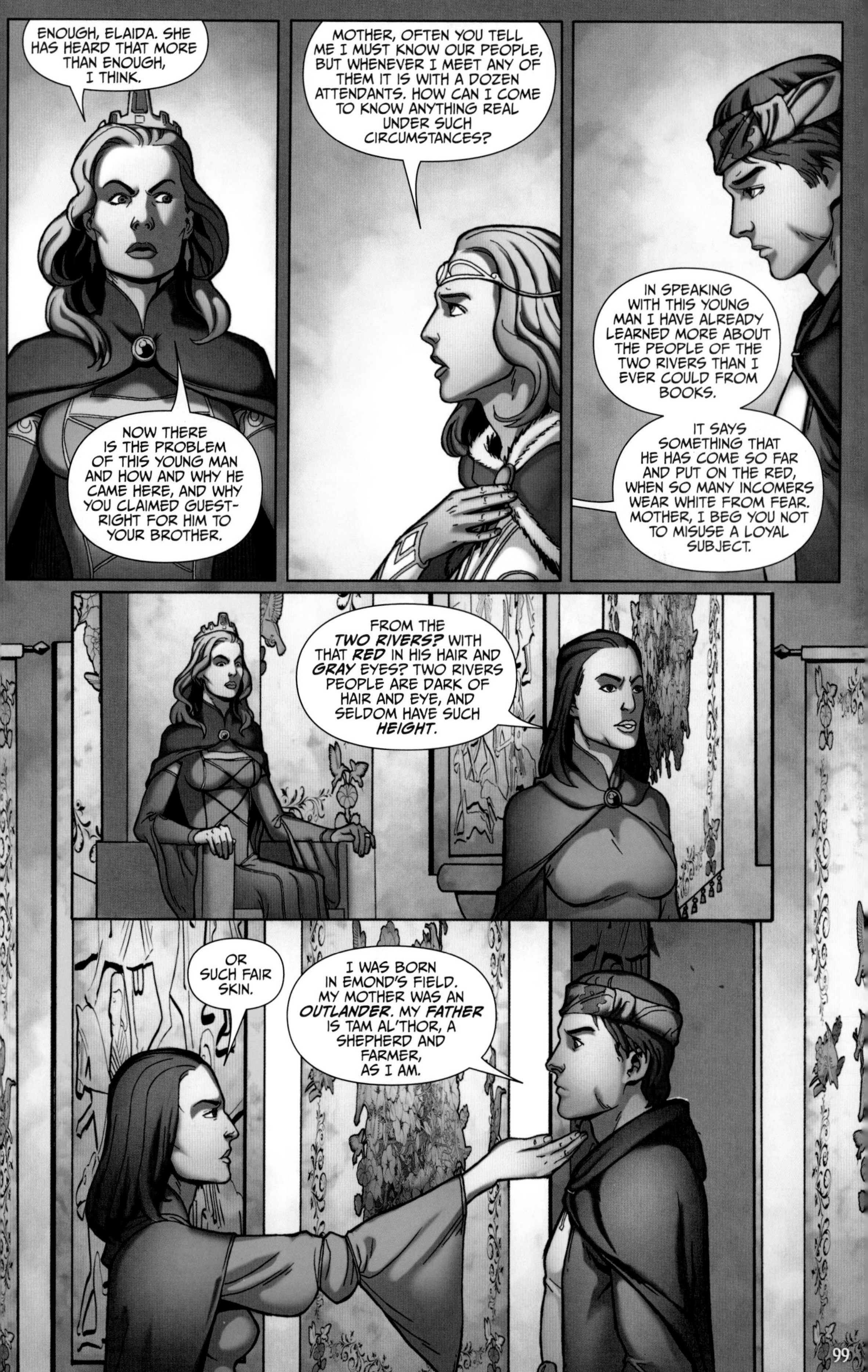
ENOUGH, ELAIDA. SHE HAS HEARD THAT MORE THAN ENOUGH, I THINK.
NOW THERE IS THE PROBLEM OF THIS YOUNG MAN AND HOW AND WHY HE CAME HERE, AND WHY YOU CLAIMED GUEST-RIGHT FOR HIM TO YOUR BROTHER.
MOTHER, OFTEN YOU TELL ME I MUST KNOW OUR PEOPLE, BUT WHENEVER I MEET ANY OF THEM IT IS WITH A DOZEN ATTENDANTS. HOW CAN I COME TO KNOW ANYTHING REAL UNDER SUCH CIRCUMSTANCES?
IN SPEAKING WITH THIS YOUNG MAN I HAVE ALREADY LEARNED MORE ABOUT THE PEOPLE OF THE TWO RIVERS THAN I EVER COULD FROM BOOKS.
IT SAYS SOMETHING THAT HE HAS COME SO FAR AND PUT ON THE RED, WHEN SO MANY INCOMERS WEAR WHITE FROM FEAR. MOTHER, I BEG YOU NOT TO MISUSE A LOYAL SUBJECT.
FROM THE *TWO RIVERS?* WITH THAT *RED* IN HIS HAIR AND *GRAY* EYES? TWO RIVERS PEOPLE ARE DARK OF HAIR AND EYE, AND SELDOM HAVE SUCH *HEIGHT*.
OR SUCH FAIR SKIN.
I WAS BORN IN EMOND'S FIELD. MY MOTHER WAS AN *OUTLANDER*. MY *FATHER* IS TAM AL'THOR, A SHEPHERD AND FARMER, AS I AM.

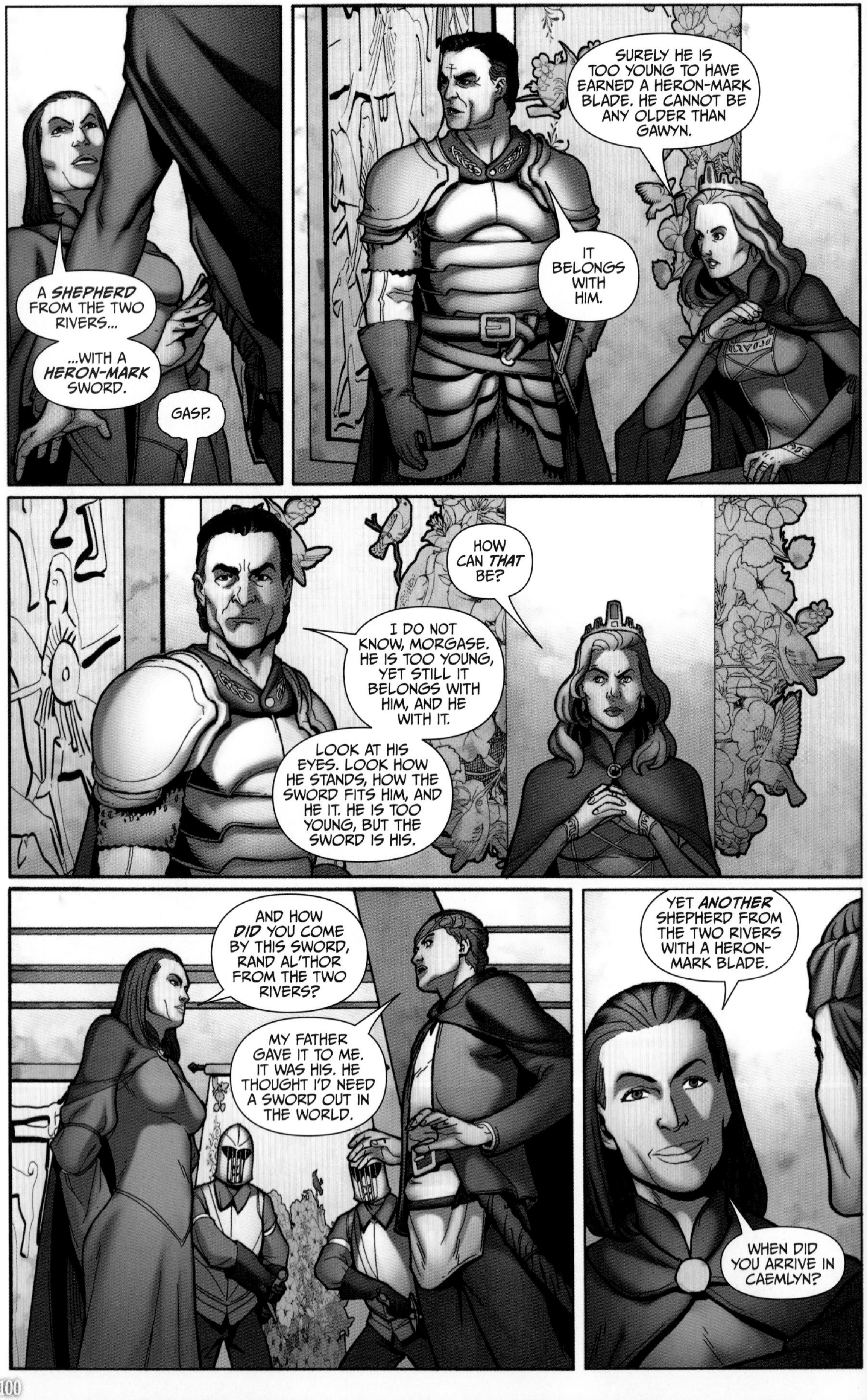
A *SHEPHERD* FROM THE TWO RIVERS...
...WITH A *HERON-MARK* SWORD.
GASP.
SURELY HE IS TOO YOUNG TO HAVE EARNED A HERON-MARK BLADE. HE CANNOT BE ANY OLDER THAN GAWYN.
IT BELONGS WITH HIM.
HOW CAN *THAT* BE?
I DO NOT KNOW, MORGASE. HE IS TOO YOUNG, YET STILL IT BELONGS WITH HIM, AND HE WITH IT.
LOOK AT HIS EYES. LOOK HOW HE STANDS, HOW THE SWORD FITS HIM, AND HE IT. HE IS TOO YOUNG, BUT THE SWORD IS HIS.
AND HOW *DID* YOU COME BY THIS SWORD, RAND AL'THOR FROM THE TWO RIVERS?
MY FATHER GAVE IT TO ME. IT WAS HIS. HE THOUGHT I'D NEED A SWORD OUT IN THE WORLD.
YET *ANOTHER* SHEPHERD FROM THE TWO RIVERS WITH A HERON-MARK BLADE.
WHEN DID YOU ARRIVE IN CAEMLYN?

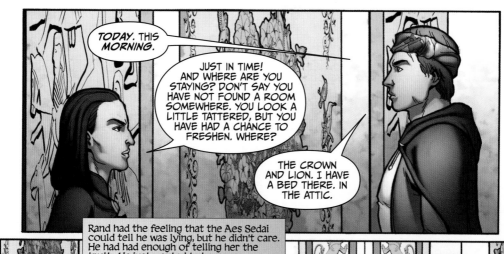

TODAY. THIS MORNING.

JUST IN TIME! AND WHERE ARE YOU STAYING? DON'T SAY YOU HAVE NOT FOUND A ROOM SOMEWHERE. YOU LOOK A LITTLE TATTERED, BUT YOU HAVE HAD A CHANCE TO FRESHEN. WHERE?

THE CROWN AND LION. I HAVE A BED THERE. IN THE ATTIC.

Rand had the feeling that the Aes Sedai could tell he was lying, but he didn't care. He had had enough of telling her the truth. He just wanted to be gone.

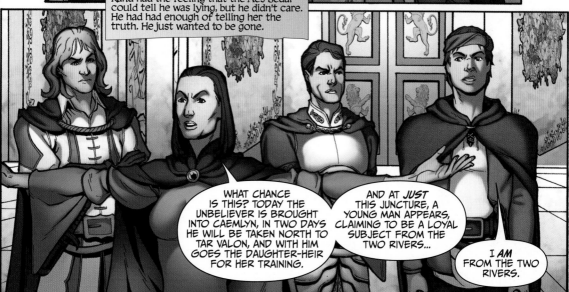

WHAT CHANCE IS THIS? TODAY THE UNBELIEVER IS BROUGHT INTO CAEMLYN, IN TWO DAYS HE WILL BE TAKEN NORTH TO TAR VALON, AND WITH HIM GOES THE DAUGHTER-HEIR FOR HER TRAINING.

AND AT *JUST* THIS JUNCTURE, A YOUNG MAN APPEARS, CLAIMING TO BE A LOYAL SUBJECT FROM THE TWO RIVERS...

I *AM* FROM THE TWO RIVERS.

...WITH A STORY CALCULATED TO ENTICE ELAYNE, AND BEARING A HERON-MARK BLADE.

HE DOES NOT WEAR AN ARMBAND OR COCKADE TO PROCLAIM HIS ALLEGIANCE, BUT WRAPPINGS THAT CAREFULLY CONCEAL THE HERON FROM INQUISITIVE EYES. WHAT CHANCE THIS, MORGASE?

WHAT ARE YOU NAMING HIM? *DARKFRIEND?* ONE OF *LOGAIN'S* FOLLOWERS?

THE DARK ONE STIRS IN SHAYOL GHUL. THE SHADOW LIES ACROSS THE PATTERN, AND THE FUTURE IS BALANCED ON THE POINT OF A PIN.

THIS ONE IS *DANGEROUS.*

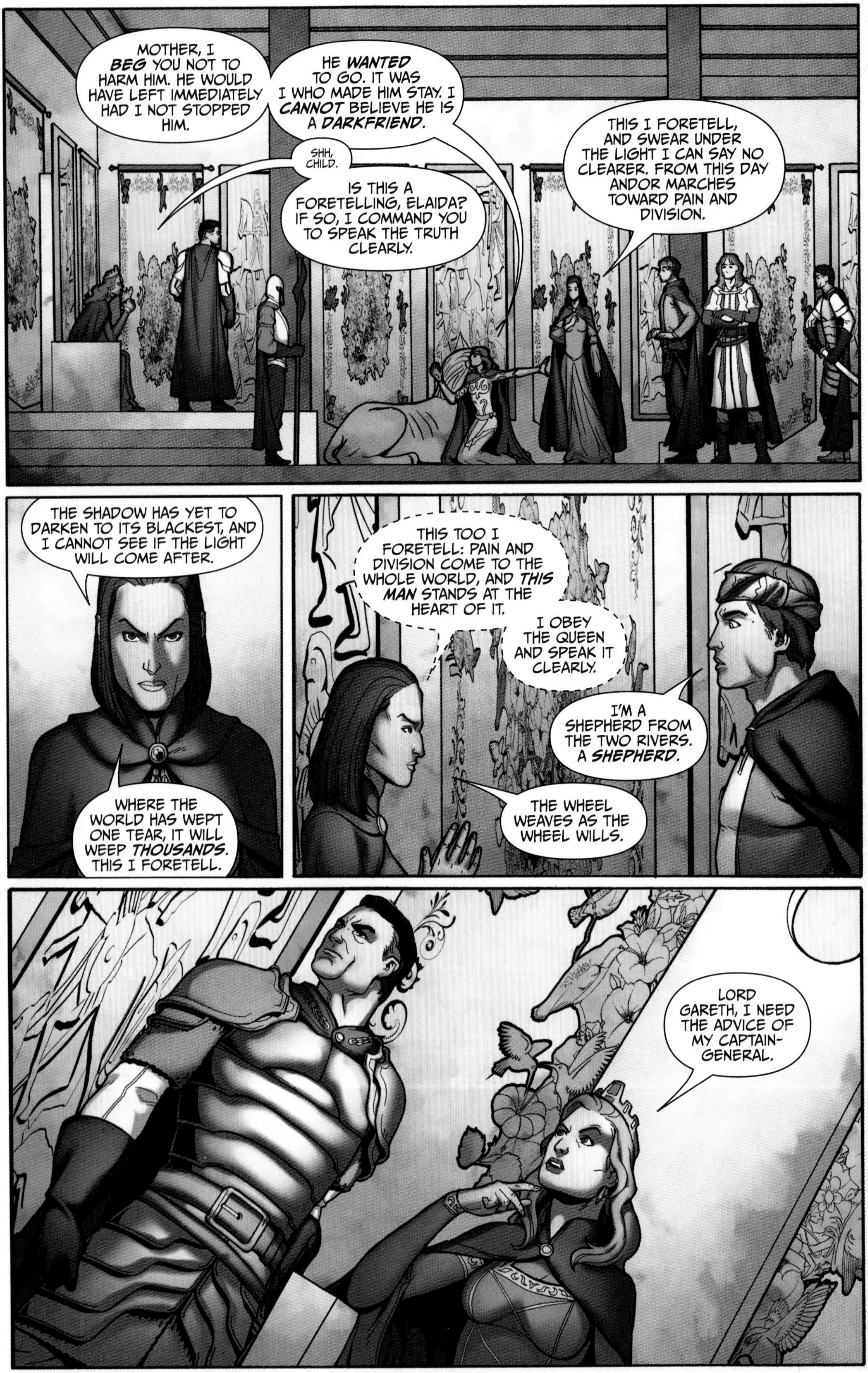
MOTHER, I BEG YOU NOT TO HARM HIM. HE WOULD HAVE LEFT IMMEDIATELY HAD I NOT STOPPED HIM.
HE WANTED TO GO. IT WAS I WHO MADE HIM STAY. I CANNOT BELIEVE HE IS A DARKFRIEND.
SHH, CHILD.
IS THIS A FORETELLING, ELAIDA? IF SO, I COMMAND YOU TO SPEAK THE TRUTH CLEARLY.
THIS I FORETELL, AND SWEAR UNDER THE LIGHT I CAN SAY NO CLEARER. FROM THIS DAY ANDOR MARCHES TOWARD PAIN AND DIVISION.
THE SHADOW HAS YET TO DARKEN TO ITS BLACKEST, AND I CANNOT SEE IF THE LIGHT WILL COME AFTER.
WHERE THE WORLD HAS WEPT ONE TEAR, IT WILL WEEP THOUSANDS. THIS I FORETELL.
THIS TOO I FORETELL: PAIN AND DIVISION COME TO THE WHOLE WORLD, AND THIS MAN STANDS AT THE HEART OF IT.
I OBEY THE QUEEN AND SPEAK IT CLEARLY.
I'M A SHEPHERD FROM THE TWO RIVERS. A SHEPHERD.
THE WHEEL WEAVES AS THE WHEEL WILLS.
LORD GARETH, I NEED THE ADVICE OF MY CAPTAIN-GENERAL.

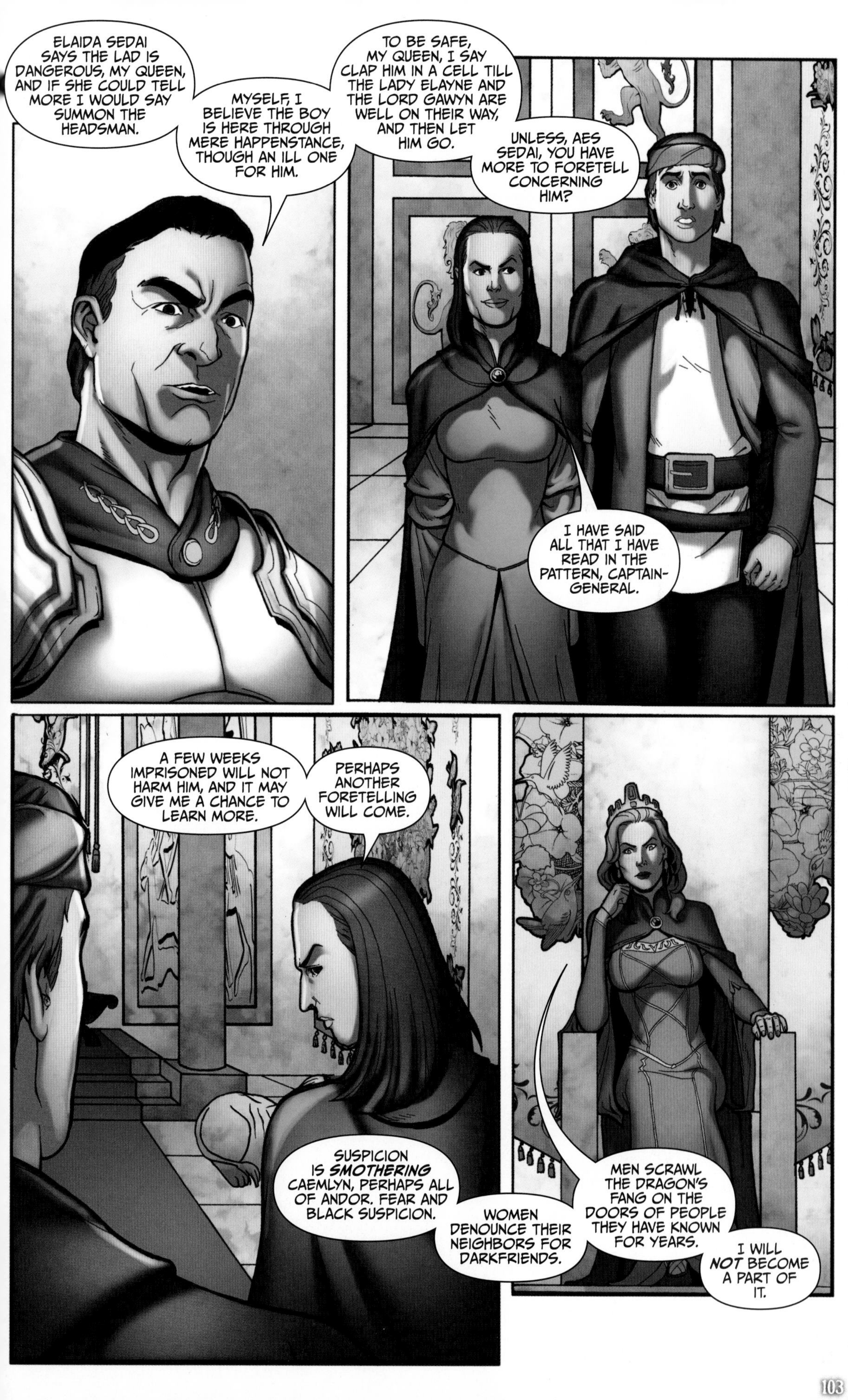
ELAIDA SEDAI SAYS THE LAD IS DANGEROUS, MY QUEEN, AND IF SHE COULD TELL MORE I WOULD SAY SUMMON THE HEADSMAN.
MYSELF, I BELIEVE THE BOY IS HERE THROUGH MERE HAPPENSTANCE, THOUGH AN ILL ONE FOR HIM.
TO BE SAFE, MY QUEEN, I SAY CLAP HIM IN A CELL TILL THE LADY ELAYNE AND THE LORD GAWYN ARE WELL ON THEIR WAY, AND THEN LET HIM GO.
UNLESS, AES SEDAI, YOU HAVE MORE TO FORETELL CONCERNING HIM?
I HAVE SAID ALL THAT I HAVE READ IN THE PATTERN, CAPTAIN-GENERAL.
A FEW WEEKS IMPRISONED WILL NOT HARM HIM, AND IT MAY GIVE ME A CHANCE TO LEARN MORE.
PERHAPS ANOTHER FORETELLING WILL COME.
SUSPICION IS *SMOTHERING* CAEMLYN, PERHAPS ALL OF ANDOR. FEAR AND BLACK SUSPICION.
WOMEN DENOUNCE THEIR NEIGHBORS FOR DARKFRIENDS.
MEN SCRAWL THE DRAGON'S FANG ON THE DOORS OF PEOPLE THEY HAVE KNOWN FOR YEARS.
I WILL *NOT* BECOME A PART OF IT.

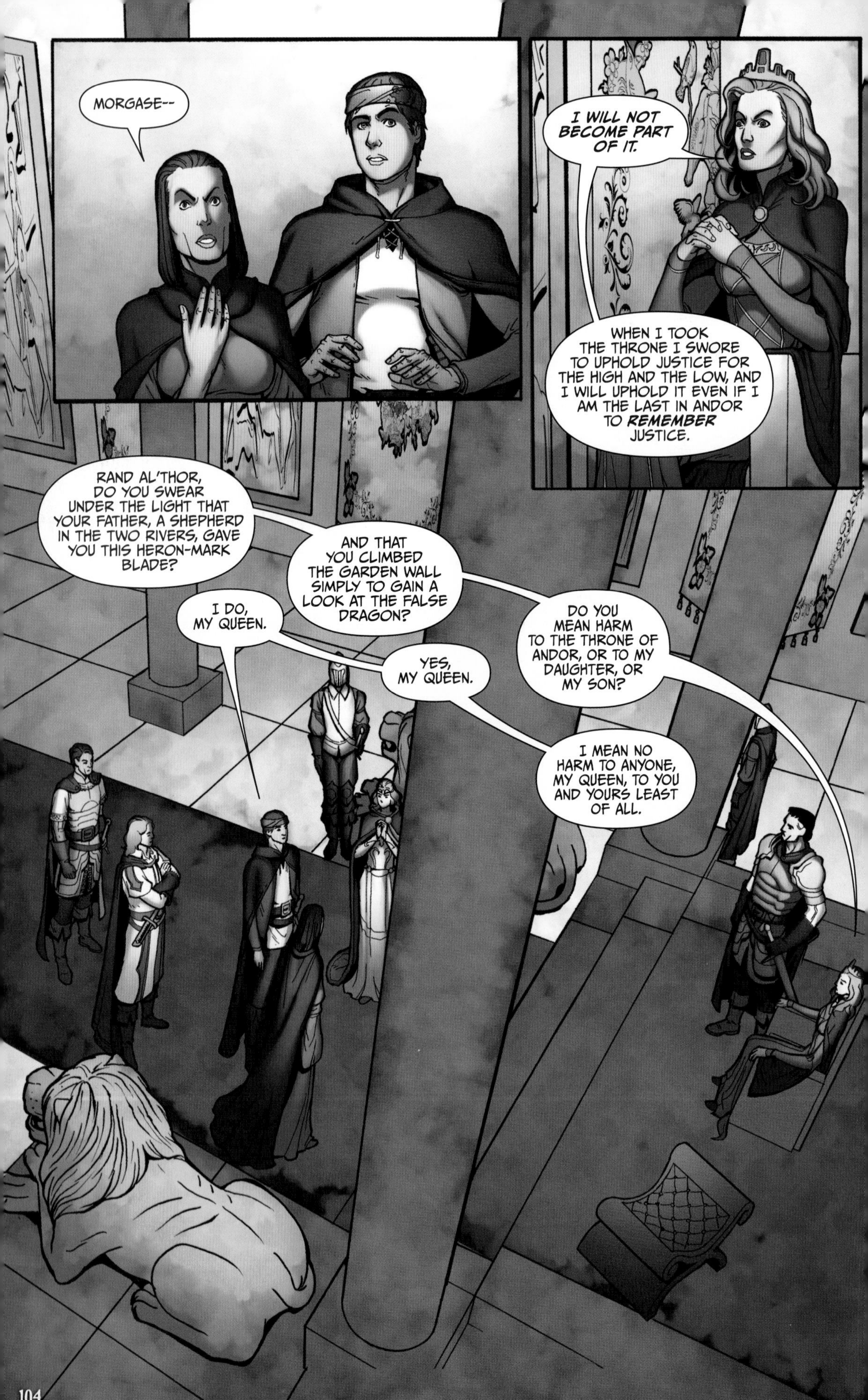
MORGASE--
I WILL NOT BECOME PART OF IT.
WHEN I TOOK THE THRONE I SWORE TO UPHOLD JUSTICE FOR THE HIGH AND THE LOW, AND I WILL UPHOLD IT EVEN IF I AM THE LAST IN ANDOR TO *REMEMBER* JUSTICE.
RAND AL'THOR, DO YOU SWEAR UNDER THE LIGHT THAT YOUR FATHER, A SHEPHERD IN THE TWO RIVERS, GAVE YOU THIS HERON-MARK BLADE?
I DO, MY QUEEN.
AND THAT YOU CLIMBED THE GARDEN WALL SIMPLY TO GAIN A LOOK AT THE FALSE DRAGON?
YES, MY QUEEN.
DO YOU MEAN HARM TO THE THRONE OF ANDOR, OR TO MY DAUGHTER, OR MY SON?
I MEAN NO HARM TO ANYONE, MY QUEEN, TO YOU AND YOURS LEAST OF ALL.

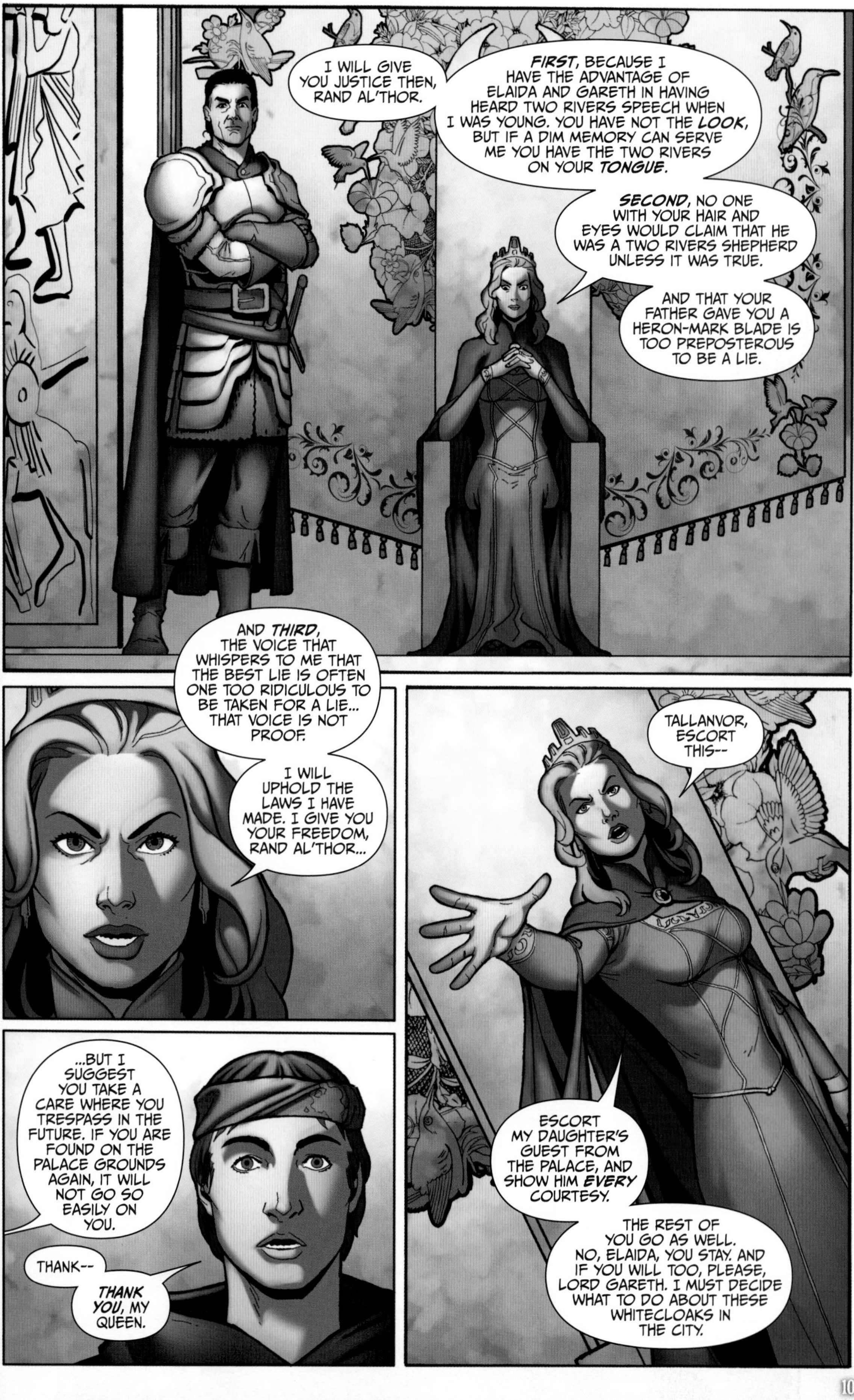
I WILL GIVE YOU JUSTICE THEN, RAND AL'THOR.
FIRST, BECAUSE I HAVE THE ADVANTAGE OF ELAIDA AND GARETH IN HAVING HEARD TWO RIVERS SPEECH WHEN I WAS YOUNG. YOU HAVE NOT THE LOOK, BUT IF A DIM MEMORY CAN SERVE ME YOU HAVE THE TWO RIVERS ON YOUR TONGUE.
SECOND, NO ONE WITH YOUR HAIR AND EYES WOULD CLAIM THAT HE WAS A TWO RIVERS SHEPHERD UNLESS IT WAS TRUE.
AND THAT YOUR FATHER GAVE YOU A HERON-MARK BLADE IS TOO PREPOSTEROUS TO BE A LIE.
AND THIRD, THE VOICE THAT WHISPERS TO ME THAT THE BEST LIE IS OFTEN ONE TOO RIDICULOUS TO BE TAKEN FOR A LIE... THAT VOICE IS NOT PROOF.
I WILL UPHOLD THE LAWS I HAVE MADE. I GIVE YOU YOUR FREEDOM, RAND AL'THOR...
...BUT I SUGGEST YOU TAKE A CARE WHERE YOU TRESPASS IN THE FUTURE. IF YOU ARE FOUND ON THE PALACE GROUNDS AGAIN, IT WILL NOT GO SO EASILY ON YOU.
THANK--
THANK YOU, MY QUEEN.
TALLANVOR, ESCORT THIS--
ESCORT MY DAUGHTER'S GUEST FROM THE PALACE, AND SHOW HIM EVERY COURTESY.
THE REST OF YOU GO AS WELL. NO, ELAIDA, YOU STAY. AND IF YOU WILL TOO, PLEASE, LORD GARETH. I MUST DECIDE WHAT TO DO ABOUT THESE WHITECLOAKS IN THE CITY.

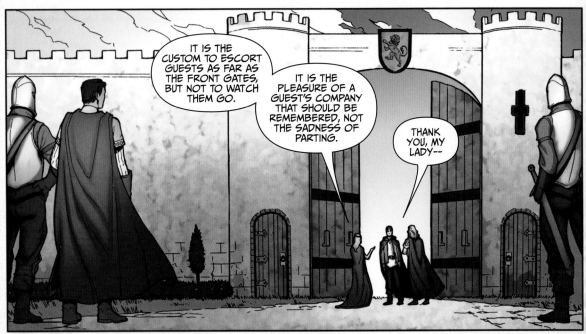

IT IS THE CUSTOM TO ESCORT GUESTS AS FAR AS THE FRONT GATES, BUT NOT TO WATCH THEM GO.

IT IS THE PLEASURE OF A GUEST'S COMPANY THAT SHOULD BE REMEMBERED, NOT THE SADNESS OF PARTING.

THANK YOU, MY LADY--

--FOR *EVERYTHING.*

CUSTOM IN THE TWO RIVERS IS FOR A GUEST TO BRING A SMALL GIFT. I'M AFRAID I HAVE NOTHING. ALTHOUGH... APPARENTLY I DID TEACH YOU SOMETHING OF TWO RIVERS FOLK.

IF I HAD TOLD MOTHER I THINK YOU ARE *HANDSOME,* SHE CERTAINLY WOULD HAVE HAD YOU LOCKED IN A CELL.

FARE YOU WELL, RAND AL'THOR.

DO NOT TRY TO BANDY WORDS WITH HER, SHE WILL WIN EVERY TIME.

MY LORD-- WHEN I TOLD YOU I WAS FROM THE TWO RIVERS YOU WERE SURPRISED. AND EVERYBODY ELSE, YOUR MOTHER, ELAIDA SEDAI, LORD GARETH...

WRAP A *SHOUFA* AROUND YOUR HEAD, RAND, AND YOU WOULD BE THE IMAGE OF AN *AIELMAN.* ODD, SINCE MOTHER SEEMS TO THINK YOU *SOUND LIKE* A TWO RIVERS MAN.

I WISH WE COULD HAVE COME TO KNOW EACH OTHER, RAND AL'THOR. FARE YOU WELL.

Rand barely registered Gawyn walking away-- the young lord's words stuck in his head: "the image of an Aielman."

An *Aielman?*

chapter five

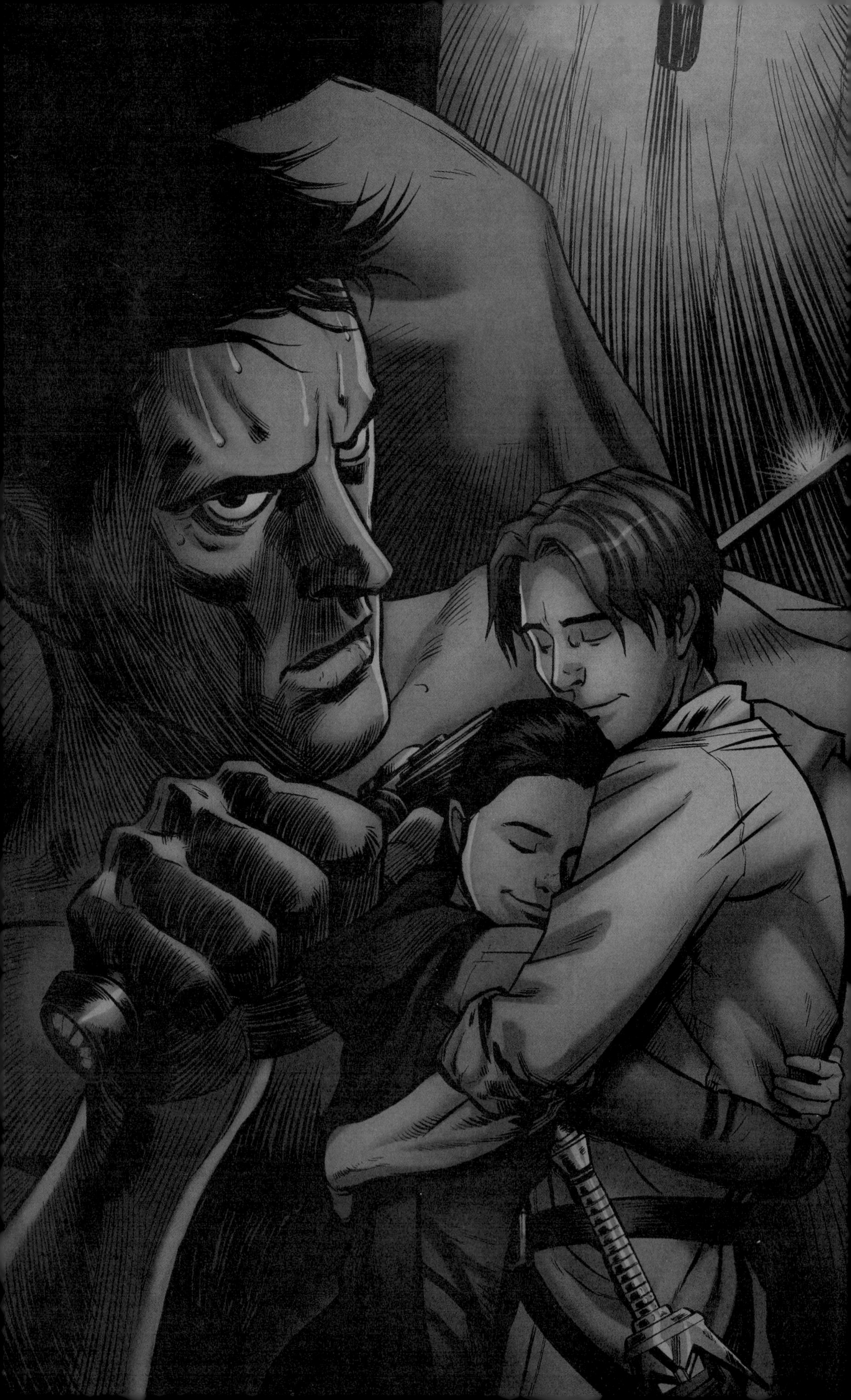

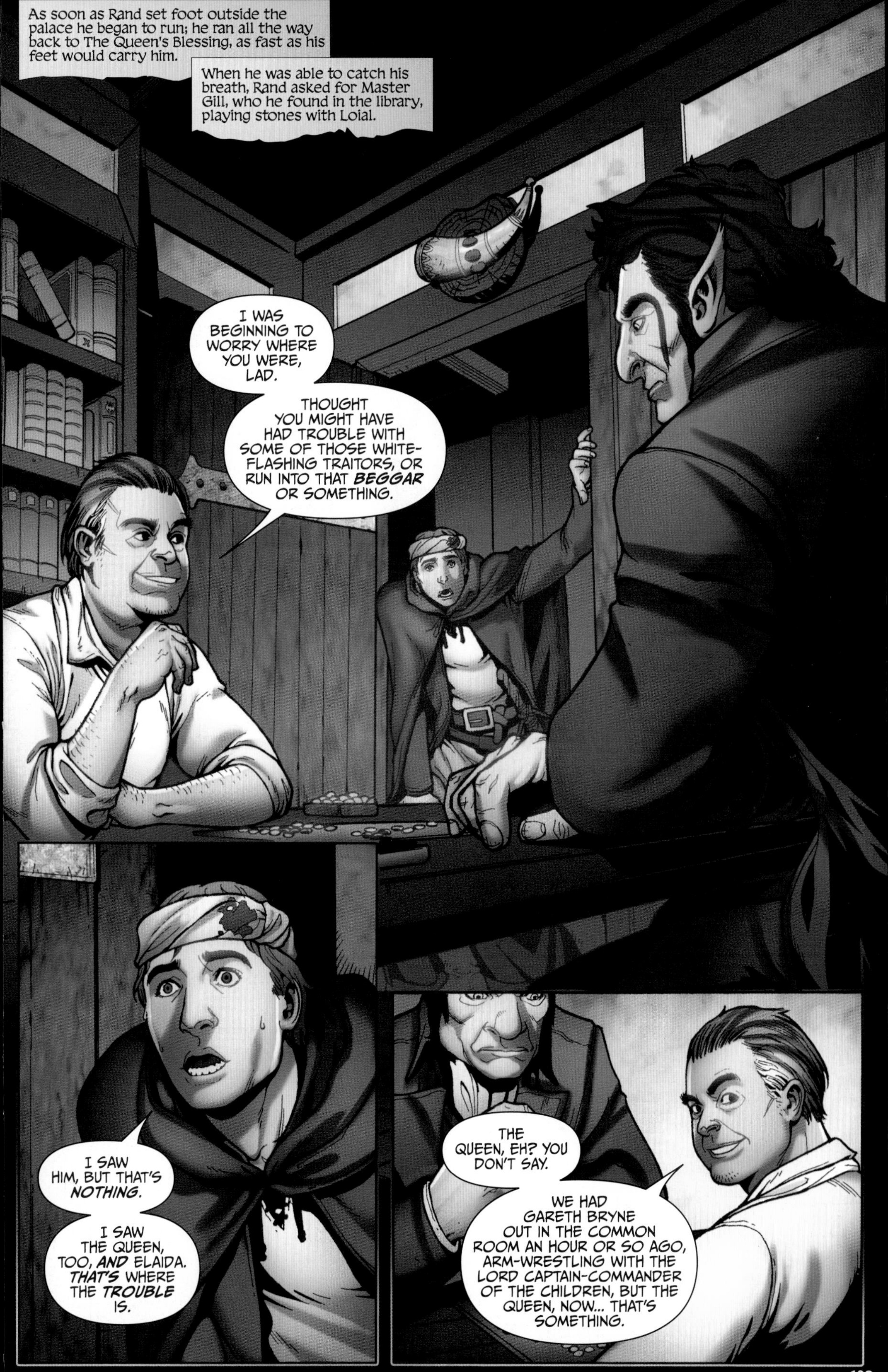
As soon as Rand set foot outside the palace he began to run; he ran all the way back to The Queen's Blessing, as fast as his feet would carry him.
When he was able to catch his breath, Rand asked for Master Gill, who he found in the library, playing stones with Loial.
I WAS BEGINNING TO WORRY WHERE YOU WERE, LAD.
THOUGHT YOU MIGHT HAVE HAD TROUBLE WITH SOME OF THOSE WHITE-FLASHING TRAITORS, OR RUN INTO THAT *BEGGAR* OR SOMETHING.
I SAW HIM, BUT THAT'S *NOTHING*.
I SAW THE QUEEN, TOO, *AND* ELAIDA. *THAT'S* WHERE THE *TROUBLE* IS.
THE QUEEN, EH? YOU DON'T SAY.
WE HAD GARETH BRYNE OUT IN THE COMMON ROOM AN HOUR OR SO AGO, ARM-WRESTLING WITH THE LORD CAPTAIN-COMMANDER OF THE CHILDREN, BUT THE QUEEN, NOW... THAT'S SOMETHING.

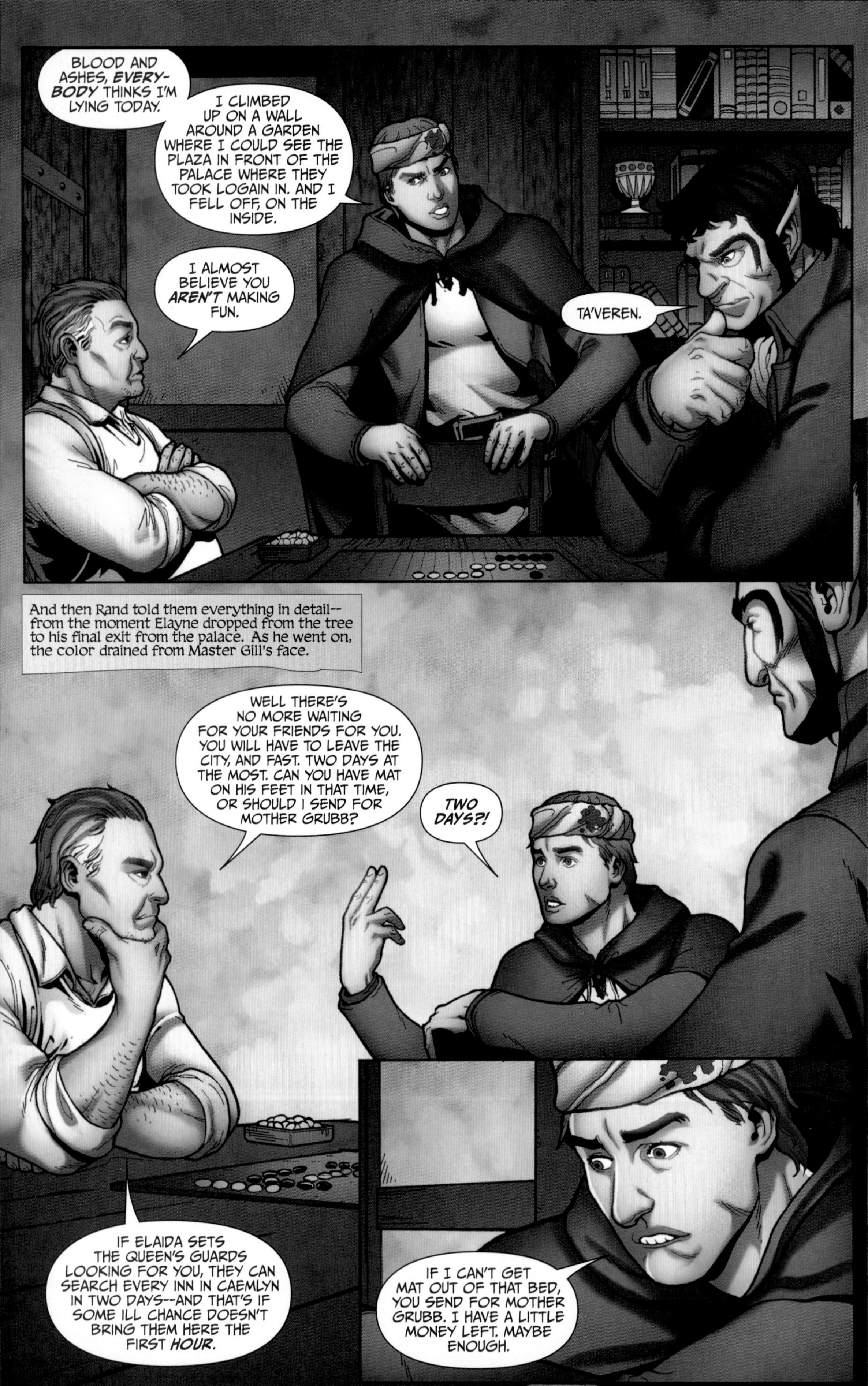

BLOOD AND ASHES, EVERY-BODY THINKS I'M LYING TODAY.
I CLIMBED UP ON A WALL AROUND A GARDEN WHERE I COULD SEE THE PLAZA IN FRONT OF THE PALACE WHERE THEY TOOK LOGAIN IN. AND I FELL OFF, ON THE INSIDE.
I ALMOST BELIEVE YOU AREN'T MAKING FUN.
TA'VEREN.
And then Rand told them everything in detail--from the moment Elayne dropped from the tree to his final exit from the palace. As he went on, the color drained from Master Gill's face.
WELL THERE'S NO MORE WAITING FOR YOUR FRIENDS FOR YOU. YOU WILL HAVE TO LEAVE THE CITY, AND FAST. TWO DAYS AT THE MOST. CAN YOU HAVE MAT ON HIS FEET IN THAT TIME, OR SHOULD I SEND FOR MOTHER GRUBB?
TWO DAYS?!
IF ELAIDA SETS THE QUEEN'S GUARDS LOOKING FOR YOU, THEY CAN SEARCH EVERY INN IN CAEMLYN IN TWO DAYS--AND THAT'S IF SOME ILL CHANCE DOESN'T BRING THEM HERE THE FIRST HOUR.
IF I CAN'T GET MAT OUT OF THAT BED, YOU SEND FOR MOTHER GRUBB. I HAVE A LITTLE MONEY LEFT. MAYBE ENOUGH.

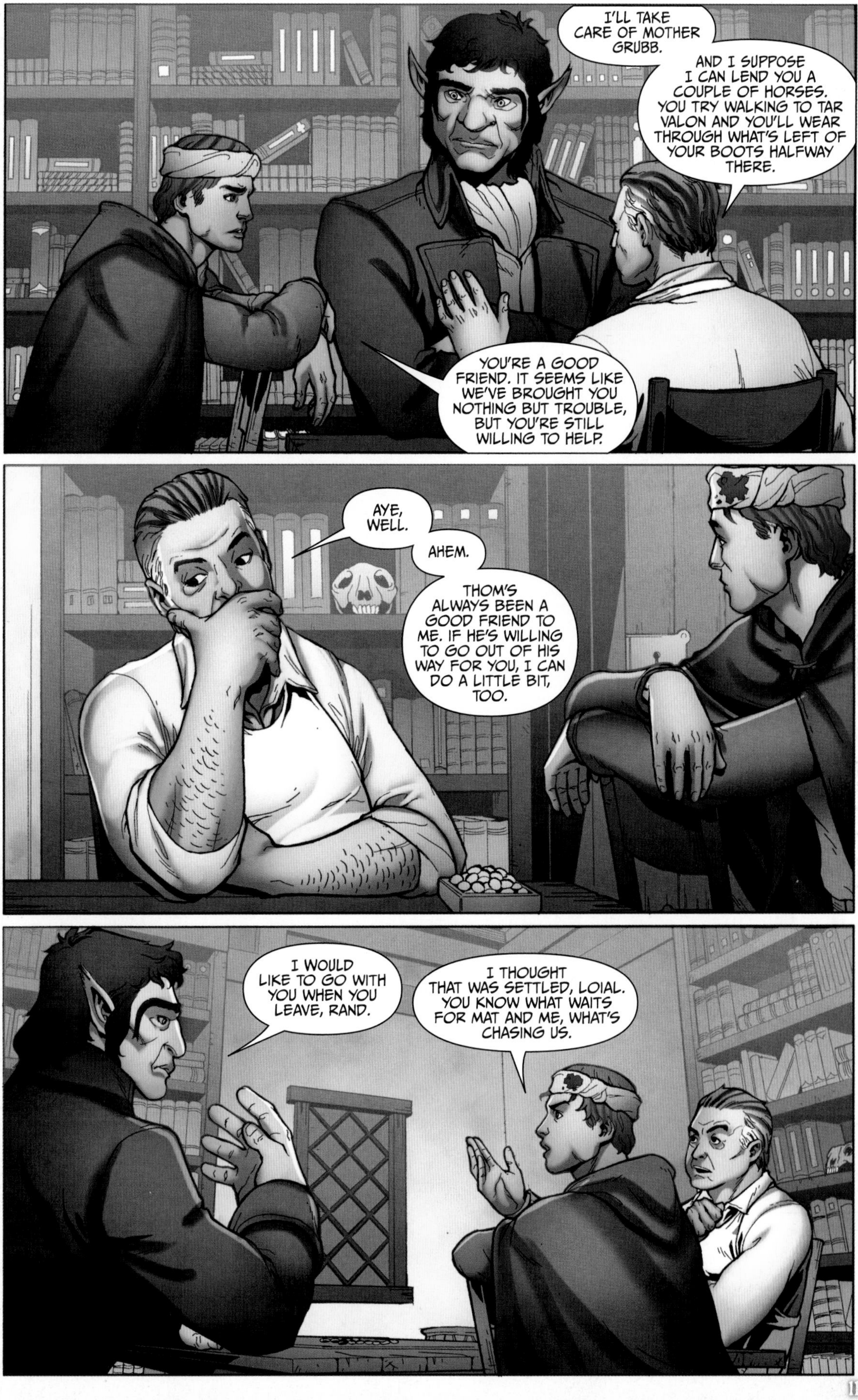
I'LL TAKE CARE OF MOTHER GRUBB.
AND I SUPPOSE I CAN LEND YOU A COUPLE OF HORSES. YOU TRY WALKING TO TAR VALON AND YOU'LL WEAR THROUGH WHAT'S LEFT OF YOUR BOOTS HALFWAY THERE.
YOU'RE A GOOD FRIEND. IT SEEMS LIKE WE'VE BROUGHT YOU NOTHING BUT TROUBLE, BUT YOU'RE STILL WILLING TO HELP.
AYE, WELL.
AHEM.
THOM'S ALWAYS BEEN A GOOD FRIEND TO ME. IF HE'S WILLING TO GO OUT OF HIS WAY FOR YOU, I CAN DO A LITTLE BIT, TOO.
I WOULD LIKE TO GO WITH YOU WHEN YOU LEAVE, RAND.
I THOUGHT THAT WAS SETTLED, LOIAL. YOU KNOW WHAT WAITS FOR MAT AND ME, WHAT'S CHASING US.

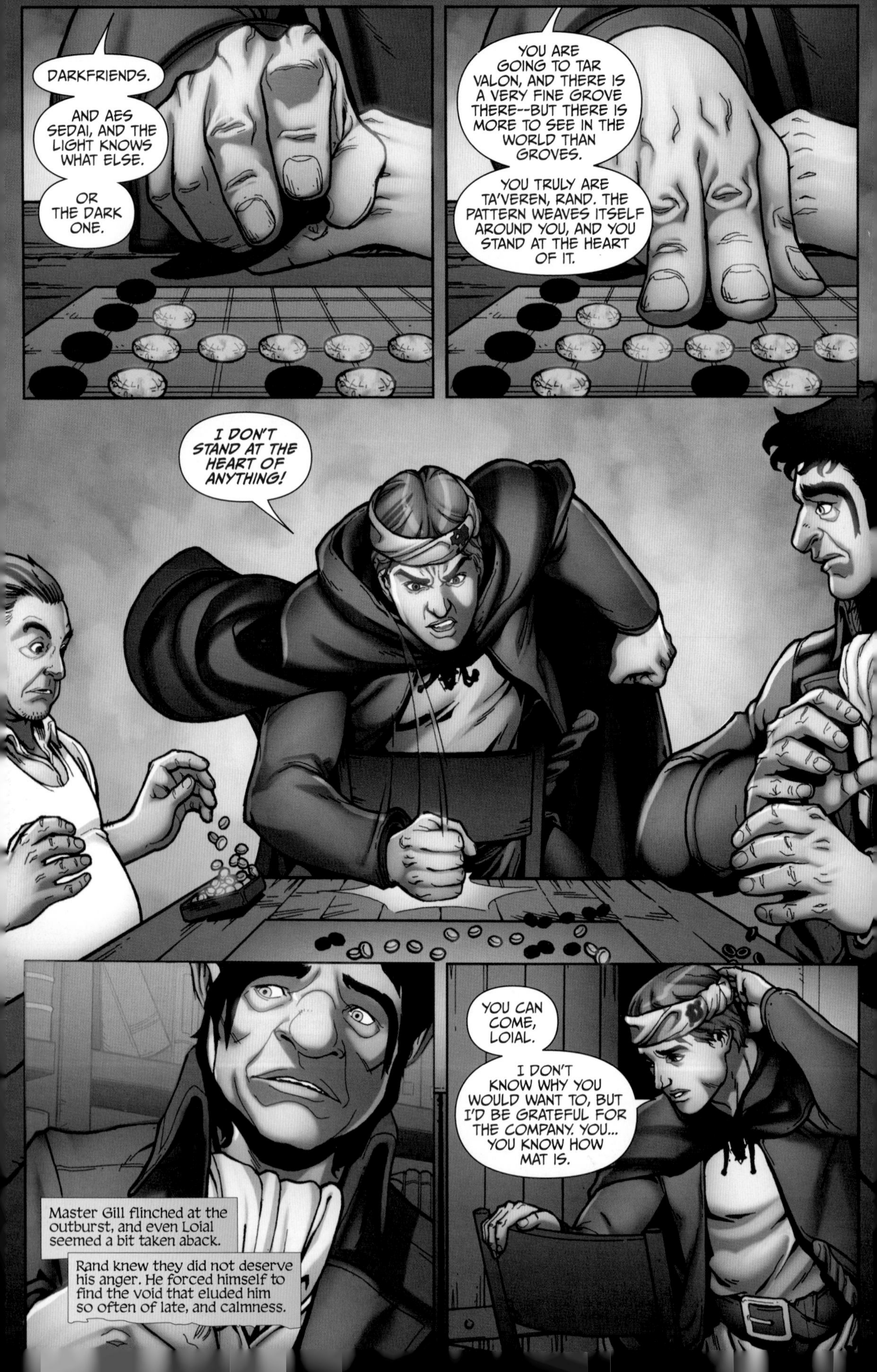
DARKFRIENDS.
AND AES SEDAI, AND THE LIGHT KNOWS WHAT ELSE.
OR THE DARK ONE.
YOU ARE GOING TO TAR VALON, AND THERE IS A VERY FINE GROVE THERE--BUT THERE IS MORE TO SEE IN THE WORLD THAN GROVES.
YOU TRULY ARE TA'VEREN, RAND. THE PATTERN WEAVES ITSELF AROUND YOU, AND YOU STAND AT THE HEART OF IT.
I DON'T STAND AT THE HEART OF ANYTHING!
Master Gill flinched at the outburst, and even Loial seemed a bit taken aback.
Rand knew they did not deserve his anger. He forced himself to find the void that eluded him so often of late, and calmness.
YOU CAN COME, LOIAL.
I DON'T KNOW WHY YOU WOULD WANT TO, BUT I'D BE GRATEFUL FOR THE COMPANY. YOU... YOU KNOW HOW MAT IS.

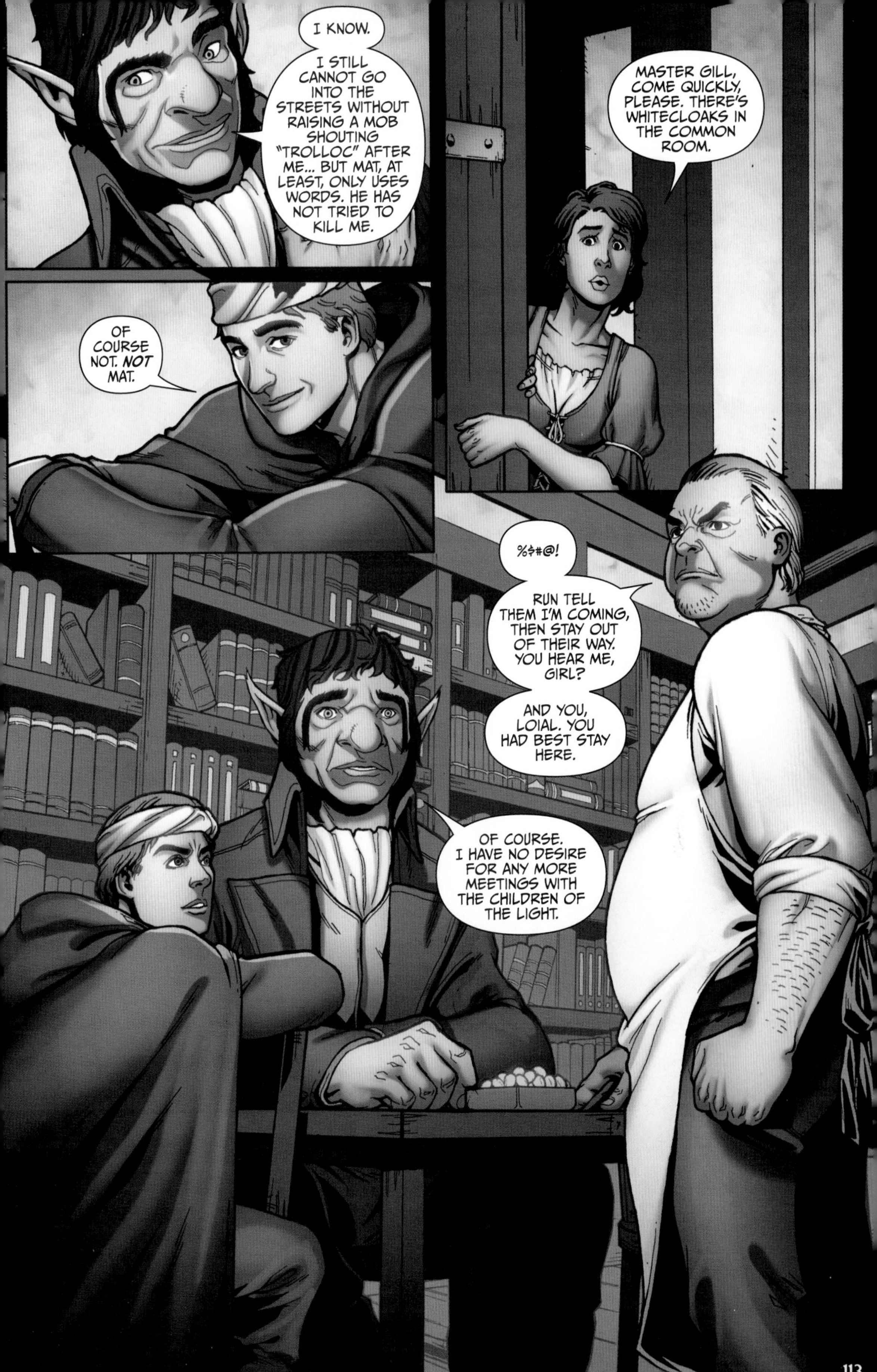
I KNOW.
I STILL CANNOT GO INTO THE STREETS WITHOUT RAISING A MOB SHOUTING "TROLLOC" AFTER ME... BUT MAT, AT LEAST, ONLY USES WORDS. HE HAS NOT TRIED TO KILL ME.
MASTER GILL, COME QUICKLY, PLEASE. THERE'S WHITECLOAKS IN THE COMMON ROOM.
OF COURSE NOT. *NOT* MAT.
%$#@!
RUN TELL THEM I'M COMING, THEN STAY OUT OF THEIR WAY. YOU HEAR ME, GIRL?
AND YOU, LOIAL. YOU HAD BEST STAY HERE.
OF COURSE. I HAVE NO DESIRE FOR ANY MORE MEETINGS WITH THE CHILDREN OF THE LIGHT.

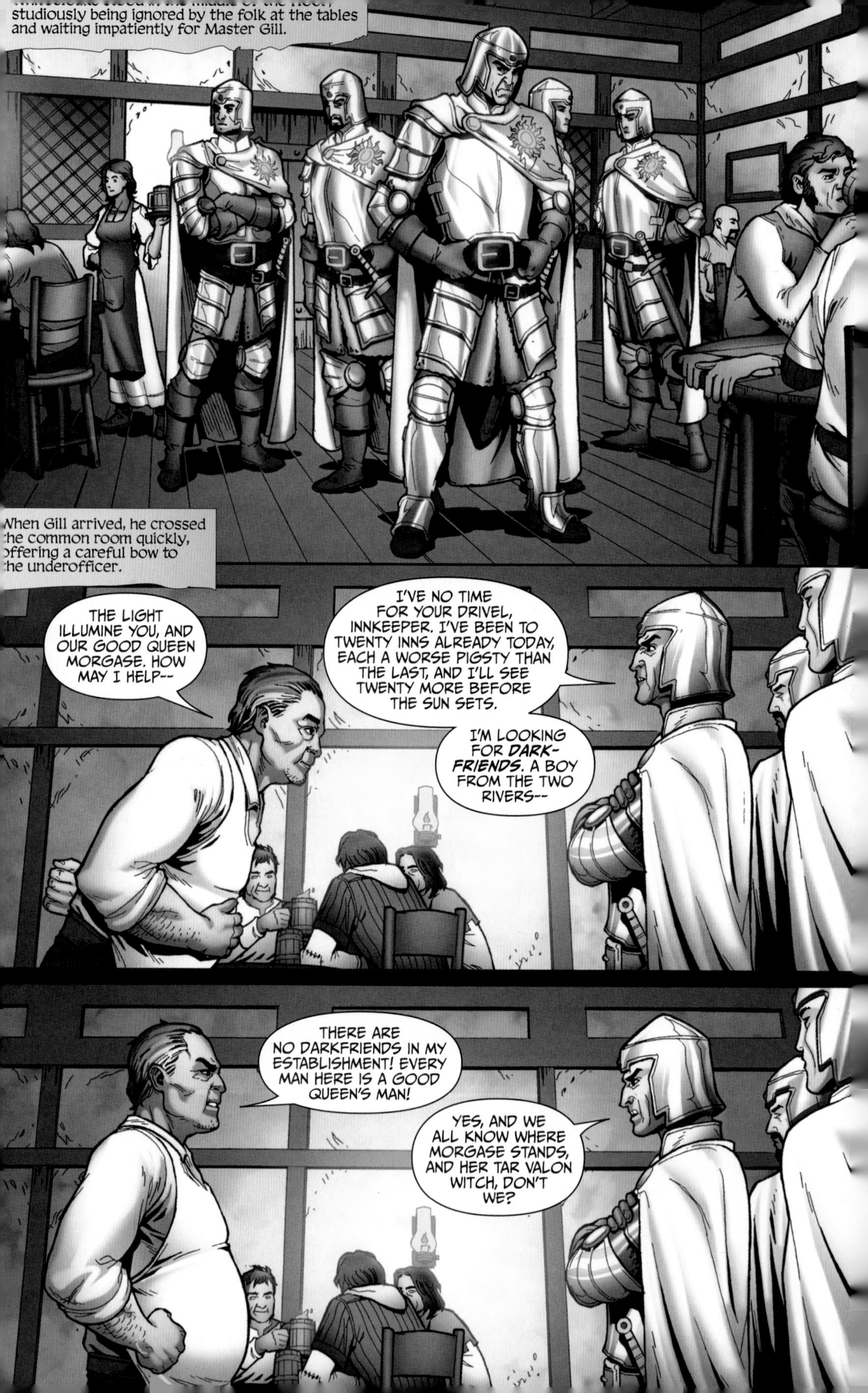

studiously being ignored by the folk at the tables
and waiting impatiently for Master Gill.
When Gill arrived, he crossed the common room quickly, offering a careful bow to the underofficer.
THE LIGHT ILLUMINE YOU, AND OUR GOOD QUEEN MORGASE. HOW MAY I HELP--
I'VE NO TIME FOR YOUR DRIVEL, INNKEEPER. I'VE BEEN TO TWENTY INNS ALREADY TODAY, EACH A WORSE PIGSTY THAN THE LAST, AND I'LL SEE TWENTY MORE BEFORE THE SUN SETS.
I'M LOOKING FOR *DARK-FRIENDS*. A BOY FROM THE TWO RIVERS--
THERE ARE NO DARKFRIENDS IN MY ESTABLISHMENT! EVERY MAN HERE IS A GOOD QUEEN'S MAN!
YES, AND WE ALL KNOW WHERE MORGASE STANDS, AND HER TAR VALON WITCH, DON'T WE?

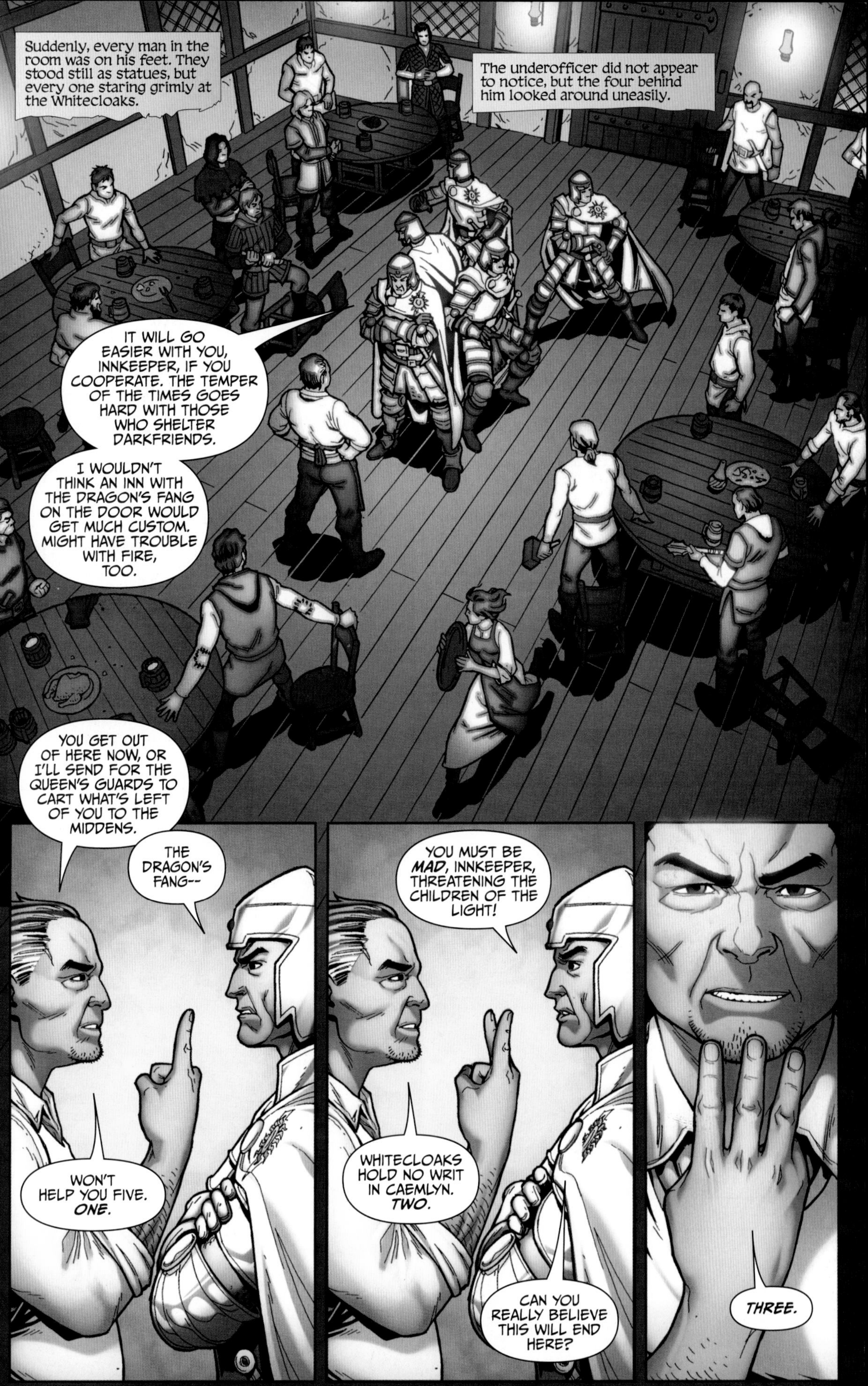
Suddenly, every man in the room was on his feet. They stood still as statues, but every one staring grimly at the Whitecloaks.
The underofficer did not appear to notice, but the four behind him looked around uneasily.
IT WILL GO EASIER WITH YOU, INNKEEPER, IF YOU COOPERATE. THE TEMPER OF THE TIMES GOES HARD WITH THOSE WHO SHELTER DARKFRIENDS.
I WOULDN'T THINK AN INN WITH THE DRAGON'S FANG ON THE DOOR WOULD GET MUCH CUSTOM. MIGHT HAVE TROUBLE WITH FIRE, TOO.
YOU GET OUT OF HERE NOW, OR I'LL SEND FOR THE QUEEN'S GUARDS TO CART WHAT'S LEFT OF YOU TO THE MIDDENS.
THE DRAGON'S FANG--
WON'T HELP YOU FIVE. *ONE.*
YOU MUST BE *MAD*, INNKEEPER, THREATENING THE CHILDREN OF THE LIGHT!
WHITECLOAKS HOLD NO WRIT IN CAEMLYN. *TWO.*
CAN YOU REALLY BELIEVE THIS WILL END HERE?
THREE.

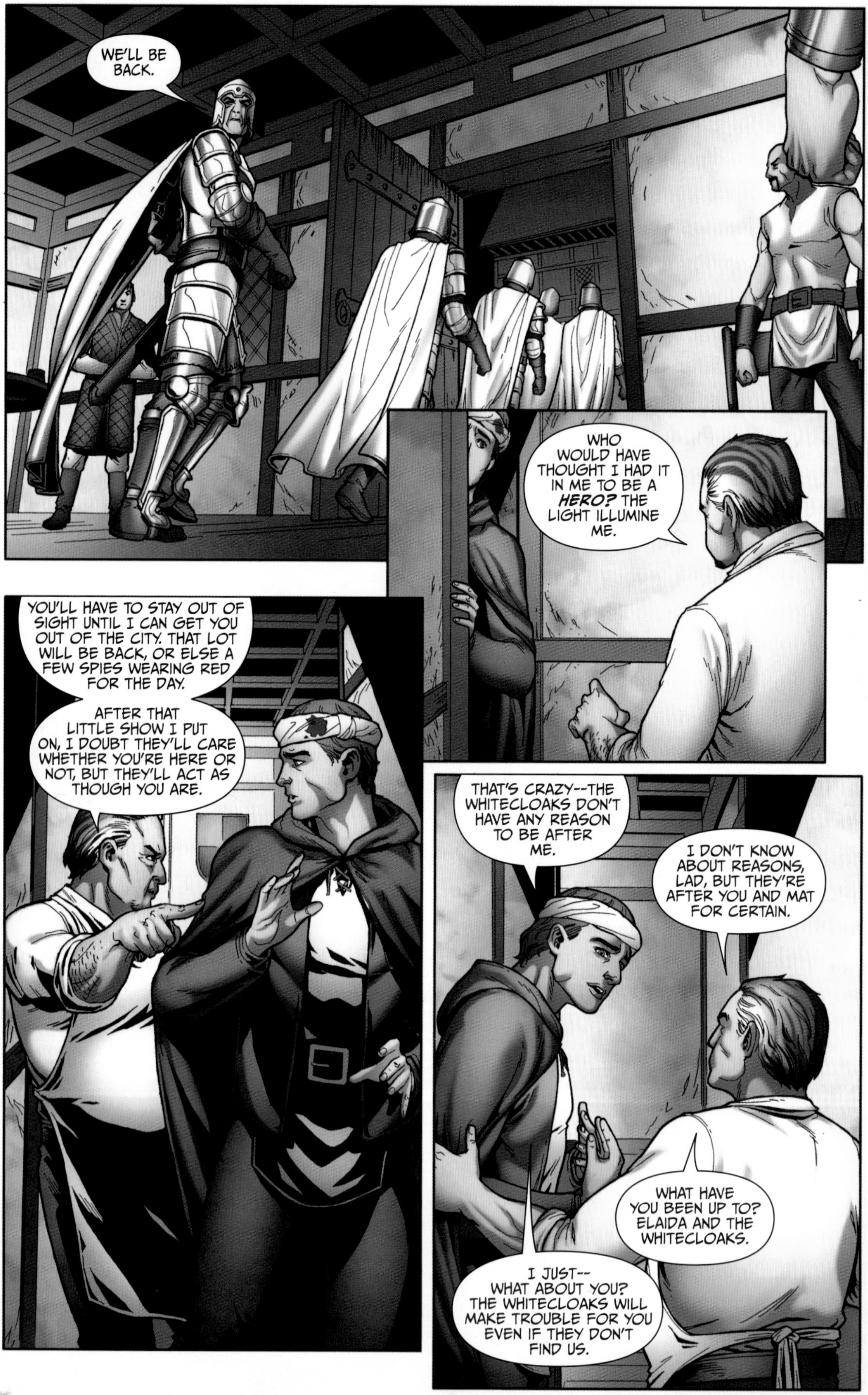
WE'LL BE BACK.
WHO WOULD HAVE THOUGHT I HAD IT IN ME TO BE A *HERO?* THE LIGHT ILLUMINE ME.
YOU'LL HAVE TO STAY OUT OF SIGHT UNTIL I CAN GET YOU OUT OF THE CITY. THAT LOT WILL BE BACK, OR ELSE A FEW SPIES WEARING RED FOR THE DAY.
AFTER THAT LITTLE SHOW I PUT ON, I DOUBT THEY'LL CARE WHETHER YOU'RE HERE OR NOT, BUT THEY'LL ACT AS THOUGH YOU ARE.
THAT'S CRAZY--THE WHITECLOAKS DON'T HAVE ANY REASON TO BE AFTER ME.
I DON'T KNOW ABOUT REASONS, LAD, BUT THEY'RE AFTER YOU AND MAT FOR CERTAIN.
WHAT HAVE YOU BEEN UP TO? ELAIDA AND THE WHITECLOAKS.
I JUST-- WHAT ABOUT YOU? THE WHITECLOAKS WILL MAKE TROUBLE FOR YOU EVEN IF THEY DON'T FIND US.

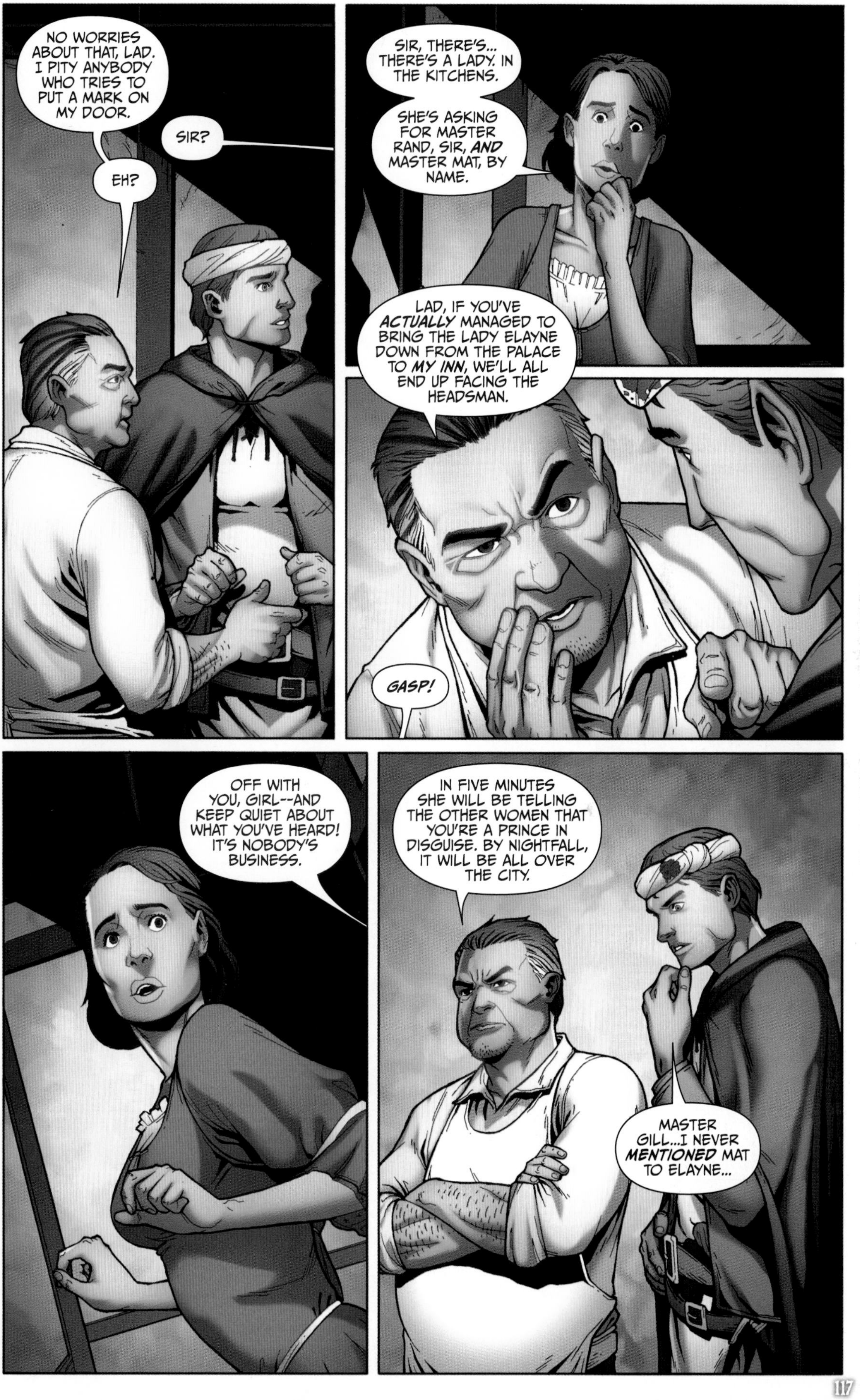
NO WORRIES ABOUT THAT, LAD. I PITY ANYBODY WHO TRIES TO PUT A MARK ON MY DOOR.
SIR?
EH?
SIR, THERE'S... THERE'S A LADY. IN THE KITCHENS.
SHE'S ASKING FOR MASTER RAND, SIR, AND MASTER MAT, BY NAME.
LAD, IF YOU'VE ACTUALLY MANAGED TO BRING THE LADY ELAYNE DOWN FROM THE PALACE TO MY INN, WE'LL ALL END UP FACING THE HEADSMAN.
GASP!
OFF WITH YOU, GIRL--AND KEEP QUIET ABOUT WHAT YOU'VE HEARD! IT'S NOBODY'S BUSINESS.
IN FIVE MINUTES SHE WILL BE TELLING THE OTHER WOMEN THAT YOU'RE A PRINCE IN DISGUISE. BY NIGHTFALL, IT WILL BE ALL OVER THE CITY.
MASTER GILL...I NEVER MENTIONED MAT TO ELAYNE...

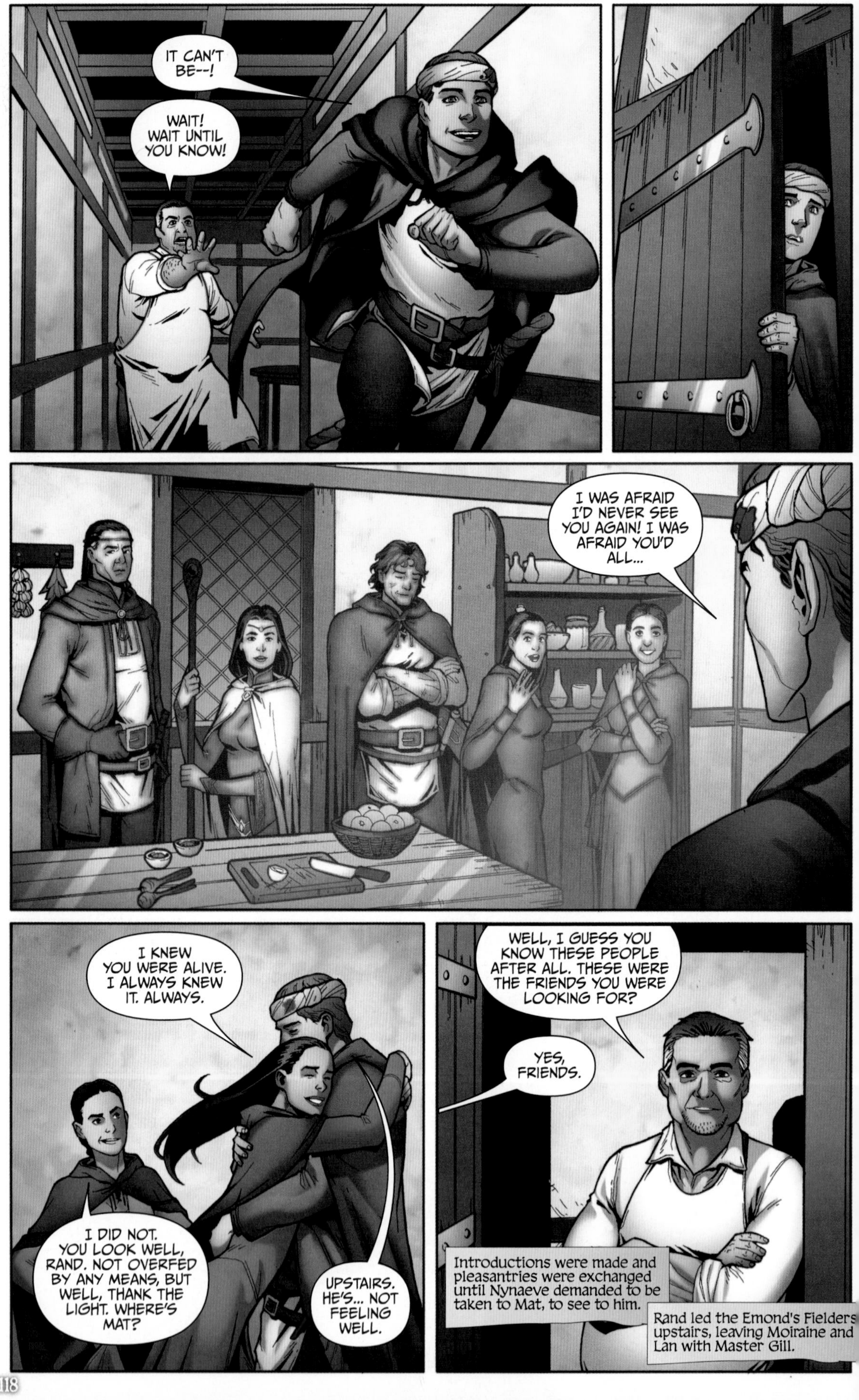
IT CAN'T BE--!
WAIT! WAIT UNTIL YOU KNOW!
I WAS AFRAID I'D NEVER SEE YOU AGAIN! I WAS AFRAID YOU'D ALL...
I KNEW YOU WERE ALIVE. I ALWAYS KNEW IT. ALWAYS.
I DID NOT. YOU LOOK WELL, RAND. NOT OVERFED BY ANY MEANS, BUT WELL, THANK THE LIGHT. WHERE'S MAT?
UPSTAIRS. HE'S... NOT FEELING WELL.
WELL, I GUESS YOU KNOW THESE PEOPLE AFTER ALL. THESE WERE THE FRIENDS YOU WERE LOOKING FOR?
YES, FRIENDS.
Introductions were made and pleasantries were exchanged until Nynaeve demanded to be taken to Mat, to see to him.
Rand led the Emond's Fielders upstairs, leaving Moiraine and Lan with Master Gill.

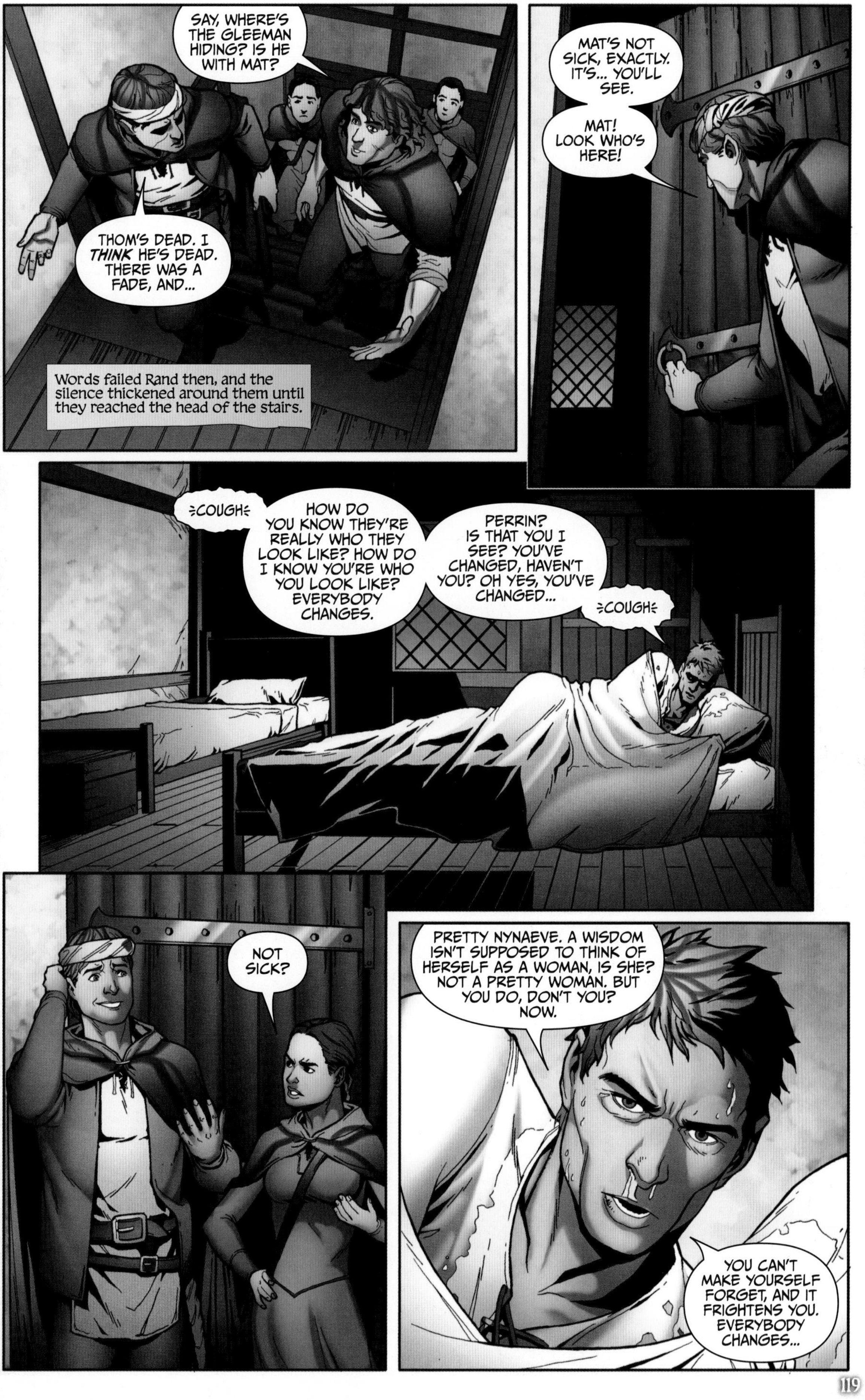
SAY, WHERE'S THE GLEEMAN HIDING? IS HE WITH MAT?
THOM'S DEAD. I *THINK* HE'S DEAD. THERE WAS A FADE, AND...
Words failed Rand then, and the silence thickened around them until they reached the head of the stairs.
MAT'S NOT SICK, EXACTLY. IT'S... YOU'LL SEE.
MAT! LOOK WHO'S HERE!
≡COUGH≡
HOW DO YOU KNOW THEY'RE REALLY WHO THEY LOOK LIKE? HOW DO I KNOW YOU'RE WHO YOU LOOK LIKE? EVERYBODY CHANGES.
PERRIN? IS THAT YOU I SEE? YOU'VE CHANGED, HAVEN'T YOU? OH YES, YOU'VE CHANGED...
≡COUGH≡
NOT SICK?
PRETTY NYNAEVE. A WISDOM ISN'T SUPPOSED TO THINK OF HERSELF AS A WOMAN, IS SHE? NOT A PRETTY WOMAN. BUT YOU DO, DON'T YOU? NOW.
YOU CAN'T MAKE YOURSELF FORGET, AND IT FRIGHTENS YOU. EVERYBODY CHANGES...

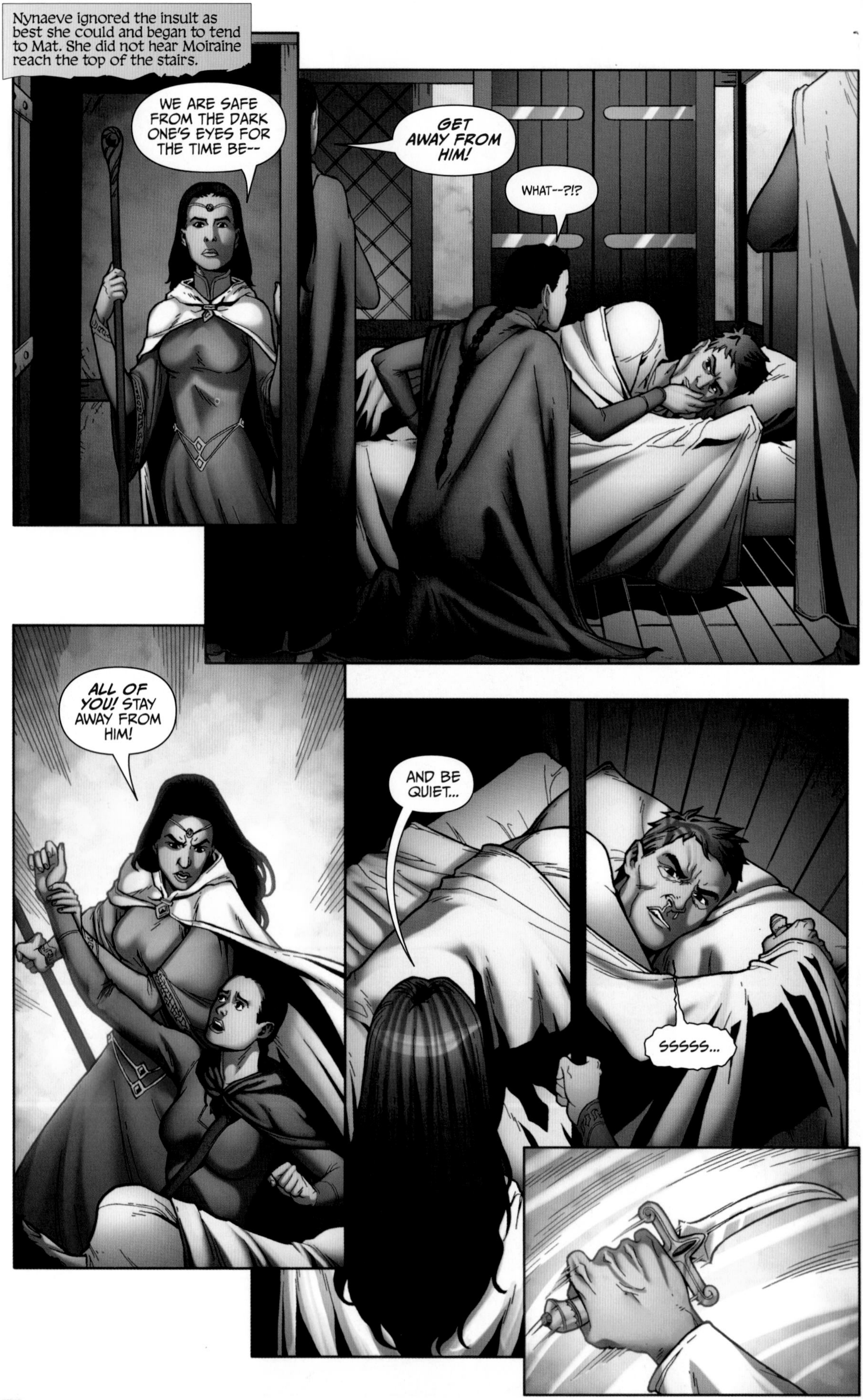

Nynaeve ignored the insult as best she could and began to tend to Mat. She did not hear Moiraine reach the top of the stairs.
WE ARE SAFE FROM THE DARK ONE'S EYES FOR THE TIME BE--
GET AWAY FROM HIM!
WHAT--?!?
ALL OF YOU! STAY AWAY FROM HIM!
AND BE QUIET...
SSSSS...

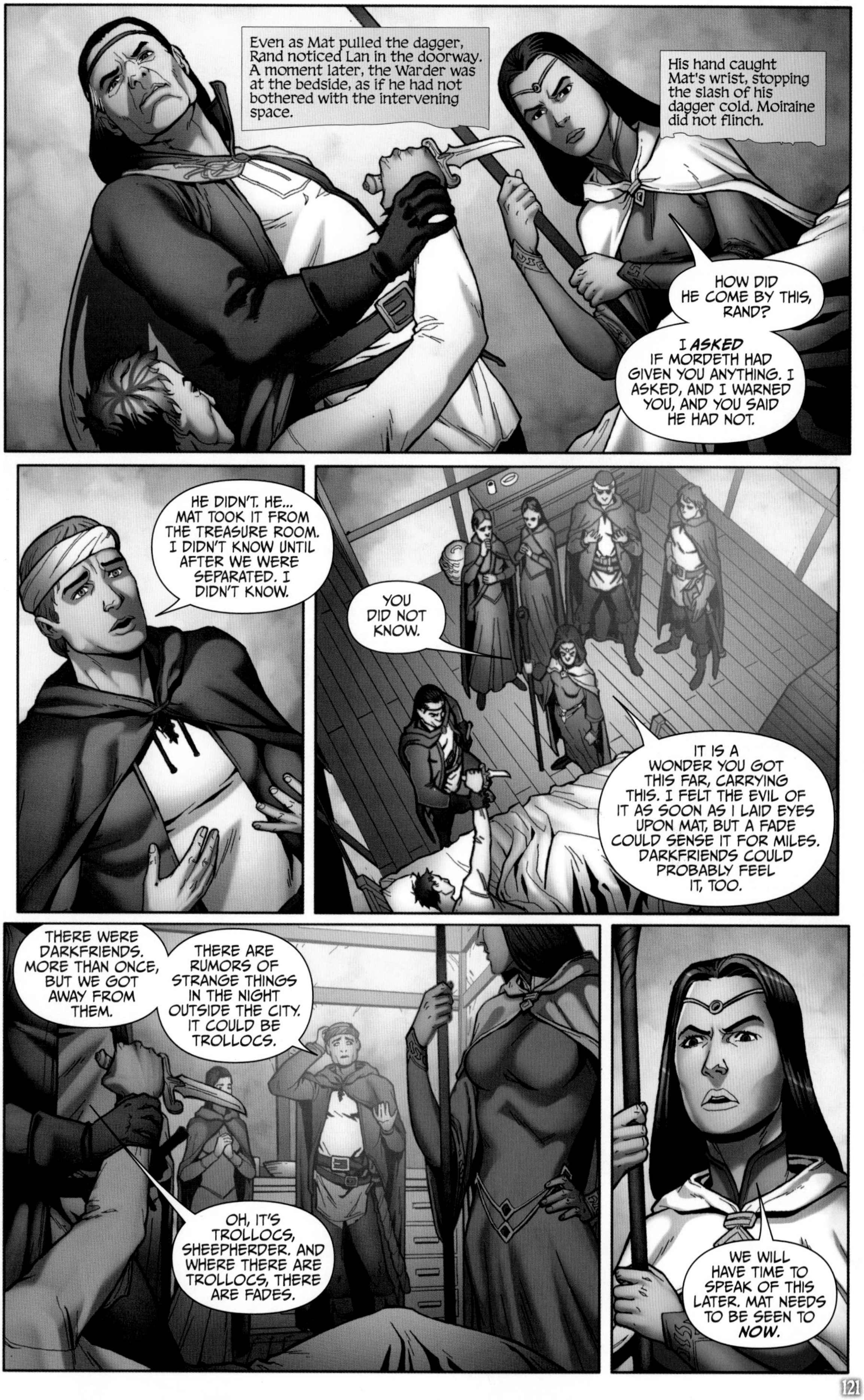
Even as Mat pulled the dagger, Rand noticed Lan in the doorway. A moment later, the Warder was at the bedside, as if he had not bothered with the intervening space.
His hand caught Mat's wrist, stopping the slash of his dagger cold. Moiraine did not flinch.
HOW DID HE COME BY THIS, RAND?
I ***ASKED*** IF MORDETH HAD GIVEN YOU ANYTHING. I ASKED, AND I WARNED YOU, AND YOU SAID HE HAD NOT.
HE DIDN'T. HE... MAT TOOK IT FROM THE TREASURE ROOM. I DIDN'T KNOW UNTIL AFTER WE WERE SEPARATED. I DIDN'T KNOW.
YOU DID NOT KNOW.
IT IS A WONDER YOU GOT THIS FAR, CARRYING THIS. I FELT THE EVIL OF IT AS SOON AS I LAID EYES UPON MAT, BUT A FADE COULD SENSE IT FOR MILES. DARKFRIENDS COULD PROBABLY FEEL IT, TOO.
THERE WERE DARKFRIENDS. MORE THAN ONCE, BUT WE GOT AWAY FROM THEM.
THERE ARE RUMORS OF STRANGE THINGS IN THE NIGHT OUTSIDE THE CITY. IT COULD BE TROLLOCS.
OH, IT'S TROLLOCS, SHEEPHERDER. AND WHERE THERE ARE TROLLOCS, THERE ARE FADES.
WE WILL HAVE TIME TO SPEAK OF THIS LATER. MAT NEEDS TO BE SEEN TO ***NOW.***

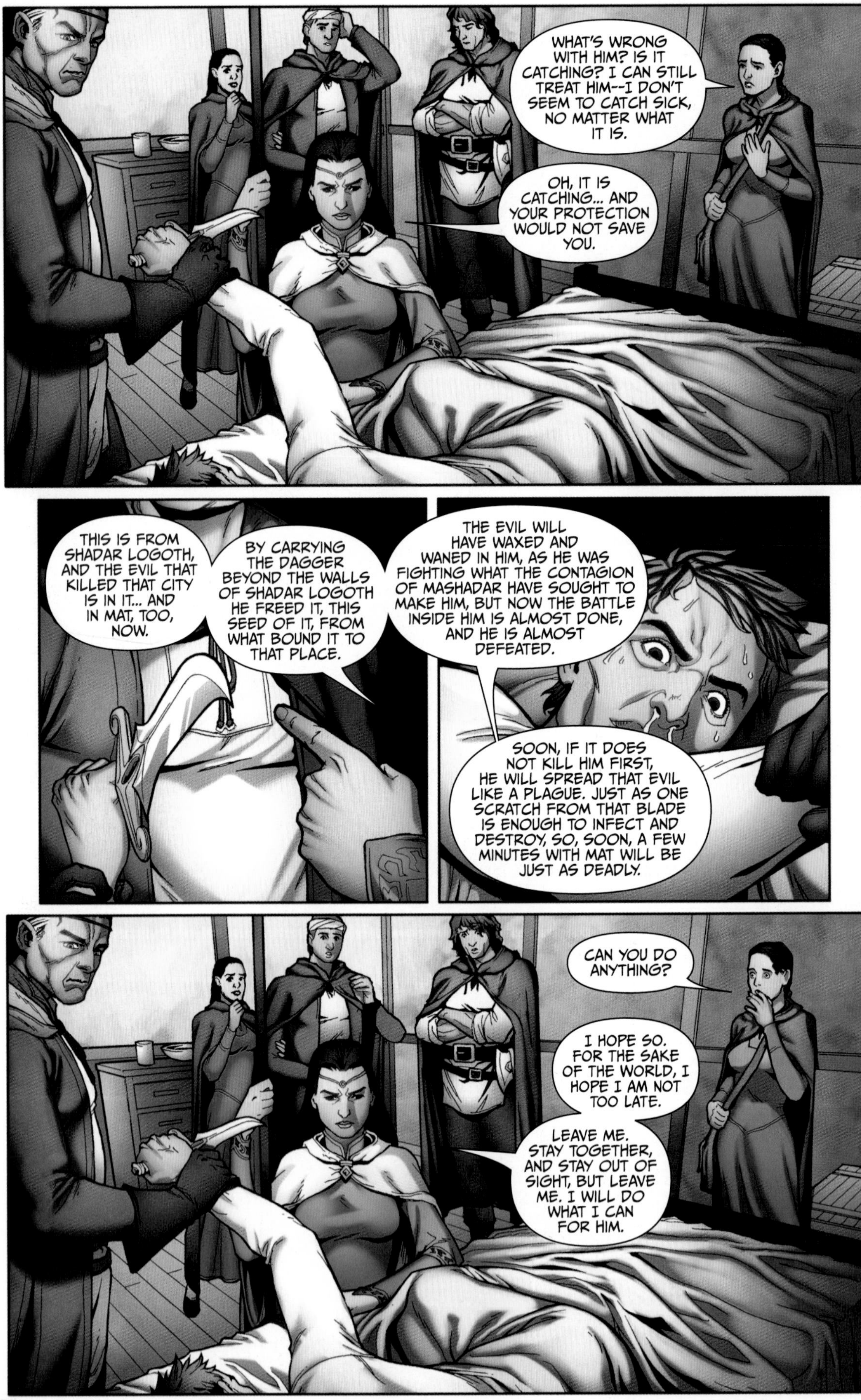
WHAT'S WRONG WITH HIM? IS IT CATCHING? I CAN STILL TREAT HIM--I DON'T SEEM TO CATCH SICK, NO MATTER WHAT IT IS.
OH, IT IS CATCHING... AND YOUR PROTECTION WOULD NOT SAVE YOU.
THIS IS FROM SHADAR LOGOTH, AND THE EVIL THAT KILLED THAT CITY IS IN IT... AND IN MAT, TOO, NOW.
BY CARRYING THE DAGGER BEYOND THE WALLS OF SHADAR LOGOTH HE FREED IT, THIS SEED OF IT, FROM WHAT BOUND IT TO THAT PLACE.
THE EVIL WILL HAVE WAXED AND WANED IN HIM, AS HE WAS FIGHTING WHAT THE CONTAGION OF MASHADAR HAVE SOUGHT TO MAKE HIM, BUT NOW THE BATTLE INSIDE HIM IS ALMOST DONE, AND HE IS ALMOST DEFEATED.
SOON, IF IT DOES NOT KILL HIM FIRST, HE WILL SPREAD THAT EVIL LIKE A PLAGUE. JUST AS ONE SCRATCH FROM THAT BLADE IS ENOUGH TO INFECT AND DESTROY, SO, SOON, A FEW MINUTES WITH MAT WILL BE JUST AS DEADLY.
CAN YOU DO ANYTHING?
I HOPE SO. FOR THE SAKE OF THE WORLD, I HOPE I AM NOT TOO LATE.
LEAVE ME. STAY TOGETHER, AND STAY OUT OF SIGHT, BUT LEAVE ME. I WILL DO WHAT I CAN FOR HIM.

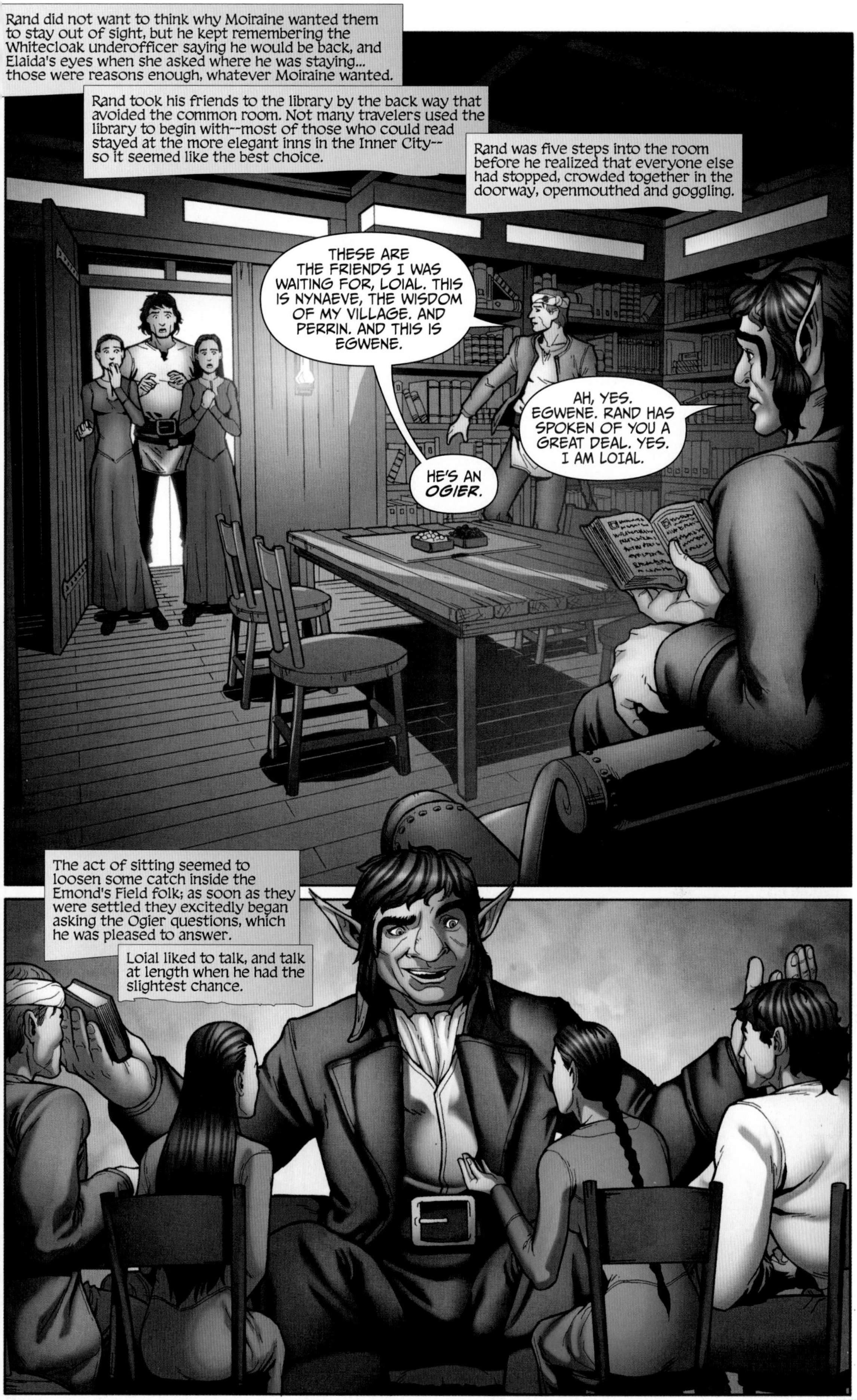
Rand did not want to think why Moiraine wanted them to stay out of sight, but he kept remembering the Whitecloak underofficer saying he would be back, and Elaida's eyes when she asked where he was staying... those were reasons enough, whatever Moiraine wanted.
Rand took his friends to the library by the back way that avoided the common room. Not many travelers used the library to begin with--most of those who could read stayed at the more elegant inns in the Inner City--so it seemed like the best choice.
Rand was five steps into the room before he realized that everyone else had stopped, crowded together in the doorway, openmouthed and goggling.
THESE ARE THE FRIENDS I WAS WAITING FOR, LOIAL. THIS IS NYNAEVE, THE WISDOM OF MY VILLAGE. AND PERRIN. AND THIS IS EGWENE.
HE'S AN *OGIER*.
AH, YES. EGWENE. RAND HAS SPOKEN OF YOU A GREAT DEAL. YES. I AM LOIAL.
The act of sitting seemed to loosen some catch inside the Emond's Field folk; as soon as they were settled they excitedly began asking the Ogier questions, which he was pleased to answer.
Loial liked to talk, and talk at length when he had the slightest chance.

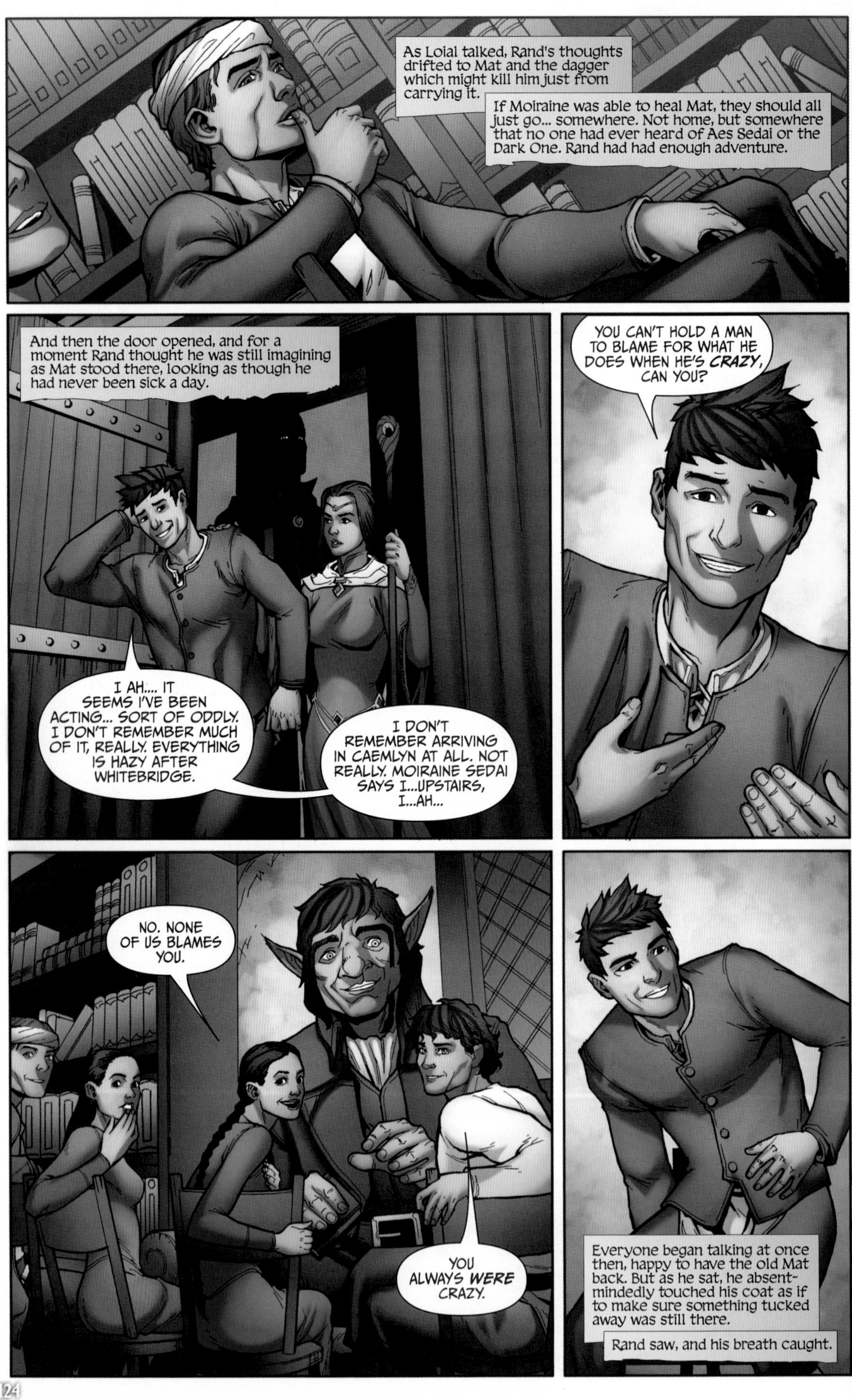
As Loial talked, Rand's thoughts drifted to Mat and the dagger which might kill him just from carrying it.
If Moiraine was able to heal Mat, they should all just go... somewhere. Not home, but somewhere that no one had ever heard of Aes Sedai or the Dark One. Rand had had enough adventure.
And then the door opened, and for a moment Rand thought he was still imagining as Mat stood there, looking as though he had never been sick a day.
I AH.... IT SEEMS I'VE BEEN ACTING... SORT OF ODDLY. I DON'T REMEMBER MUCH OF IT, REALLY. EVERYTHING IS HAZY AFTER WHITEBRIDGE.
I DON'T REMEMBER ARRIVING IN CAEMLYN AT ALL. NOT REALLY. MOIRAINE SEDAI SAYS I...UPSTAIRS, I...AH...
YOU CAN'T HOLD A MAN TO BLAME FOR WHAT HE DOES WHEN HE'S *CRAZY*, CAN YOU?
NO. NONE OF US BLAMES YOU.
YOU ALWAYS ***WERE*** CRAZY.
Everyone began talking at once then, happy to have the old Mat back. But as he sat, he absent-mindedly touched his coat as if to make sure something tucked away was still there.
Rand saw, and his breath caught.

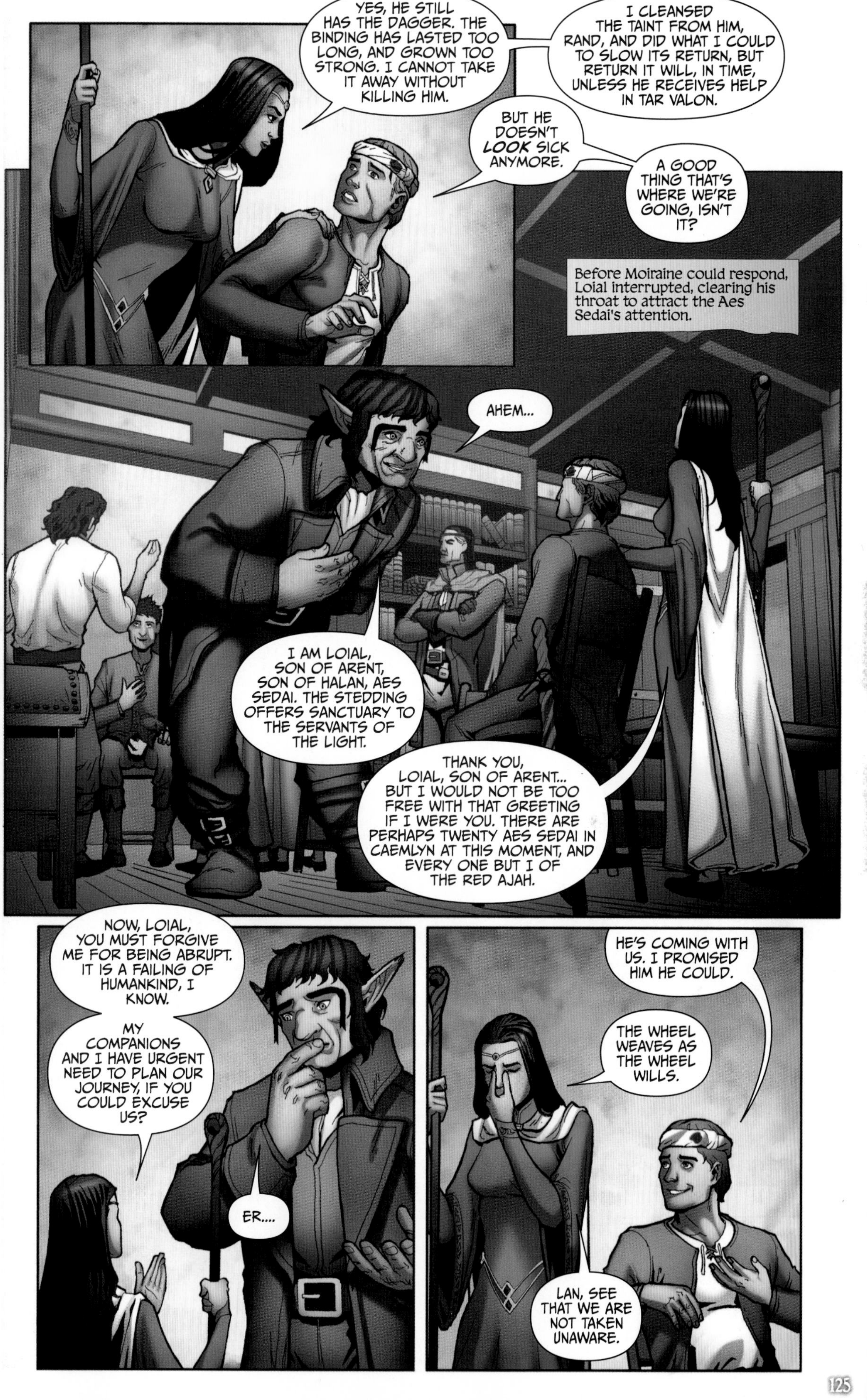
YES, HE STILL HAS THE DAGGER. THE BINDING HAS LASTED TOO LONG, AND GROWN TOO STRONG. I CANNOT TAKE IT AWAY WITHOUT KILLING HIM.
I CLEANSED THE TAINT FROM HIM, RAND, AND DID WHAT I COULD TO SLOW ITS RETURN, BUT RETURN IT WILL, IN TIME, UNLESS HE RECEIVES HELP IN TAR VALON.
BUT HE DOESN'T *LOOK* SICK ANYMORE.
A GOOD THING THAT'S WHERE WE'RE GOING, ISN'T IT?
Before Moiraine could respond, Loial interrupted, clearing his throat to attract the Aes Sedai's attention.
AHEM...
I AM LOIAL, SON OF ARENT, SON OF HALAN, AES SEDAI. THE STEDDING OFFERS SANCTUARY TO THE SERVANTS OF THE LIGHT.
THANK YOU, LOIAL, SON OF ARENT... BUT I WOULD NOT BE TOO FREE WITH THAT GREETING IF I WERE YOU. THERE ARE PERHAPS TWENTY AES SEDAI IN CAEMLYN AT THIS MOMENT, AND EVERY ONE BUT I OF THE RED AJAH.
NOW, LOIAL, YOU MUST FORGIVE ME FOR BEING ABRUPT. IT IS A FAILING OF HUMANKIND, I KNOW.
MY COMPANIONS AND I HAVE URGENT NEED TO PLAN OUR JOURNEY, IF YOU COULD EXCUSE US?
ER....
HE'S COMING WITH US. I PROMISED HIM HE COULD.
THE WHEEL WEAVES AS THE WHEEL WILLS.
LAN, SEE THAT WE ARE NOT TAKEN UNAWARE.

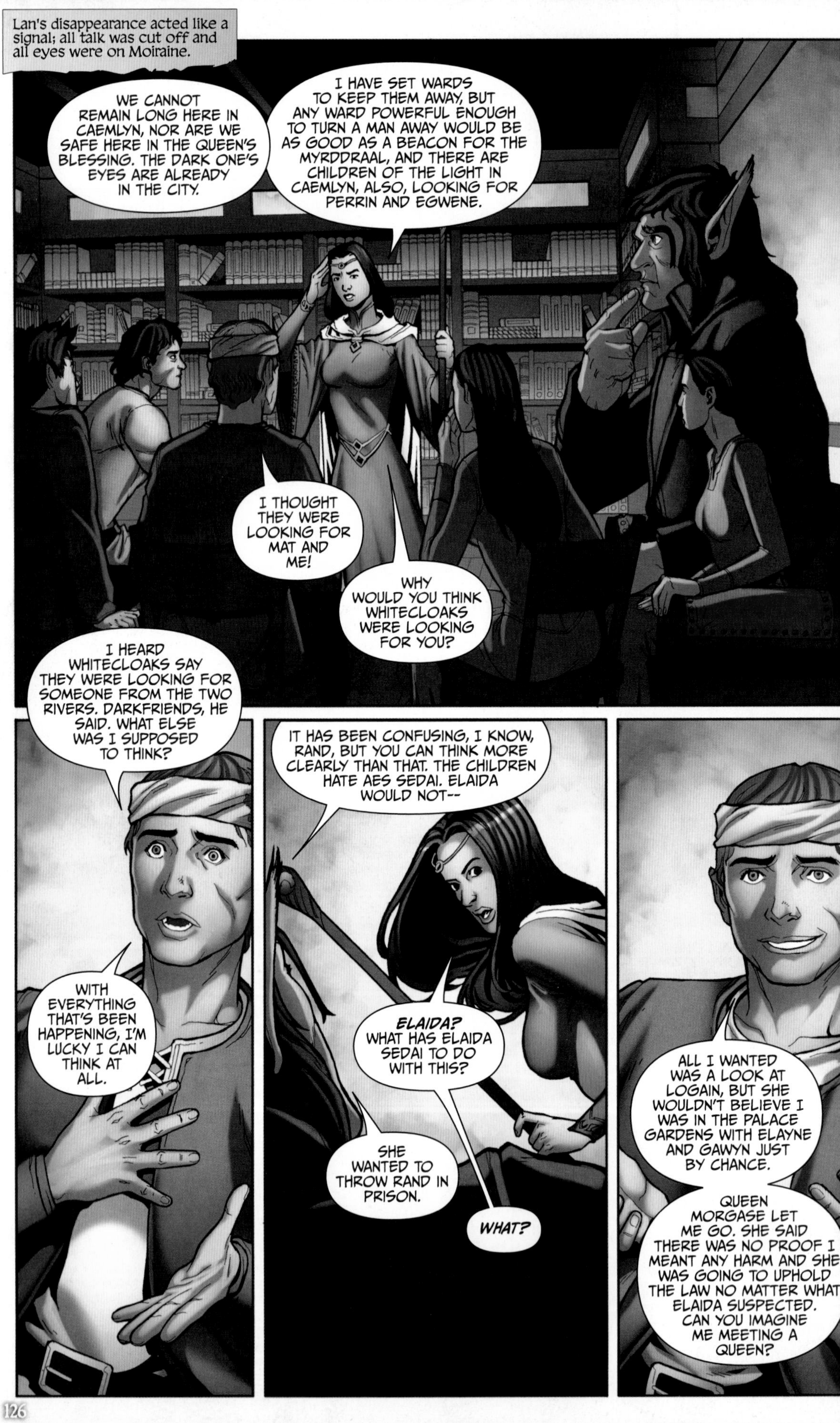

Lan's disappearance acted like a signal; all talk was cut off and all eyes were on Moiraine.
WE CANNOT REMAIN LONG HERE IN CAEMLYN, NOR ARE WE SAFE HERE IN THE QUEEN'S BLESSING. THE DARK ONE'S EYES ARE ALREADY IN THE CITY.
I HAVE SET WARDS TO KEEP THEM AWAY, BUT ANY WARD POWERFUL ENOUGH TO TURN A MAN AWAY WOULD BE AS GOOD AS A BEACON FOR THE MYRDDRAAL, AND THERE ARE CHILDREN OF THE LIGHT IN CAEMLYN, ALSO, LOOKING FOR PERRIN AND EGWENE.
I THOUGHT THEY WERE LOOKING FOR MAT AND ME!
WHY WOULD YOU THINK WHITECLOAKS WERE LOOKING FOR YOU?
I HEARD WHITECLOAKS SAY THEY WERE LOOKING FOR SOMEONE FROM THE TWO RIVERS. DARKFRIENDS, HE SAID. WHAT ELSE WAS I SUPPOSED TO THINK?
WITH EVERYTHING THAT'S BEEN HAPPENING, I'M LUCKY I CAN THINK AT ALL.
IT HAS BEEN CONFUSING, I KNOW, RAND, BUT YOU CAN THINK MORE CLEARLY THAN THAT. THE CHILDREN HATE AES SEDAI. ELAIDA WOULD NOT--
ELAIDA? WHAT HAS ELAIDA SEDAI TO DO WITH THIS?
SHE WANTED TO THROW RAND IN PRISON.
WHAT?
ALL I WANTED WAS A LOOK AT LOGAIN, BUT SHE WOULDN'T BELIEVE I WAS IN THE PALACE GARDENS WITH ELAYNE AND GAWYN JUST BY CHANCE.
QUEEN MORGASE LET ME GO. SHE SAID THERE WAS NO PROOF I MEANT ANY HARM AND SHE WAS GOING TO UPHOLD THE LAW NO MATTER WHAT ELAIDA SUSPECTED. CAN YOU IMAGINE ME MEETING A QUEEN?

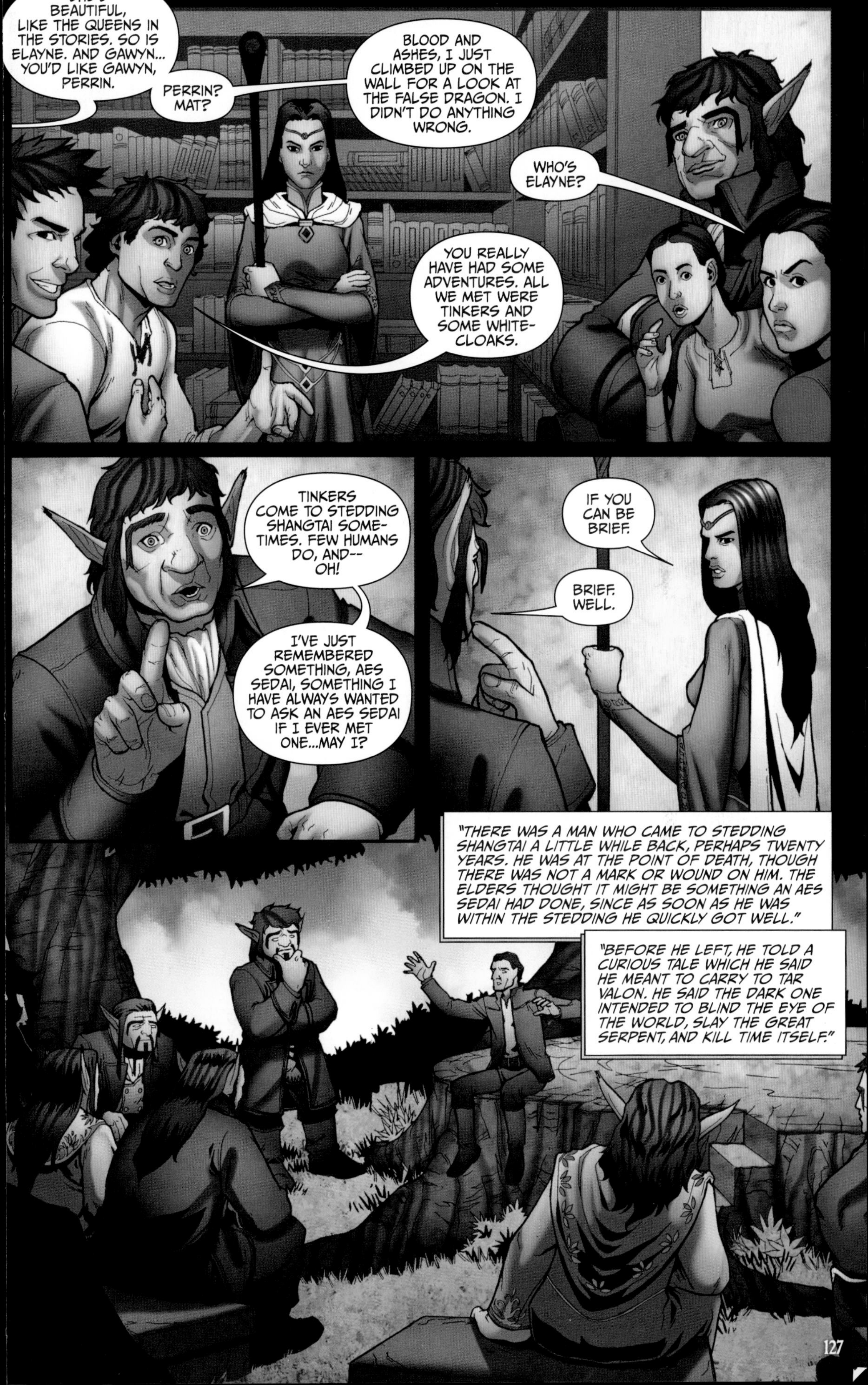
SHE'S BEAUTIFUL, LIKE THE QUEENS IN THE STORIES. SO IS ELAYNE. AND GAWYN... YOU'D LIKE GAWYN, PERRIN.
PERRIN? MAT?
BLOOD AND ASHES, I JUST CLIMBED UP ON THE WALL FOR A LOOK AT THE FALSE DRAGON. I DIDN'T DO ANYTHING WRONG.
WHO'S ELAYNE?
YOU REALLY HAVE HAD SOME ADVENTURES. ALL WE MET WERE TINKERS AND SOME WHITE-CLOAKS.
TINKERS COME TO STEDDING SHANGTAI SOME-TIMES. FEW HUMANS DO, AND-- OH!
I'VE JUST REMEMBERED SOMETHING, AES SEDAI, SOMETHING I HAVE ALWAYS WANTED TO ASK AN AES SEDAI IF I EVER MET ONE...MAY I?
IF YOU CAN BE BRIEF.
BRIEF. WELL.
"THERE WAS A MAN WHO CAME TO STEDDING SHANGTAI A LITTLE WHILE BACK, PERHAPS TWENTY YEARS. HE WAS AT THE POINT OF DEATH, THOUGH THERE WAS NOT A MARK OR WOUND ON HIM. THE ELDERS THOUGHT IT MIGHT BE SOMETHING AN AES SEDAI HAD DONE, SINCE AS SOON AS HE WAS WITHIN THE STEDDING HE QUICKLY GOT WELL."
"BEFORE HE LEFT, HE TOLD A CURIOUS TALE WHICH HE SAID HE MEANT TO CARRY TO TAR VALON. HE SAID THE DARK ONE INTENDED TO BLIND THE EYE OF THE WORLD, SLAY THE GREAT SERPENT, AND KILL TIME ITSELF."

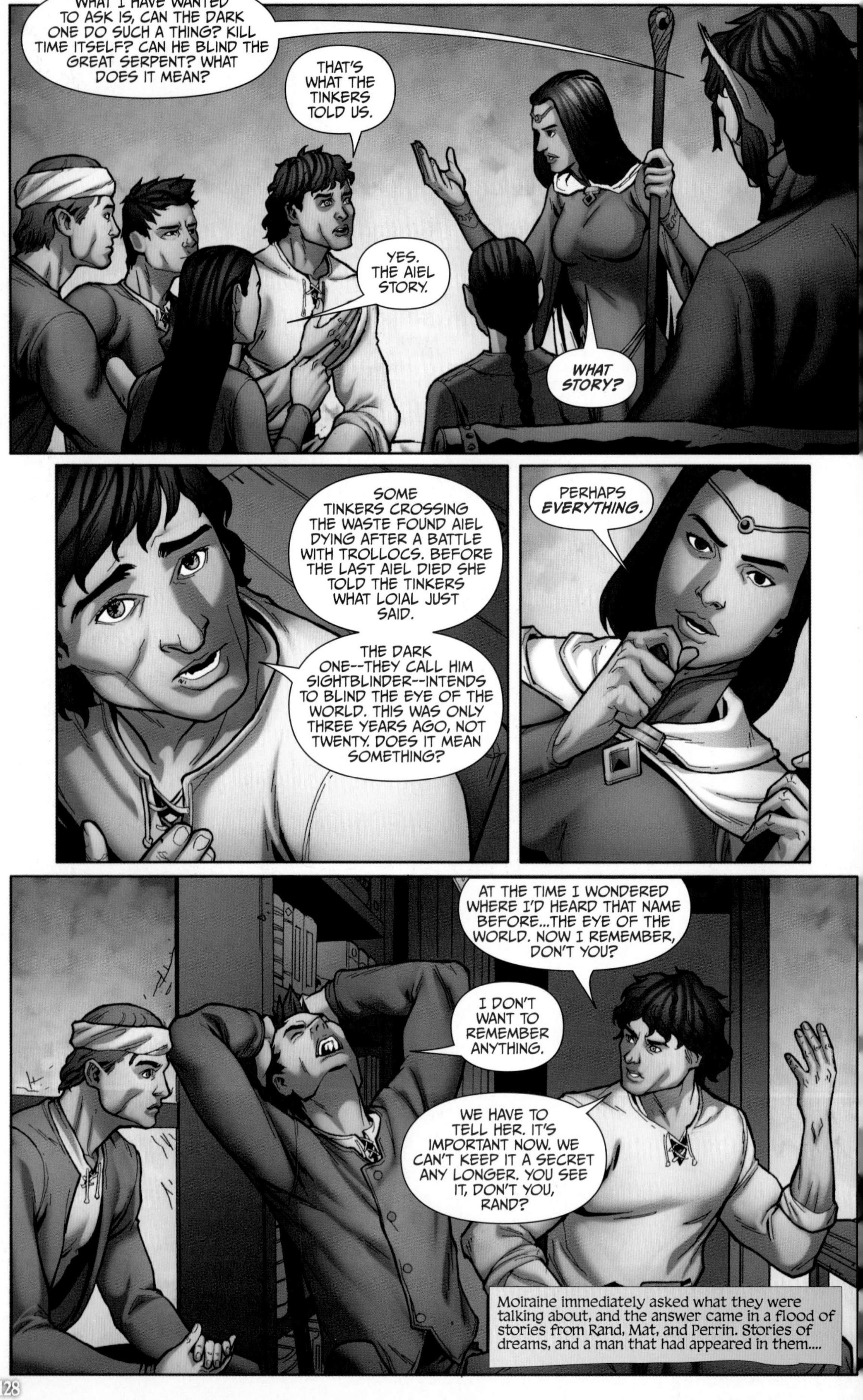
WHAT I HAVE WANTED TO ASK IS, CAN THE DARK ONE DO SUCH A THING? KILL TIME ITSELF? CAN HE BLIND THE GREAT SERPENT? WHAT DOES IT MEAN?
THAT'S WHAT THE TINKERS TOLD US.
YES. THE AIEL STORY.
WHAT STORY?
SOME TINKERS CROSSING THE WASTE FOUND AIEL DYING AFTER A BATTLE WITH TROLLOCS. BEFORE THE LAST AIEL DIED SHE TOLD THE TINKERS WHAT LOIAL JUST SAID.
THE DARK ONE--THEY CALL HIM SIGHTBLINDER--INTENDS TO BLIND THE EYE OF THE WORLD. THIS WAS ONLY THREE YEARS AGO, NOT TWENTY. DOES IT MEAN SOMETHING?
PERHAPS EVERYTHING.
AT THE TIME I WONDERED WHERE I'D HEARD THAT NAME BEFORE...THE EYE OF THE WORLD. NOW I REMEMBER, DON'T YOU?
I DON'T WANT TO REMEMBER ANYTHING.
WE HAVE TO TELL HER. IT'S IMPORTANT NOW. WE CAN'T KEEP IT A SECRET ANY LONGER. YOU SEE IT, DON'T YOU, RAND?
Moiraine immediately asked what they were talking about, and the answer came in a flood of stories from Rand, Mat, and Perrin. Stories of dreams, and a man that had appeared in them....

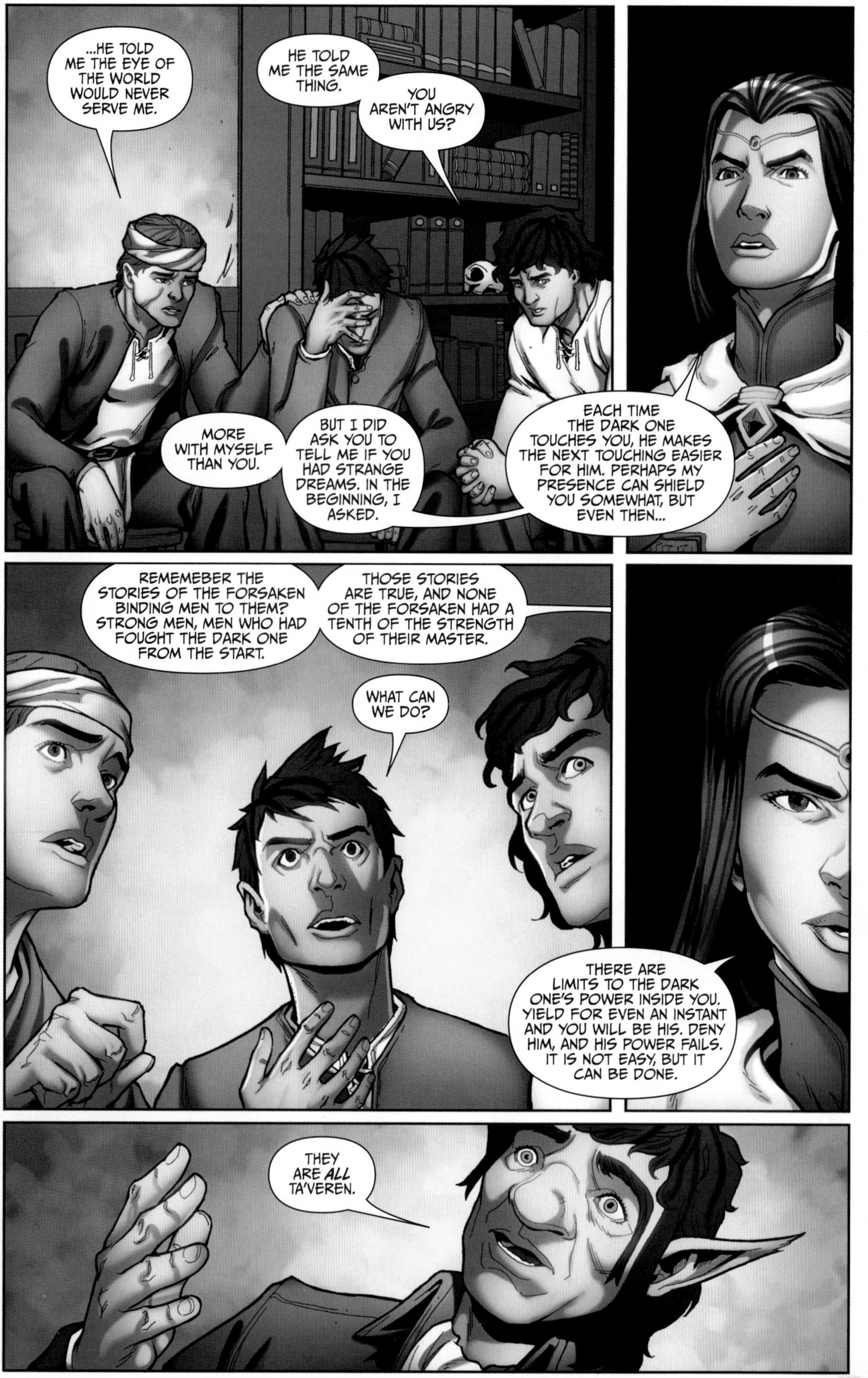

...HE TOLD ME THE EYE OF THE WORLD WOULD NEVER SERVE ME.
HE TOLD ME THE SAME THING.
YOU AREN'T ANGRY WITH US?
MORE WITH MYSELF THAN YOU.
BUT I DID ASK YOU TO TELL ME IF YOU HAD STRANGE DREAMS. IN THE BEGINNING, I ASKED.
EACH TIME THE DARK ONE TOUCHES YOU, HE MAKES THE NEXT TOUCHING EASIER FOR HIM. PERHAPS MY PRESENCE CAN SHIELD YOU SOMEWHAT, BUT EVEN THEN...
REMEMEBER THE STORIES OF THE FORSAKEN BINDING MEN TO THEM? STRONG MEN, MEN WHO HAD FOUGHT THE DARK ONE FROM THE START.
THOSE STORIES ARE TRUE, AND NONE OF THE FORSAKEN HAD A TENTH OF THE STRENGTH OF THEIR MASTER.
WHAT CAN WE DO?
THERE ARE LIMITS TO THE DARK ONE'S POWER INSIDE YOU. YIELD FOR EVEN AN INSTANT AND YOU WILL BE HIS. DENY HIM, AND HIS POWER FAILS. IT IS NOT EASY, BUT IT CAN BE DONE.
THEY ARE *ALL* TA'VEREN.

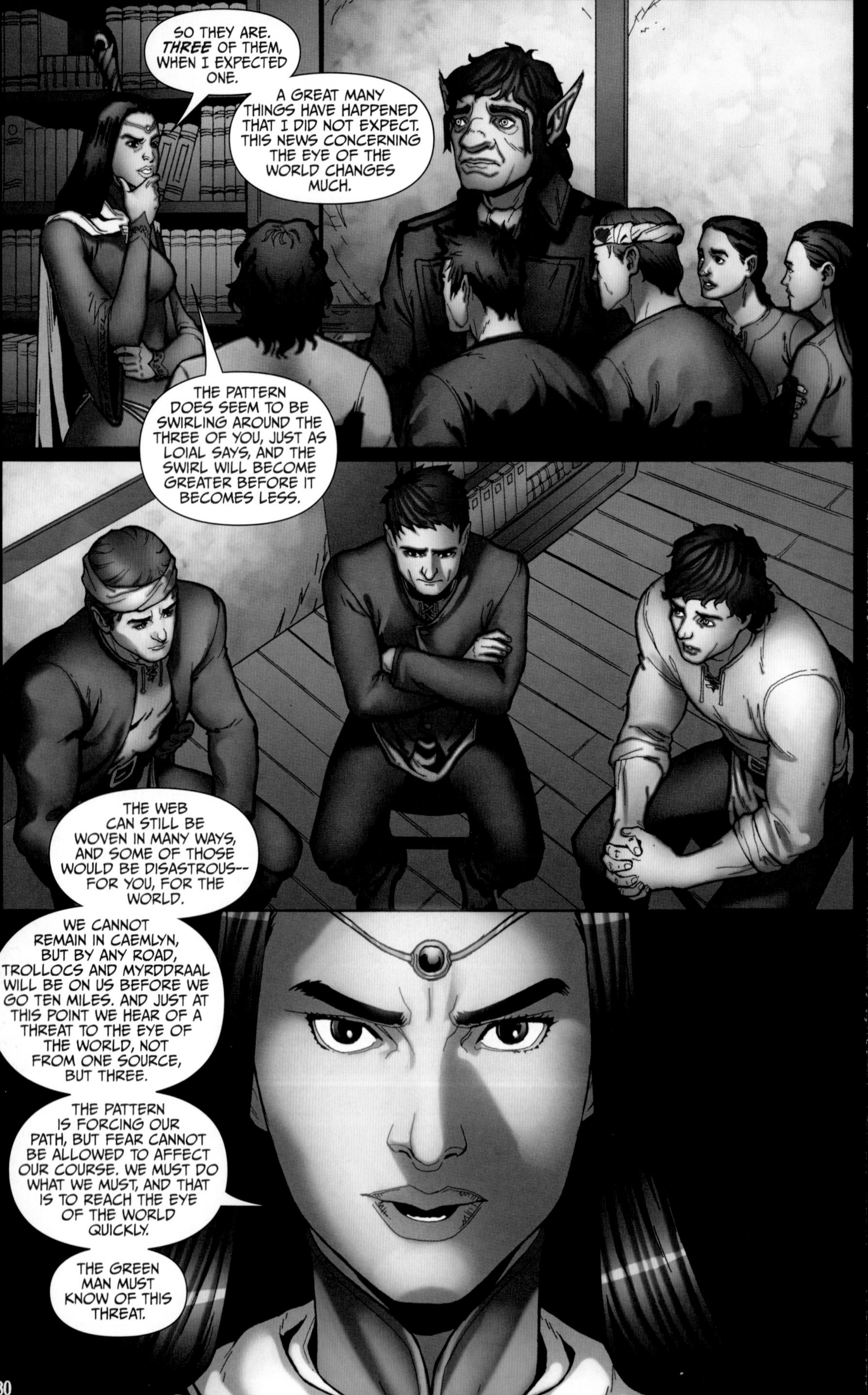
SO THEY ARE. *THREE* OF THEM, WHEN I EXPECTED ONE.
A GREAT MANY THINGS HAVE HAPPENED THAT I DID NOT EXPECT. THIS NEWS CONCERNING THE EYE OF THE WORLD CHANGES MUCH.
THE PATTERN DOES SEEM TO BE SWIRLING AROUND THE THREE OF YOU, JUST AS LOIAL SAYS, AND THE SWIRL WILL BECOME GREATER BEFORE IT BECOMES LESS.
THE WEB CAN STILL BE WOVEN IN MANY WAYS, AND SOME OF THOSE WOULD BE DISASTROUS-- FOR YOU, FOR THE WORLD.
WE CANNOT REMAIN IN CAEMLYN, BUT BY ANY ROAD, TROLLOCS AND MYRDDRAAL WILL BE ON US BEFORE WE GO TEN MILES. AND JUST AT THIS POINT WE HEAR OF A THREAT TO THE EYE OF THE WORLD, NOT FROM ONE SOURCE, BUT THREE.
THE PATTERN IS FORCING OUR PATH, BUT FEAR CANNOT BE ALLOWED TO AFFECT OUR COURSE. WE MUST DO WHAT WE MUST, AND THAT IS TO REACH THE EYE OF THE WORLD QUICKLY.
THE GREEN MAN MUST KNOW OF THIS THREAT.

chapter six

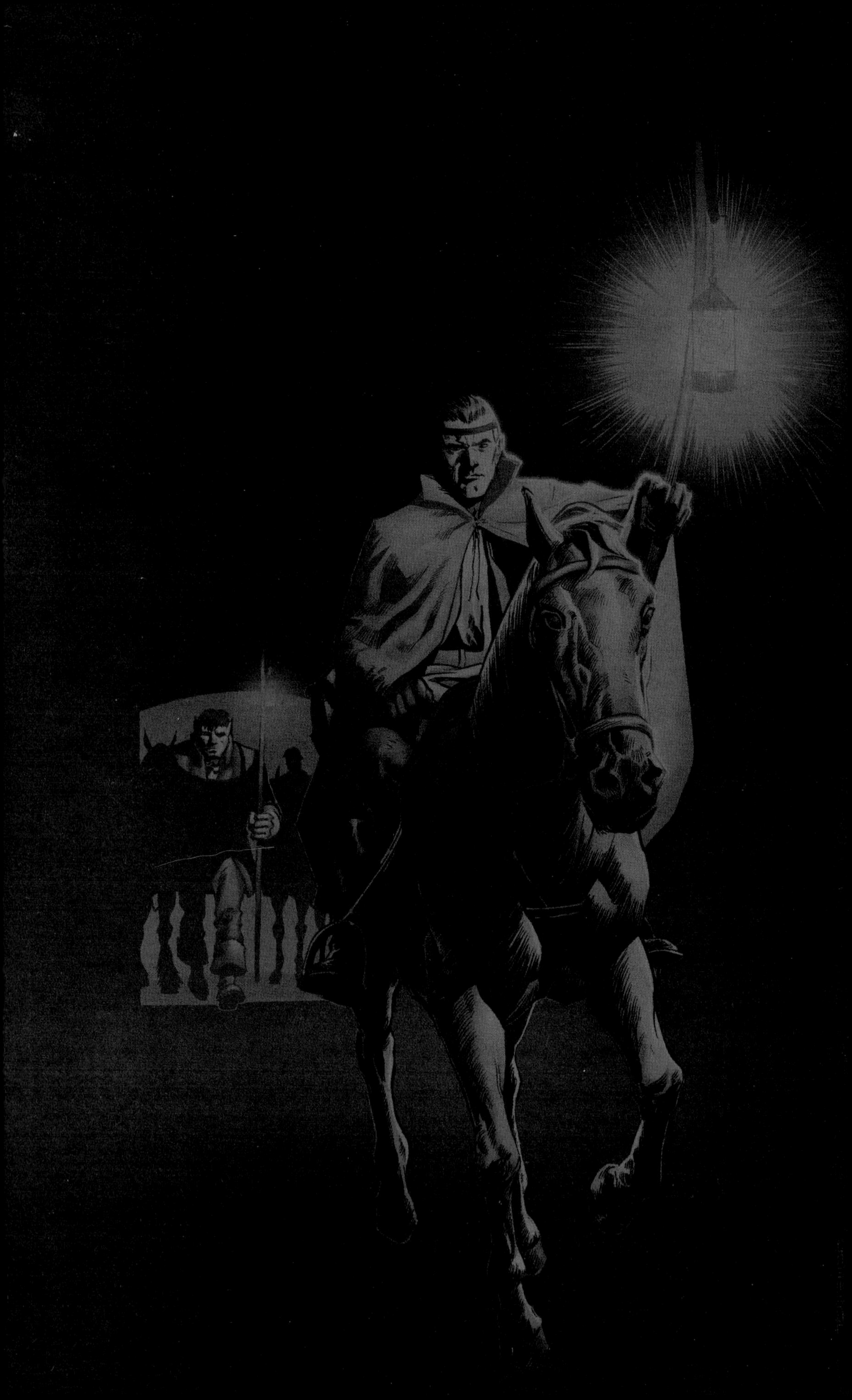

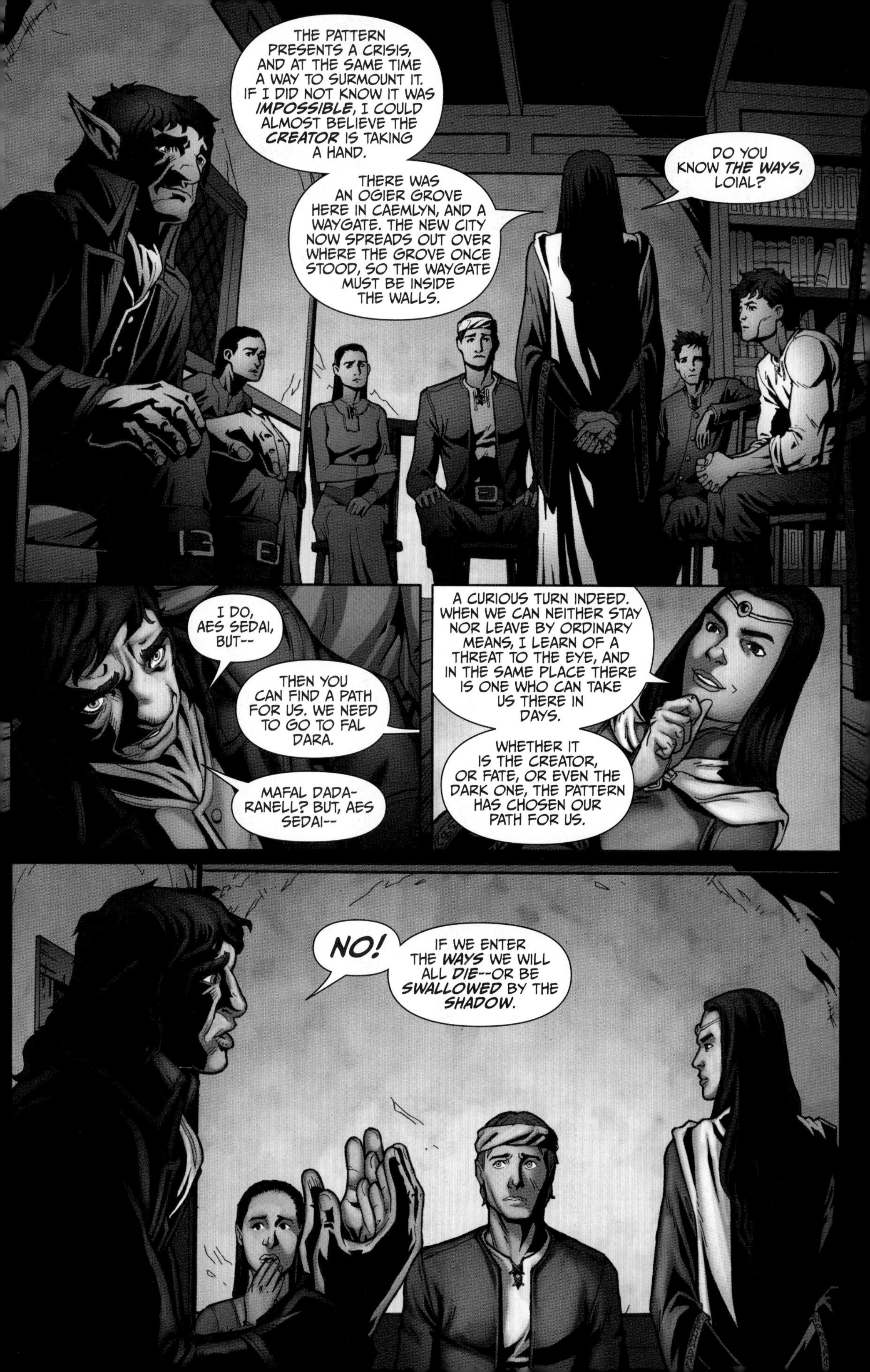
THE PATTERN PRESENTS A CRISIS, AND AT THE SAME TIME A WAY TO SURMOUNT IT. IF I DID NOT KNOW IT WAS *IMPOSSIBLE*, I COULD ALMOST BELIEVE THE *CREATOR* IS TAKING A HAND.
THERE WAS AN OGIER GROVE HERE IN CAEMLYN, AND A WAYGATE. THE NEW CITY NOW SPREADS OUT OVER WHERE THE GROVE ONCE STOOD, SO THE WAYGATE MUST BE INSIDE THE WALLS.
DO YOU KNOW *THE WAYS*, LOIAL?
I DO, AES SEDAI, BUT--
THEN YOU CAN FIND A PATH FOR US. WE NEED TO GO TO FAL DARA.
MAFAL DADARANELL? BUT, AES SEDAI--
A CURIOUS TURN INDEED. WHEN WE CAN NEITHER STAY NOR LEAVE BY ORDINARY MEANS, I LEARN OF A THREAT TO THE EYE, AND IN THE SAME PLACE THERE IS ONE WHO CAN TAKE US THERE IN DAYS.
WHETHER IT IS THE CREATOR, OR FATE, OR EVEN THE DARK ONE, THE PATTERN HAS CHOSEN OUR PATH FOR US.
NO!
IF WE ENTER THE *WAYS* WE WILL ALL *DIE*--OR BE *SWALLOWED* BY THE *SHADOW*.

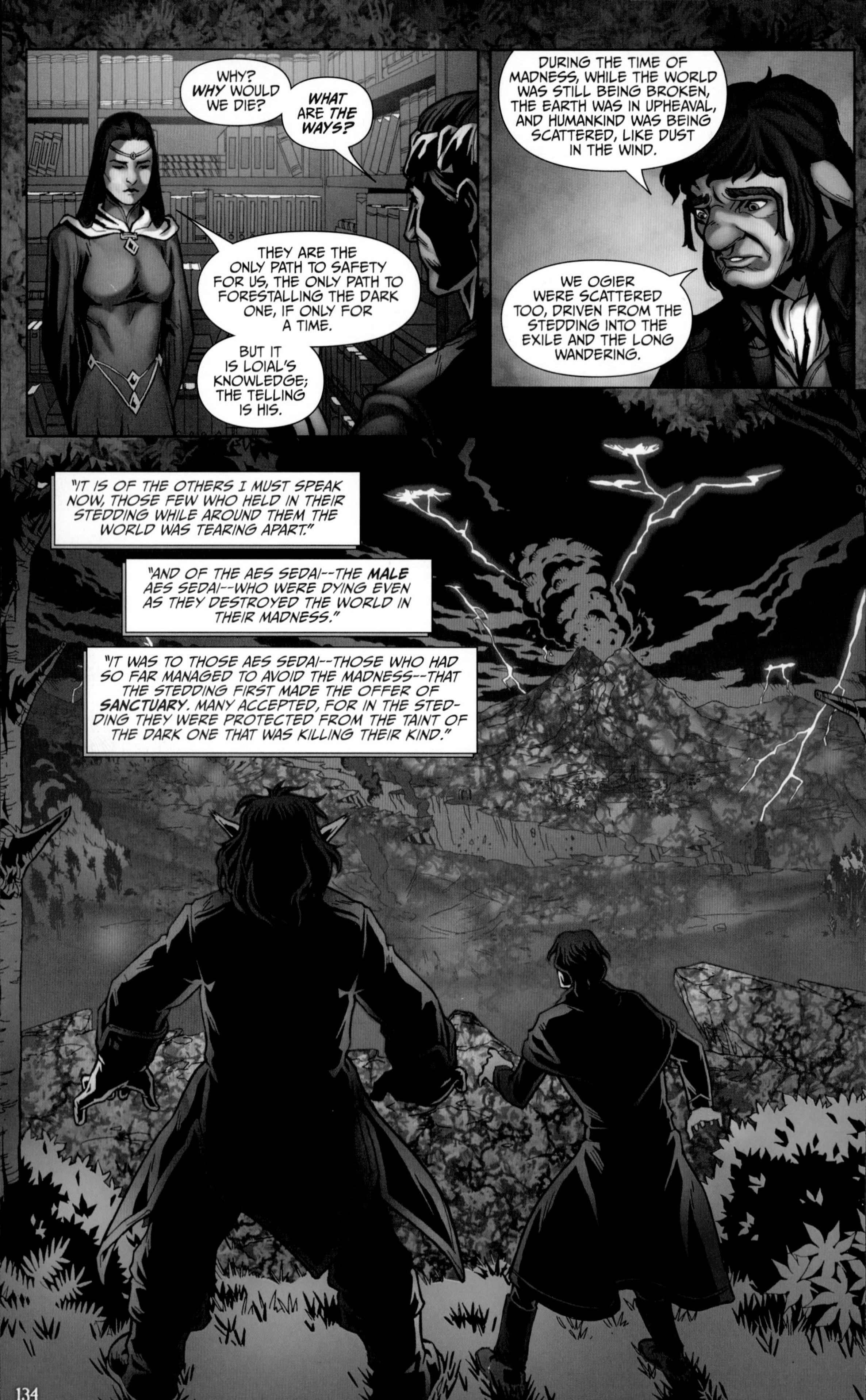
WHY? WHY WOULD WE DIE?
WHAT ARE THE WAYS?
THEY ARE THE ONLY PATH TO SAFETY FOR US, THE ONLY PATH TO FORESTALLING THE DARK ONE, IF ONLY FOR A TIME.
BUT IT IS LOIAL'S KNOWLEDGE; THE TELLING IS HIS.
DURING THE TIME OF MADNESS, WHILE THE WORLD WAS STILL BEING BROKEN, THE EARTH WAS IN UPHEAVAL, AND HUMANKIND WAS BEING SCATTERED, LIKE DUST IN THE WIND.
WE OGIER WERE SCATTERED TOO, DRIVEN FROM THE STEDDING INTO THE EXILE AND THE LONG WANDERING.
"IT IS OF THE OTHERS I MUST SPEAK NOW, THOSE FEW WHO HELD IN THEIR STEDDING WHILE AROUND THEM THE WORLD WAS TEARING APART."
"AND OF THE AES SEDAI--THE MALE AES SEDAI--WHO WERE DYING EVEN AS THEY DESTROYED THE WORLD IN THEIR MADNESS."
"IT WAS TO THOSE AES SEDAI--THOSE WHO HAD SO FAR MANAGED TO AVOID THE MADNESS--THAT THE STEDDING FIRST MADE THE OFFER OF SANCTUARY. MANY ACCEPTED, FOR IN THE STEDDING THEY WERE PROTECTED FROM THE TAINT OF THE DARK ONE THAT WAS KILLING THEIR KIND."

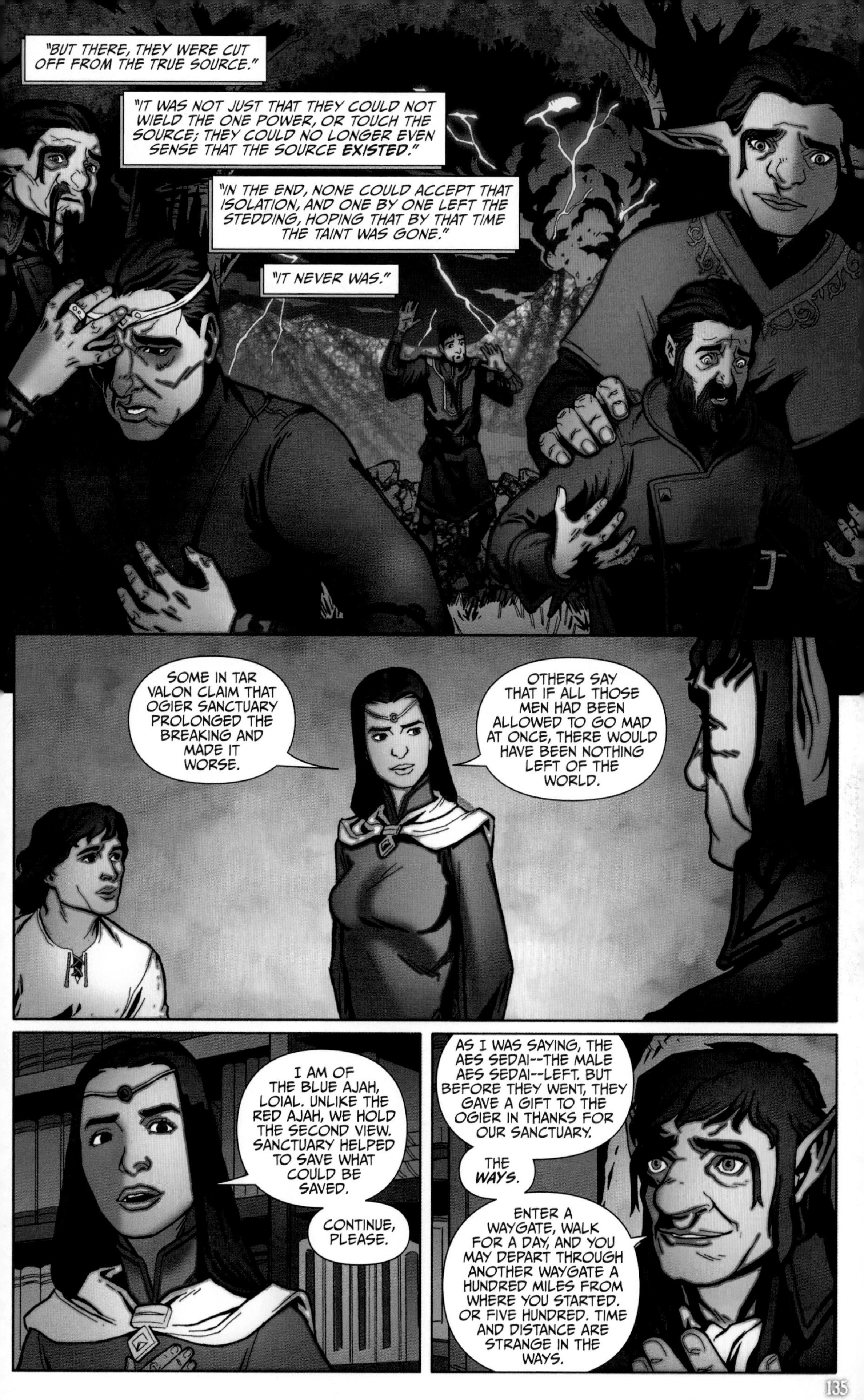

"BUT THERE, THEY WERE CUT OFF FROM THE TRUE SOURCE."
"IT WAS NOT JUST THAT THEY COULD NOT WIELD THE ONE POWER, OR TOUCH THE SOURCE; THEY COULD NO LONGER EVEN SENSE THAT THE SOURCE **EXISTED**."
"IN THE END, NONE COULD ACCEPT THAT ISOLATION, AND ONE BY ONE LEFT THE STEDDING, HOPING THAT BY THAT TIME THE TAINT WAS GONE."
"IT NEVER WAS."
SOME IN TAR VALON CLAIM THAT OGIER SANCTUARY PROLONGED THE BREAKING AND MADE IT WORSE.
OTHERS SAY THAT IF ALL THOSE MEN HAD BEEN ALLOWED TO GO MAD AT ONCE, THERE WOULD HAVE BEEN NOTHING LEFT OF THE WORLD.
I AM OF THE BLUE AJAH, LOIAL. UNLIKE THE RED AJAH, WE HOLD THE SECOND VIEW. SANCTUARY HELPED TO SAVE WHAT COULD BE SAVED.
CONTINUE, PLEASE.
AS I WAS SAYING, THE AES SEDAI--THE MALE AES SEDAI--LEFT. BUT BEFORE THEY WENT, THEY GAVE A GIFT TO THE OGIER IN THANKS FOR OUR SANCTUARY.
THE *WAYS*.
ENTER A WAYGATE, WALK FOR A DAY, AND YOU MAY DEPART THROUGH ANOTHER WAYGATE A HUNDRED MILES FROM WHERE YOU STARTED. OR FIVE HUNDRED. TIME AND DISTANCE ARE STRANGE IN THE WAYS.

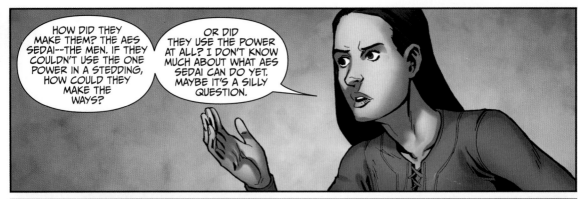

HOW DID THEY MAKE THEM? THE AES SEDAI--THE MEN. IF THEY COULDN'T USE THE ONE POWER IN A STEDDING, HOW COULD THEY MAKE THE WAYS?

OR DID THEY USE THE POWER AT ALL? I DON'T KNOW MUCH ABOUT WHAT AES SEDAI CAN DO YET. MAYBE IT'S A SILLY QUESTION.

EACH STEDDING HAS A WAYGATE ON ITS BORDER, BUT OUTSIDE. YOUR QUESTION IS NOT SILLY.

YOU'VE FOUND THE SEED OF WHY WE *DARE NOT* TRAVEL THE WAYS. THEY WERE MADE BY MEN WIELDING POWER FOULED BY THE DARK ONE.

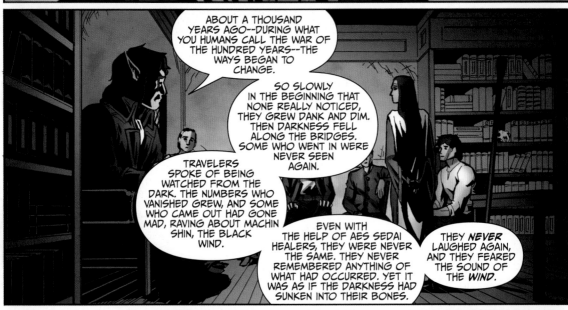

ABOUT A THOUSAND YEARS AGO--DURING WHAT YOU HUMANS CALL THE WAR OF THE HUNDRED YEARS--THE WAYS BEGAN TO CHANGE.

SO SLOWLY IN THE BEGINNING THAT NONE REALLY NOTICED, THEY GREW DANK AND DIM. THEN DARKNESS FELL ALONG THE BRIDGES. SOME WHO WENT IN WERE NEVER SEEN AGAIN.

TRAVELERS SPOKE OF BEING WATCHED FROM THE DARK. THE NUMBERS WHO VANISHED GREW, AND SOME WHO CAME OUT HAD GONE MAD, RAVING ABOUT MACHIN SHIN, THE BLACK WIND.

EVEN WITH THE HELP OF AES SEDAI HEALERS, THEY WERE NEVER THE SAME. THEY NEVER REMEMBERED ANYTHING OF WHAT HAD OCCURRED. YET IT WAS AS IF THE DARKNESS HAD SUNKEN INTO THEIR BONES.

THEY *NEVER* LAUGHED AGAIN, AND THEY FEARED THE SOUND OF THE *WIND*.

AND YOU EXPECT US TO FOLLOW YOU INTO THAT? YOU MUST BE MAD!

WHICH WOULD YOU CHOOSE INSTEAD? THE WHITECLOAKS WITHIN CAEMLYN, OR THE TROLLOCS WITHOUT?

REMEMBER THAT MY PRESENCE IN ITSELF GIVES *SOME* PROTECTION FROM THE DARK ONE'S WORKS.

BY EDICT OF THE ELDERS, ALL THE ELDERS OF ALL THE STEDDING, NONE MAY, HUMAN OR OGIER, USE THE WAYS.

YOU HAVE NOT EXPLAINED TO ME WHY I SHOULD BREAK THE EDICT OF THE ELDERS. AND I HAVE NO DESIRE TO ENTER THE WAYS.

HUMANKIND AND OGIER--EVERYTHING THAT LIVES--WE ARE AT WAR WITH THE DARK ONE. THE GREATER PART OF THE WORLD DOES NOT EVEN KNOW IT YET, AND MOST OF THE FEW WHO DO FIGHT SKIRMISHES AND BELIEVE THEY ARE BATTLES.

WHAT CAN WE DO? WHY ARE WE SO IMPORTANT? WHY DO WE HAVE TO GO?

ONE THING WE CAN DO. WE CAN TRY. WHAT SEEMS LIKE CHANCE IS OFTEN THE PATTERN.

THREE THREADS HAVE COME TOGETHER HERE, EACH GIVING A WARNING: THE EYE. IT CANNOT BE CHANCE. IT IS THE PATTERN.

WHILE THE WORLD REFUSES TO BELIEVE, THE DARK ONE MAY BE AT THE BRINK OF VICTORY. THERE IS ENOUGH POWER IN THE EYE OF THE WORLD TO UNDO HIS PRISON. IF THE DARK ONE HAS FOUND SOME WAY TO BEND THE EYE OF THE WORLD TO HIS USE...

YOU DID NOT CHOOSE, YOU WERE CHOSEN. YOU ARE HERE, WHERE THE DANGER IS KNOWN. YOU CAN STEP ASIDE, AND PERHAPS DOOM THE WORLD.

RUNNING AND HIDING WILL NOT SAVE YOU FROM THE WEAVING OF THE PATTERN.

OR, YOU CAN *TRY*.

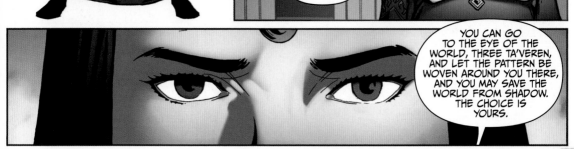

YOU CAN GO TO THE EYE OF THE WORLD, THREE TA'VEREN, AND LET THE PATTERN BE WOVEN AROUND YOU THERE, AND YOU MAY SAVE THE WORLD FROM SHADOW. THE CHOICE IS YOURS.

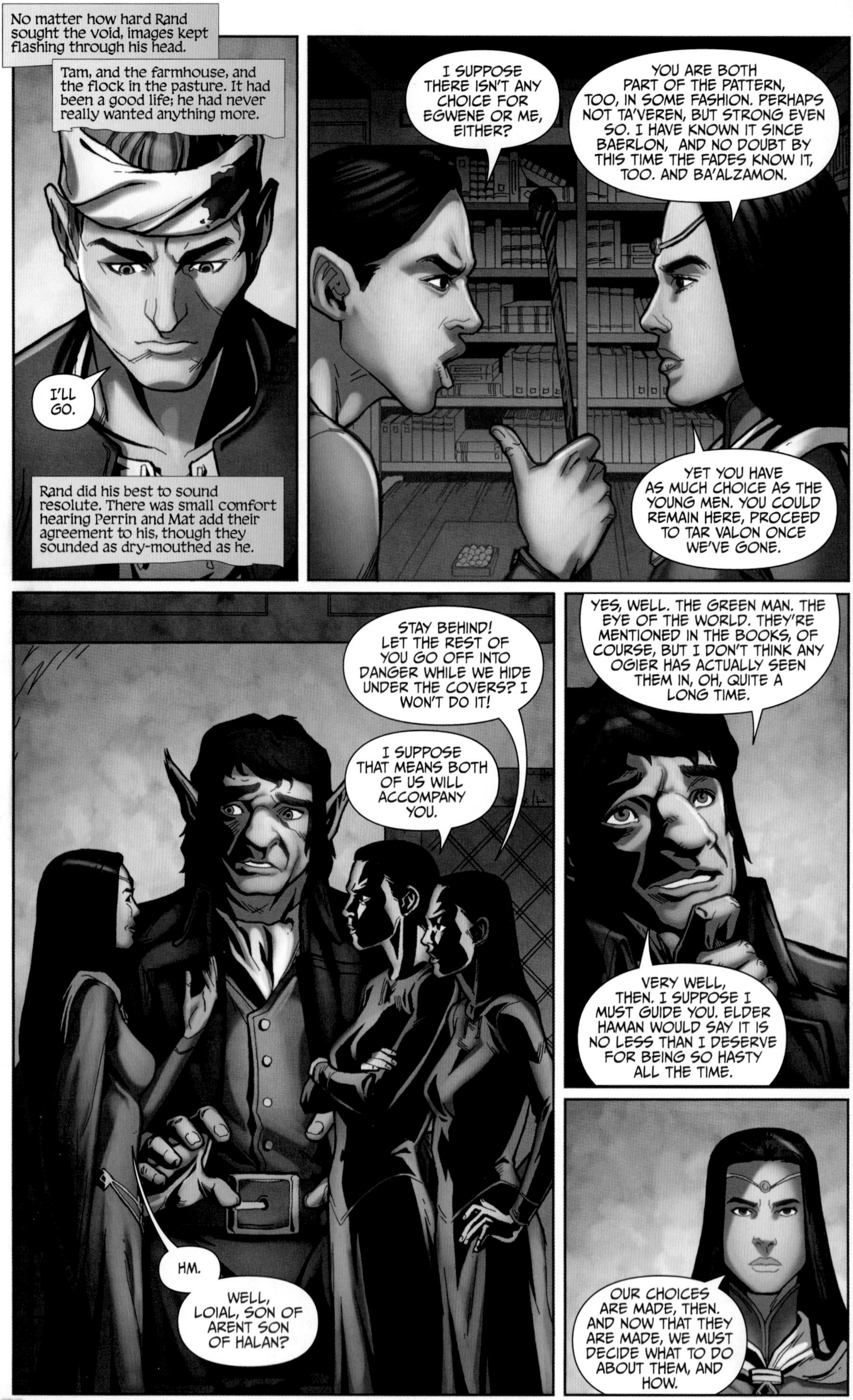

No matter how hard Rand sought the void, images kept flashing through his head.
Tam, and the farmhouse, and the flock in the pasture. It had been a good life; he had never really wanted anything more.
I'LL GO.
Rand did his best to sound resolute. There was small comfort hearing Perrin and Mat add their agreement to his, though they sounded as dry-mouthed as he.
I SUPPOSE THERE ISN'T ANY CHOICE FOR EGWENE OR ME, EITHER?
YOU ARE BOTH PART OF THE PATTERN, TOO, IN SOME FASHION. PERHAPS NOT TA'VEREN, BUT STRONG EVEN SO. I HAVE KNOWN IT SINCE BAERLON, AND NO DOUBT BY THIS TIME THE FADES KNOW IT, TOO. AND BA'ALZAMON.
YET YOU HAVE AS MUCH CHOICE AS THE YOUNG MEN. YOU COULD REMAIN HERE, PROCEED TO TAR VALON ONCE WE'VE GONE.
STAY BEHIND! LET THE REST OF YOU GO OFF INTO DANGER WHILE WE HIDE UNDER THE COVERS? I WON'T DO IT!
I SUPPOSE THAT MEANS BOTH OF US WILL ACCOMPANY YOU.
HM.
WELL, LOIAL, SON OF ARENT SON OF HALAN?
YES, WELL. THE GREEN MAN. THE EYE OF THE WORLD. THEY'RE MENTIONED IN THE BOOKS, OF COURSE, BUT I DON'T THINK ANY OGIER HAS ACTUALLY SEEN THEM IN, OH, QUITE A LONG TIME.
VERY WELL, THEN. I SUPPOSE I MUST GUIDE YOU. ELDER HAMAN WOULD SAY IT IS NO LESS THAN I DESERVE FOR BEING SO HASTY ALL THE TIME.
OUR CHOICES ARE MADE, THEN. AND NOW THAT THEY ARE MADE, WE MUST DECIDE WHAT TO DO ABOUT THEM, AND HOW.

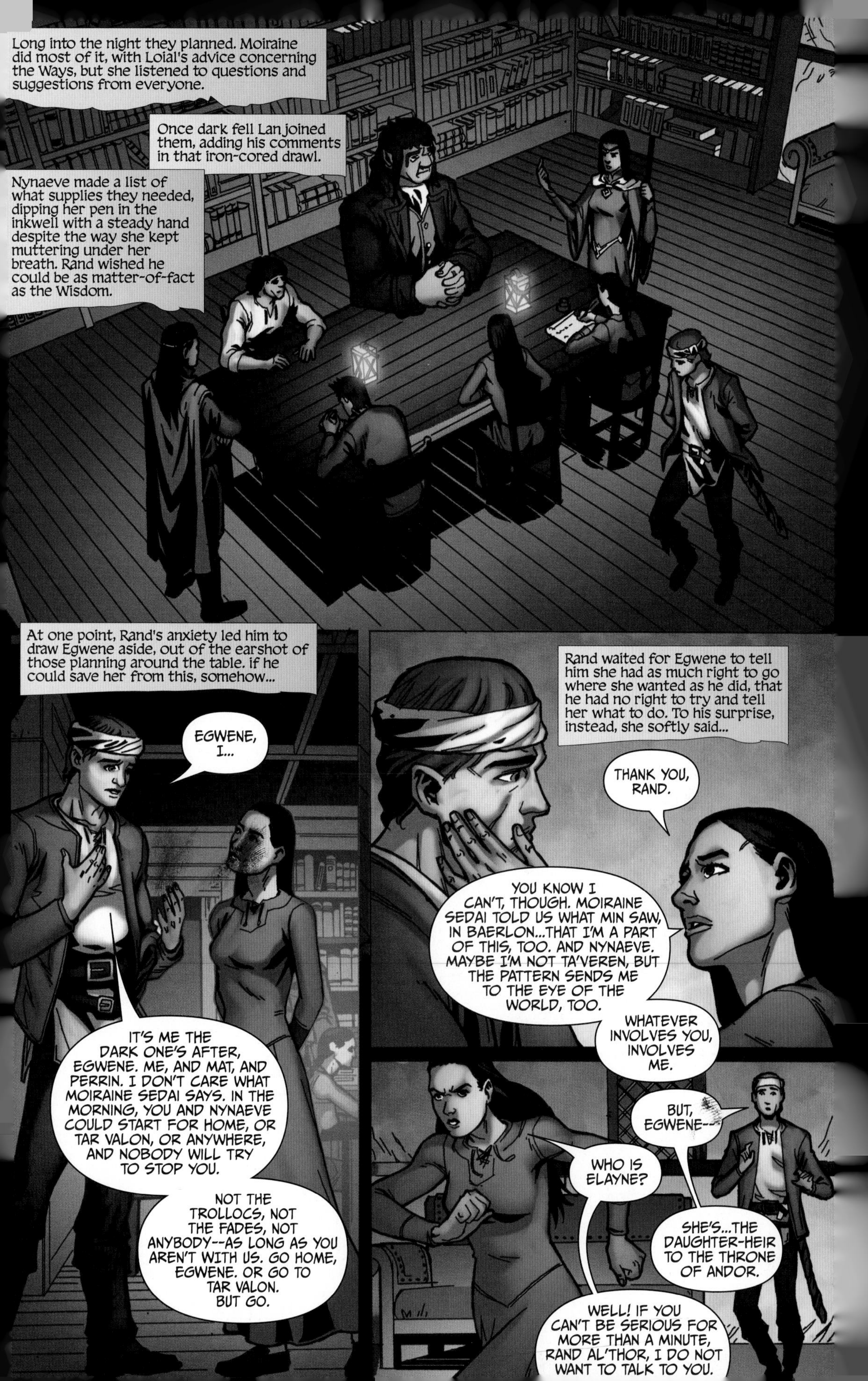

Long into the night they planned. Moiraine did most of it, with Loial's advice concerning the Ways, but she listened to questions and suggestions from everyone.
Once dark fell Lan joined them, adding his comments in that iron-cored drawl.
Nynaeve made a list of what supplies they needed, dipping her pen in the inkwell with a steady hand despite the way she kept muttering under her breath. Rand wished he could be as matter-of-fact as the Wisdom.
At one point, Rand's anxiety led him to draw Egwene aside, out of the earshot of those planning around the table. if he could save her from this, somehow...
EGWENE, I...
IT'S ME THE DARK ONE'S AFTER, EGWENE. ME, AND MAT, AND PERRIN. I DON'T CARE WHAT MOIRAINE SEDAI SAYS. IN THE MORNING, YOU AND NYNAEVE COULD START FOR HOME, OR TAR VALON, OR ANYWHERE, AND NOBODY WILL TRY TO STOP YOU.
NOT THE TROLLOCS, NOT THE FADES, NOT ANYBODY--AS LONG AS YOU AREN'T WITH US. GO HOME, EGWENE. OR GO TO TAR VALON. BUT GO.
Rand waited for Egwene to tell him she had as much right to go where she wanted as he did, that he had no right to try and tell her what to do. To his surprise, instead, she softly said...
THANK YOU, RAND.
YOU KNOW I CAN'T, THOUGH. MOIRAINE SEDAI TOLD US WHAT MIN SAW, IN BAERLON...THAT I'M A PART OF THIS, TOO. AND NYNAEVE. MAYBE I'M NOT TA'VEREN, BUT THE PATTERN SENDS ME TO THE EYE OF THE WORLD, TOO.
WHATEVER INVOLVES YOU, INVOLVES ME.
BUT, EGWENE--
WHO IS ELAYNE?
SHE'S...THE DAUGHTER-HEIR TO THE THRONE OF ANDOR.
WELL! IF YOU CAN'T BE SERIOUS FOR MORE THAN A MINUTE, RAND AL'THOR, I DO NOT WANT TO TALK TO YOU.

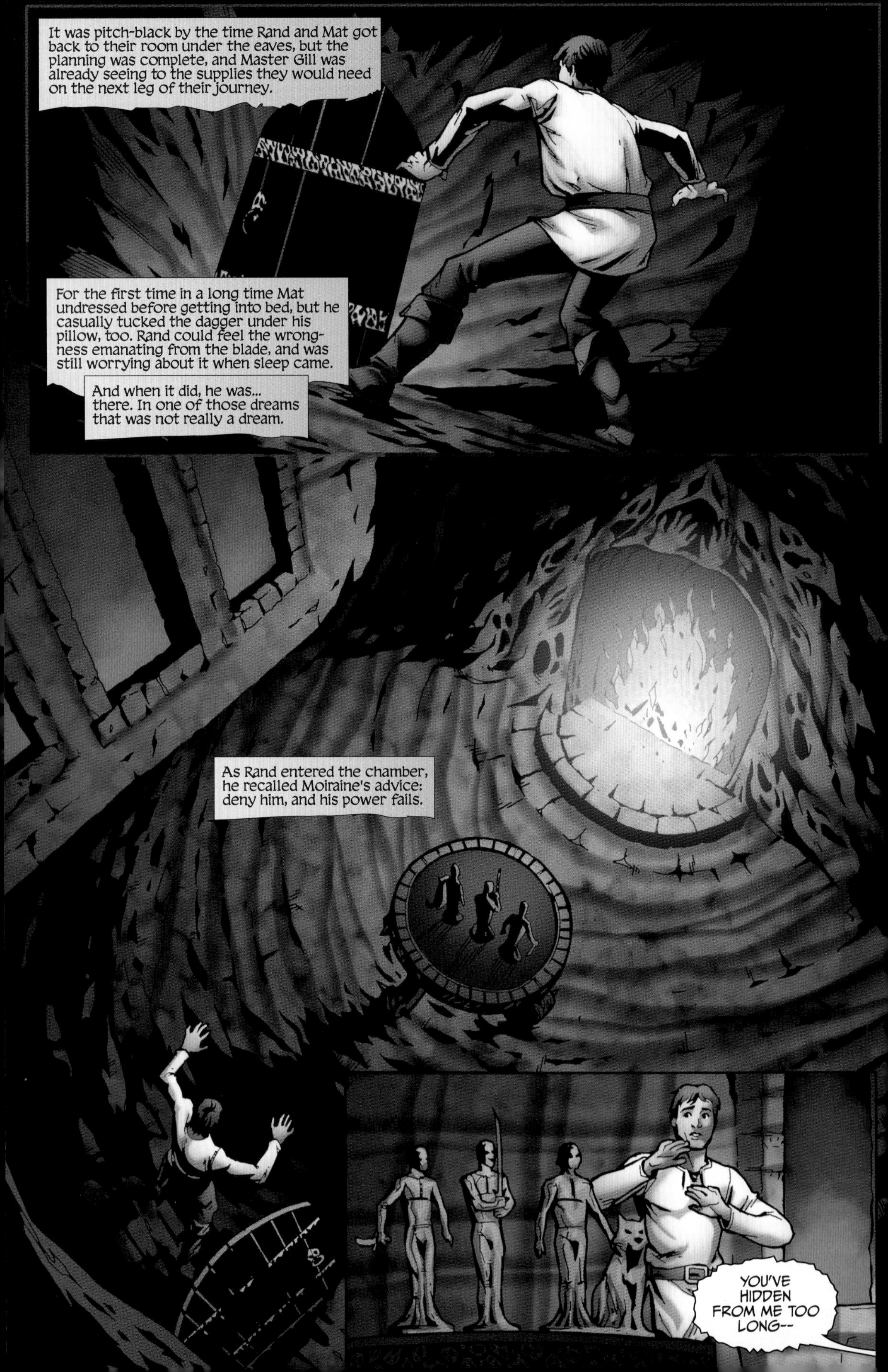
It was pitch-black by the time Rand and Mat got back to their room under the eaves, but the planning was complete, and Master Gill was already seeing to the supplies they would need on the next leg of their journey.
For the first time in a long time Mat undressed before getting into bed, but he casually tucked the dagger under his pillow, too. Rand could feel the wrong-ness emanating from the blade, and was still worrying about it when sleep came.
And when it did, he was... there. In one of those dreams that was not really a dream.
As Rand entered the chamber, he recalled Moiraine's advice: deny him, and his power fails.
YOU'VE HIDDEN FROM ME TOO LONG--

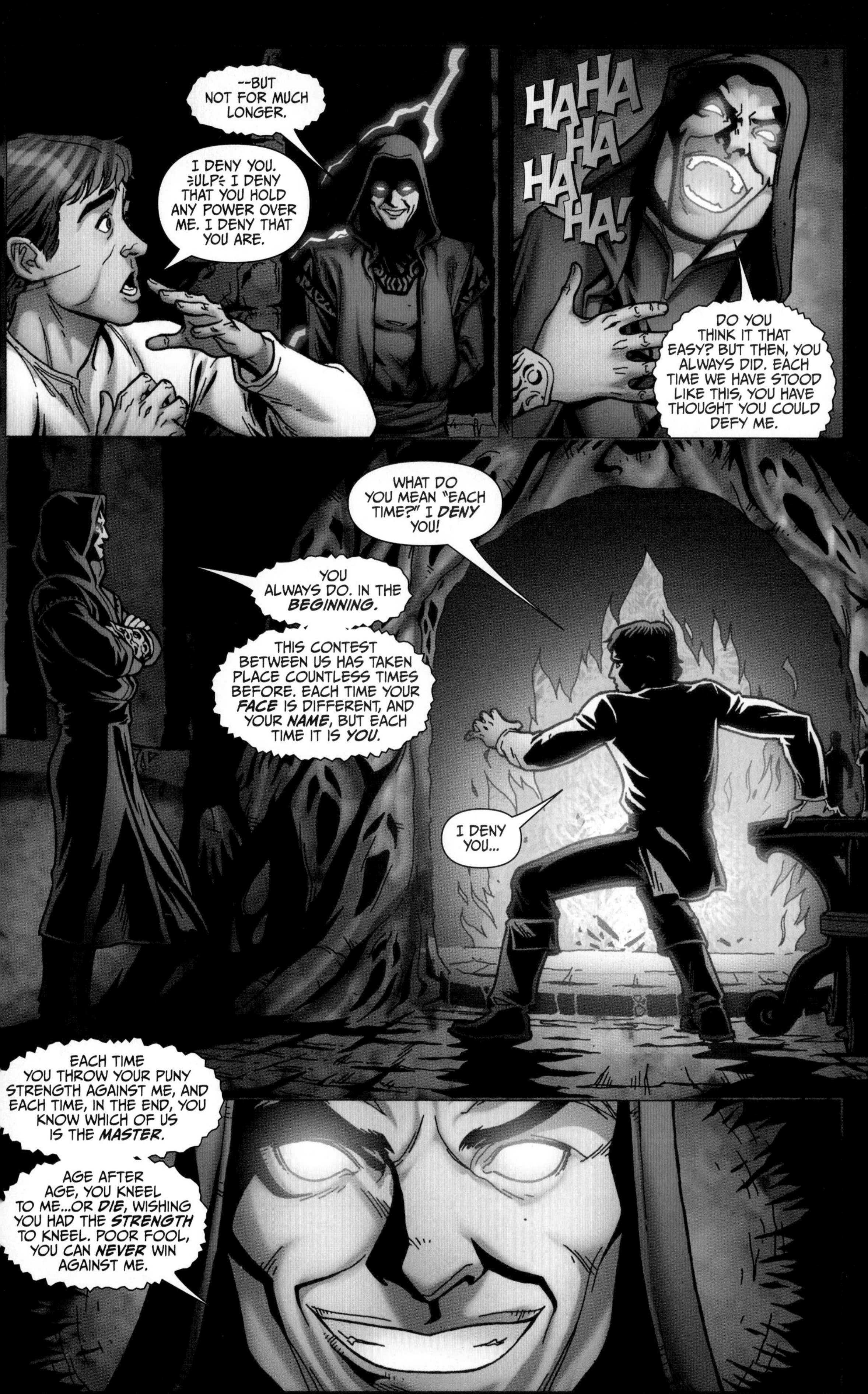
--BUT NOT FOR MUCH LONGER.
I DENY YOU. ≈ULP≈ I DENY THAT YOU HOLD ANY POWER OVER ME. I DENY THAT YOU ARE.
HAHA HA HA HA!
DO YOU THINK IT THAT EASY? BUT THEN, YOU ALWAYS DID. EACH TIME WE HAVE STOOD LIKE THIS, YOU HAVE THOUGHT YOU COULD DEFY ME.
WHAT DO YOU MEAN "EACH TIME?" I DENY YOU!
YOU ALWAYS DO. IN THE BEGINNING.
THIS CONTEST BETWEEN US HAS TAKEN PLACE COUNTLESS TIMES BEFORE. EACH TIME YOUR FACE IS DIFFERENT, AND YOUR NAME, BUT EACH TIME IT IS YOU.
I DENY YOU...
EACH TIME YOU THROW YOUR PUNY STRENGTH AGAINST ME, AND EACH TIME, IN THE END, YOU KNOW WHICH OF US IS THE MASTER.
AGE AFTER AGE, YOU KNEEL TO ME...OR DIE, WISHING YOU HAD THE STRENGTH TO KNEEL. POOR FOOL, YOU CAN NEVER WIN AGAINST ME.

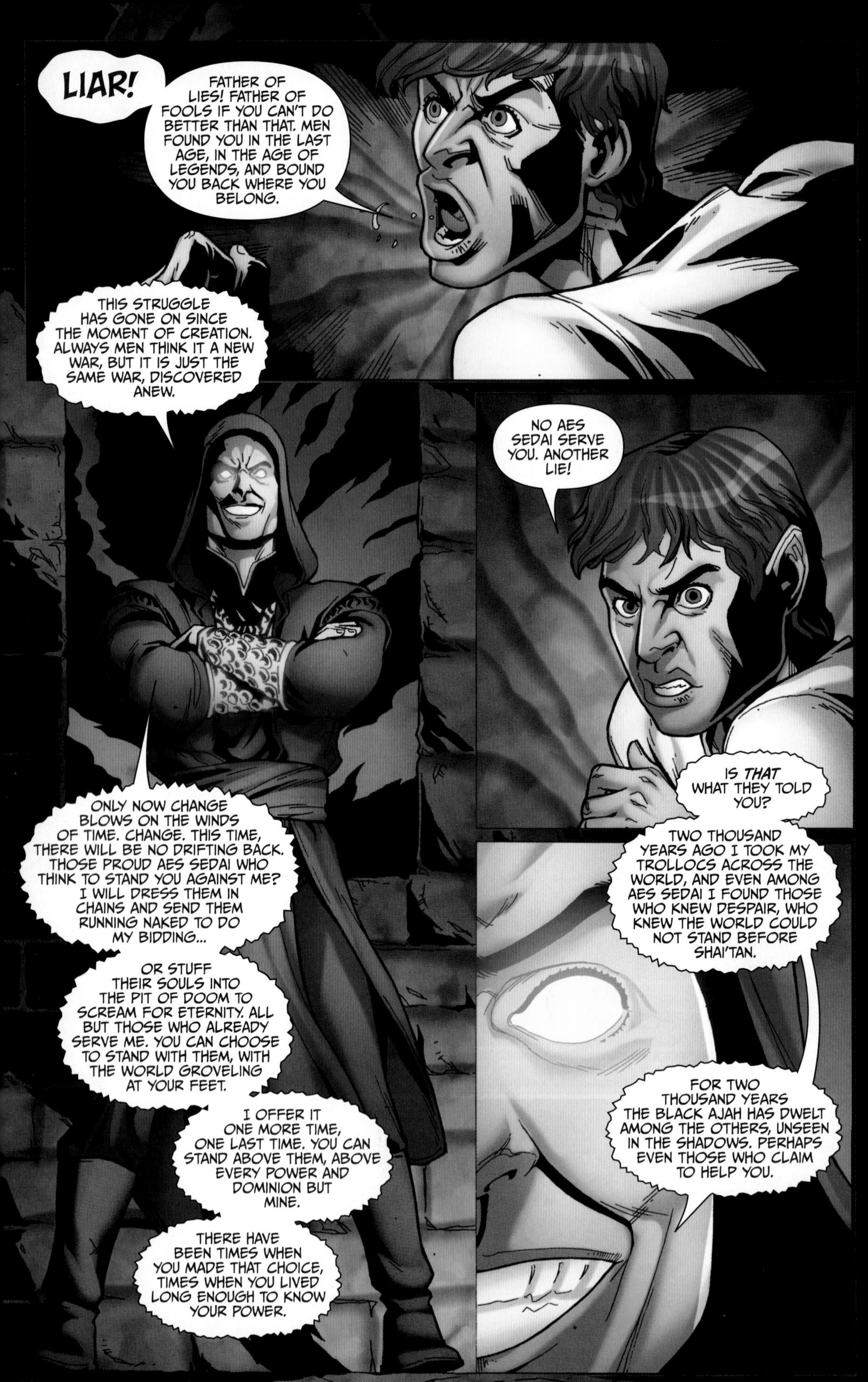
LIAR!
FATHER OF LIES! FATHER OF FOOLS IF YOU CAN'T DO BETTER THAN THAT. MEN FOUND YOU IN THE LAST AGE, IN THE AGE OF LEGENDS, AND BOUND YOU BACK WHERE YOU BELONG.
THIS STRUGGLE HAS GONE ON SINCE THE MOMENT OF CREATION. ALWAYS MEN THINK IT A NEW WAR, BUT IT IS JUST THE SAME WAR, DISCOVERED ANEW.
ONLY NOW CHANGE BLOWS ON THE WINDS OF TIME. CHANGE. THIS TIME, THERE WILL BE NO DRIFTING BACK. THOSE PROUD AES SEDAI WHO THINK TO STAND YOU AGAINST ME? I WILL DRESS THEM IN CHAINS AND SEND THEM RUNNING NAKED TO DO MY BIDDING...
OR STUFF THEIR SOULS INTO THE PIT OF DOOM TO SCREAM FOR ETERNITY. ALL BUT THOSE WHO ALREADY SERVE ME. YOU CAN CHOOSE TO STAND WITH THEM, WITH THE WORLD GROVELING AT YOUR FEET.
I OFFER IT ONE MORE TIME, ONE LAST TIME. YOU CAN STAND ABOVE THEM, ABOVE EVERY POWER AND DOMINION BUT MINE.
THERE HAVE BEEN TIMES WHEN YOU MADE THAT CHOICE, TIMES WHEN YOU LIVED LONG ENOUGH TO KNOW YOUR POWER.
NO AES SEDAI SERVE YOU. ANOTHER LIE!
IS *THAT* WHAT THEY TOLD YOU?
TWO THOUSAND YEARS AGO I TOOK MY TROLLOCS ACROSS THE WORLD, AND EVEN AMONG AES SEDAI I FOUND THOSE WHO KNEW DESPAIR, WHO KNEW THE WORLD COULD NOT STAND BEFORE SHAI'TAN.
FOR TWO THOUSAND YEARS THE BLACK AJAH HAS DWELT AMONG THE OTHERS, UNSEEN IN THE SHADOWS. PERHAPS EVEN THOSE WHO CLAIM TO HELP YOU.

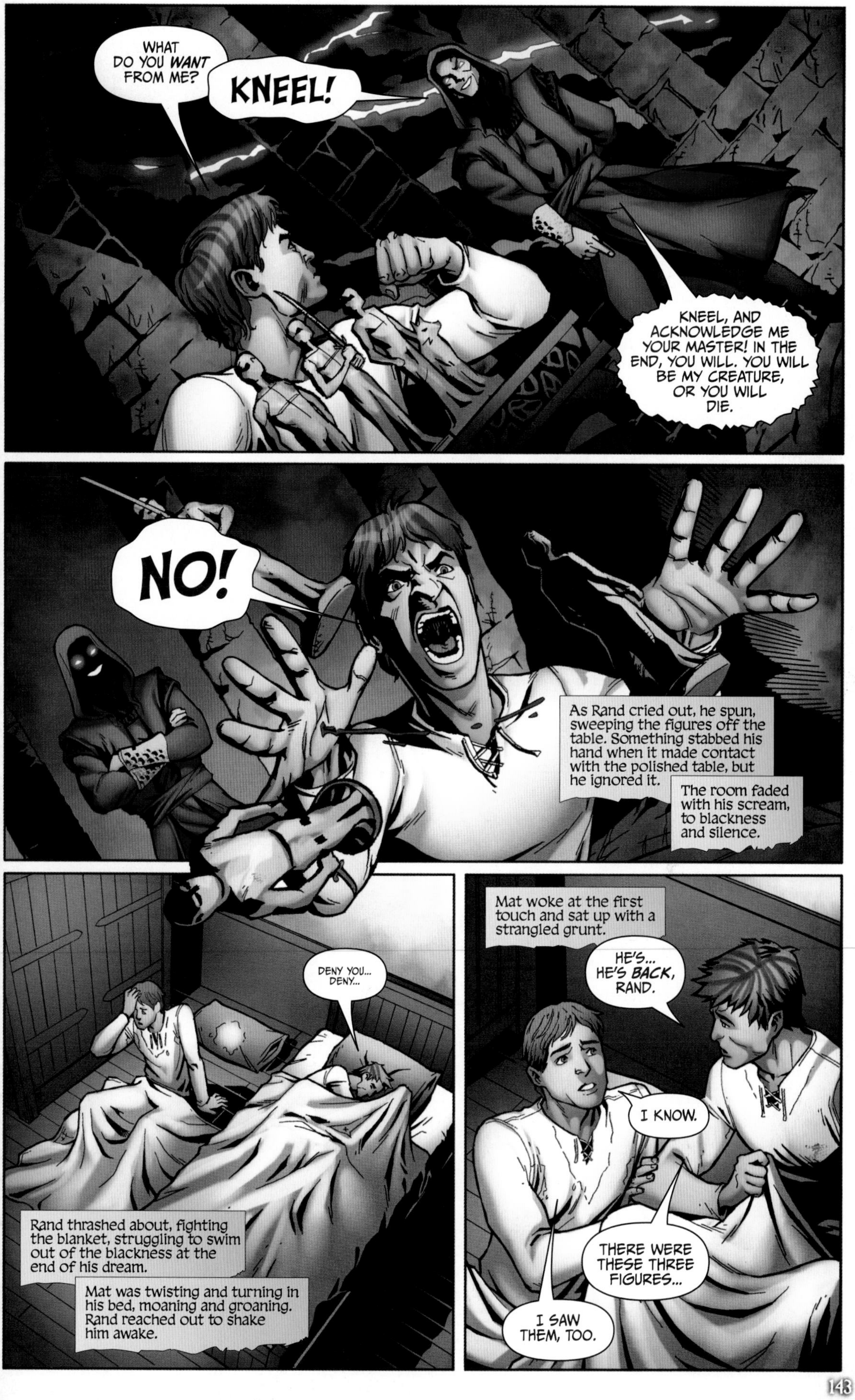
WHAT DO YOU WANT FROM ME?
KNEEL!
KNEEL, AND ACKNOWLEDGE ME YOUR MASTER! IN THE END, YOU WILL. YOU WILL BE MY CREATURE, OR YOU WILL DIE.
NO!
As Rand cried out, he spun, sweeping the figures off the table. Something stabbed his hand when it made contact with the polished table, but he ignored it.
The room faded with his scream, to blackness and silence.
DENY YOU... DENY...
Rand thrashed about, fighting the blanket, struggling to swim out of the blackness at the end of his dream.
Mat was twisting and turning in his bed, moaning and groaning. Rand reached out to shake him awake.
Mat woke at the first touch and sat up with a strangled grunt.
HE'S... HE'S BACK, RAND.
I KNOW.
THERE WERE THESE THREE FIGURES...
I SAW THEM, TOO.

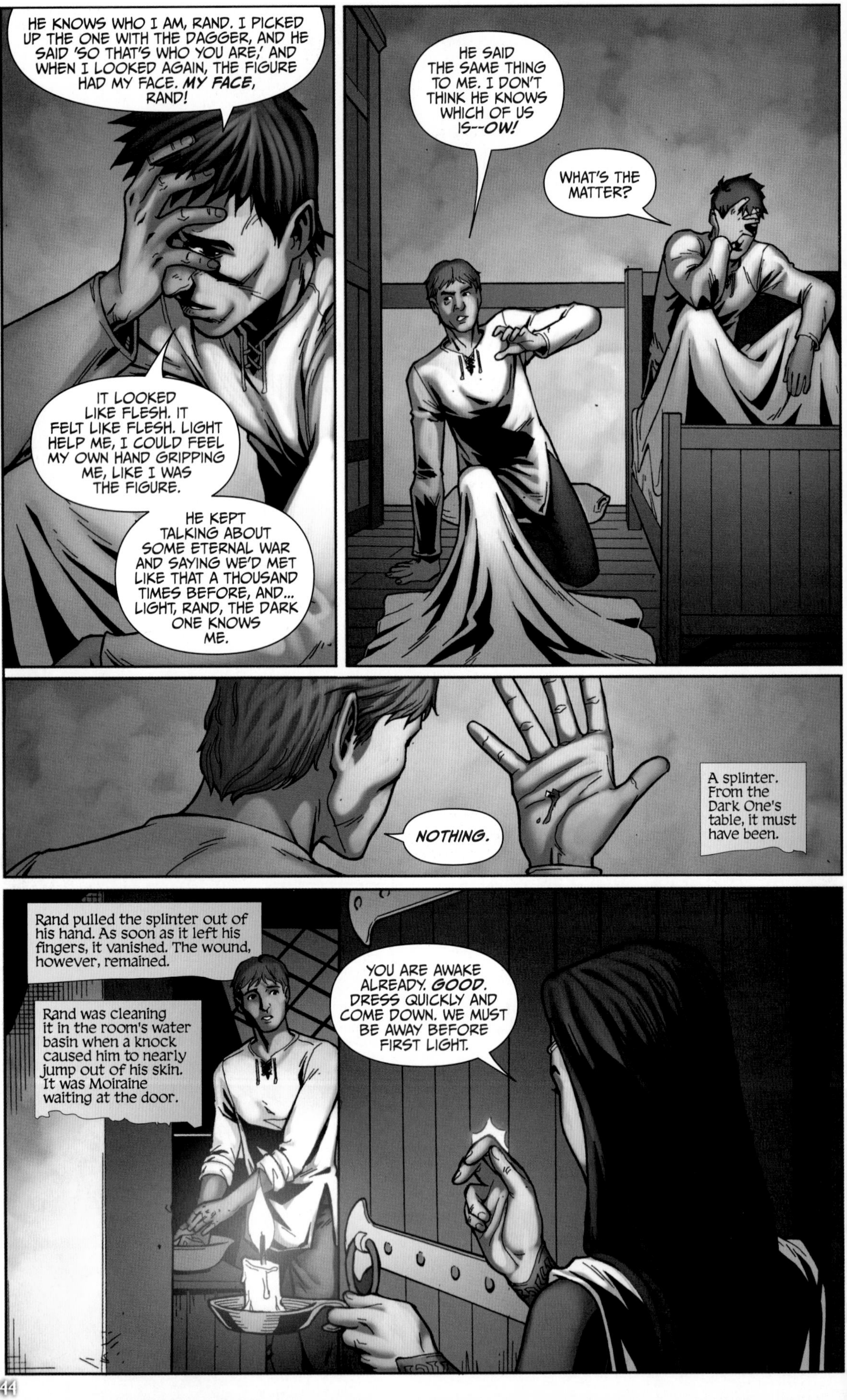
HE KNOWS WHO I AM, RAND. I PICKED UP THE ONE WITH THE DAGGER, AND HE SAID 'SO THAT'S WHO YOU ARE,' AND WHEN I LOOKED AGAIN, THE FIGURE HAD MY FACE. MY FACE, RAND!
IT LOOKED LIKE FLESH. IT FELT LIKE FLESH. LIGHT HELP ME, I COULD FEEL MY OWN HAND GRIPPING ME, LIKE I WAS THE FIGURE.
HE KEPT TALKING ABOUT SOME ETERNAL WAR AND SAYING WE'D MET LIKE THAT A THOUSAND TIMES BEFORE, AND... LIGHT, RAND, THE DARK ONE KNOWS ME.
HE SAID THE SAME THING TO ME. I DON'T THINK HE KNOWS WHICH OF US IS--OW!
WHAT'S THE MATTER?
NOTHING.
A splinter. From the Dark One's table, it must have been.
Rand pulled the splinter out of his hand. As soon as it left his fingers, it vanished. The wound, however, remained.
Rand was cleaning it in the room's water basin when a knock caused him to nearly jump out of his skin. It was Moiraine waiting at the door.
YOU ARE AWAKE ALREADY. GOOD. DRESS QUICKLY AND COME DOWN. WE MUST BE AWAY BEFORE FIRST LIGHT.

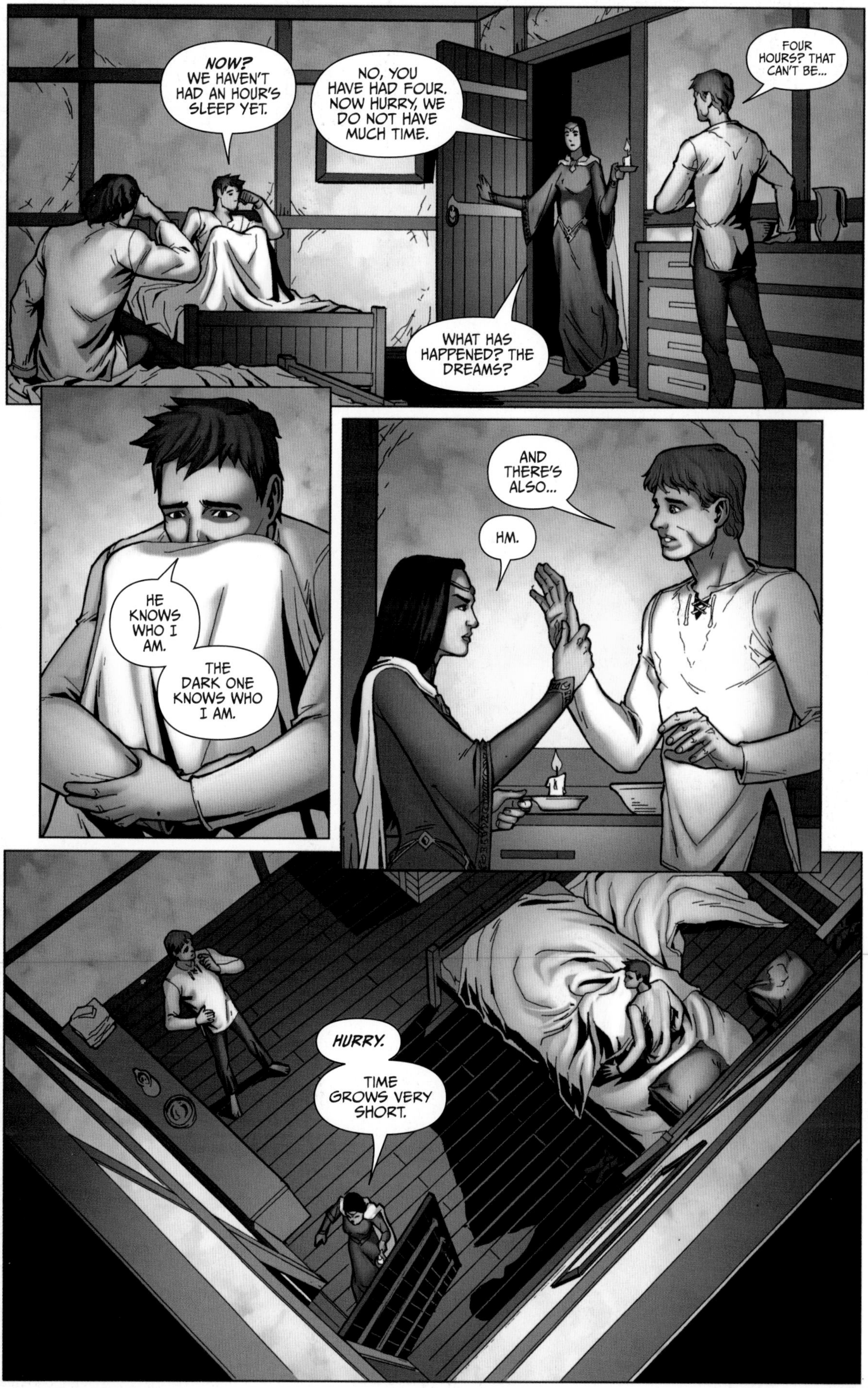
NOW? WE HAVEN'T HAD AN HOUR'S SLEEP YET.
NO, YOU HAVE HAD FOUR. NOW HURRY, WE DO NOT HAVE MUCH TIME.
FOUR HOURS? THAT CAN'T BE...
WHAT HAS HAPPENED? THE DREAMS?
HE KNOWS WHO I AM.
THE DARK ONE KNOWS WHO I AM.
AND THERE'S ALSO...
HM.
HURRY.
TIME GROWS VERY SHORT.

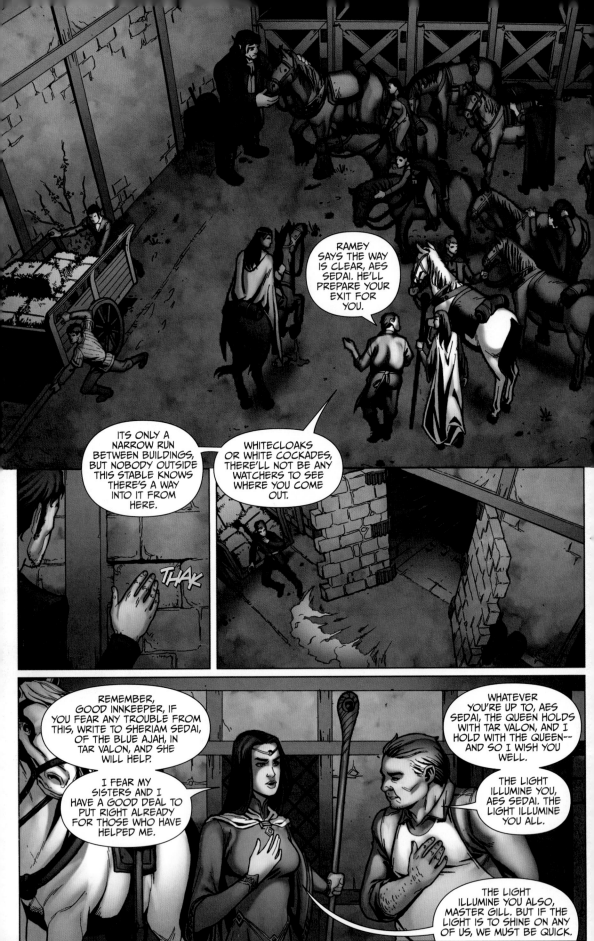

RAMEY SAYS THE WAY IS CLEAR, AES SEDAI. HE'LL PREPARE YOUR EXIT FOR YOU.

ITS ONLY A NARROW RUN BETWEEN BUILDINGS, BUT NOBODY OUTSIDE THIS STABLE KNOWS THERE'S A WAY INTO IT FROM HERE.

WHITECLOAKS OR WHITE COCKADES, THERE'LL NOT BE ANY WATCHERS TO SEE WHERE YOU COME OUT.

THAK

REMEMBER, GOOD INNKEEPER, IF YOU FEAR ANY TROUBLE FROM THIS, WRITE TO SHERIAM SEDAI, OF THE BLUE AJAH, IN TAR VALON, AND SHE WILL HELP.

I FEAR MY SISTERS AND I HAVE A GOOD DEAL TO PUT RIGHT ALREADY FOR THOSE WHO HAVE HELPED ME.

WHATEVER YOU'RE UP TO, AES SEDAI, THE QUEEN HOLDS WITH TAR VALON, AND I HOLD WITH THE QUEEN-- AND SO I WISH YOU WELL.

THE LIGHT ILLUMINE YOU, AES SEDAI. THE LIGHT ILLUMINE YOU ALL.

THE LIGHT ILLUMINE YOU ALSO, MASTER GILL. BUT IF THE LIGHT IS TO SHINE ON ANY OF US, WE MUST BE QUICK.

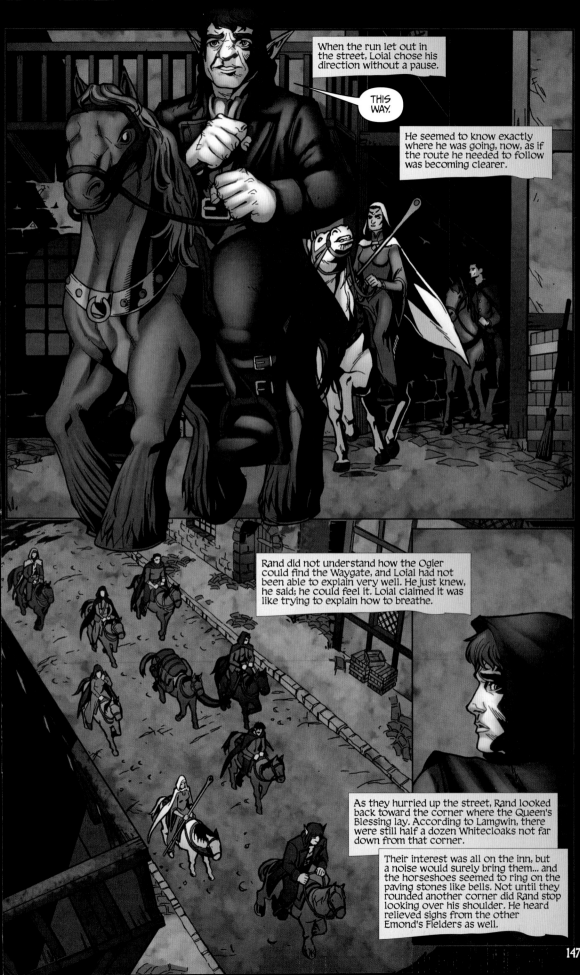

When the run let out in the street, Loial chose his direction without a pause.

THIS WAY.

He seemed to know exactly where he was going, now, as if the route he needed to follow was becoming clearer.

Rand did not understand how the Ogier could find the Waygate, and Loial had not been able to explain very well. He just knew, he said; he could feel it. Loial claimed it was like trying to explain how to breathe.

As they hurried up the street, Rand looked back toward the corner where the Queen's Blessing lay. According to Lamgwin, there were still half a dozen Whitecloaks not far down from that corner.

Their interest was all on the inn, but a noise would surely bring them... and the horseshoes seemed to ring on the paving stones like bells. Not until they rounded another corner did Rand stop looking over his shoulder. He heard relieved sighs from the other Emond's Fielders as well.

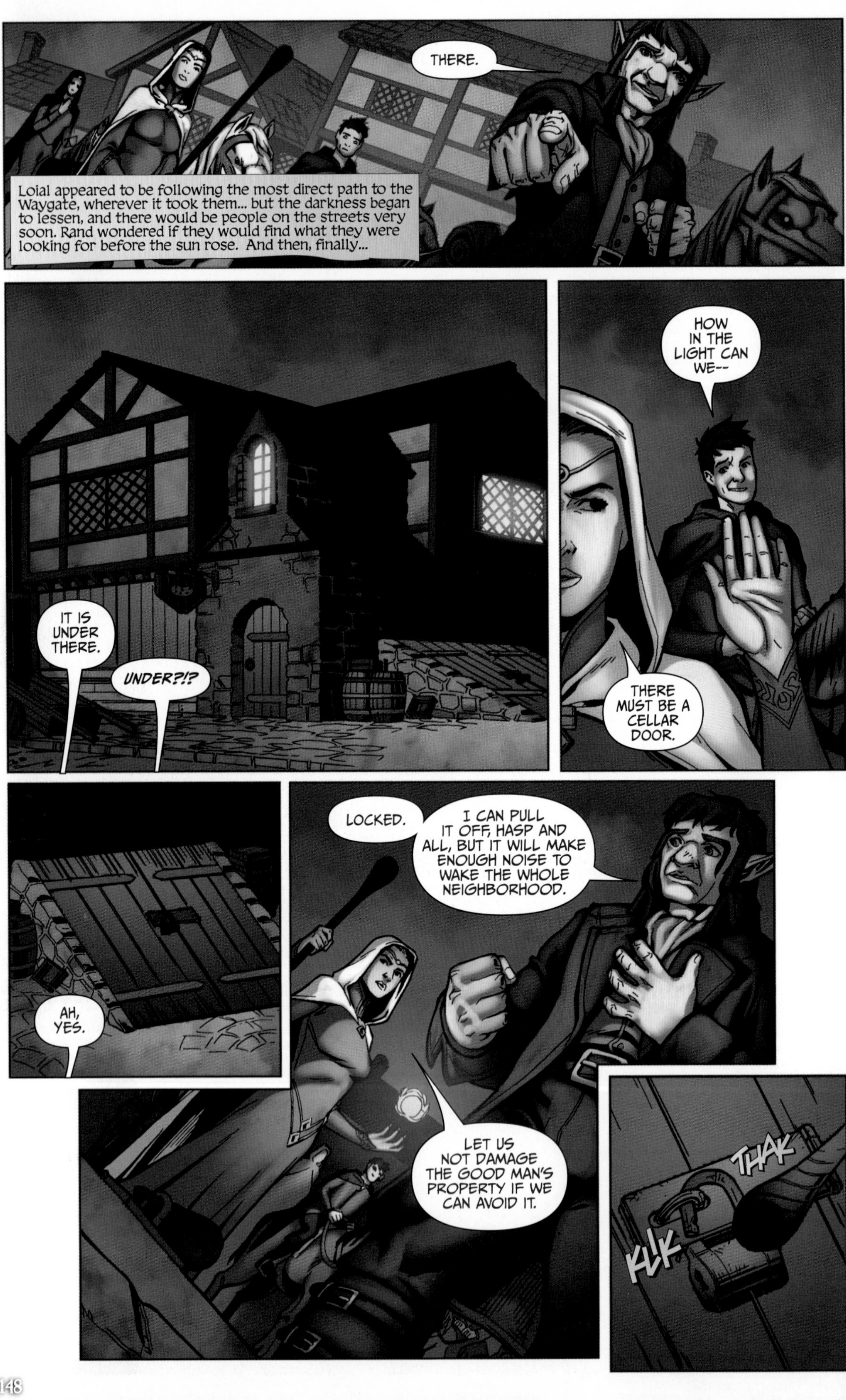

THERE.
Loial appeared to be following the most direct path to the Waygate, wherever it took them... but the darkness began to lessen, and there would be people on the streets very soon. Rand wondered if they would find what they were looking for before the sun rose. And then, finally...
IT IS UNDER THERE.
UNDER?!?
HOW IN THE LIGHT CAN WE--
THERE MUST BE A CELLAR DOOR.
AH, YES.
LOCKED.
I CAN PULL IT OFF, HASP AND ALL, BUT IT WILL MAKE ENOUGH NOISE TO WAKE THE WHOLE NEIGHBORHOOD.
LET US NOT DAMAGE THE GOOD MAN'S PROPERTY IF WE CAN AVOID IT.
THAK
KLIK

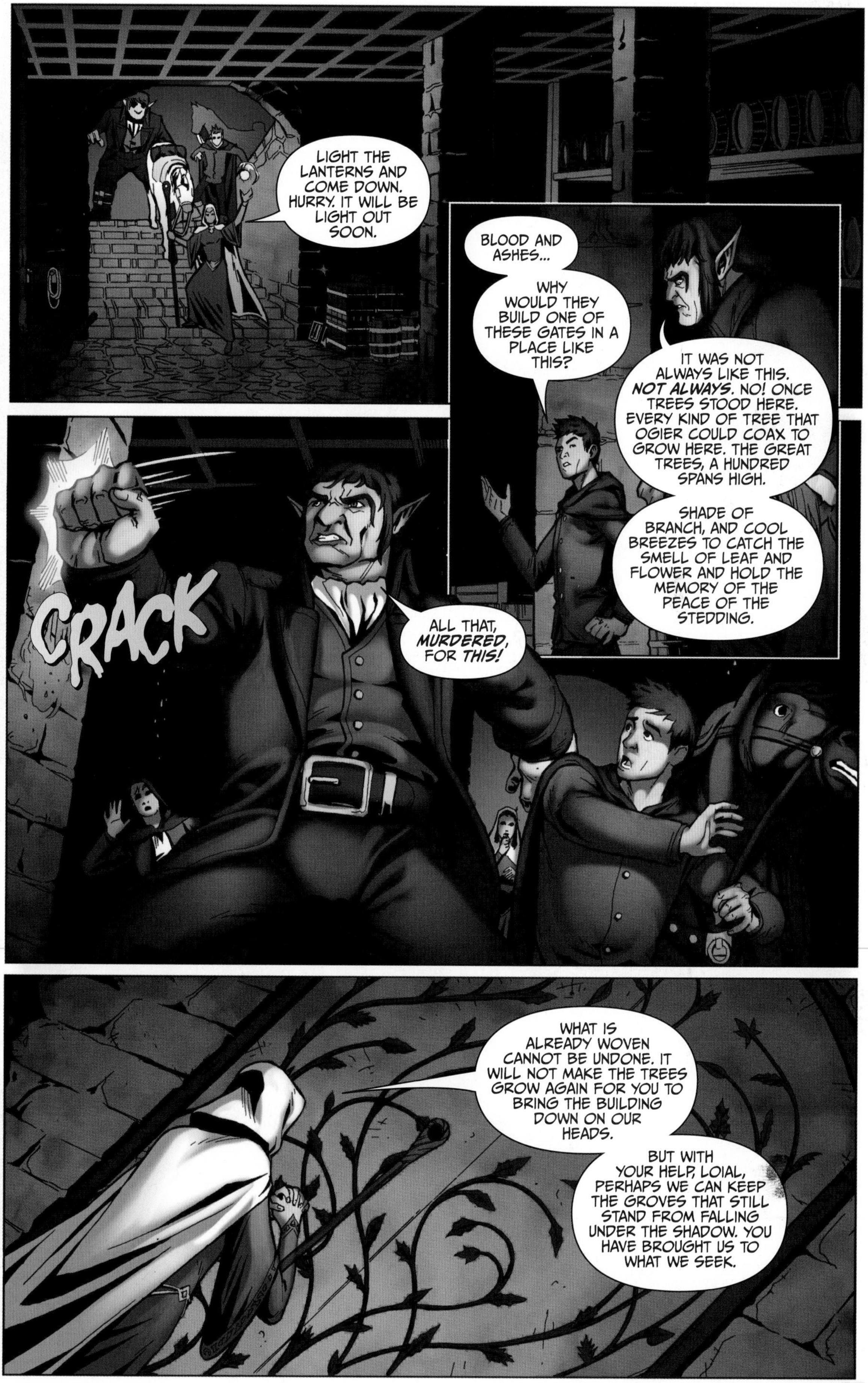
LIGHT THE LANTERNS AND COME DOWN. HURRY. IT WILL BE LIGHT OUT SOON.
BLOOD AND ASHES...
WHY WOULD THEY BUILD ONE OF THESE GATES IN A PLACE LIKE THIS?
IT WAS NOT ALWAYS LIKE THIS. ***NOT ALWAYS***. NO! ONCE TREES STOOD HERE. EVERY KIND OF TREE THAT OGIER COULD COAX TO GROW HERE. THE GREAT TREES, A HUNDRED SPANS HIGH.
SHADE OF BRANCH, AND COOL BREEZES TO CATCH THE SMELL OF LEAF AND FLOWER AND HOLD THE MEMORY OF THE PEACE OF THE STEDDING.
CRACK
ALL THAT, ***MURDERED***, FOR ***THIS!***
WHAT IS ALREADY WOVEN CANNOT BE UNDONE. IT WILL NOT MAKE THE TREES GROW AGAIN FOR YOU TO BRING THE BUILDING DOWN ON OUR HEADS.
BUT WITH YOUR HELP, LOIAL, PERHAPS WE CAN KEEP THE GROVES THAT STILL STAND FROM FALLING UNDER THE SHADOW. YOU HAVE BROUGHT US TO WHAT WE SEEK.

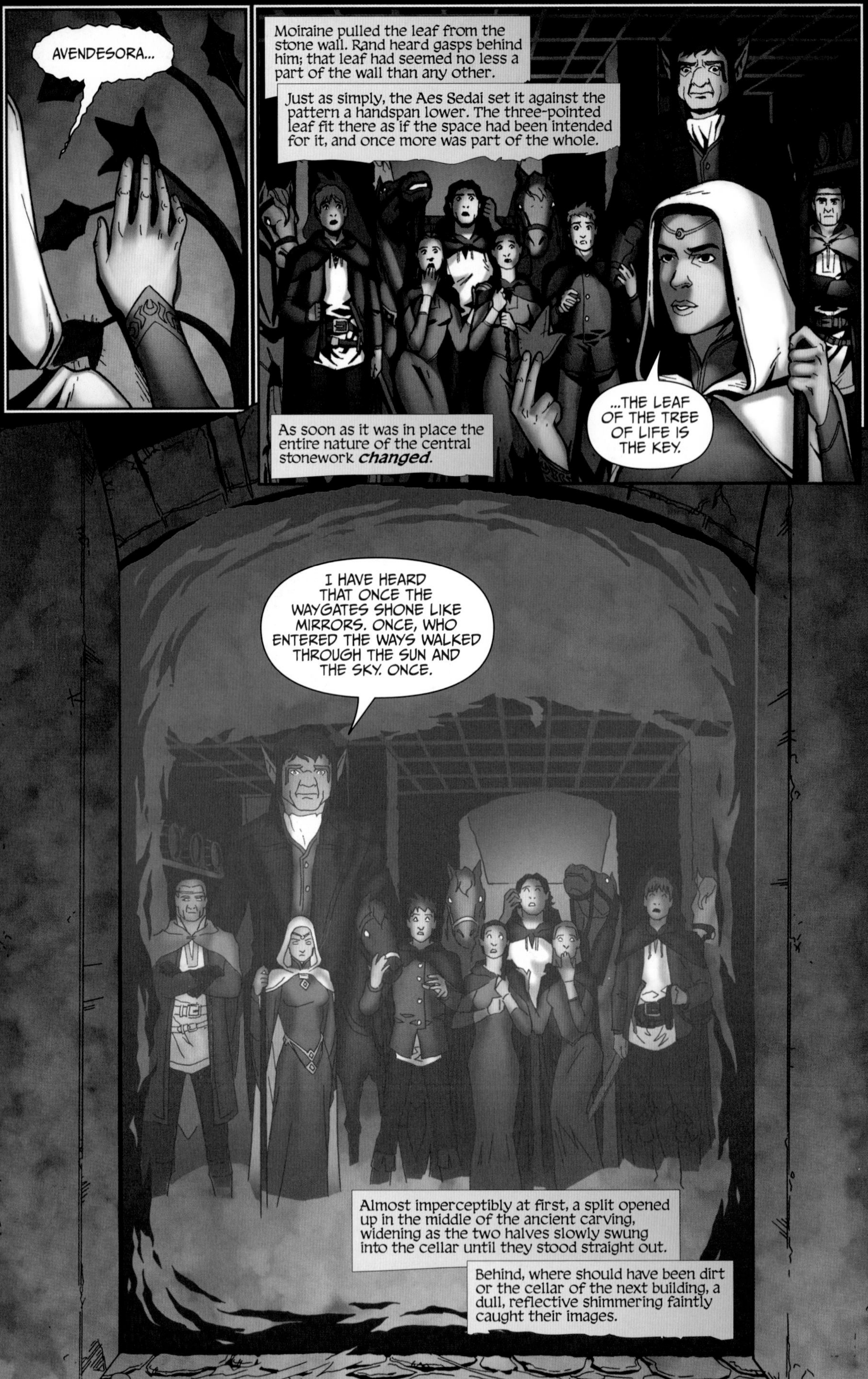
AVENDESORA...
Moiraine pulled the leaf from the stone wall. Rand heard gasps behind him; that leaf had seemed no less a part of the wall than any other.
Just as simply, the Aes Sedai set it against the pattern a handspan lower. The three-pointed leaf fit there as if the space had been intended for it, and once more was part of the whole.
...THE LEAF OF THE TREE OF LIFE IS THE KEY.
As soon as it was in place the entire nature of the central stonework *changed*.
I HAVE HEARD THAT ONCE THE WAYGATES SHONE LIKE MIRRORS. ONCE, WHO ENTERED THE WAYS WALKED THROUGH THE SUN AND THE SKY. ONCE.
Almost imperceptibly at first, a split opened up in the middle of the ancient carving, widening as the two halves slowly swung into the cellar until they stood straight out.
Behind, where should have been dirt or the cellar of the next building, a dull, reflective shimmering faintly caught their images.

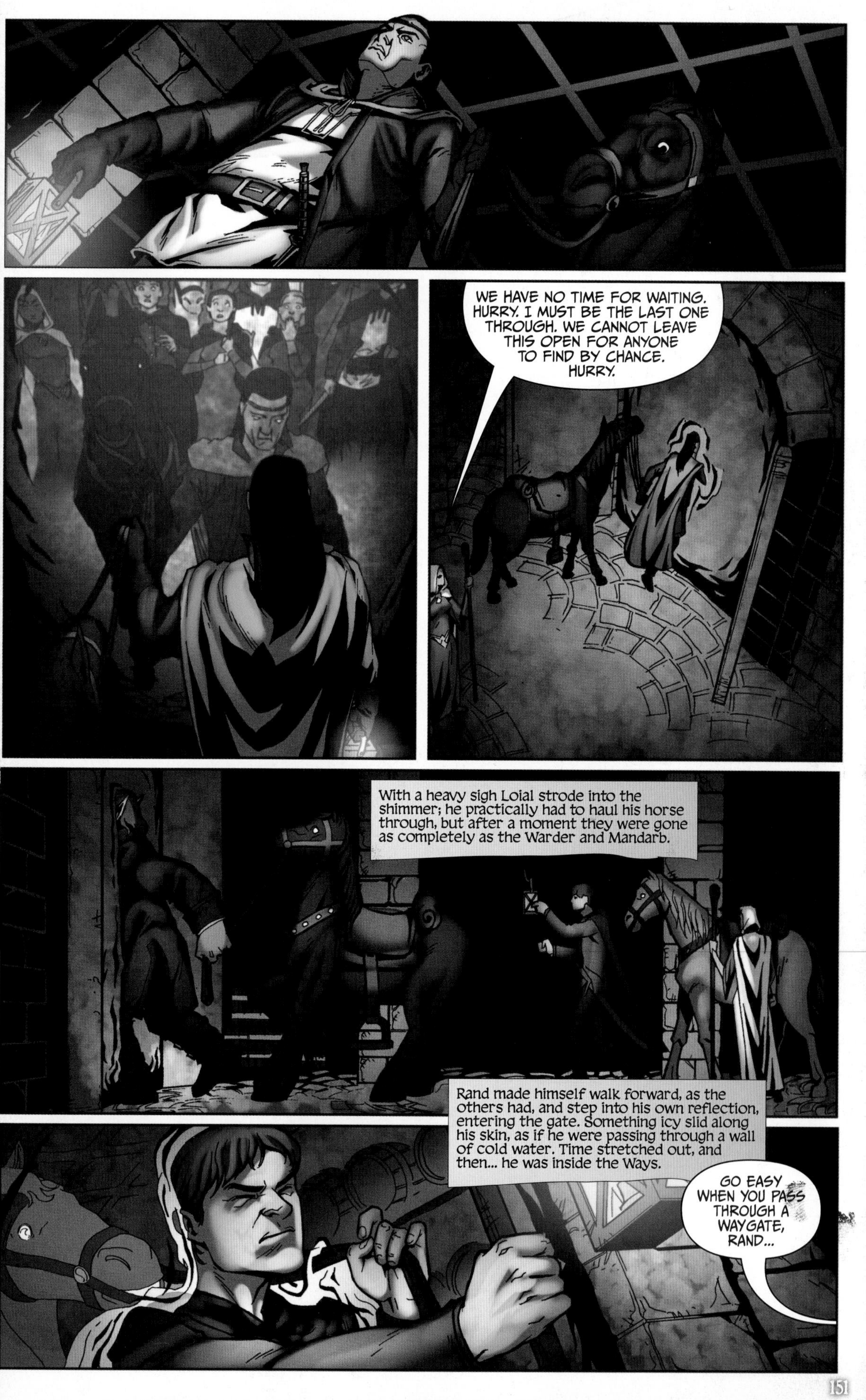
WE HAVE NO TIME FOR WAITING. HURRY. I MUST BE THE LAST ONE THROUGH. WE CANNOT LEAVE THIS OPEN FOR ANYONE TO FIND BY CHANCE. HURRY.
With a heavy sigh Loial strode into the shimmer; he practically had to haul his horse through, but after a moment they were gone as completely as the Warder and Mandarb.
Rand made himself walk forward, as the others had, and step into his own reflection, entering the gate. Something icy slid along his skin, as if he were passing through a wall of cold water. Time stretched out, and then... he was inside the Ways.
GO EASY WHEN YOU PASS THROUGH A WAYGATE, RAND...

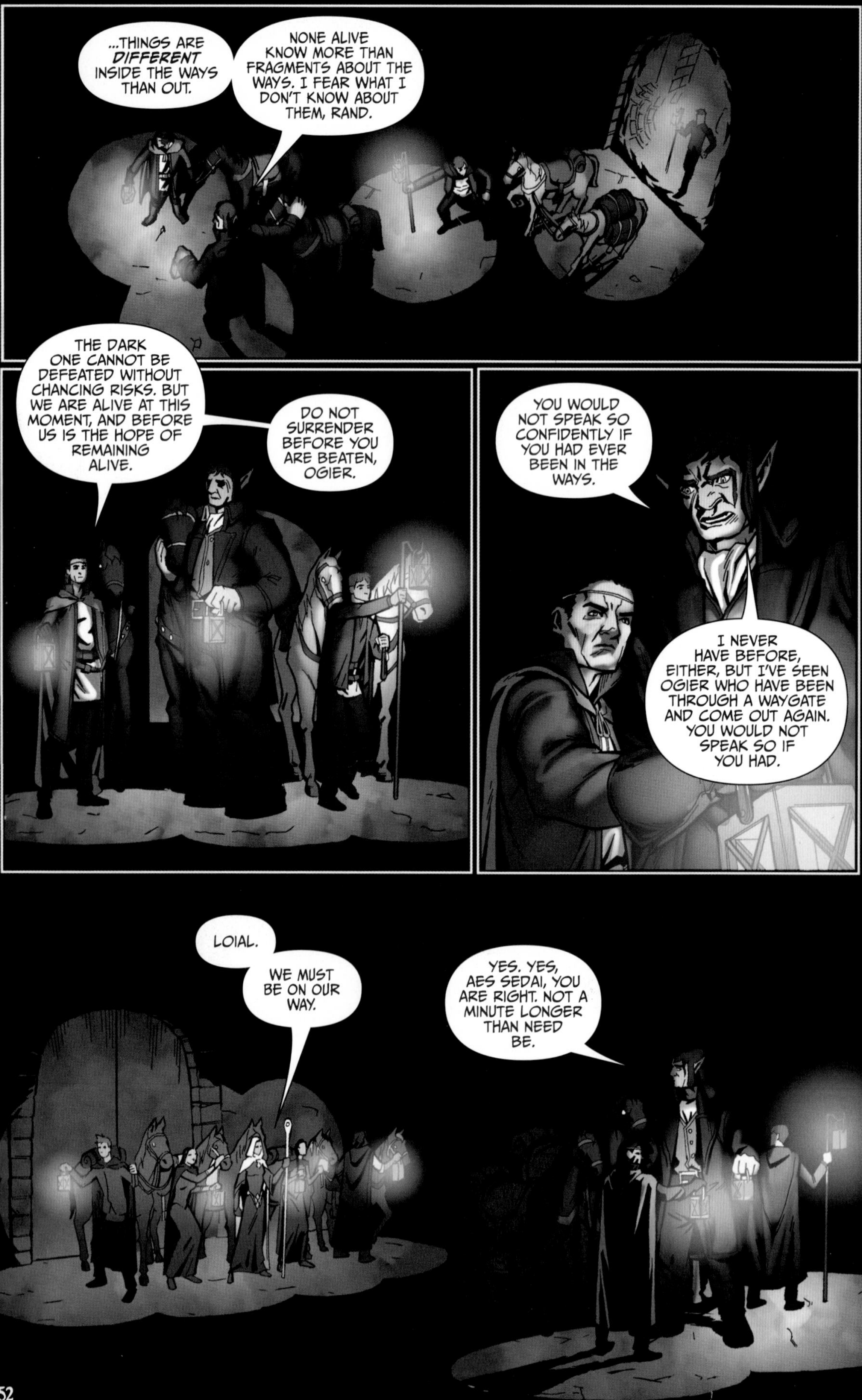

...THINGS ARE *DIFFERENT* INSIDE THE WAYS THAN OUT.
NONE ALIVE KNOW MORE THAN FRAGMENTS ABOUT THE WAYS. I FEAR WHAT I DON'T KNOW ABOUT THEM, RAND.
THE DARK ONE CANNOT BE DEFEATED WITHOUT CHANCING RISKS. BUT WE ARE ALIVE AT THIS MOMENT, AND BEFORE US IS THE HOPE OF REMAINING ALIVE.
DO NOT SURRENDER BEFORE YOU ARE BEATEN, OGIER.
YOU WOULD NOT SPEAK SO CONFIDENTLY IF YOU HAD EVER BEEN IN THE WAYS.
I NEVER HAVE BEFORE, EITHER, BUT I'VE SEEN OGIER WHO HAVE BEEN THROUGH A WAYGATE AND COME OUT AGAIN. YOU WOULD NOT SPEAK SO IF YOU HAD.
LOIAL.
WE MUST BE ON OUR WAY.
YES. YES, AES SEDAI, YOU ARE RIGHT. NOT A MINUTE LONGER THAN NEED BE.

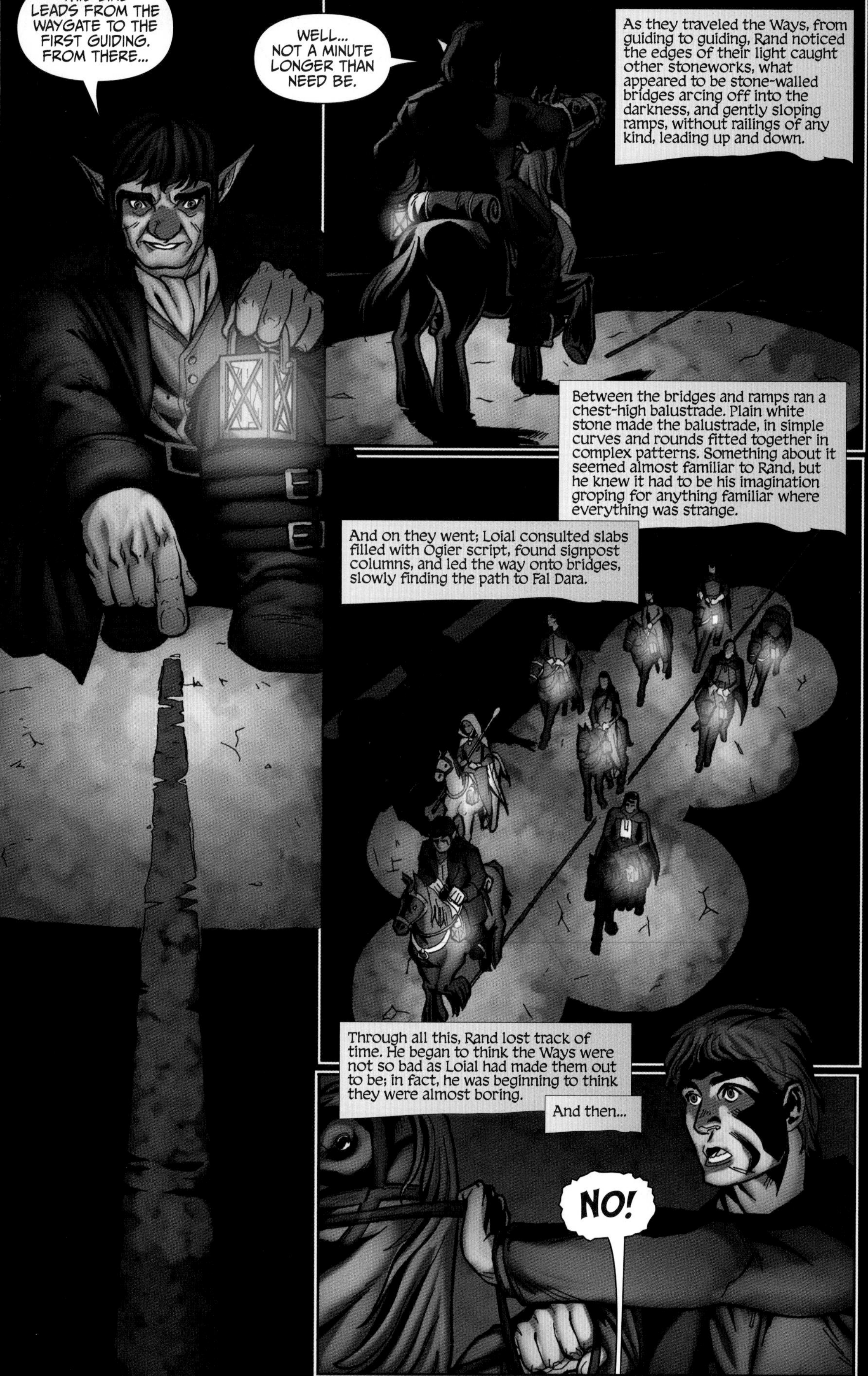
LEADS FROM THE WAYGATE TO THE FIRST GUIDING. FROM THERE...
WELL... NOT A MINUTE LONGER THAN NEED BE.
As they traveled the Ways, from guiding to guiding, Rand noticed the edges of their light caught other stoneworks, what appeared to be stone-walled bridges arcing off into the darkness, and gently sloping ramps, without railings of any kind, leading up and down.
Between the bridges and ramps ran a chest-high balustrade. Plain white stone made the balustrade, in simple curves and rounds fitted together in complex patterns. Something about it seemed almost familiar to Rand, but he knew it had to be his imagination groping for anything familiar where everything was strange.
And on they went; Loial consulted slabs filled with Ogier script, found signpost columns, and led the way onto bridges, slowly finding the path to Fal Dara.
Through all this, Rand lost track of time. He began to think the Ways were not so bad as Loial had made them out to be; in fact, he was beginning to think they were almost boring.
And then...
NO!

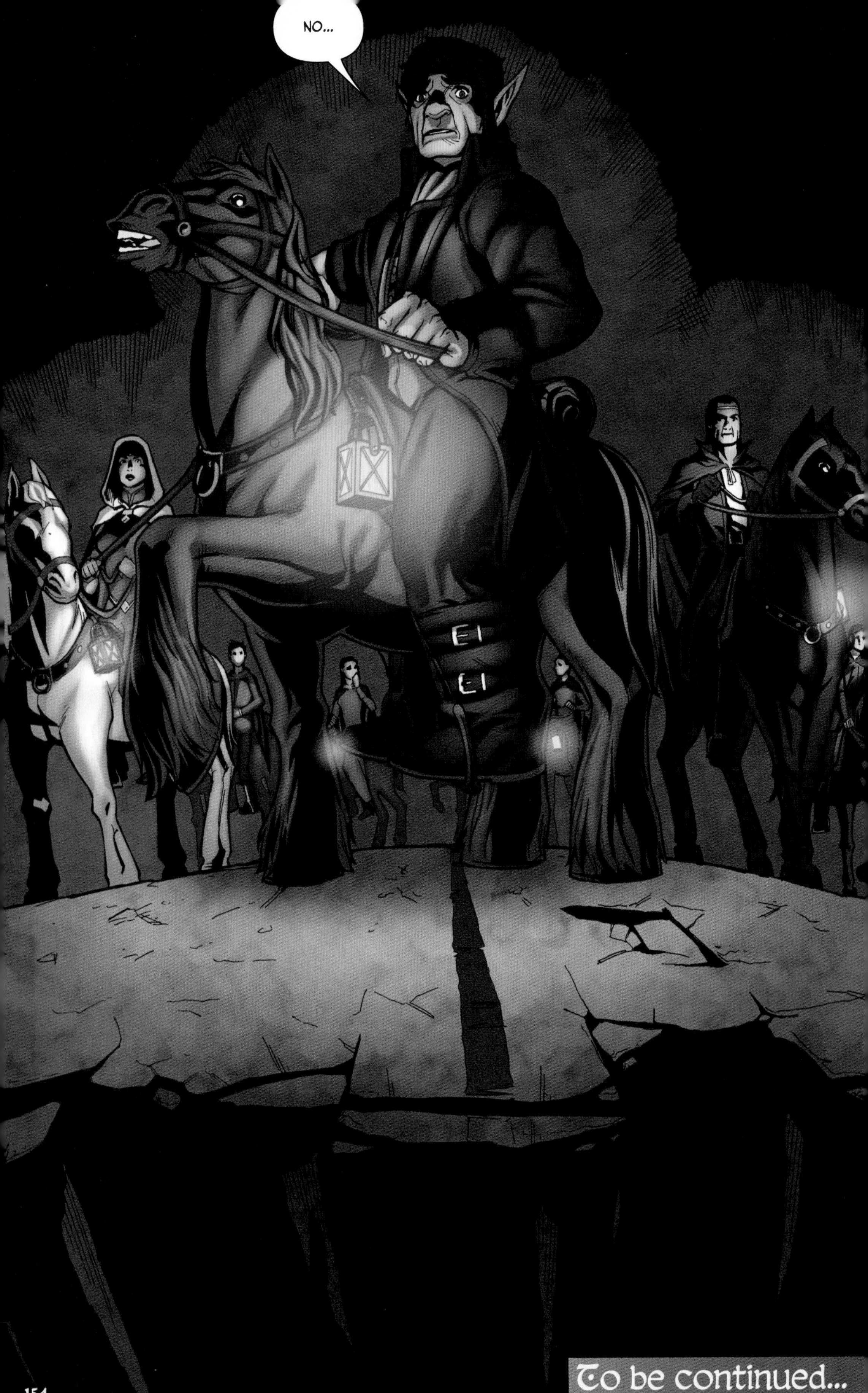
NO...
To be continued...

cover gallery

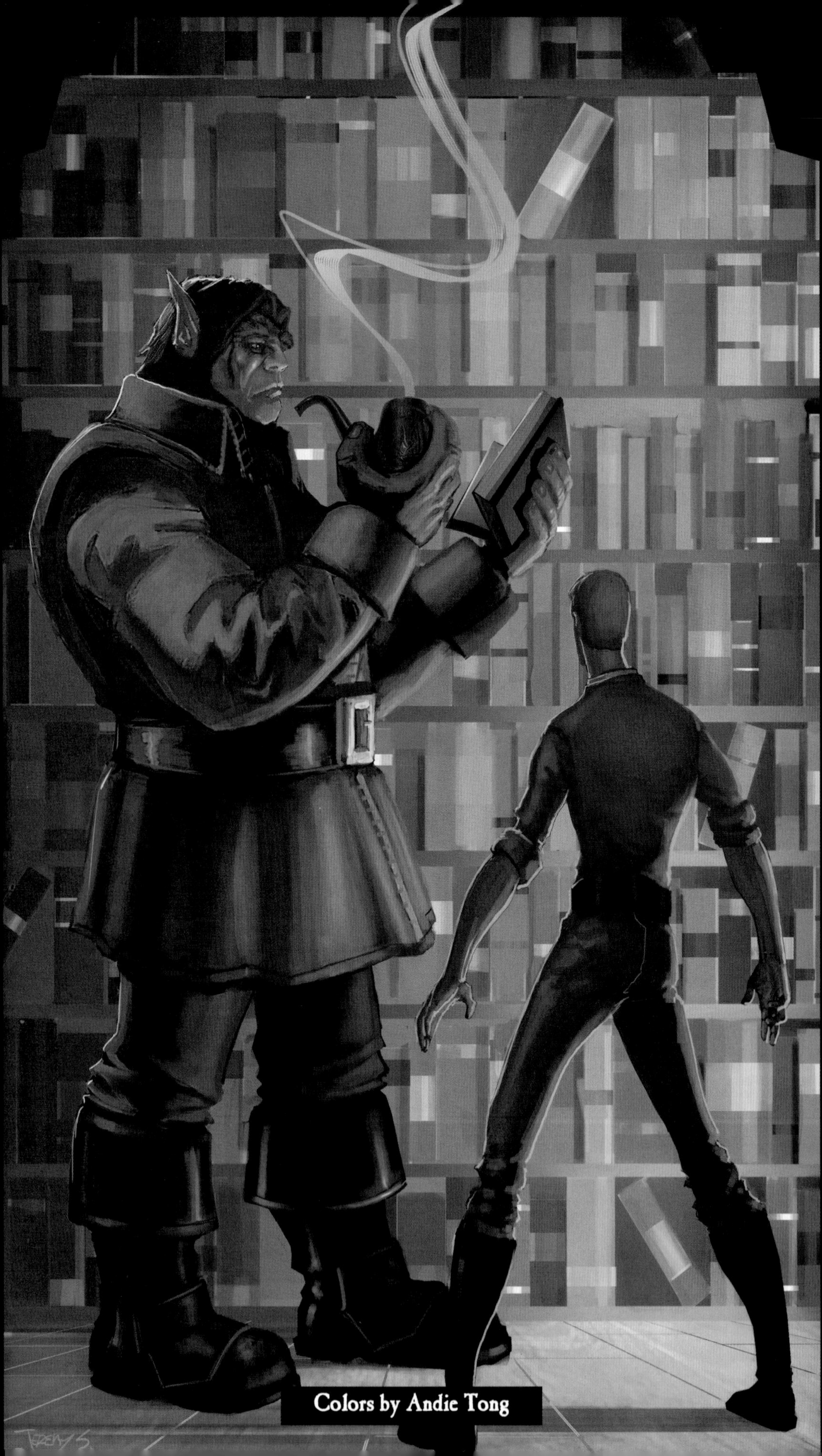

Colors by Andie Tong

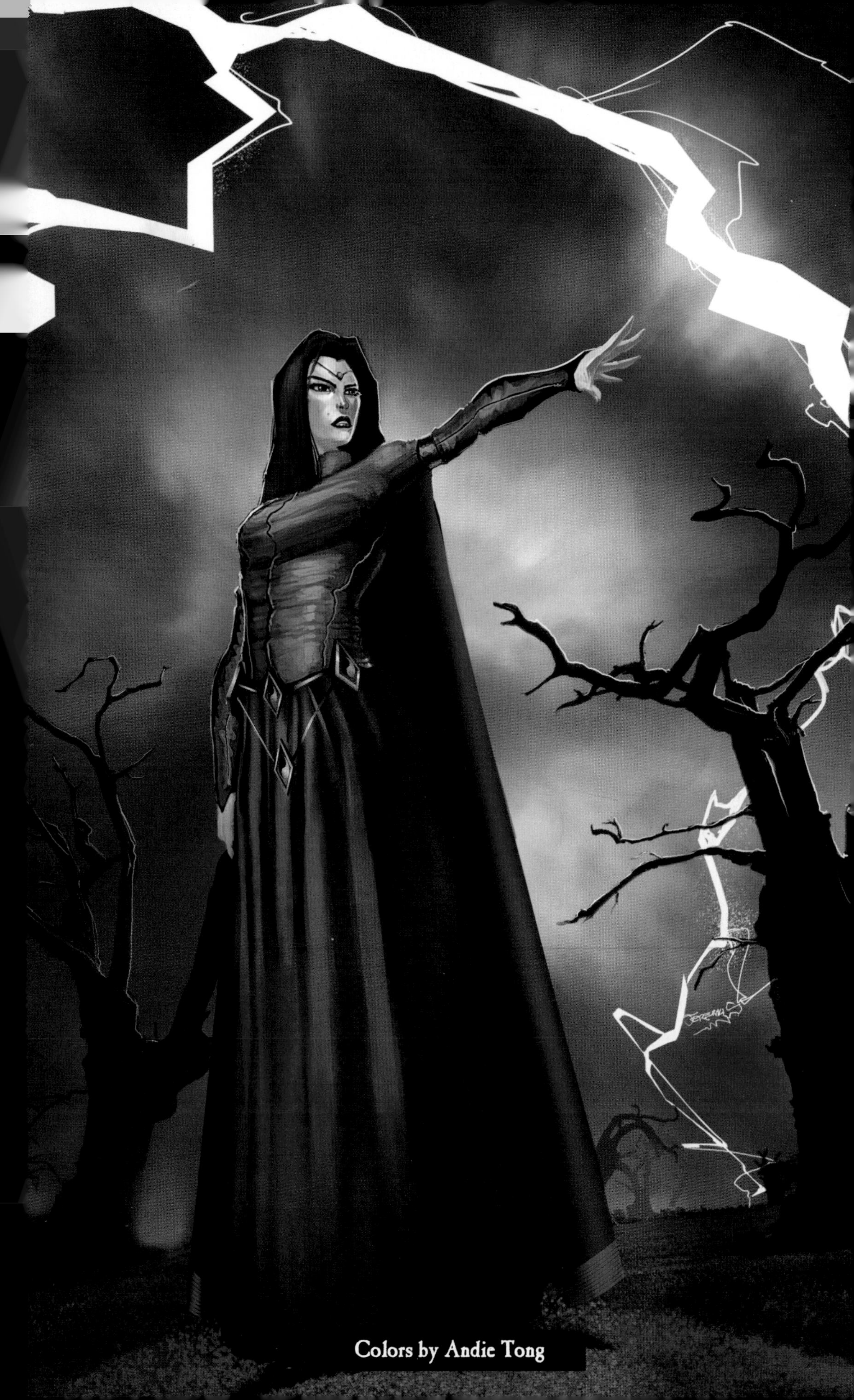

Colors by Andie Tong

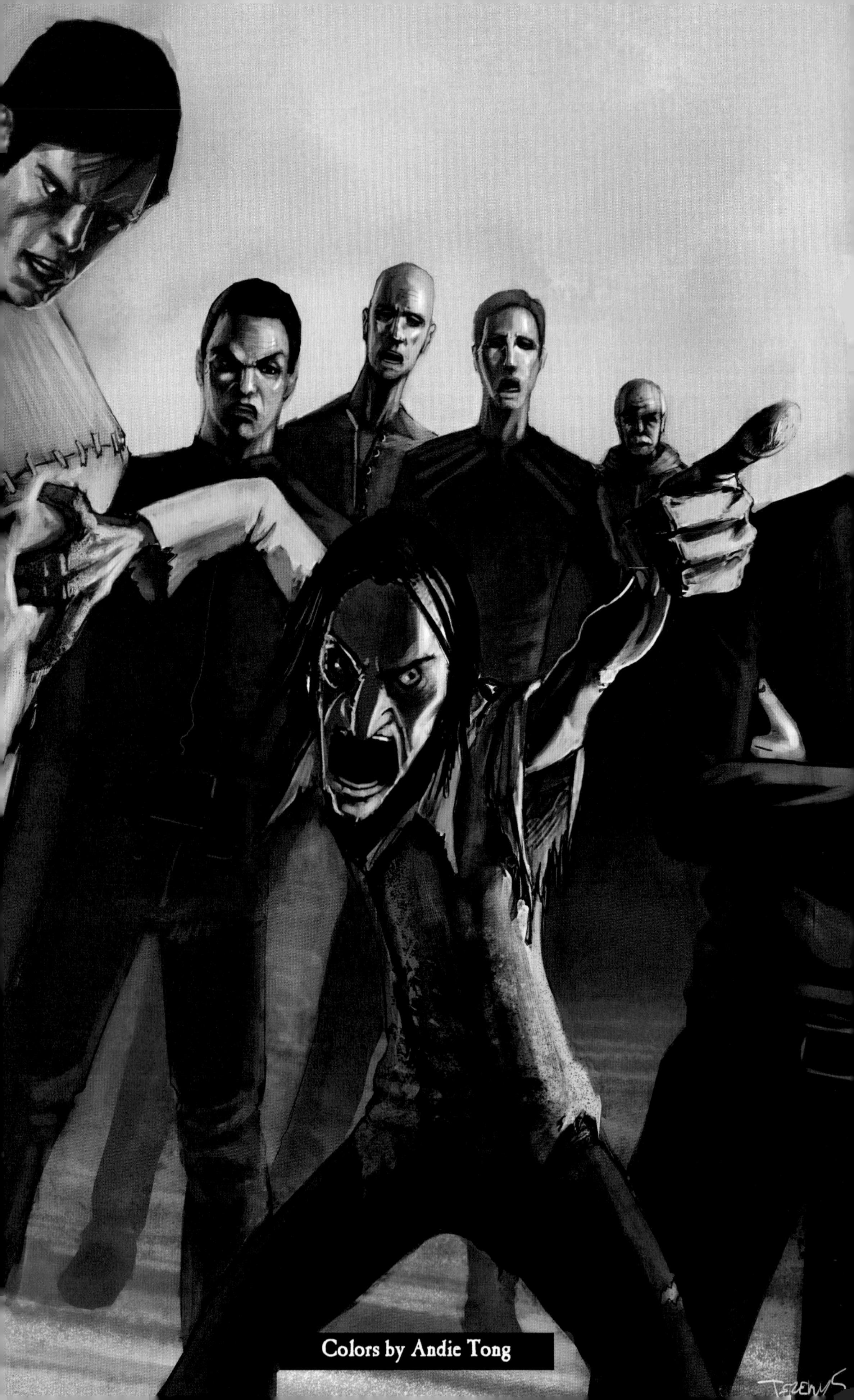

Colors by Andie Tong

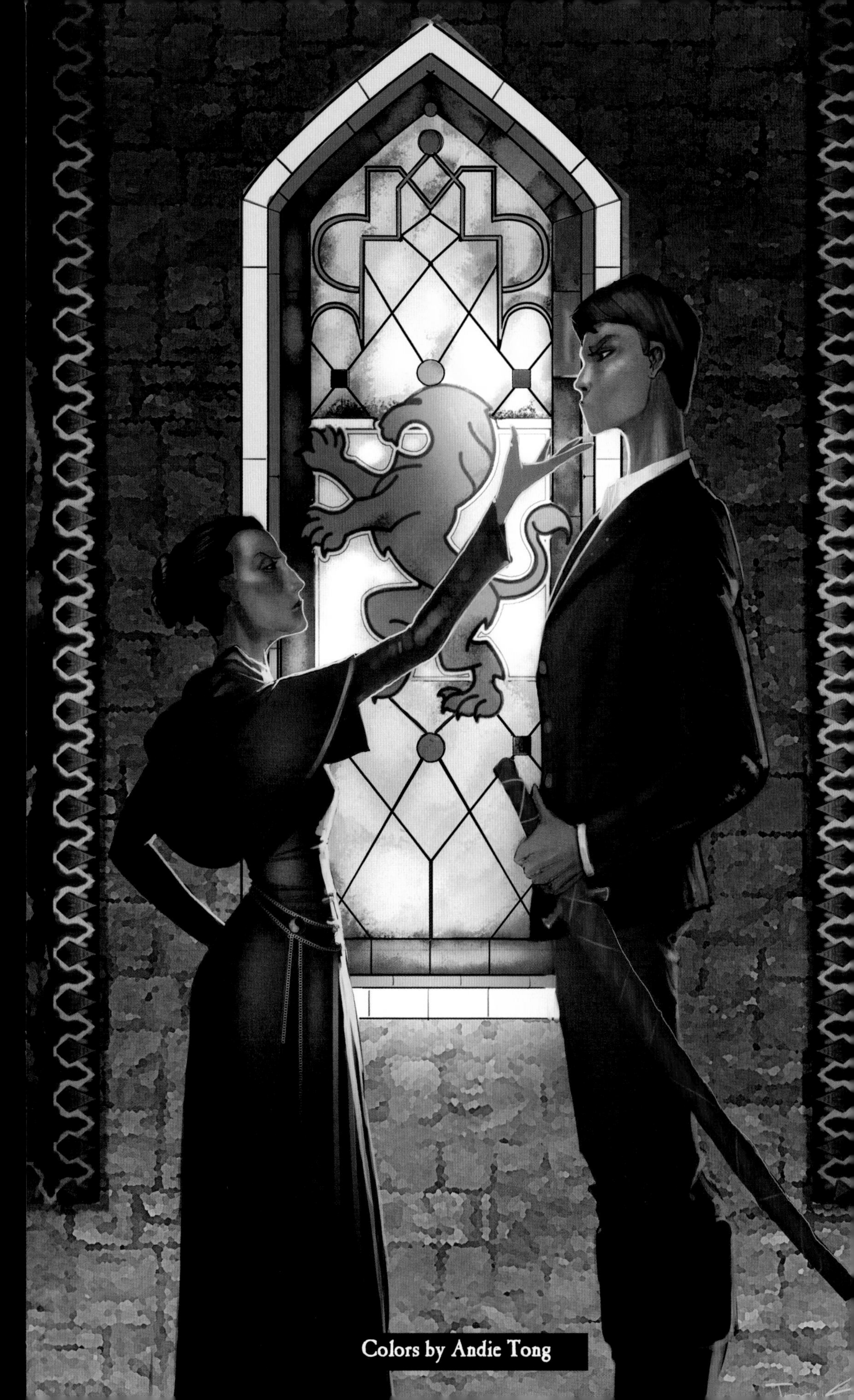

Colors by Andie Tong

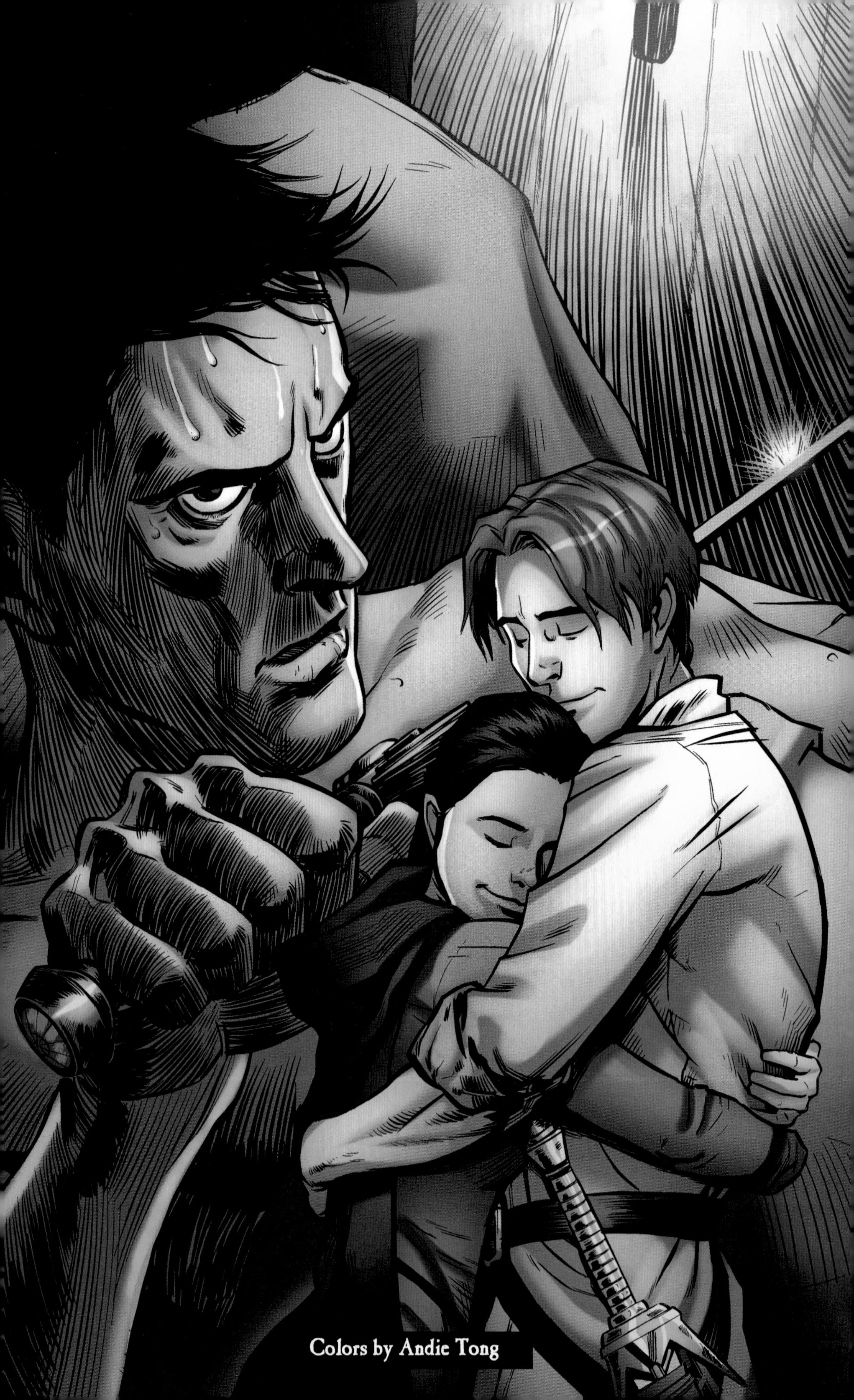

Colors by Andie Tong

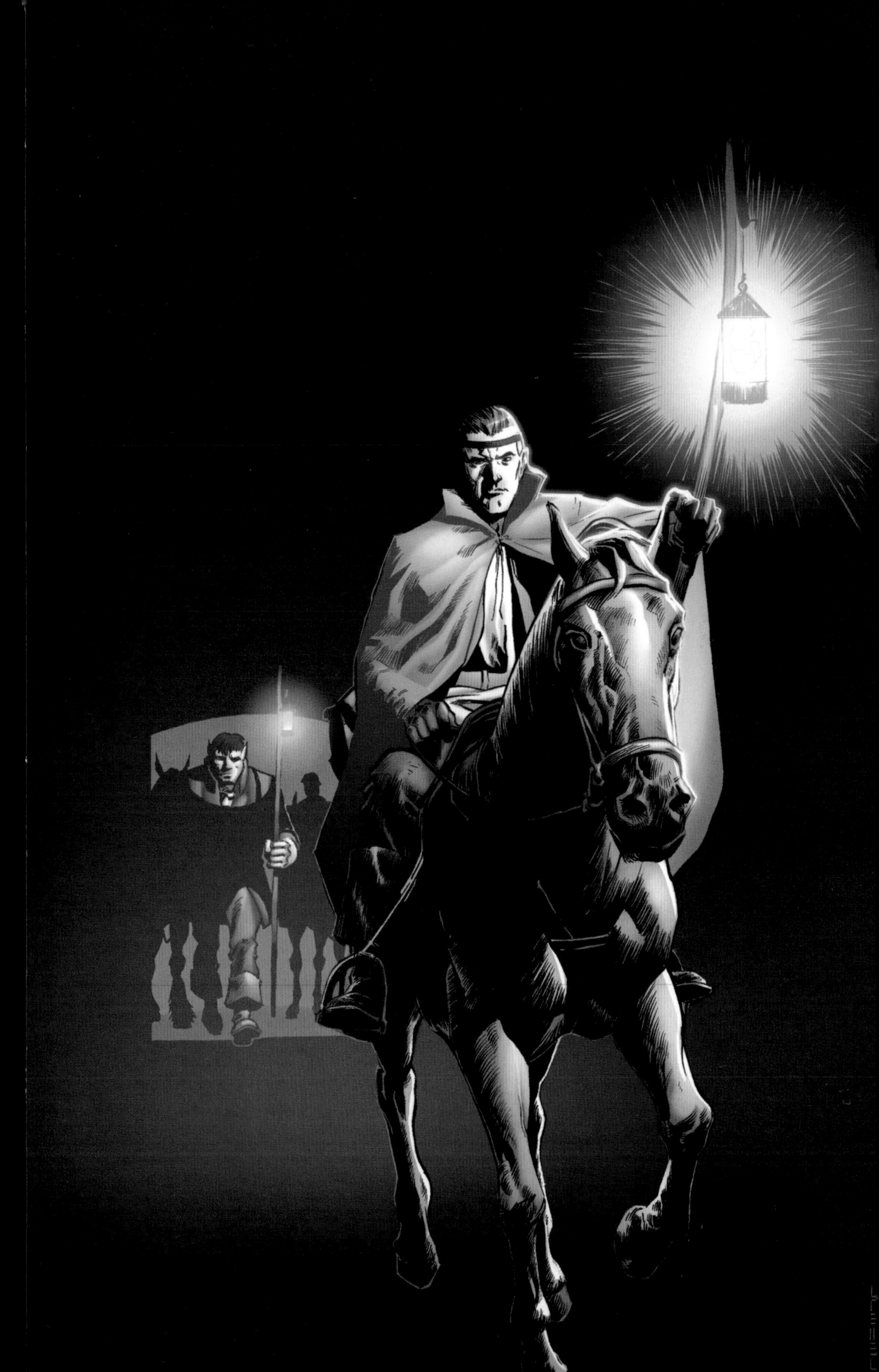

Colors by Andie Tong

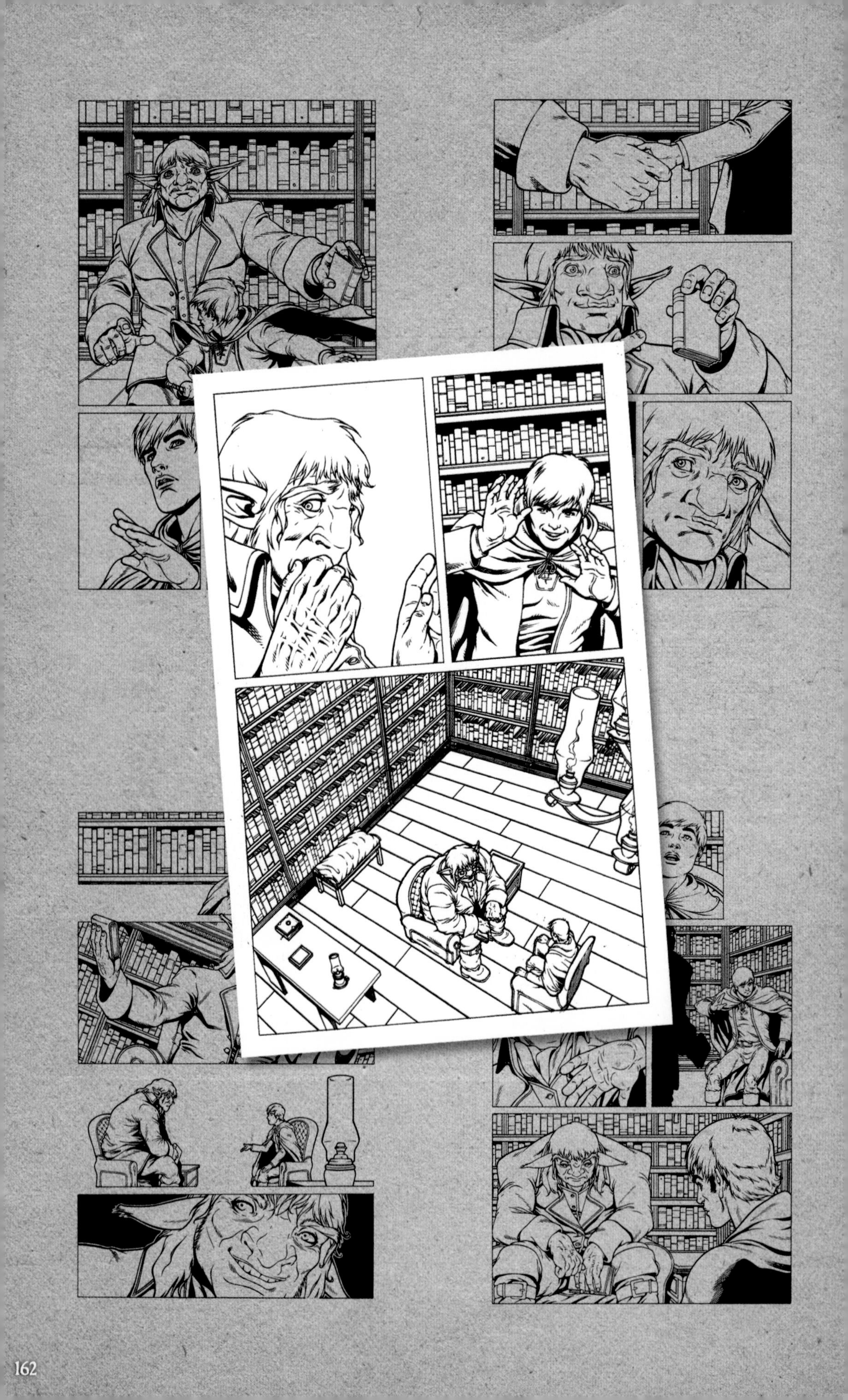

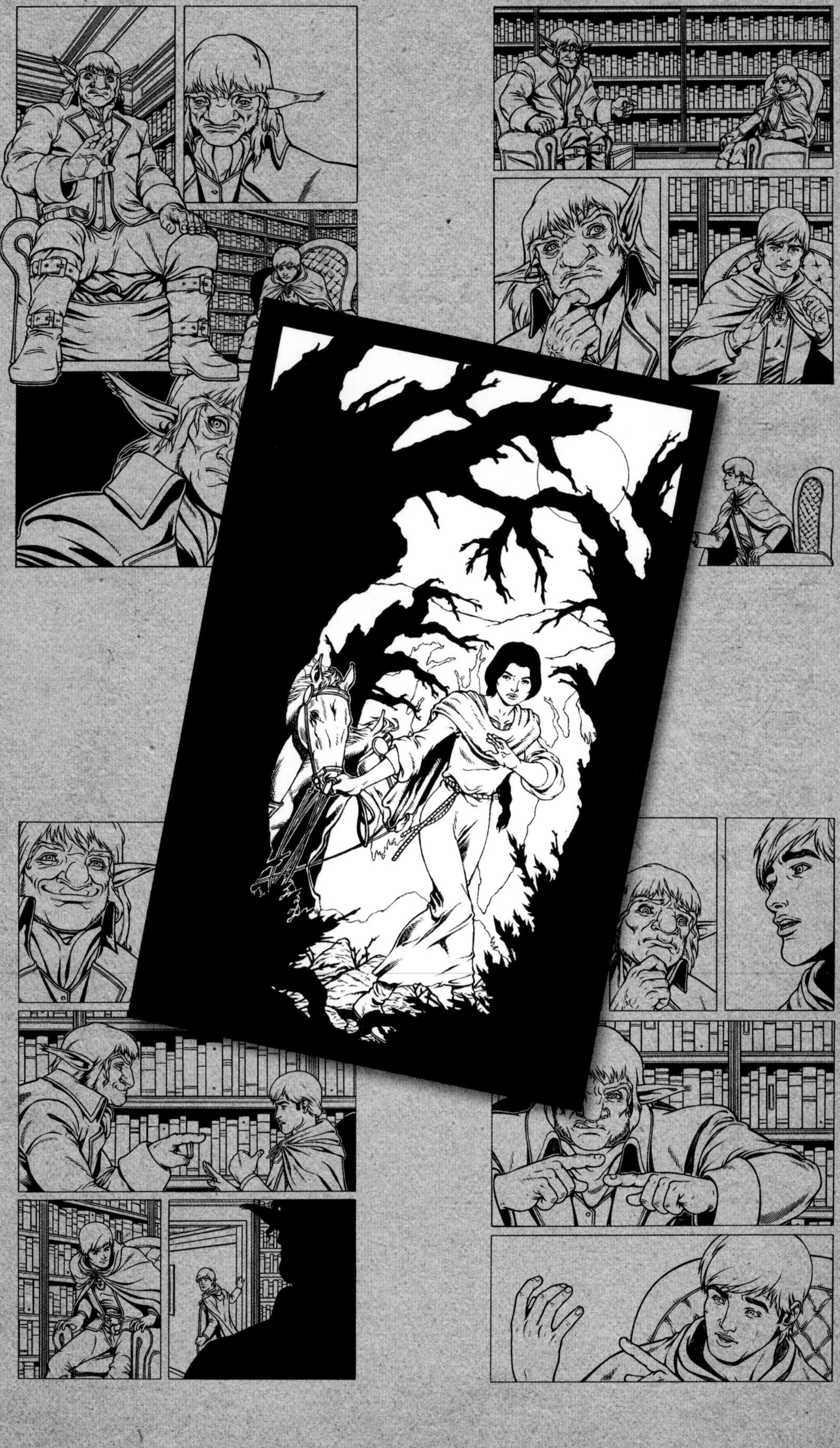

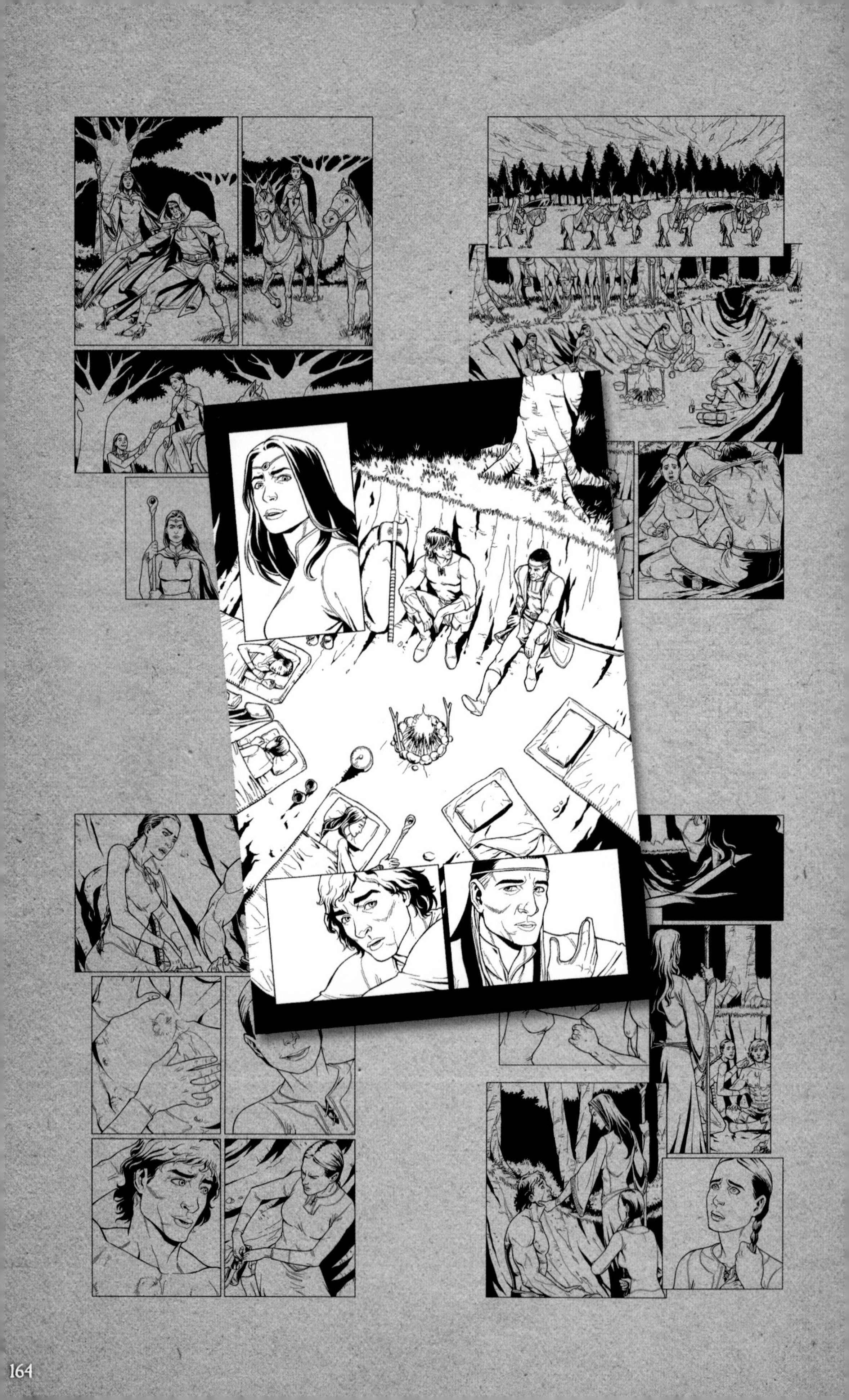

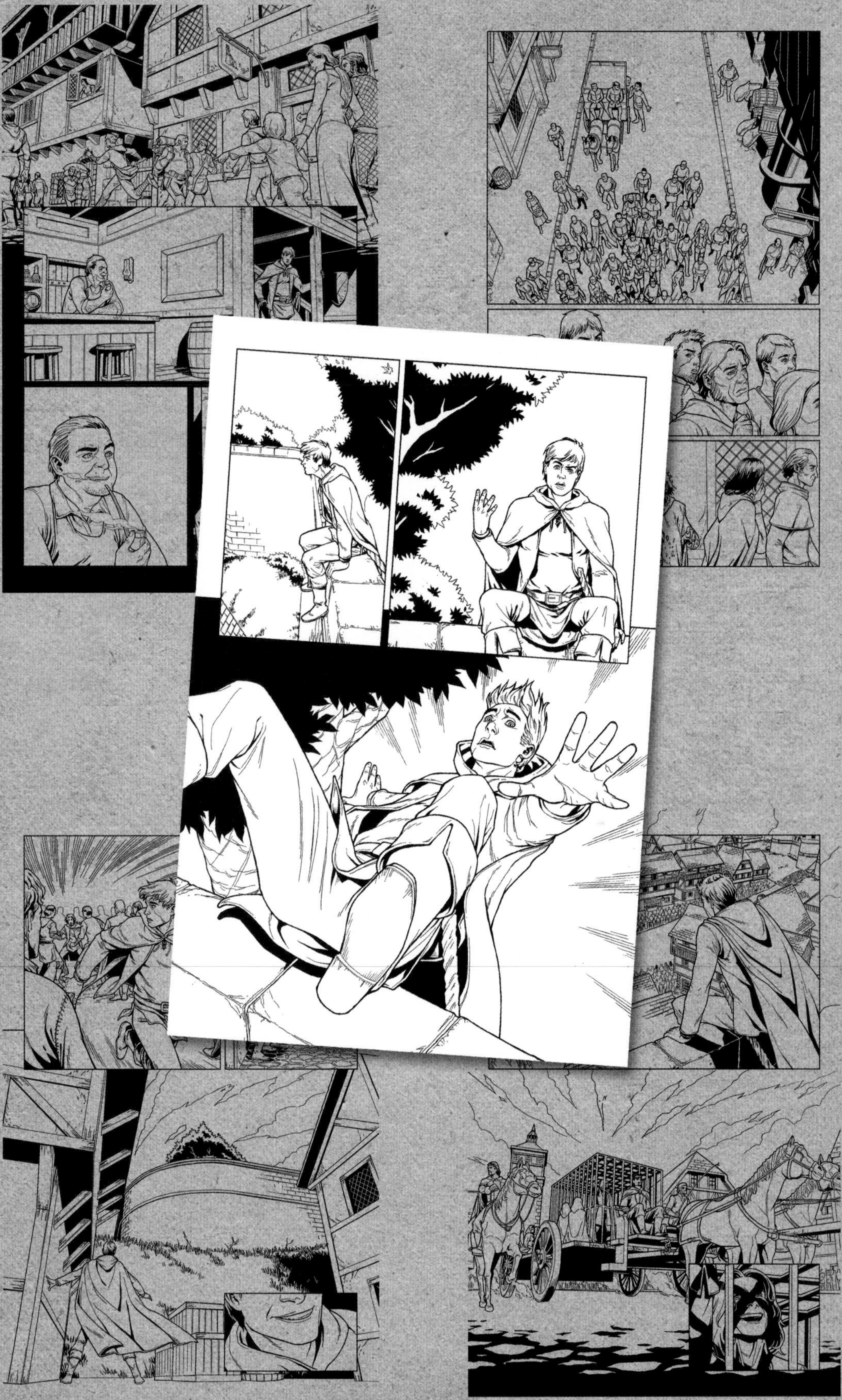

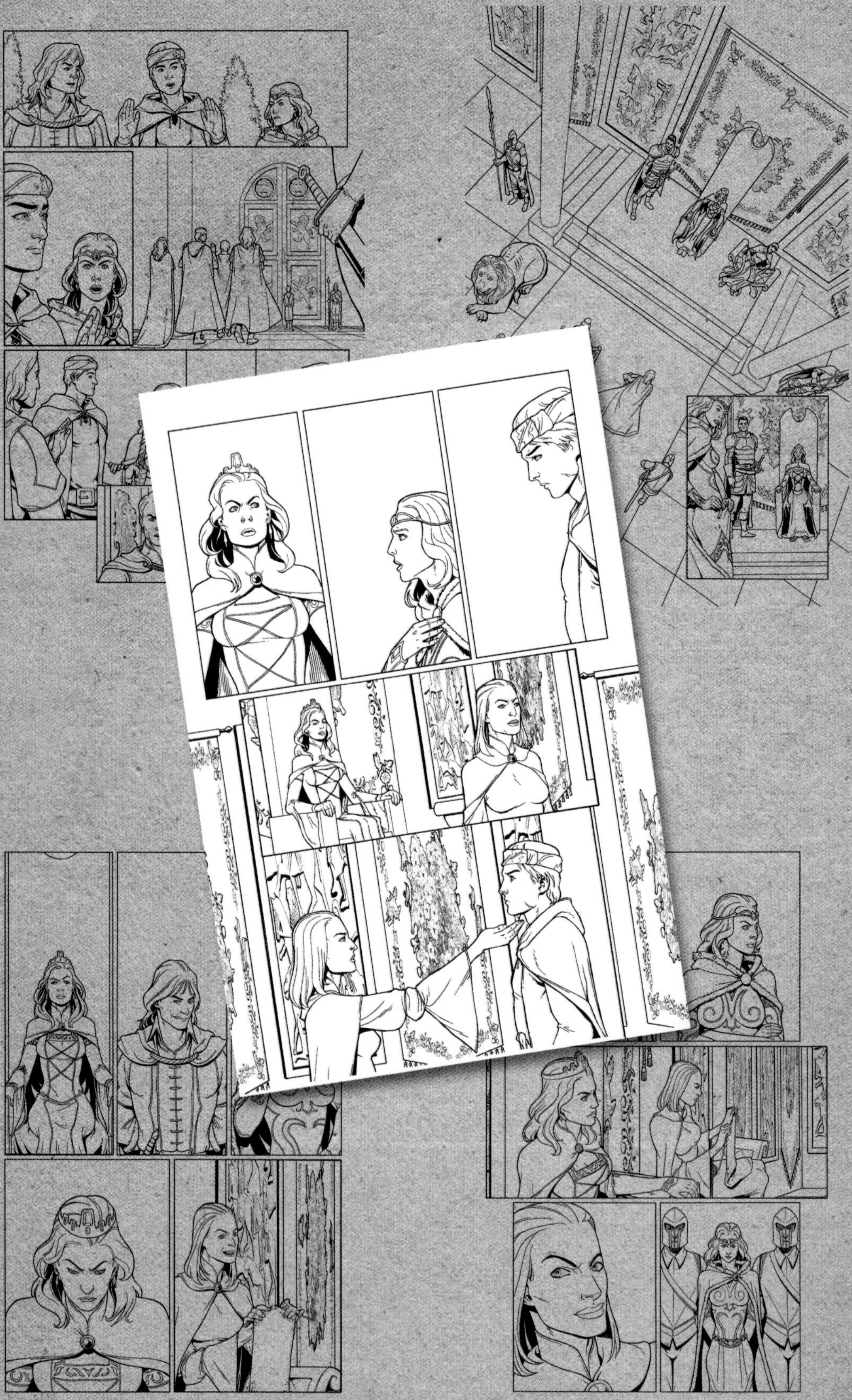

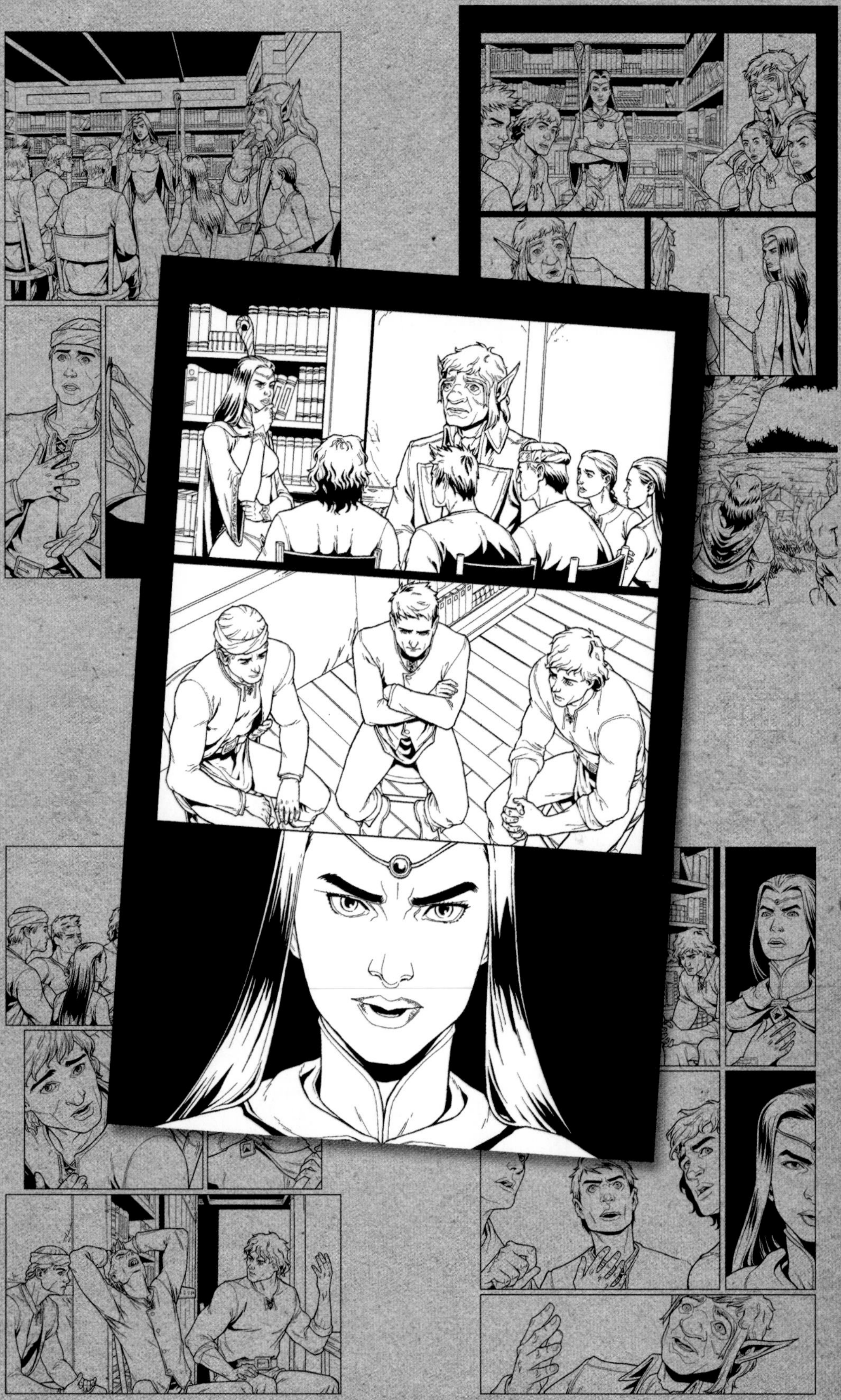

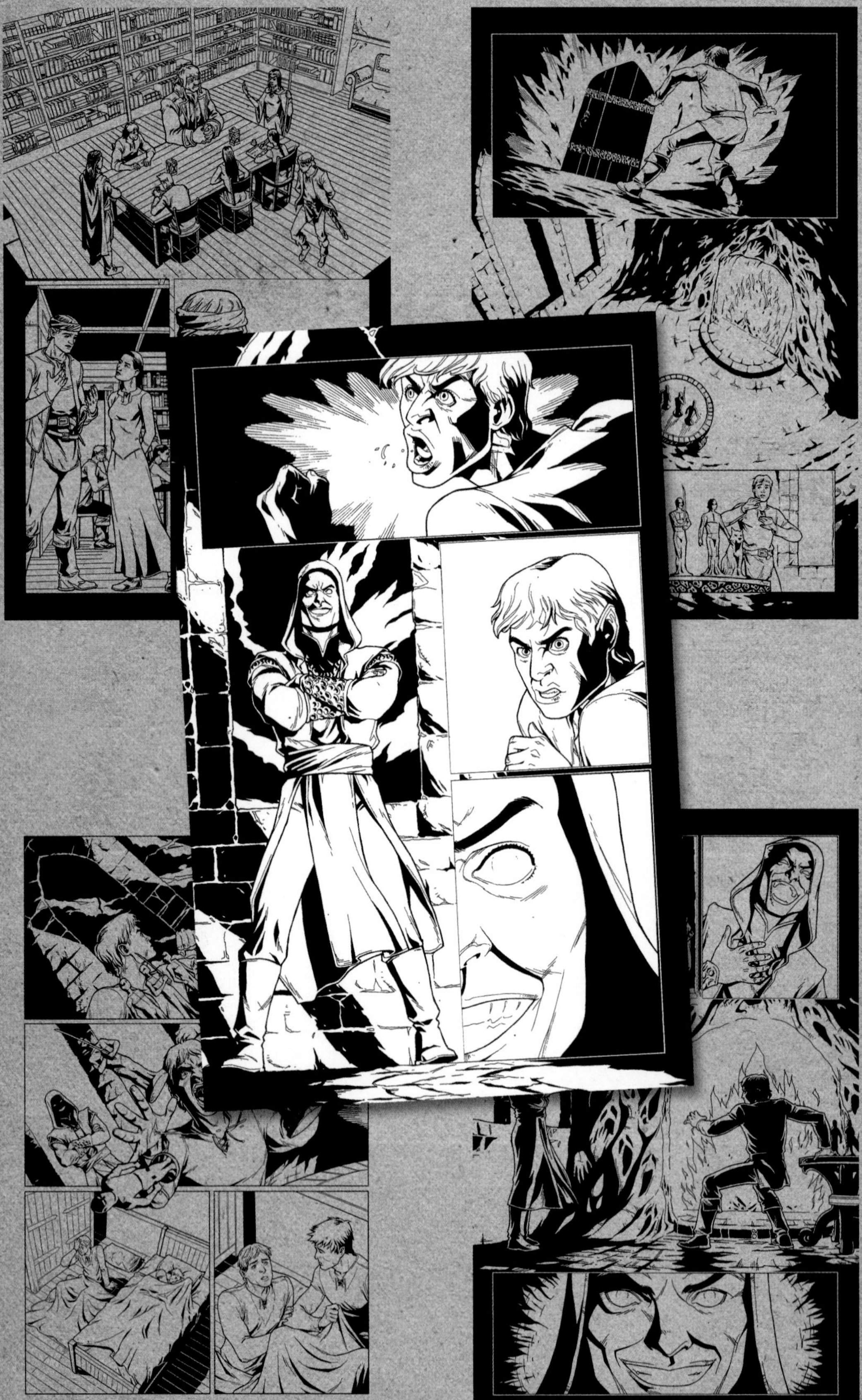

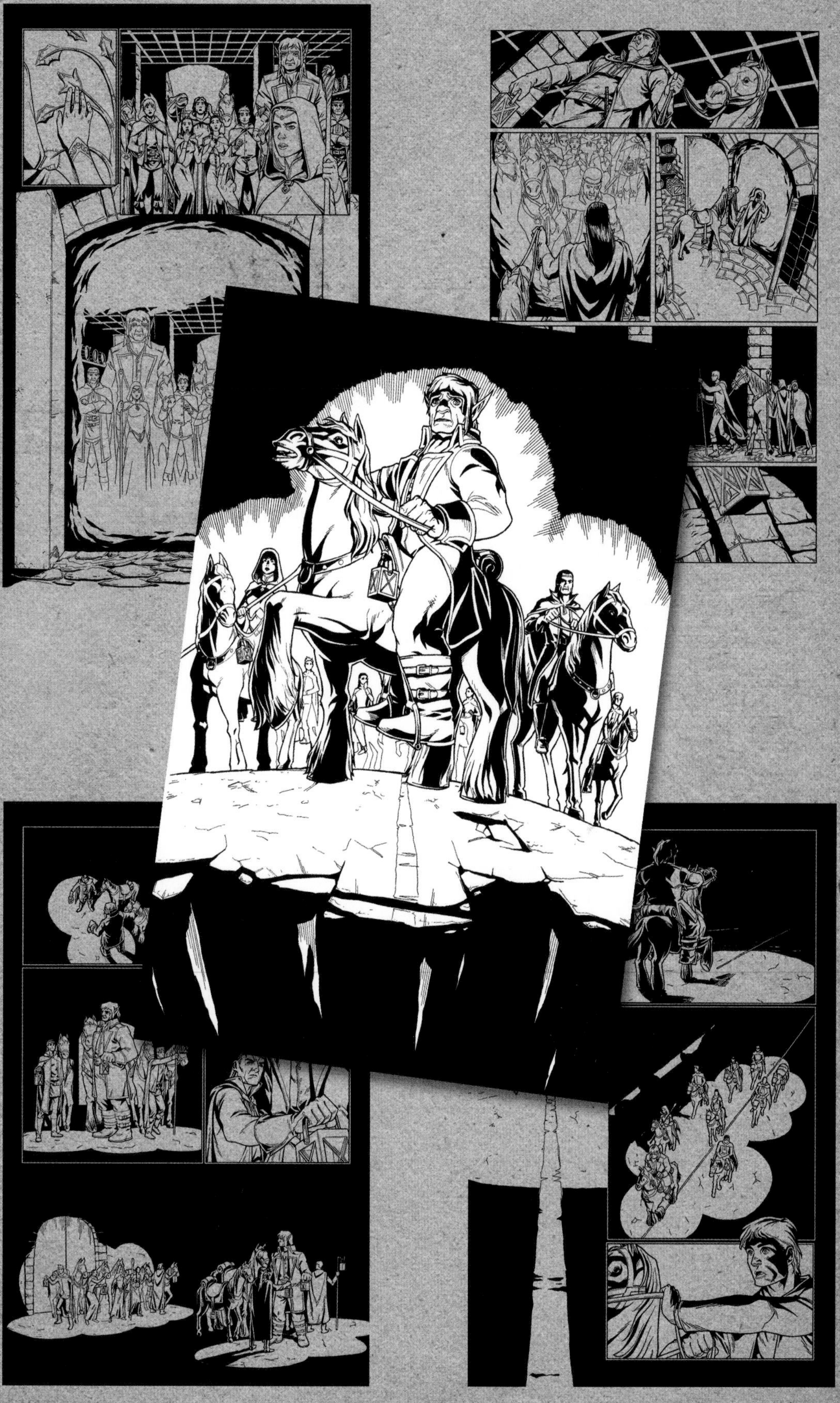

biographies

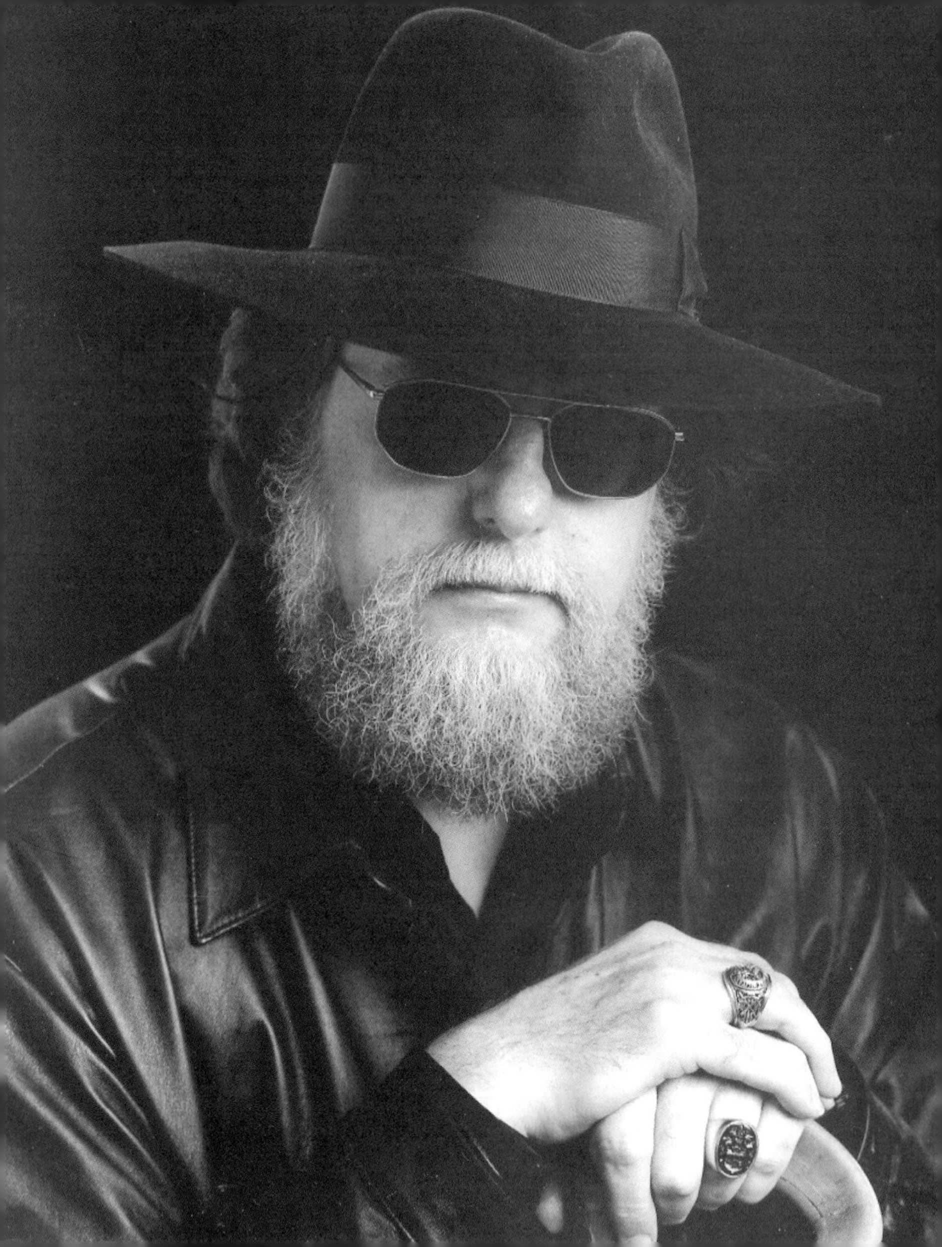

ROBERT JORDAN

Mr. Jordan was born in 1948 in Charleston, South Carolina. He taught himself to read when he was four with the incidental aid of a twelve-years-older brother, and was tackling Mark Twain and Jules Verne by five. He was a graduate of The Citadel, the Military College of South Carolina, with a degree in physics. He served two tours in Vietnam with the U. S. Army; among his decorations are the Distinguished Flying Cross with bronze oak leaf cluster, the Bronze Star with "V" and bronze oak leaf cluster, and two Vietnamese Gallantry Crosses with palm. A history buff, he also wrote dance and theater criticism and enjoyed the outdoor sports of hunting, fishing, and sailing, and the indoor sports of poker, chess, pool, and pipe collecting. He began writing in 1977 and went on to write The Wheel of Time®, one of the most important and bestselling series in the history of fantasy publishing with more than 14 million copies sold in North America, and countless more sold abroad. Robert Jordan died on September 16, 2007, after a courageous battle with the rare blood disease amyloidosis.

CHUCK DIXON

Mr. Dixon has worked for every major comic book publisher as a professional comic book writer. His credits include *The Hobbit* graphic novel, *The Punisher, Birds of Prey, Batman, Catwoman, Green Arrow, Green Lantern, Star Wars, Simpsons* comics, and the comic adaptation of *Dean Koontz's Frankenstein.*

Chuck currently resides in Florida.

ANDIE TONG

Mr. Tong started off as a multimedia designer in 1997 and eventually migrated full-time to comics in 2006. Since then he has worked on titles such as *Tron: Betrayal, Spectacular Spider-Man UK, Batman Strikes, Smallville, TMNT, Masters of the Universe,* and *Starship Troopers,* working for companies such as Disney, Marvel, DC, Panini, Dark Horse, as well as doing commercial illustration for Nike, Universal, CBS, Mattel, and Hasbro. When he gets the chance, Andie concept designs for various companies and also juggles illustration duties on a range of children's picture storybooks for HarperCollins.

Mr. Tong currently resides in Singapore.

FRANCIS NUGUIT

Philippine-based artist Francis R.V. Nuguit, a fine-arts graduate, has worked as a graphic, package, and web designer for several different companies before breaking in as a comic book illustrator. He has worked on a few creator-owned and indie titles such as *Hitless* and *Control Under Fire (Bloodlines)*. He did some character concept art as well, before he started working on the *Wheel of Time: Eye of the World* series.

NICOLAS CHAPUIS

Mr. Chapuis was born in 1985 and decided to freelance as a comic book colorist after earning a degree in graphic design. His work includes *Robert Jordan's The Wheel of Time, Jonathan Stroud's Bartimaeus: The Amulet of Samarkand,* and *Richard Starking's Elephantmen*.

BILL TORTOLINI

Already an accomplished art director and graphic designer, Mr. Tortolini began lettering comics more than a decade ago and has worked with many of the comic book industry's top creators and publishers.

Current and past projects include: *Stephen King's Talisman, Anita Blake: Vampire Hunter, Army of Darkness, Random Acts of Violence, Wolverine, Back to Brooklyn, The Hedge Knight, Archie Comics, Riftwar, Battlestar Galactica, The Warriors, The Wheel of Time, The Dresden Files, Transformers, Star Trek: The Next Generation, G.I. Joe, The Last Resort,* and many others.

Mr. Tortolini resides in Billerica, Massachusetts, with his wife and three children, and his sometimes loyal dog, Oliver.